Succeeding Generations

Succeeding Generations:
Realizing the Dream
of Families in Business

Ivan Lansberg

Harvard Business School Press
Boston, Massachusetts

Printed in the United States of America
03   02   01   00   99   5   4   3   2   1

LIBRARY OF CONGRESS CATALOGING-IN-PUBLICATION DATA

Lansberg, Ivan, 1954–
    Succeeding generations : realizing the dream of families in business / Ivan Lansberg.
        p.   cm.
    Includes bibliographical references and index.
    ISBN 0-87584-742-0 (alk. paper)
    1. Family-owned business enterprises—Management.   I. Title.
    HD62.25.L36   1999
    658′.045—dc21   98-52228
                                                                          CIP

The paper used in this publication meets the requirements of the American National Standard
for Permanence of Paper for Printed Library Materials Z39.49-1984.

To Margarita,
my partner and soul mate.
Without you
there would be nothing.

Contents

Preface

MY approach in this book results from the three roles that have defined my personal involvement with family businesses: as the academic interested in the generation, validation, and dissemination of ideas; as the consultant seeking to improve the lives of business families that I work with; and as the son who grew up in a family enterprise and has experienced firsthand many of the joys and pains that go with success and failure in these companies.

In 1954 my father founded "Segurosca," an insurance brokerage company that later became Grupo Lansberg in Venezuela. In its heyday, Grupo Lansberg was one of the largest insurance brokerage companies in the Spanish-speaking world. Although I never had a managerial role in the family business, I was a participant in the sessions it held at least twice a year for five years with Richard Beckhard, one the leading thinkers in field of organizational development, and his then-wife, Elaine Kepner, a specialist in Gestalt psychology, to discuss and plan my father's succession. The sessions were exciting. I was still in graduate school when the planning process started and I was captivated by the issues we had to address in our family and business as we attempted to plan for this transition.

Unfortunately, the process did not work out as we had hoped. My brother and a professional non-family executive took charge at a time when the economy of the country was falling apart. Instead of battening down the hatches in the face of the impending storm, they pursued a growth strategy and failed. In the aftermath, the anointed successors left the company and my father returned to manage a business that was, by then, a fraction of its former size.

This experience was a painful and important part of my education. It taught me that all the planning in the world does not guarantee success in negotiating generational transitions, that planning is doomed unless certain fundamental ingredients are present in the family mix and business environment. It also opened my eyes to the true complexity of these processes and broadened my ability to empathize with the dilemmas that my clients face.

Nevertheless, I am persuaded that despite its limitations, planning increases the odds of success enormously. My family's experience influenced my choice of a career. When I became aware of the paucity of studies in this field, I was driven to search for answers. I care deeply about the issues discussed in this book because I know the price of failure. On the other hand, I find some comfort in the ancient truth that through adversity, learning and deeper understanding seem to crystallize. Experience—as a learned business owner once said— is what you have when you get what you never expected.

For those who do reach the destination, the rewards are well worth the effort. For parents, passing on to their offspring all they have worked for and built in their lifetimes is the best way to perpetuate their hopes and dreams into the future. For the successors, there is no more satisfying challenge than to preserve and build on what has been entrusted to them and then to pass it on to their own children. Indeed, there may be nothing more basic in the human instinct and ethos. The urge to work with family may go as far back as the Stone Age when people hunted and gathered in tribes. It has deep roots in agricultural societies in which families have farmed the land together for hundreds of years. In today's highly mobile modern societies that tend to scatter families, a business in which family members spend a lifetime working together to achieve common goals and values remains one of the few institutions in which these instincts can still be expressed.

Acknowledgments

It is said that writing is a lonely business—and, indeed, it is. It is also true, at least in my case, that this book reflects the effort, support, and ideas of many people who made its completion possible.

Howard Muson, the editor of this book, has been a friend and writing mentor. His editorial input was truly invaluable. Not only did he help me design the underlying structure of the book, but his unwavering commitment to the principle of "Occam's Razor" pushed me to draw a distinction between the important and the peripheral ideas in the book. Howard also located many of the real world examples I use in the book. His editing gave the writing a more accessible style and tone. Above all, Howard has been extraordinarily generous and patient, never letting me forget whose book this was.

I am grateful to my mentors, Dick Beckhard, formerly of the Sloan School at MIT; Morton Deutsch, professor emeritus at Columbia; and the late Dan Levinson of Yale. I first met Dick Beckhard in Venezuela when I was sixteen years old. Dick stimulated my early interest in applied behavioral science and in family businesses in particular. Many of the underlying ideas regarding the nature of systems and of organizational change that are at the heart of this book I have learned from Dick. Much of my thinking regarding the nature of structural conflict in family companies and the conditions that foster (or inhibit) collaboration in sibling and cousin teams is rooted in Morton Deutsch's work. Mort instilled in me a deep appreciation for the notion that there is nothing more practical than a good theory. Even though I met Dan Levinson only a few years before his untimely death in 1994, his influence on my thinking has been extensive. His developmental model and, especially, his idea of the Dream are central to this book.

I have also been blessed with the support and talent of some wonderful colleagues. Kelin Gersick, my dear friend and business partner, has continuously encouraged me to finish the book. Kelin read many of the early versions of the manuscript, challenged me to develop my ideas further, and gave me comments and questions which deepened both my understanding of the issues in this book and, more important, of myself. I have also learned much from my friend John Ward, of Loyola University of Chicago. Over the past ten years I have been fortunate to have been able to collaborate with John in many executive programs. He has been tremendously generous with his ideas, and his enthusiasm for this book and his feedback on the manuscript are much appreciated.

I would also like to thank my colleagues at the Harvard Business School Press for shepherding this book along. Carol Franco, Hollis Heimbouch, and Howard Stevenson enthusiastically endorsed the field of family business and were early supporters of this project. Nikki

Sabin and Janet Coleman offered many useful suggestions on how the manuscript could be streamlined and shortened. I'm especially grateful to By Barnes, of the Harvard Business School faculty, who provided me with extraordinarily helpful comments which greatly strengthened the book.

Other colleagues have participated in many of the research studies executive programs and consultation projects that have informed the ideas in this book, including Michele Desjardins, Katherine Grady, Susana Feldman, Barbara Dunn, Mary Lou Phillips, John Davis, Sharon Rogolsky, Edith Perrow, Alden Lank, Rod Correll, Erika Morgan, Jon Martinez, Joe Astrachan, and Philippe and Nan-b de Gaspe Beaubien. Mari Firth, our assistant at Lansberg, Gersick and Associates, patiently plowed through revisions, greatly improved the graphics, proofread chapters, and kept the manuscript (and me) organized. My heartfelt thanks to them all.

I would like to extend my gratitude to the many business families that have been my real teachers. Their willingness to entrust me with their Dreams and concerns, as well as their courage in tackling the challenges posed by generational transition, has been inspiring. It has been a privilege to get to know them and to work with them. I am especially grateful to the Lombardi family for their willingness to share their experience for the benefit of others.

Finally, I would like to thank my own family. This book has taken me nearly ten years to complete. During that time, my parents' life has been shaken by the downturn in our family's business and in the economy of Venezuela, our country of origin. Throughout this upheaval they have remained loving toward each other and extraordinarily supportive of my brother, my sister, and me. My mother, Josette Senior de Lansberg, has always shown great confidence in me. Her trust is a spring of strength. My father, Ivan Lansberg Henriquez, has been by far my most important teacher: His contagious thirst for knowledge, his gift for teaching and writing, and his integrity and perseverance, as well as his capacity to retain his sense of humor and perspective even during the most trying times, are his true legacy to us.

Margarita, my wife and partner, has been a constant source of love and encouragement. She read and gave me her thoughts on many versions of the manuscript; she nudged me when I needed nudging; she gave me space when I needed space; she nurtured my Dream and never stopped believing that someday the book would actually get done. I want to give thanks to my sons Daniel and Simon Emilio for their loving patience with me during all those days I spent writing. I am grateful to Daniel for his helpful comments and suggestions on important parts of the manuscript. I am thankful to Simon for not refraining from asking, "Papi, want to play?" His zest for life helped me keep my work in perspective.

Guilford, August 10, 1998

Introduction

BUILDING a successful business takes an enormous amount of energy, talent, hard work—and luck. Indeed, research suggests that the vast majority of startup ventures fail within the first five years.[1] Founders face formidable odds and must be relentlessly determined. Small wonder that those who succeed, through years of effort, are treated as heroes by their families and their communities.

Every successful business is, in a way, a small miracle. Family companies that are successfully passed down from one generation to another and continue to thrive represent an even greater achievement. The low survival rate of family firms is well known. Less than 30 percent of family firms last into the second generation and, of these, only about 10 percent make it to the third.[2] Yet some of the world's greatest companies have managed to reinvent the miracle in every generation. The family owners of these enterprises overcome numerous obstacles—wars and depressions, natural catastrophes, adverse shifts in markets, the sudden deaths of key leaders—in order to continue building on what their forebears have bequeathed to them. These robust organizations include European companies such as BMW in Germany, Lego in Denmark, Ikea in Sweden, and Beretta in Italy; Japanese companies such as Matsushita and the Kikkoman Corp.; Canadian companies such as Seagram; and leading privately held firms in the United States such as S.C. Johnson & Son, Cargill, Levi Strauss & Co., Mars, the Bechtel Group, Hallmark Cards, Milliken & Co., and many that are publicly traded but family established, such as Ford Motor Company, Campbell Soup, and the New York Times Company.

This book is about how such family companies and myriad others, less well known, have managed generational transitions. Every mom-and-pop grocery store as well as family-controlled multinational shares this challenge with kings and queens, prime ministers and presidents, sultans and popes, who down through the centuries have had to arrange for an orderly transfer of power from one generation to another without discord and feuding and civil war. The stakes in a successful business are often just that high.

Even though the vast majority of businesses in America can be described as family owned or family controlled, our knowledge about how these firms are successfully passed down to the next generation remains embryonic. This book will argue that leadership change in family businesses takes not one form but many, and that the literature has not succeeded in portraying the true complexity of the universe of family companies because it focuses on only one type of succession, in which a single dominant leader (historically, usually a father) passes a business to another single leader (most often a son).

I can best illustrate what I mean with an anecdote. A number of years ago I was a faculty member at the Institute for Management Development (IMD) in Lausanne, Switzerland, where I taught a series of seminars on succession and continuity in family businesses. I expected the seminar participants, all owners of European family companies—some of which go back three hundred years—to be a challenging group. Nevertheless, I was puzzled by the participants' fidgeting and frowning at one of the first sessions. Different individuals, moreover, became restless at different times during my presentation.

When I inquired about the reasons, a few participants volunteered that some of my points simply did not apply to them. It soon became apparent that the participants were having different reactions because their situations varied in fundamental ways. While all were deeply interested in the topic of "succession," their primary issues of concern varied according to the leadership structure of their companies and the type of generational transition they were facing.

Many of the participants controlled all, or a majority, of the stock in their companies and ran the business as well. Of these controlling owners, some were founding entrepreneurs planning a succession for the first time. Others were sons who had inherited their positions through the tradition of primogeniture and were seeking to avoid the kinds of mistakes they felt their fathers had made when authority was transferred to them.

Still others in the audience were more or less equal partners with brothers and sisters in their companies. These sibling partners were dealing with the complexities of turning over their businesses to their heirs in their respective families—in most cases, a loosely connected group of cousins, each of whom would inherit only a fraction of the company's shares. Yet another group at the seminar was in older mega-businesses that had been led for several generations by cousins who were all direct descendants of the founders. Leaders of these cousin consortiums were concerned with preserving the family values and control in companies that had become increasingly corporate and dependent on non-family managers. They were also interested in learning how approaches to management succession developed by highly respected public companies might be applied to their firms.

These seminars challenged me to reassess my thinking about succession. In my research as well as in my consulting practice, I had encountered many situations in which the traditional formulation about continuity planning—the controlling-owner to controlling-owner pattern—simply did not apply. As my experience in Lausanne showed, there are at least three basic types of ownership structures in family companies: the controlling owner, the sibling partnership, and the cousin consortium. How the ownership control is allocated has important consequences on the type of leadership structure that ultimately emerges—but even these are "pure models." The reality is considerably more complex. A company reaching this crossroads can go in three directions: It can recycle its existing structure, move toward a more complex structure, or adopt a simpler structure.

Although survey data is lacking, the demographic arrow inexorably points in the direction of more complexity rather than less. Family companies tend to become more complex in later generations as the family tree branches out and the business expands. Throughout the world, the generation of post–World War II business founders is rapidly fading from the scene. By all accounts it is the generation in human history that has created the most wealth (about $10 trillion in the United States alone). Much of that wealth, which is tied up in family enterprises, will be passed down to their baby-boomer children within the next ten to fifteen years. As the succeeding generations take charge of these businesses they are being confronted with issues that were never a part of their parents' experiences, including collective ownership, shared leadership responsibilities, and multifamily succession. Now the participants are not just fathers and sons, but mothers and daughters as well. In addition, the widespread disillusionment with large corporate bureaucracies in recent years, the uncertainties and anxieties of working in public companies, has made joining the family business a more attractive career option for young people. The greater numbers attracted to such careers place a heavy burden on the family business to provide an expanding workplace within which family members may realize their career and lifestyle aspirations.

Although the leadership structure of family companies takes various forms, which may evolve over generations, certain tasks must be accomplished in every transition. In each instance, some person or group in the new generation takes charge, and some person or group in the older generation gives up control. Together, in a dialogue that may stretch over a period of years, the two generations must negotiate the hardest issues: They must decide what type of leadership structure is desirable and feasible, given the talents and skills of the successors; they must create career development plans for the candidates and test each one's ability to lead and produce results; they must design a legitimate process for selecting the next leader or leaders from among the group of candidates; and they must assist the new leaders in establishing their credibility and authority with a variety of stakeholders.

Succession, however, is about more than the evolution of systems and structures. It is also about the continuous process of change in people's lives, the development and maturation of individuals as they move through life. Early in the life of a young business family, when children are growing up, parents begin to think about how the enterprise they have built will outlive them and continue to nurture their descendants. As the time for passing the baton approaches, these thoughts become more conscious and formal. When three or four generations of family members are involved, multiple successions may be taking place simultaneously. A snapshot of the events in a third-generation company at a moment in time might show one succession nearing an end while another enters a consolidation phase and a third is just beginning.

What unites people and structures in the moving stream of a family business is the individual and collective aspirations of family members. Family enterprises are highly personal systems that evoke the same depth of feeling in the participants that most people reserve for their children and their marriages. Too often, elaborate strategic and succession plans go unrealized because these deeper psychological factors have not been taken into consideration.

A central theoretical assumption of this book is that what drives all successions is a vision of the future, hammered out over time, that embraces the aspirations of both the senior and the junior generations as well as those of their forebears. This vision—which I call a Shared Dream—generates the excitement and energy that every family must have to do the hard work of succession planning.

The concept of a Shared Dream draws heavily on the psychological literature on human development, especially on the work of Daniel Levinson, the late Yale University psychologist. Levinson's landmark *Seasons of a Man's Life* described the power of the Dream in the unfolding maturation of the individual over time, an imagined possibility that gives meaning to the person's life and guides his or her fundamental choices. The notion of a Dream impelling entrepreneurs to build empires is familiar in the business literature. The powerful imagery of the American Dream is often invoked to describe the aspirations of the poor immigrants who come to America and build a successful business, thereby providing a better life for their children and for future generations.

Although Levinson saw the Dream as shaped in part by one's interaction with society, his work focused on its critical role in the individual's development. In this book, I shall expand on the original construct and use it to explain the process through which business families formulate a compelling vision of the future necessary for negotiating the passage to the next generation. It is my contention that family business continuity requires that the individual Dreams of different generations be woven together into a shared, collective Dream. This Shared Dream sets the context within which succession in both ownership and management can take place effectively. In every family that owns a successful company, the enterprise has a tremendous impact on the career choices of younger family members, and every young person must come to terms with the dominating influence of the business in the family, especially when the parents' Dream involves having them own and manage it.

Like the movements of tectonic plates beneath the earth's surface, the process of succession in families is pushed along by an ongoing, inevitable dialogue between generations, in which seniors and juniors grope toward some common vision of the future that will enable them to work together to achieve continuity. This dialogue is not only essential for the successful transfer of a business, but largely shapes the structure of ownership and leadership in the next generation. Investing time and resources in formulating elaborate strategic and succession plans without first addressing the Dreams and aspirations of family members is likely to be both wasteful and ineffective. Every plan requires a vision of the future. In a family enterprise, such a vision cannot be constructed without first addressing the Dreams of those who will control the system in the next generation.

Over the past fifteen years, I have consulted with over one hundred family companies in the United States and abroad. *Succeeding Generations* represents what I have learned about the succession process in the course of that work. I have carefully documented my observations of many firms and, with their consent, have used several as examples in this book (with names and other details disguised). In addition, my analyses are informed by some of my own research as well as by other empirical studies on family businesses.

Succeeding Generations should be useful to the growing numbers of professional advisers and academics seeking a fuller understanding of the emotional and political forces at work in succession planning. The typology of successions that it offers may help them organize their thinking about the diversity of the clientele they serve and about the conditions affecting the odds of continuity in the systems they work with. I also expect the book will help widen the horizons of many business owners who perhaps are not yet fully aware of the range of options available to them in planning for the future.

My conclusions address some of the misconceptions held by many business owners. One assumption, for example, is that succession occurs at the moment when the torch is passed to a new leader or leaders. Succession is a process, not an event. Thinking of generational transitions as simply the selection of a new leader is far too limiting. This book therefore makes a distinction between "succession," which suggests a single event, and "continuity," which sees planning for generational transitions as a lifelong, ongoing process.

Successful leadership transitions depend upon planning, but, as we will see, planning alone is no guarantee of success. In a family company, the business organization itself tends to be an extension of the personalities of the family owners. These powerful emotional undercurrents sometimes block the progress of planning, but they can, if properly mobilized, also provide the energy that propels it forward. As a social psychologist, I pay close attention to situational factors that shape people's emotions as well as their behavior in a particular set of circumstances. In succession planning, I see my role as helping to create a context in which a family can make the necessary changes in its circumstances to succeed in transferring the leadership to a new generation.

My purpose in *Succeeding Generations* is not to present a standardized step-by-step guideline for how succession planning should be done, but rather to offer a deeper analysis of how the succession process unfolds in its many permutations. Throughout the book I provide detailed examples of how family companies have successfully managed these transitions and I draw out many lessons for practice. My principal points may thus be summarized:

Succession is a journey, with the choice of destination determined by the family's Shared Dream. To succeed, the family has to keep the final destination in mind and understand what it needs to do to get there. Whatever the destination, family members must ask some basic questions: Do we have the resources? Will it satisfy the aspirations of key constituents? Can we enhance our capacity to work together in the future scenario? The challenges of the journey are compounded when it involves not just a changing of the guard but a fundamental change in the leadership and ownership structure.

The key to understanding where true power lies in a family company is ownership. As a business owner once told me, "the golden rule of family business is that those who own the gold rule." Whether the stock is owned by one person, or is divided 50–50 between two family members, or fractionated among many, is the critical determinant of power and behavior in a family company and of the kind of structure that is likely to be viable in the next generation.

Succession is driven by a biological clock. The ages of the senior leaders of the business and of their designated successors determine the timing of succession. The relative ages of the participants also powerfully affect what is possible for the family to achieve at any given stage of the planning process. To appreciate the influence of age on succession therefore requires an understanding of the psychology of human development. Such is the power of this well-developed body of research, that simply knowing the ages of the principals in a family business is often enough to accurately predict the succession issues they are struggling with at any given time.

Shared leadership can work—under the right conditions. Parents often dream of having all their offspring working together harmoniously in the company, but they tend to believe collective leadership is doomed to fail. More complex systems, such as sibling partnerships and cousin consortiums, are indeed more difficult to manage. However, human nature is much more plastic than many people assume, and many families that aspire to group leadership and ownership often find ways of collaborating and managing conflict. There is hard evidence that such systems can work under the right conditions, and this book will elucidate those conditions.

A leadership transition offers an ideal opportunity to reformulate the company's direction and renew its energies. Too often in selecting new leaders, family businesses look to past needs rather than future needs. But the leadership style and strategic goals of the previous generation may be out of synch with a world of constantly changing market conditions and competitive demands. Success in any enterprise can breed complacency, and one of the main reasons for the decline of many family companies is a waning of entrepreneurial vigor and a failure to make periodic reassessments of strategic direction. The final choice of successors must be preceded by a strategic planning exercise that will suggest the most important requirements for the new leadership.

Efforts to tightly control ownership and decision making in a family company contain the seeds of their own destruction. Continuity in large complex family companies depends on establishing open forums to enlist the support of family shareholders. The different constituencies in a family business—managers, shareholders, and other family members—must understand their separate rights and responsibilities and avoid infringing on the domains of the other groups. In the long run, the continuity of the enterprise requires establishing the structures through which each constituency can assert its legitimate interests and concerns. I will describe in detail the functioning of the principal governance structures in a family company—the board of directors, the family council, and the shareholders' assembly—and how the three can work together in preparing for succession and continuity.

Ultimately, continuity in a family company depends on instilling a sense of stewardship in every generation. The pitfalls that prevent planning and cause the downfall of many family businesses are well known: the ego-mania and reluctance to delegate of founding entrepreneurs; the old rivalries that spill over into the business; the political infighting that sometimes divides branches of the extended family; the perks and family "toys and hobbies" that deplete companies of the cash needed to stay afloat; the unconscious resistance of aging leaders against stepping aside. All these factors can conspire against continuity unless the lesson is instilled in young people from an early age that the family business is not there to be milked for all it's worth: They are the fortunate custodians of a legacy that has been created and kept alive by the hard work of others. As stewards, their responsibility is to pass on to their descendants a company that is even stronger and more admired than the one that was vouchsafed to them by their elders.

PART I

Family Business Forms

CHAPTER 1

Designing New Road Maps
for the Journey

I N thinking about succession, family business owners and the professionals who advise them have generally had only one road map to follow: The literature in the field has been largely limited to transitions from one controlling owner to another controlling owner (CO to CO). This has virtually eliminated from view a large number of family businesses that either have a system of multiple leaders or would prefer to transfer the company in the next generation to a leadership *group*.

The deep-rooted bias in favor of CO-to-CO successions conforms to the hierarchical patterns of authority that the public has come to accept as the norm in business. Every business is supposed to have one, and only one, boss who is the ultimate decision maker. Executive committees, offices of the president, or other such arrangements that convey the idea that leadership responsibilities are shared, are seen as suboptimal compromises. Clients, suppliers, and even employees often do not understand them.

Having a single leader does tend to be less complicated from the point of view of corporate decision making. When power is concentrated in the hands of one individual, major decisions can be made quickly and informally. When there are several owner-managers looking after the business, leadership responsibilities may become diffuse, sometimes leading to slow and ineffective action. To many family business owners rule by one leader seems clean and simple, while a system of multiple leaders is messy and complex (if not dangerous!).

I held this same bias for many years—until I began to meet more and more brothers and sisters or groups of cousins who professed to run their businesses as equal partners. Members of these families told me that they made all major decisions as a group, by consensus. Skeptical, I would sometimes ask them, "But who is *really* in charge here? Who has the final say when push comes to shove?" The reply was usually, "*We* are the leaders here." I was still suspicious of these claims, believing the formal team structure was merely a way of allowing weaker family members to accept the rule of a stronger brother or sister without hurt feelings. When I observed these businesses closely, I found that in some of them, indeed, the "we" was really an "I." There was a perception that power was shared, but one person was actually the ultimate decision maker.

In other shared leadership arrangements, however, I could not identify an "ultimate boss." While responsibilities were often divided—with each partner having virtual autonomy within his or her own bailiwick—decisions that involved the company as a whole were reached by consensus. The partners were loath to make a major investment or divestiture, for example, unless all were in agreement. In their titles and perks, in the size of their offices and other trappings of power, they were careful to preserve their equality. They often invented ingenious techniques for getting along, fostering agreement on potentially divisive issues, and maintaining unity. As we shall see, some of the rules that sibling partners adopt in order to minimize conflict seem to violate many rules of sound administration. Indeed, members of sibling partnerships are often sensitive about how their idiosyncratic organizational structures and quirky rules look to outsiders.

Some years ago a group of scientists studied the bumblebee and concluded that, according to basic principles of aerodynamics, it could not possibly fly. Of course, we know that although bumblebees may not be as aerodynamically designed as mosquitoes, they do, in fact, fly. Although the sibling and cousin partnerships I observed were often as strangely designed as bumblebees, they did, in fact, fly. Some of these partners had been together for twenty-five years or more. They were making money and having fun.

This realization led me to question the lack of attention to collective systems in the family business literature. Why had these systems been ignored for so long? How and why do shared leadership arrangements come about, and what does it take to make them work? Why were they becoming more numerous?

This chapter traces what appears to be a major shift in attitudes toward shared leadership systems. An interest in shared leadership in family companies grows out of the preference of many parents for shared ownership—that is, for dividing their assets more or less equally among members of the next generation. I will cite evidence that, in their succession planning, a growing number of family business owners are showing an interest in collective systems and many are already experimenting with them. If these statistics are any indication, many family companies are headed into terra incognita. My experience and the research I have conducted suggest the challenges associated with these kinds of transitions have been greatly underestimated.

Clearly, collective systems are not feasible for every family and company. They are almost certain to fail when siblings' or cousins' relationships are riddled with destructive family conflict and rivalry. Furthermore, the controlling owner structure has undeniable advantages—a parsimonious governance and leadership arrangement is unquestionably simpler to manage. If all family trees could be pruned at every succeeding generation so that only one of the heirs would inherit ownership and management responsibilities, most generational transitions would probably be smoother. But pruning the tree is not always economically or emotionally feasible in a family business.

The Prevailing Wisdom

Both researchers and practitioners in the family business field have tended to embrace the prevailing view in general management literature that collective authority systems are unworkable. For example, Christensen, in his pioneering study of succession in family businesses, described partnerships as feasible mostly as interim arrangements—structures that work for a limited period of time until an appropriate successor can be found.[1] Similarly, Harry Levinson in his classic *Harvard Business Review* article warned against the perils of sibling partnerships:

If the brothers own equal shares in the organization and both are members of the board, as is frequently the case, the problems are compounded. On the board they can argue policy from equally strong positions. However, when they return to operations in which one is subordinate to the other, the subordinate one, usually the junior brother, finds it extremely difficult to think of himself in a subordinate role. . . .[2]

Note that Levinson's assumes that the two brothers should not be equals in operations. Instead, he offers the following solution: "If one or more brothers is on the board, then only one, as a rule, should be an operating executive." Levinson does leave the door open a crack when he says that under rare conditions ("if the brothers work well together") deviations from this rule may be possible. His message, however, is resoundingly clear: Stay away from arrangements in which siblings have to collaborate in both management and ownership roles.

In their classic *The Family Owned Business*, Benjamin Becker and Fred Tillman unambivalently delineate the benefits of having a single leader:

Every family business must have a boss. . . . The family business owner should consider designating an individual in the business to be the final decision-maker after the owner relinquishes the managerial reins. Feelings are likely to be hurt by the selection, but this step still should be taken. . . . If there are two or more family members in the business, a family business owner should not hesitate to vest—during his lifetime—adequate managerial powers in the most competent family member to avoid possible conflicts.[3]

More recent authors are even more explicit about the hazards of shared ownership and management arrangements. Consider the advice by Benjamin Benson and associates, all senior consultants to family businesses, in a popular book aimed at the family business owner. About shared management they say: "In our experience, most businesses need one leader with ultimate authority. Some owners, unable to reach a decision on which child should be the successor, allow them to fight it out, usually with destructive results."[4] On shared ownership: "Multifamily ownership requires such a unique combination of people, attitudes, and skills, and the odds are so high against success that some consultants categorically advise that rather than attempting to continue the business . . . [it] should be sold."[5] And finally, "The proliferation of stockholders is a principal reason for the high mortality rate of family businesses."[6] Throughout their book, Benson and his coauthors argue for a twofold solution to the succession problem. First, choose a single successor to lead the company.

Second, concentrate the voting control of the company in the hands of the successor.

Similarly, in a column in *Family Business* magazine, Léon Danco writes: "Solutions that call for sharing of power—equal multiple partnerships, co-presidencies, rotating the presidency—are mostly naive fantasies. . . . In my experience a family business can have only one leader."[7] Danco is considered by many to be the pioneer in family business consulting. Although he is not an academic researcher, he has been practicing in the field for almost forty years and his ideas have had a far-reaching impact on both the theory and practice of succession planning. His popular book *Beyond Survival*, which is addressed to the single owner-manager and focuses almost entirely on succession planning, provides many practical ideas that have become standard practice in the field. These include the need to develop a board with competent independent directors; the importance of training and selecting a successor; and the necessity of developing a retirement plan and of handing over power to the successor during the lifetime of the entrepreneur.[8]

All of these are sound prescriptions. However, implementing them becomes incrementally more difficult the further removed a given family business is from the entrepreneurial stage, in which a single individual is usually in full control. Companies tend to become more complex in later generations; as the business expands, the family tree branches out and the ownership becomes more fragmented. For the elders, this greatly increases the challenges involved in deciding such questions as: Who is most qualified to lead the business in the next generation? How many family members seeking jobs can be accommodated in the company? What is the most efficient structure for managing all this complexity? Likewise, juniors in the company must appreciate that circumstances in the business and family may have changed significantly and that following the management formulas of their elders may be a recipe for disaster. To succeed in their turn at the helm, the younger generation may have to consider wholly new management styles and structures.

The substance of the issues thus changes significantly in the more complex business forms. The process of selecting successors can also differ depending on whether the person doing the selecting is the father or mother of the candidates, a brother or sister, an uncle or a cousin—and will be different still if the decision makers are themselves a group or if they are choosing a group of successors rather than a single leader. Choosing successors by group consensus can be a political nightmare in these later-generation family companies. Imagine a second-generation family company with three siblings, equal owners, all in leadership roles. Those three are likely to be involved in training and evaluating one another's children. Can they do so with a reasonable degree of impartiality? Or will each promote his or her own children over those of the others? How the top positions are distributed among the various branches of a family—and how each family divides its shares with their offspring—will have a direct impact on the overall balance of power among the cousins. Whatever arrangements are reached regarding succession, the family must necessarily address these added complexities.

Similarly, the very fact that there is a *team* of leaders that must step down in order for the next generation to take charge makes the succession process significantly different. Should the current leaders be replaced with another management team? How likely is it that similar collaborative relationships can be replicated among the cousins? Should the family company revert back to a single leader? And, if so, how does the shared leadership pattern established by the predecessors affect the mandate of the new leader? What expectations does the structure that operated in the past create for the structure that will operate in the future? These are all important considerations that must be taken into account in the context of alternative types of successions.

Alternatives to the Controlling
Owner Model

The evidence that shared leadership arrangements are increasingly common is beginning to mount. In a 1997 survey of 3,000 family firms across the United States, 11.2 percent of the respondents reported having more than one CEO at the helm. Another 1 percent said they had more than two CEOs. More importantly, the survey reports that over 42 percent of respondents think that co-CEOs are a possible leadership solution for their companies in the next generation.[9] A survey reported in the *Wall Street Journal* suggests that family business owners actually consider a broad range of leadership arrangements when thinking about succession. In this study, 15 percent of those business owners sampled explicitly planned to form an executive committee of two or more children; 40 percent were considering recruiting the help of the board of directors or of an external third party in choosing between a single successor and several. Only 35 percent of those interviewed had settled on grooming only one successor candidate.[10]

Statistics that I have collected at conferences in recent years also indicate the diversity of owners' choices and preferences. Of the 401 companies in the sample, a majority of single, controlling owners aspire to move their companies to sibling partnerships in the next generation—nearly twice as many as favor passing the business to another single leader. Presumably, many of these owners want to see their children function as a team in the second generation. The other notable point is that 54 of the 127 (42%) owners now functioning as part of sibling partnerships wish to retain the same structure in the next generation rather than move toward a more complex form of organization—the cousin consortium—which is the next natural step in the generational progression. What this suggests is that the seniors feel that the structure they know will work best for business in the next generation as well.

From the Fuggers of the Italian Renaissance, to the Rothschilds in the nineteenth century, to the Rockefellers and du Ponts in this century, some of the world's greatest business empires have been built by family partnerships. Through the mass media today, the public hears mostly about powerful family companies that have imploded because of sibling rivalries and intra-family feuds. But there are numerous examples of siblings and cousins who have worked together for years and achieved notable success.

One example is the Asplundh Tree Expert Co., a company that trims trees for telephone and electrical utility companies in all fifty states of the United States and in eight foreign countries. Based in Willow Grove, Pennsylvania, the company was founded by three brothers, Griffith, Carl, and Lester Asplundh, who got into tree-trimming in order to finance their educations after their Swedish immigrant father died. For many years, according to *Forbes* magazine, Griffith oversaw the tree-trimming operations, Carl took care of the books, and Les provided technical expertise and managed research and development. By 1968, the three founders were either dead or retired and a new generation had taken over. Both the ownership and the leadership structure were becoming more complex. Barr Asplundh, Griffith's son, was elected president and seven brothers and cousins were on the board of directors. Edward Asplundh, Carl's son, became president next in 1982, and Chris Asplundh, the youngest member of the second generation, succeeded Edward in 1992. Today Asplundh is owned by 132 shareholders—all of them members of the Asplundh family. Revenues have expanded from $100 million in 1984 to $900 million in 1995. The board consists entirely of family members. Sixteen family members work in the company, admitted only after satisfying stiff educational and training requirements—described by *Forbes* as a system of "disciplined nepotism." Multiple ownership and plural leadership have clearly worked for Asplundh.[11]

Nordstrom, the upscale department store chain based in Seattle, is another highly visible example of how these complex systems can be successfully managed. The company was founded as a shoe store in 1901 by Swedish immigrant John Nordstrom and a partner whom he later bought out. John's sons, Everett, Lloyd, and Elmer Nordstrom, took over the business during the Depression of the 1930s. They realized that their ability to work as a team was crucial to the success of the business. Everett, the oldest, was the natural choice for president, but he took the position on the condition that the posts of president, vice president, and secretary-treasurer would be rotated every two years. The brothers operated as a team. They discussed major options and tried to resolve differences of opinion by finding a consensus rather than by a majority vote. All three were reluctant to override the views of any one member of the group. *The Nordstrom Way* by Robert Spector and Patrick D. McCarthy recalls an episode that reveals the brothers' decision-making style. In the early 1960s, the brothers were weighing a diversification into women's apparel through purchase of the Best stores in Seattle. Elmer, the middle brother, dissented, saying, "We really don't know the apparel business. I think we should do what we know how to do and expand, maybe into San Francisco, with shoe stores." Lloyd, who had spent four years negotiating for purchase of the Best stores, replied, "Fine, we won't do it." That apparently surprised Elmer, who then said, "Wait a minute. If you guys want to do it, then we'll do it." Jim Nordstrom, a member of the third-generation partnership, was present during the conversation and it made a big impression on him. "They got into a heck of an argument, trying to honor the other guy's wishes. I thought that was a good lesson to all of us."[12]

Jim's generation had to convince their fathers that they had the right stuff to run the business and could get along as well as had Everett, Lloyd, and Elmer. The brothers were skeptical and wanted to protect their estates by selling the company to an established retailer. Jim and two of his cousins, Bruce Nordstrom and John Nordstrom, and Lloyd's son-in-law, Jack McMillan, argued that they could run the business better than any of the large companies with whom the brothers were negotiating. They presented a detailed business plan, proposing to buy the stores from their seniors by taking the company public. The seniors agreed. The four Nordstrom cousins ran the company as a team, just as their elders had done, sharing authority and making decisions by consensus. They continued to diversify the merchandise offered in the stores, built a nationwide reputation for exceptional customer service, and expanded into major cities across the country. During their tenure, which neared an end in 1995 (Jim Nordstrom died the following year), Nordstrom sales zoomed from $57 million to $4 billion. Now a team of fourth-generation cousins is being groomed to follow in their path. Six cousins who have been working in the company, all in their thirties, were named copresidents in 1996; they report to a pair of long-time non-family executives who serve as cochairmen.

Observed from the outside, it is often difficult to discern what accounts for the viability of these collective family systems. The partners have usually reached unique compromises and adaptations that enable them to disagree without destroying the partnership. The bumblebee is designed a little differently in each case, but still seems to fly! Barbara Hollander, the late family business consultant, wrote about a chain of retail credit clothing stores in Wheeling, West Virginia, that for three decades was run by her father, Sam Stone, and her two uncles, Mark and Arthur. The three brothers were equal owners of Richards, Inc. (named after Hollander's brother) and functioned as equals on an executive team. Sam, who fulfilled the controller role and oversaw finance, was the acknowledged leader, but over time, Arthur, the youngest brother, who headed operations, became a strong figure.

All three brothers were committed to the goal of making the business grow, and to maintaining equality in all important decisions affecting the welfare of the firm. Yet they recognized that each needed to rule in his own domain. Luckily, the business permitted each to have a high degree of autonomy. They operated out of offices in different cities. But whenever major business decisions had to be made, they would fly to New York and "check out the figures" over their mother's kitchen table.[13]

Hollander was impressed by the unity achieved by her father and uncles, who were all good friends when they retired. She was convinced that sibling partnerships could function effectively, "but only with better planning by both the founder and his offspring than most firms normally do."

Much of the literature on team building is pertinent to sibling partnerships. But sibling teams do have a number of qualities that make them distinctive as performance units. These partnerships often have more going for them than other kinds of teams. The knowledge of one's brothers and sisters that comes from growing up in the same household—an awareness and appreciation of one another's goals, attitudes, and reactions to specific circumstances—can lead to synergies and decisiveness in managing a business together. When this shared history is blended with a common sense of purpose and complementary skills, the mixture can be phenomenally powerful.

I worked with two brothers who inherited a multibillion-dollar textile manufacturing company from their father. The older brother had little formal education, entering the company right after high school. The younger brother had a degree in chemical engineering, which was very important to the company. The company carried the father's name—which was the same as the older brother's—so it was changed when the younger brother joined the business. The brothers were fifty–fifty owners and copresidents; for legal reasons, each also held the title of chairman in alternate years. They described the company as "bicephalous"—that is, a body with two heads. These brothers had passionate battles because of their differences in style and approach. The older brother tended to be conservative and risk-averse. The younger brother was much more entrepreneurial. Privately, each brother wished that the business had only one leader—himself. What neither fully appreciated was how their different mindsets improved the quality of top-management decisions, with one brother's venturesome attitude spurring the company's spectacular growth and the other's prudence providing a brake on excessive risks. Such was the continuing dialogue between the two that each had incorporated much of the other's mindset in his own thinking.

The Trend to Plural Leadership

The predominant focus on the CO-to-CO succession, with its tacit commitment to monocracy, has had a number of consequences for both research and practice. From the standpoint of research, it has meant that until very recently few studies have been done on whether collective systems can work and under what conditions. From the perspective of practice it has limited the extent to which deviations from monocracy are considered feasible alternatives. The controlling owner focus has curbed the development of a full appreciation among family business researchers of the wide variety of governance structures and leadership arrangements that actually exist.

Many such arrangements seem to defy long accepted dicta of management theory and practice, including: that in the ideal work setting job responsibilities should be clearly defined; that the equal distribution of salaries and rewards is demotivating and dysfunctional; and that strict meritocracy is better than even restrained favoritism. While many of these dicta are true in the sense that they make organizational life tidier and easier to manage, they should not necessarily be held as strict standards of what is feasible or desirable for a given family or a given business. Human behavior and organizational life are, in fact, much more malleable than that.

Many economic and technological developments over the past twenty years have begun to overturn long held management concepts. The principles underlying the orderly hierarchies envisioned by Max Weber, so often held as the ideal in the context of family business, are now regarded by many as outdated. International competition and more demanding standards of quality from consumers have heightened the need for flexibility in production. Large companies are being asked to produce high quality products and services more cost effectively. Many have risen to the challenge through the use of high technology, increasingly skilled labor, and new organizational forms that foster high commitment and cooperation. These state-of-the-art management arrangements are, in fact, inherently messier: they encourage worker autonomy through job descriptions that are broad, rather than specific; they foster cooperation through teamwork, and the egalitarian distribution of rewards and incentives, like gain-sharing; and they attempt to encourage commitment through various forms of shared leadership and ownership. Many of these new techniques are found in smaller sibling and cousin owned and managed family businesses.

We may be holding family businesses to a conceptual double standard. Frequently criticized for their informality and lack of professionalism, these businesses are compared unfavorably with the highly rationalized organizational structures of large public companies. At the same time, however, large companies today are struggling to "demassify," decentralize, and recapture the virtues of smallness. To prevent bureaucratic hardening of the arteries, they are granting more decision-making autonomy to their various business units.

Alvin Toffler, the futurologist, suggested in his *Power Shift* that small and medium-sized family companies offer a number of strategic advantages that make them ideally suited for the economic conditions of the future. These presumed advantages include a high degree of production flexibility, the efficient long-term use of capital, considerable managerial discretion, and an ongoing commitment to the quality of products and services. Toffler argues that traditional hierarchies with their tidy job descriptions and elaborate personnel and production manuals are rapidly becoming extinct.[14]

The virtues of smallness and flexibility are confirmed in Hermann Simon's study of firms that he calls "hidden champions." Simon, an international consultant and researcher, examined companies in fourteen countries that were either number one or number two in the world (or in Europe) in the market niches they served. These companies were relentlessly devoted to product quality and service. Of 122 German firms surveyed by Simon, a total of 76 percent were privately held, which means that were very likely family firms. The majority had been in business for generations: 23.5 percent were founded between 1845 and 1919, 40.5 percent in the postwar growth period from 1945 to 1969. Surprisingly, although many of these firms were dominated by a single authoritarian leader—a "monomaniac with a mission"—more than 80 percent were formally led by executive teams combining family owner-managers with non-family executives.[15]

The trend to plural leadership is also evident in the executive suites of large public companies. In a study of 270 randomly selected companies including family as well as non-family firms, Vancil found that the percentage of firms managed by a single senior executive has declined significantly since 1964. Most companies today are managed by a "duo" in which two executives, a chairman and a president or CEO, split senior responsibilities. Vancil also points out that "by 1984 the second most common [senior management] structure consisted of three or more executives, each carrying one or more of the top five titles." In these cases, "the team collectively is responsible for the health and survival of the company, resulting in a shared fate."[16] According to Vancil's study, the move toward more shared senior leadership arrangements has resulted from the increasing complexities that most senior executives face in today's business environment. The multiple demands placed on senior executives can be better handled by a leadership team.

Generational transitions are about change, particularly when the destination of the journey is much different from the one with which the family members are familiar. Until very recently, companies planning to travel to less familiar destinations have had few road maps. The more that academic researchers and practitioners studied the predominant CO pattern of leadership, the better they understood it, and the more they became wedded to it as the only feasible path to follow in succession. New research suggests that an increasing number of family companies are run by more or less equal partners, and that many others are contemplating moving toward shared ownership and leadership. In the next chapter, I will outline a typology of family companies, a classification scheme that will be helpful in understanding the range of possible options in moving from one type to another.

CHAPTER 2

A Typology of Successions

IN chapter 1, I argued that long-standing biases in the family business field have blocked understanding of the complexities of succession that these companies face now and in the future. I also suggested that the stubborn adherence to an idealized monocratic succession needlessly curtails the range of options that are considered feasible in any family business. In this chapter I will present a typology of succession in family companies that captures the full range of potential transitions that can and do occur. The first step in bringing order to this multifaceted subject is to understand the fundamental forms of family business. The second is to develop a framework for organizing the possible types of successions that can occur when moving from one basic form to another during generational transitions.

The framework I propose is based on the assumption that ownership is the most useful variable for distinguishing among the different family business forms. Legitimate decision-making authority derives, in the final analysis, from property rights that the law confers upon the shareholders. While in theory this is true in all businesses, large public companies have such fragmented and remote ownership that de facto control over governance issues is primarily in the hands of senior management.[1] In contrast, ownership control in privately held family businesses, and in publicly traded companies that are controlled by families, is usually in the hands of a relatively small group of shareholders, most

27

Figure 2-1   Basic Family Forms

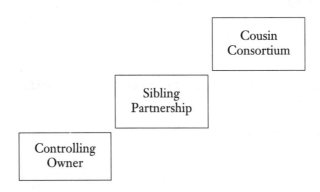

of whom are—by definition—closely related. The influence of the owners in these companies is direct and pervasive. However, in many larger companies, especially those whose stock is publicly traded, the family may exert its influence indirectly through mechanisms such as holding companies and complex systems of trusts. In working with older, multigenerational companies, I have found that one can rarely assess the family's full holdings strictly from stock in the hands of individual family members. As Zeitlin[2] has showed, legendary families such the du Ponts, Mellons, Fords, and Rockefellers often own sizable numbers of shares through their banking and insurance institutions as well as elaborate networks of interlocking holding companies.

Whether or not the owners are working in management, they hold the ultimate power in the company. This assumption in no way diminishes the importance of managerial authority in many companies. The point is simply that in family businesses, the traditional distinction between ownership and management is at best blurred, so that, when the chips are down, ownership rights typically prevail over managerial authority.

When viewed from the vantage point of the ownership distribution, and hence of influence over governance, family businesses come in three fundamental forms: the controlling owner business, the sibling partnership, and the cousin consortium (see Figure 2-1).[3]

Historically, these basic forms of family companies have been associated with the generational stage that the company is in, so that a controlling owner business in the first generation becomes a sibling partnership in the second, and a cousin consortium in the third.

An historical example of this classic evolution is E. I. du Pont de Nemours and Company, now the largest producer of chemicals in the United States. The company was founded in 1802, with the help of French capital, by Eleuthère Irénée du Pont de Nemours. After his death in 1834, the company went from a single controlling owner structure to a sibling partnership when du Pont's sons, Alfred, Alexis, and Henry, took over the company, buying out the other partners in order to ensure family control. Then, in 1902, three du Pont cousins, Pierre, Alfred, and Coleman, bought Du Pont. Pierre bought out Coleman's share and became the controlling owner for a time with his two brothers, but after them the stock was held by numerous cousins through a holding company, Christiana Securities. The holding company was dissolved during the modern era when a well respected non-family CEO, Irving Shapiro, sought to reduce the family's influence. His efforts notwithstanding, the du Pont descendants continue to control the largest bloc of shares in the company and a number of family members still hold seats on the board.[4]

Although there is often a correlation between business form and generational stage, the progression does not always follow a predetermined sequence. For example, some of the most famous family companies were founded not by a single entrepreneur but by a pair of siblings or a sibling team—Bloomingdale's department store and the Cargill grain empire started as sibling partnerships. Similarly, there are family businesses that have existed for generations as controlling owner businesses. For example, the Beretta family, the Italian gun makers, have scrupulously passed stock down in a direct line to a single capo through thirteen generations; in fact, the present CEO, Ugo Gussalli Beretta, was adopted by his uncle so that the succession could remain in the same family.[5]

Before examining the variety of transitions that can occur, it will be helpful to briefly describe these three basic forms of family business, paying particular attention to the structural features of each.

The Controlling Owner Form

Perhaps no author has captured the reality—and the folklore—of the controlling owner business better than Léon Danco. In reading Danco, one quickly realizes that the distinguishing feature of these types of family companies is the centrality of the controlling owner:

Figure 2-2   The Controlling Owner Form: The Business

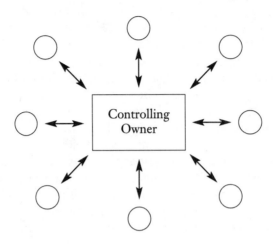

[The controlling owner] has an organization chart that resembles a spider. He sits in the middle of the web and periodically goes out to confer with the plant foreman or the warehouse superintendent or the sales manager. But it is still "me" and "him," one-on-one. Nobody gets together to set objectives or compare data. . . Nobody tells the boss he shouldn't behave that way. For employees to say so would be mutiny. Their jobs depend upon compliance with his basic management philosophy. . . . Loyalty and tenure provide the moves up the organization ladder.[6]

Controlling owners are inextricably involved with all aspects of their business. They have a deep understanding of the products and services the company delivers and they serve as the company's link to critical external resources such as banks, suppliers, and clients. They personally sign for loans extended to the business and offer their assets as collateral. As Danco suggests, the controlling owner organization is usually designed like a wheel with owner at the hub. Information about everything from paper clips to major acquisitions flows towards the center, and decisions then radiate outward to managers and employees on the rim (see Figure 2-2).

This structure works well during the early stages of growth of the business in which quick adaptations to customer needs and market requirements are critical. If the business grows in size and complexity, however, this structure becomes overloaded—as does the controlling

Figure 2-3 The Controling Owner Stage: The Family

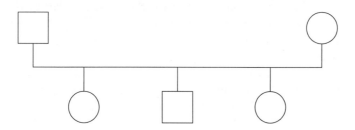

owner himself. Beyond a certain threshold of complexity, the control-ling owner can no longer keep up with the information-processing requirements of the business and is forced to delegate. Delegation, however, does not come easily to most controlling owners. Typically, they retain control of all critical decisions, regardless of the size of the company. As Ward and others have pointed out, controlling owner businesses often lack a functioning board of directors. Typically, if there is a board it is a rubber stamp board that caters to the wishes of the controlling owner.

Although many controlling owners are often too busy running their businesses to spend much time with their families, the fact that they command the economics of the family makes them powerful in that system. The business usually has an important psychological pres-ence in the family, and the controlling owner determines which family members get jobs and share in the benefits. Typically, the family at this stage is still relatively simple in its structure and resembles what is gen-erally thought of as a nuclear family with father, mother, and children at various stages of their development (see Figure 2-3).

When the controlling owner is also the founder of the business, he or she acquires a symbolic stature that permeates many aspects of the business's culture.[7] In these firms the organizational culture often reflects the founder's psychology and world view. This special stature of founders has some important consequences for succession. For one thing, founders are a hard act to follow. For another, the succession from the founder to a second generation is a particular challenge because the family business lacks experience in planning for the depar-ture of the top leader and the process of taking charge by a new leader.

Not all controlling owner businesses are first-generation compa-nies. Ownership and management control may be transferred to a single heir in any generation. Typically, this occurs when only one member of the next generation is interested in the business, or when parents believe the wisest course is to turn the business over to the child that they view as the most competent and provide the others with alternative assets such as real estate or (in their estate) the proceeds of life insurance; or the owners may simply have a strong belief that concentrating ownership and control in the hands of a single individual is necessary to ensure coherence in policy and efficiency in management.

The Sibling Partnership Form

In this type of family business—favored by many parents who wish to see their children working as a team—the ownership structure is divided more or less equally among a group of siblings. In its pure form no one has a clear advantage over the others, and ways must be found to share influence over decision making.

Shared ownership implies that the siblings are accountable to each other and need to acknowledge, directly or indirectly, one another's needs, perspectives, and preferences. Coordinating the input of the various siblings can be time-consuming and frustrating. This is particularly the case when some of the sibling partners are not involved with the management of the company. In these situations, those siblings who are in the business are more knowledgeable and often have more influence over governance decisions than those who are only shareholders. Maintaining a workable balance of power among the siblings is a fundamental challenge in these systems.

Sibling partnerships come in two fundamental forms: the first-among-equals form and the shared leadership arrangement.[8] The first-among-equals form involves a group in which there is one acknowledged leader. Lead siblings in these types of partnerships cannot and do not act unilaterally. On the contrary, these siblings learn early on to behave in consultative ways and to work toward consensus by continuously brokering deals with the others. In some family companies, the lead sibling's role is formally recognized and differentiated through titles and perks, while in others he or she is allowed to influence the other siblings only informally. In order for this form of sibling partnership to be stable and effective, the leader must prove his or her managerial abilities to the other siblings; the others need to know that their economic interests are advanced by granting the lead sibling relatively more authority. While exerting their authority in the business, lead

Figure 2-4   The Sibling Partnership Form: The Business

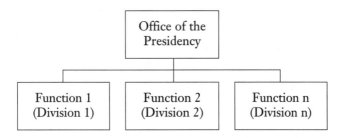

siblings in turn must continuously struggle to avoid assuming the role of a parent in their relations with brothers and sisters. For whenever they do, conflict inevitably arises in the partnership.

The second type of sibling partnership is the shared leadership arrangement, in which the siblings lead the company as a team. The partners in this system are not only equal shareholders but also have equal managerial authority. In some such partnerships, there is a de facto "office of the presidency" and all managerial decisions of significance are made by the siblings as a group (see Figure 2-4). Salaries and bonuses are typically divided equally, and, while there may be functional (or divisional) distinctions in the siblings' responsibilities, it is presumed that they are equals in terms of their decision-making authority. In these systems, getting employees and the outside world to understand and work with the shared leadership arrangement is often a critical challenge.

The family structure associated with sibling partnerships is considerably more complex than that of the controlling owner form. Now the family involves the parents, the siblings, and the siblings' spouses and children (see Figure 2-5).

As we shall see later, whether a sibling partnership is organized along the lines of the shared leadership form or the first-among-equals form has important implications for how succession unfolds in the next generation.

The Cousin Consortium

This form of family business is characterized by a fragmented owner-ship structure that has been divided, often over the course of several

Figure 2-5   The Sibling Partnership Phase: The Family

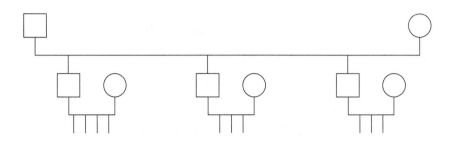

generations, among various branches of an extended family (see Figure 2-6). The distinguishing feature of this form is its dynastic character and the fact that the stock is held by a large number of cousins; in one of the companies I studied, the shareholder group was composed of more than 230 cousins, all direct descendants of the company's founder.

An endemic concern in cousin consortiums is managing the political dynamics among the various branches of an extended family. The degree of influence of any given branch often depends on three factors. First, the number of cousins in the branch: The fewer the number compared with other branches, the more stock they are likely to control and the more influence they are likely to have. Second, the ability of the cousins in a branch to form a coalition and act in a concerted way; rarely, however, does one branch own enough stock to have clear control over major decisions. Third, the number of cousins from a given branch who hold senior positions in the company: The larger a branch's representation in senior management, the greater its influence relative to other branches.

In cousin companies, senior management positions are often held by representatives of several branches of the family; in addition, there are often a large number of shareholding cousins who are not involved in the business. Families tend to grow exponentially; businesses tend to grow, at best, linearly. Over time, the size of individual shareholdings shrinks, and cousins who are not employed in the firm become increasingly concerned with the ability of the company to provide them with a steady stream of dividends. The larger the shareholder group becomes, the wider the asymmetries of information between shareholding cousins who work in the business and those who do not—a fact

Figure 2-6   The Cousin Consortium Phase: The Family

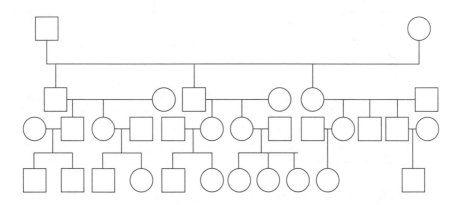

that is frequently frustrating to the cousins involved with management.

A dilemma that frequently plagues cousin consortiums is the trade-off between working capital and shareholder liquidity. On the one hand, as the business expands and ages, it demands increasing sums of working capital. On the other hand, as the ownership group grows, individuals become increasingly unable to sustain their lifestyles on the basis of their dividends. A growing number of shareholders may want to cash in their stock, but since there isn't a ready market for shares in a privately held company, management may face the need to provide some kind of buyout fund if they wish to keep the business in the family.

The spread of ages between family members in succeeding generations increasingly widens in an extended family. Whereas in a nuclear family the difference between the oldest and the youngest sibling is usually no more than ten or fifteen years, it is not unusual in a cousin consortium to see a thirty-year difference between the oldest and the youngest cousins—even when they are technically of the same generation. In a controlling owner business, management succession and ownership succession tend to occur more or less at the same time, but in cousin consortiums these two transitions tend to be decoupled. As more and more cousins mature, transfers of ownership from parents to children become a continuous process. Management succession, however, takes place at discrete intervals, whenever the top leadership is ready to retire. Thus, the ownership and management transitions are often out of sync and uncoordinated. Also, it is not unusual for each branch of the family to develop its own estate planning strategy, thus weakening the capacity of the family as a whole to continue its control of the ownership.

Unless the system has been extensively professionalized, managerial leadership in these firms is often a tenuous proposition at best. Having only a small fraction of the stock, the cousin or cousins leading this type of family firm must derive their authority from their ability to manage the business successfully and from their influence within the family. If the performance of the firm falls off, or if there is a family dispute, the cousins in the leadership may rapidly lose their ability to manage the cousin shareholders. This is particularly the case in the absence of governance structures such as a functioning board of directors.

In addition, the cousins in senior management often find that they are trapped in caretaker roles. As their individual shareholdings become diluted over generations, they cannot expect the substantial rewards that are an important part of the motivation of a controlling owner. For example, the chief cousin in a consortium that I studied explained how frustrated he felt by the many constraints imposed on his autonomy by his shareholder cousins. This man told me he could no longer function as an entrepreneur. He also resented the enormous amounts of time he had to devote to informing his cousins and convincing them of the reasons for his strategic decisions.

It is important to keep in mind that the shareholders in a typical cousin consortium often do not behave like capitalists in the traditional sense. They have acquired their shares through inheritance and, if they are not active in the business, they may be psychologically detached from it, ignorant of its operations, and risk-averse. Many are interested only in the size and frequency of dividends. Often, they do not have even a rudimentary understanding of the basic economic principles governing corporate investments.

Cousins in charge of the business can invest considerable effort in trying to organize the nonparticipating cousins into a coherent and economically rational shareholder group. When professional managers are in charge, the task of keeping cousin shareholders committed to the company is particularly difficult. The case of the Dorrance family of Campbell's Soup, the diversified food giant, makes this problem abundantly clear. In the late 1980s, with Campbell's profits slipping, a group of dissident cousins threatened to sell their stock, which might have precipitated the sale of the $6.6 billion, publicly traded company. The dissidents calmed down during the 1990s after a new CEO, David

Johnson, changed the company's strategy and strengthened profits.

Cousin consortiums are often diversified into a number of different business units controlled by a family holding company. The distribution of cousins among the various business units is often not random. Frequently the business units are managed by a mix of cousin and professional non-family managers. It is not unusual for a tradition to develop in which the descendants of each branch play a more dominant role in one or another business unit. Thus, a specialization by family branch develops. In some companies, the original business continues to be the dominant enterprise, while in others it has been phased out or relegated to a minor role.

The holding company is in turn controlled by an often elaborate governance structure that includes a board with representatives from various branches of the family as well as outside directors, a family council, a shareholders' assembly, and a family foundation (see Figure 2-7). In these systems, the function of such an elaborate governance structure is to regulate the relationships among an increasingly complex group of family shareholders with varying economic needs and interests. These structures also define the boundaries separating ownership, management, and family decisions.[9]

Transitions Between Types:
The Succession Journey

We have seen that the three basic forms of family business—the controlling owner business, the sibling partnership, and the cousin consortium—are fundamentally different in structure and culture. What may work wonders in one form can, and often is, a recipe for disaster in another. Each has unique structural properties; each offers specific advantages and disadvantages; each demands different managerial skills from its leaders. As we'll see, these differences have a powerful effect on the nature of the succession transition.

The succession journey begins when the generation currently in control of a family business starts to worry about transferring ownership control and management responsibilities. It ends when these people have fully turned over the control of the business to the next generation. The basic idea underlying this framework is that the form a business has at the start of the journey, and the form it will have once the journey is completed, will profoundly affect the journey itself.

When succession involves replacing the leadership while main-

Figure 2-7   Governance Structure for Complex
                Cousin Consortiums

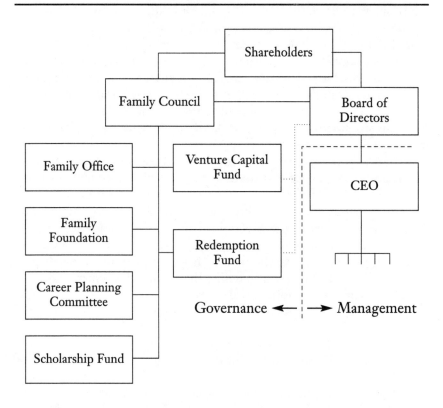

taining the basic form of the business, much of the accumulated learning from the past about how leadership and authority is exercised and how decisions are made is transferable to the future. However, when succession involves not just a changing of the guard, but also a restructuring of the fundamental form of the business, the adaptation required is of a higher order of magnitude. In this case, little of what worked effectively in the past is likely to work well in the future. In fact, in these transitions a great deal of energy must be invested in unlearning many old behavioral assumptions and organizational procedures regarded by many in the system as key determinants of success in the previous business form.

The framework that I will describe establishes a conceptual distinction between three types of succession transitions. First, there are

Figure 2-8 Succession Transitions that Recycle
the Business Form

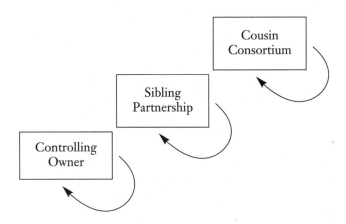

transitions that involve replacing the senior leadership without changing the fundamental form of the business—the people change but the
authority structure remains the same. I refer to these types of successions as "recycles." Three types of successions involve a recycling of
the previous business form: controlling owner to controlling owner,
sibling partnership to sibling partnership, and cousin consortium to
cousin consortium (see Figure 2-8).

When an entrepreneur successfully transfers a controlling interest in the company to one, and only one, of his children who becomes
his successor in management, the company has undergone a controlling owner to controlling owner recycle. This is the most common
form of succession, and there are numerous examples—Forbes, Inc.,
Bechtel Corp., the Beretta Company in Italy, to name a few. One of
best known is S.C. Johnson & Son, makers of Johnson Wax and the
insecticide Raid, which has had a single family member as its leader
and controlling stockholder through four successive generations. The
company's present CEO, Samuel C. Johnson, has written about the
benefits of concentrating control of the stock in the most talented
member of the family: "Our firm has been fortunate in that there has
been one logical successor in each generation. . . . When a strong
leader departs and several people fight to take that place, it is obvious
how messy the situation can become."[10]

A sibling partnership is recycled most often when one senior partner buys out the others and passes the business to his or her children, who then run it with the same basic partnership structure. The case of a Canadian company, Black & McDonald, illustrates how this can happen. Black & McDonald, which installs electrical and mechanical systems in commercial buildings across Canada, was founded in 1921 by two World War I army buddies. After buying out his partner, Mr. McDonald passed ownership to his two sons, John and Bill, who have run the company as partners for more than thirty years. Since the older brother, John McDonald, has no offspring interested in the company, he expects to leave most of his stock to the four sons of Bill McDonald, who are all planning careers with the Toronto-based firm. The two senior partners envision that Bill's sons will eventually control the company and manage it as equals, just as they did.

A sibling partnership may also be recycled when control of a company is passed from a group of older siblings to a group of younger siblings. This type of sibling-to-sibling recycle is more rare, because it requires an unusual set of circumstances. First, the younger siblings have to be willing and able to take over the company, and, second, the age spread among the siblings has to be wide enough so that the younger partners have sufficient time after they take over to make their mark—that is, the successor team has to be young enough to lead the business for an interval of years.[11]

Yet another type of succession recycle takes place when control of a business is transferred from one generation of cousins to another. Cousin-to-cousin successions tend to be associated with dynastic family businesses that move from the third to the fourth generation and beyond. In the United States, where relatively few family businesses make it to the third generation at all—and many offspring pursue careers in other fields—this type of succession is still rare. There are, however, examples of companies like Cargill and Milliken that have existed as cousin consortiums for at least one generation. In Europe, where dynastic family companies are more common, it is easier to find examples of companies such as Michelin, Lego, and Codorniu that have existed as cousin consortiums for well over three generations. Once a company becomes a cousin consortium and its stock becomes widely distributed among members of an extended family, it is usually very difficult for it to move out of that form. At this stage, changing forms requires either consolidating the stock and the control of the company in the hands of a smaller group of owners or selling significant amounts of stock to outsiders and thus weakening the family's control of the enterprise.

Figure 2-9   Three Types of Evolutionary Successions

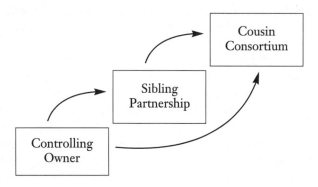

The second type of succession transition involves fundamental changes in the authority and control structure of the system. In these successions, the system experiences a metamorphic change toward greater structural complexity. I refer to this type as an evolutionary succession, meaning one in which the system evolves from a simpler form toward an increasingly complex one. There are three types of evolutionary successions: controlling owner to sibling partnership, sibling partnership to cousin consortium, and controlling owner to cousin consortium (see Figure 2-9).

The transition from a controlling owner firm to a sibling partnership requires a quantum change in the leadership structure of a family business. Decisions that were previously taken by a single individual now have to be made by a team of brothers and sisters whose economic destinies are closely intertwined. This change leads to a redefinition of the ground rules guiding how decisions are made and implemented.[12] It requires a major adaptation in the way key stakeholders interact.

When a sibling partnership is transformed into a cousin consortium, the change implies a total redefinition of the authority and governance structures of the company. As stock moves from the hands of a closely knit group of siblings to an extended cousin system, management must accommodate a diversity of needs and perspectives, and the differentiation and coordination of governance and management decisions becomes increasingly complex. The need for structures to regulate participation across family groupings becomes more pressing. This type of succession tends to occur in more mature businesses that have been around for at least three generations, and these are still relatively rare in the United States—not so in Europe, Asia, and Latin America.

The third type of evolutionary succession—when the system skips a generation and moves from a controlling owner form to a cousin consortium—is also rare. It may occur when a controlling owner is very committed to the ideal of family business continuity but has no direct offspring who are willing or able to take over the company themselves. In such cases, the controlling owner may hire a "bridge manager" to run the company for a period of time until control can be transferred directly to his or her grandchildren. These kinds of transitions are often associated with strategies to minimize the bite of inheritance taxes through the use of such mechanisms as generation-skipping trusts.[13] From a governance standpoint, a complex adaptation is required in order to facilitate the transition from the individual decision maker, during the tenures of a controlling owner and a bridge manager, to the more diffuse collective decision making by a group of cousins.

This conceptual framework identifies one last type of succession that occurs when the transition requires a structural change toward greater simplicity. I refer to this type of succession as devolutionary, meaning a succession that moves the system toward a simpler form. There are three kinds of devolutionary successions: cousin consortium to sibling partnership, sibling partnership to controlling owner business, and cousin consortium to controlling owner business. These types of successions are rare and remain poorly understood. They are rare because a significant amount of liquidity is required to concentrate the control of the stock in the hands of either a sibling branch within a cousin consortium or of a single individual in a sibling or cousin system.[14] Nonetheless, I have studied and documented several cases of these kind of transitions (see Figure 2-10).

When a cousin consortium gets too large, one or more branches of the family may decide to sell their shares to a single branch, and the business may revert to a sibling partnership. It is not unusual for branches of a cousin consortium to become disenchanted with the family business and to decide to cash out. There are also cases in which the cousins decide to split the business up into smaller independent units; when the division is done along family lines, each of these businesses can become an autonomous sibling partnership.

Similarly, there are successions that involve going from a sibling partnership to a controlling owner business. This can happen either when sibling partners decide to sell their shares in the family company

Figure 2-10   Three Types of Devolutionary Successions

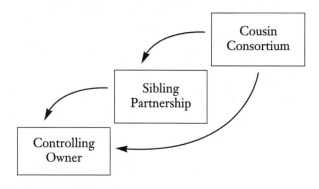

to one of the siblings or, more frequently, when siblings realize that they prefer to be in business by themselves and decide to split the company into smaller independent businesses. Quite frequently parents force their children into sibling partnerships by dividing their stock in a business equally without giving due consideration to whether or not the children can and want to be partners. What starts out as a sibling partnership gets undone as soon as the siblings have the freedom to exercise their own preference for more independence and autonomy.

A comparable change can happen in a cousin syndicate when one branch of the family buys out the other branch and installs a single family member as the leader, or, when only one heir is willing or able to take charge, the system can over time transform itself from a cousin syndicate to a controlling owner business.

The Frequency of the Different Types

No comprehensive survey has been done showing the percentages of companies that currently have one or another of the three basic family business forms, or how many plan to move to a different business form in the next generation. However, over the past four years I have been systematically collecting information at family business conferences I have led around the country in order to get a preliminary idea of the

Table 2-1 Accounts of Current and Future Ownership Distribution

	Likely Ownership in the Future			
Current Ownership	Controlling Owner	Sibling Partnership	Cousin Consortium	Total
Controlling Owner	85	161	3	249
Sibling Partnership	8	54	65	127
Cousin Consortium			25	25
Total	93	215	93	401

diversity of choices and the preferences of owners. Following a detailed explanation of the three basic family business forms, I administered a short questionnaire asking audiences to indicate which form best described the current ownership and control structure of their family business, and which form they thought would best describe their business in the next generation. Altogether, questionnaires were collected representing family business owners from 401 family companies (see Table 2-1).

Of the 401 companies in this sample, 249 (62.1% of the total) identify themselves as being controlling owner firms currently, 127 (31.7% of the total) report being sibling partnerships, and 25 (6.2% of the total) consider themselves cousin consortiums. Of the 249 controlling owner businesses, 85 (34.1%) expect that their companies will recycle the controlling owner form into the next generation, but 161 (64.6%) expect to transform themselves into sibling partnerships. Finally, only 3 out of the 249 (1.2%) expect to skip a generation and become cousin consortiums in the future.

Of the 127 sibling partnerships, 65 (51.1%) expect to evolve to cousin consortiums, while 54 (42.5%) expect to recycle the sibling partnership form. Only 8 (6.2%) of the sibling partnerships expect to devolve into controlling owner businesses. All 25 cousin consortiums expect to retain that form through the next generation, suggesting that once a company reaches the cousin consortium stage, it is much more likely to recycle that form than to devolve into either a sibling partnership or a controlling owner business.

Given the limited size and non-random nature of my sample, the findings of this survey cannot be regarded as representative of the universe of family businesses. Nevertheless, the numbers suggest that family business owners do, in fact, consider a wider array of succession options than is typically depicted in the family business literature. In addition, the data are consistent with the findings of much larger surveys. For example, a 1997 survey of 3,000 family companies conducted by Arthur Andersen found that 10 percent had two CEOs at the helm and another 1 percent had more than two CEOs. Even more surprising, 42 percent reported that it was possible their companies would have co-CEOs in the succeeding generation.

Transitional Periods

Whether a family business is recycling the same system or moving toward a different system will have a major impact on most of the substantive issues associated with the transition, including who gets involved in managing the transition, what kinds of resistance are encountered, how the seniors in control will depart, and how those taking charge will assume and consolidate their authority.

To illustrate the conflicts that shake organizations evolving from one of the three basic forms to another, it may be helpful to use a sports metaphor. Controlling owners, like singles tennis players, have to decide their own strategy, are unaccustomed to playing on a team, and thrive in situations that enable them to demonstrate their prowess and achieve personal glory. Like a tennis star, the controlling owner is likely to have large ego needs, strong views that are reflected throughout the company, and little respect for authority—particularly for umpires or for outside board members. For those reasons, it would hardly be advisable to make Jimmy Connors or Andre Agassi coach of a basketball team, which depends more on synergies among the five players, a sharing of information, team spirit, and a subordination of egos in order to achieve success. Yet in family companies going from a controlling owner to sibling ownership and management, this is exactly what happens. The "coach" is a Jimmy Connors who is often not qualified to teach teamwork.

Nor are members of the next generation open to learning it. They have, after all, been raised in a "spider organization" and may well have modeled themselves on the parent-owner, whose dominating, leader-of-the-pack entrepreneurial style emphasizes the qualities that could be disastrous in a collaborative sibling partnership. The younger family members thus face the additional challenge of trying to learn new skills in an organizational environment that is essentially hostile to the most important requirement for a successful partnership—teamwork among equals. Everyone recognizes that it was the style of the former leader that accounted for the company's success. To move toward a sibling partnership, the next generation must, in effect, unlearn those skills without any guarantee that the new, collaborative style can achieve similar results.

A similar structural mismatch occurs when a company is moving from a sibling partnership to a cousin consortium. The outgoing generation's long experience of shared authority and teamwork may have only limited application to preparing the next generation of leaders. We can compare this transition to five players on a championship basketball team trying to run a large soccer club.[15] The five know each others' habits and moves well, and have managed their relationships informally for years through face-to-face communication with a minimum of rules or formal procedures. But managing a major soccer club with multiple teams, elaborate season schedules, coaches and officials with frequently conflicting agendas, and many more players and avid fans can be considerably more complicated. The numerous players and coaches may know little—and care less—about one another's habits and needs. The league organizers may be unskilled in dealing with inter-team politics, just as sibling partners may be totally incapable of dealing with conflicts among family branches. Coordinating the multiple activities of the club requires structures, rules, and policies, all of which would be regarded as a cumbersome and unnecessary imposition by a basketball team—or a team of siblings—used to working in more informal ways. But in the transition process, again, the single most important element for success in the next generation—structure—is resisted throughout the organization. When the cousins seek advice from their elders on resolving problems among themselves, for example, they are told to just "get along" or "have a glass of wine together and work it out"—which is how the siblings did it.

Transition periods are particularly complex in evolutionary successions, because moving toward greater complexity in leadership structures increases the chances of underestimating the challenges. During these transitions, two types of structures coexist uneasily within the company, each with distinctive characteristics that often bring its supporters into conflict with leaders of the other (see Figure 2-11). The aging entrepreneur, for example, may continue to rule single-handedly while an emerging group of sibling partners attempt to establish their credibility as the future leadership team.

Figure 2-11 Transitional Periods

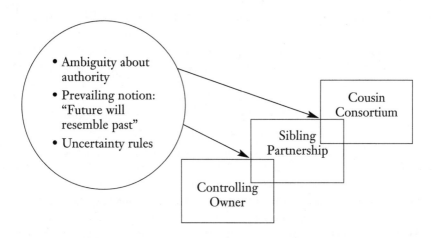

The risks of structural conflict[16] are enhanced for several reasons. Typically, the leaders currently in control are not aware of how the system requirements for the future differ from those that have worked so well for them. Hence their ability to coach and mentor the next generation is significantly compromised. Similarly, the juniors do not fully appreciate the changing structural requirements and get into trouble when they attempt to model their behavior on that of the senior leaders. In fact, the assumption that what worked well in the past will work well in the future is shared throughout the system, among non-family senior managers as well as family members. Even external stakeholders such as customers and suppliers, who are accustomed to dealing with a single leader in their business relationships, tend to resist the movement toward a sibling team.

The symptoms of the underlying clash between the values of different systems surface in varied ways. Tensions between generations become evident if the controlling owner inadvertently imposes his worldview on the sibling successor team. The seniors often feel resentful and unappreciated because others seem to regard their knowledge and experience as irrelevant for the future. There may be increasing ambiguity about who is really in charge of the company; the older leader may be making decisions that the new leaders are undermining or even reversing. Sibling rivalries may erupt if the parent, in trying to determine who in the next generation will rise to become the true leader of the system, fosters competition rather than collaboration among his or her offspring.

People in these transitional periods lose sight of the fact that the tensions they are experiencing are due largely to the overlap of two vastly different authority structures, the single leader and the leadership team. In these circumstances, they frequently end up personalizing their conflicts and blaming one another for their difficulties. Understanding succession from a contextual—or structural—standpoint helps to shift people's attention away from blaming and paves the way for more constructive problem solving. It also opens up new possibilities for interventions and learning. For example, methods can be devised for helping the seniors identify those aspects of their past experience that are transferable to the juniors and those that are not. This can be done without devaluing or dismissing the experience of the seniors. In every generational change in leadership, there are things that can be passed down from the old leaders to the new that are very valuable—understanding of the industry, values in dealing with employees, techniques for maintaining customer loyalty, to name a few. However, the fundamental assumptions about the nature of leadership and governance must be altered if the system is to evolve successfully to the desired future state. If people understand that much of what they know may not be relevant for the future, they will be more inclined to explore alternative, more adaptive, approaches. In fact, collaboration between old and new leaders can be strengthened when both generations come to the realization that they face a common challenge in adapting the organization to the needs of the future.

Simultaneous Transitions

The framework presented here has identified nine possible types of successions: three that involve a change in leadership while maintaining the same business form—recycled successions; three that involve a change in leadership while increasing the complexity of the business form—evolutionary successions; and three that involve a change in leadership while simplifying the business form—devolutionary successions.

It is important to emphasize that these nine are "pure types." The real world is even more complex than that. For example, companies do not necessarily go through only one succession at a time. Nor do generational transitions occur all at once. We can think of the transitional period as beginning when members of the next generation first enter the business, and ending when the older leaders turn over control of their stock to the new generation and retire. The timing of the change as well as the length of time required for planning are set by the ages of the key players in the family. If the children were born early, the window for planning can be quite long—as long as twenty years. Conversely, if the children were born later in the parents' lives, there may be less time for accomplishing such essential tasks as training and mentoring successors and preparing the elders for retirement. As we shall see in the Lombardi case, two or three types of successions may be occurring simultaneously in the same company—each posing a separate set of issues that must be resolved.

CHAPTER 3

The Lombardi Family Business

I first met the Lombardis[1] in 1983 when they engaged me as a consultant. The family called on me not because they were in deep trouble but because they were broad-minded enough to realize that their enterprise—and their family—had grown so large that planning for the future would not be simple. They wanted an outsider to help them sort out complex generational issues and set up structures to ensure a smooth transition in leadership.

What made the Lombardis so interesting to observe was that they were engaged, simultaneously, in two separate leadership transitions. The first was from a system controlled by a single owner, founder Paul Lombardi, Sr., to a sibling partnership of his five adult offspring. While consolidating this second-generation transition, the family was looking ahead to a third generation in which ownership would be shared by twenty-seven cousins, ranging in age from ten to thirty-five years old. A few of the cousins were already working in the company, and all were eager to prove to their elders that they have "the right stuff." Both transitions posed a range of options for the company's governance and leadership structure.

Lombardi Enterprises is a $550 million grocery and trucking company in California that includes a chain of markets, an import company, real estate interests, and a winery in the Sonoma Valley. The Lombardis are one of Northern California's best known business

51

dynasties. The father, Paul Sr., who immigrated to the United States in the late 1940s from the Tuscany, is now in his early eighties and retired. His son, Paul Jr., an intense executive in his mid-fifties with an MBA from Harvard, has been CEO of Lombardi Enterprises for fifteen years.

To the company's diverse and far-flung customers and suppliers in the Pacific Northwest, Paul Jr. is a highly effective spokesman for the family enterprise. Under his leadership, Lombardi Enterprises has grown to four or five times the size of the company built by the elder Lombardi. But Paul Jr. is not a controlling owner. He shares decision-making authority with three brothers and a sister, all of them younger. Robert, Stefano, Rita, and Frank Lombardi all own equal shares in the company with Paul Jr., and all have held positions in it for many years—as have their spouses.

The siblings readily acknowledge that Paul Jr.'s leadership has increased their own wealth and carried the company to new heights of profitability and influence. But the oldest brother still gets into trouble whenever he appears to be asserting too much power or pushing his own self-interest in the company. His equally well-educated, hard-working, and competitive siblings insist on being consulted on all major decisions. If Paul Jr. steps out of line and makes a major decision without consulting them, they will remind him, in so many words: "Forget it! You are not our parent. We are equal shareholders in this business, and we want to have a say in all important decisions that affect our assets."

Although they are worldly, middle-aged adults, the Lombardis still exhibit rivalries that can be traced far back in the family's history. Paul Jr.'s siblings can't forget that in childhood, as the oldest of the group, he sometimes assumed a parental role and bossed them around. Nevertheless, this is a family that, from an early age, has learned to cooperate and to enjoy working together for mutual goals. As adults, they have found ways to mute their differences, even joke about them, for the sake of preserving family harmony. The Lombardis have their conflicts and tensions, but in most respects they are a model sibling team. As we shall see, much of the credit for that goes to their parents, Paul Sr. and Anna Lombardi, whose presence is still powerfully felt although both are now elderly. The Lombardis are an ambitious, intense, widely traveled, interesting, spirited, and loving bunch. To appreciate their chemistry as a family, it is essential to know something about their individual personalities and aspirations. The family members (see Figure 3-1):

Figure 3-1 The Lombardi Family

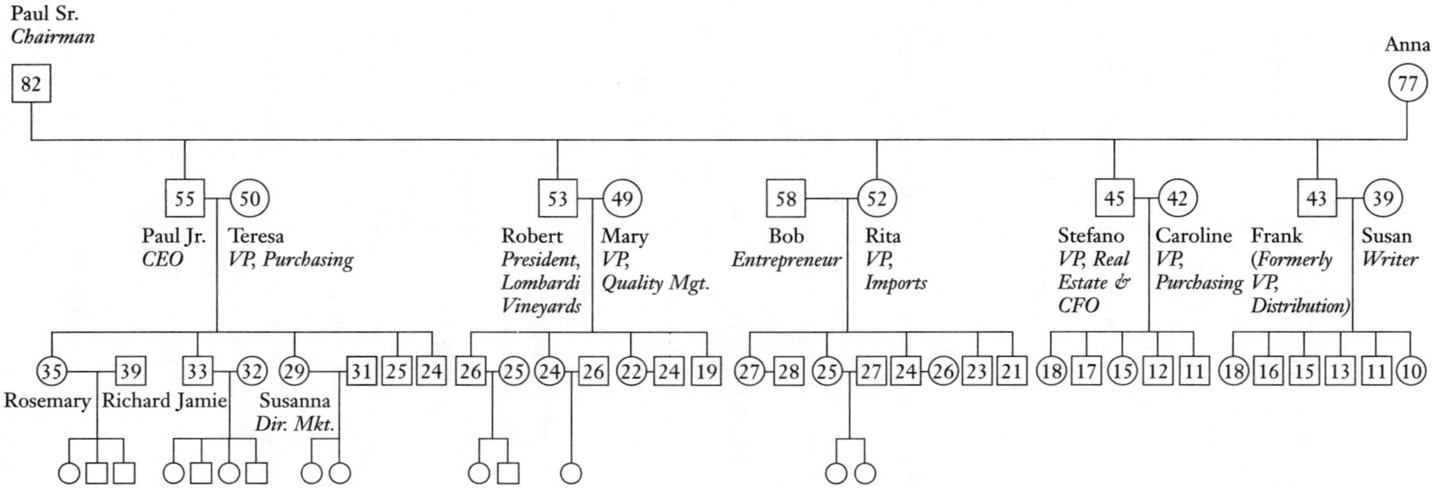

Paul Lombardi, Sr., age eighty-two, the founder of Lombardi Enterprises, was seventy-two when I first met him. The patriarch remained close to his Tuscan roots and traditions, and has never forgotten his humble beginnings. Paul Lombardi, Sr., combined charm and native shrewdness with a relentless drive to succeed. As an immigrant fruit picker, he encountered discrimination from local growers in the Sonoma Valley. He nevertheless managed to save enough money to buy a small truck farm in the valley. After failing at several ventures, he opened the produce market that was the first store in the chain, which over the years then spawned a number of related businesses. The founder's wisdom and experience is frequently invoked by his offspring. "A well-digested failure can pave the way for great success" is one of his favorite aphorisms. Another of his oft-quoted sayings in the family—"If we can dream it, we can do it"—suggests the emphasis the family places on setting ambitious goals. In recent years, the patriarch has been retired and in failing health.

Anna Lombardi, age seventy-seven, though more reserved than her husband, has always been a powerful behind-the-scenes promoter of equality and cooperation among the siblings. A woman of part-German extraction, she and Paul Sr. met and married in Europe before coming to the United States. She was her husband's bookkeeper in the early years of the produce market and exemplifies the family's work ethic. When the children were young, she attended every significant school event in which they took part, from sports to poetry readings. "My mother invented the concept of quality time," Rita says. Throughout her life, Anna Lombardi was an influence on events at Lombardi Enterprises, but her involvement has declined as age and ill health have taken their toll.

Paul Lombardi, Jr., age fifty-five, the oldest Lombardi sibling, demonstrated his business leadership as head of the company's Markets Division. Under his management, the company expanded its supermarket chain from California to other states in the Northwest, growing from twelve stores in 1979 to sixty-five stores in 1990. Although he has been "first among equals" in the second generation for fifteen years, Paul Jr. suffers from what he feels is a lack of recognition and appreciation. He often compares his authority unfavorably to that of his father, who on occasion reminds his son that he presides over a sibling partnership and is thus not free to make some decisions on his own. What Paul Jr. heard his father telling him, in effect, was, "I was a king. You are just a prince among princes."

A manager of great intensity who puts in long hours, Paul Jr. does not mince words with employees or family members who make obvious mistakes or fail to follow instructions. His temper can be volcanic, but he is usually forgiven because of his frequent kindnesses. Paul Jr. recently suffered a mild heart attack. He would like to slow down to smell the roses, and is thinking of retiring five years from now. He is married to Teresa and has five children. Teresa, a highly successful entrepreneur in her own right, has worked for years as a senior buyer for the company.

Robert Lombardi, age fifty-three, the second-oldest brother, heads the well-known Lombardi Vineyard, which produces several popular varietal wines. Although a strong and well-liked manager, Robert Lombardi seems more interested in politics. He was recently elected to the state legislature in California and aspires to run for governor one day. A graduate of Harvard's Kennedy School of Government, Robert is a liberal intellectual who has taken on the role of representing the family's social conscience. He has been active in a variety of environmental and philanthropic organizations in California. Although softer in outward manner than Paul Jr., Robert Lombardi can also be tough and confrontational when provoked. Some family members say he is driven, in part, by a need to match his older brother's business stature by achieving prominence in politics. Robert is married to Mary and they have five children. Mary worked for many years with Teresa and Rita in the purchasing department and recently has been in charge of implementing total quality programs across the company.

Rita Lombardi, age fifty-two, headed the Import Division for many years, buying the assorted handicrafts, clothing, and religious objects sold in Lombardi Markets. The only sister in the sibling group, she plays an important role (as she puts it) in "filing down male egos" and keeping the peace. She is gracious and down-to-earth, trusted by all for her fairness, good judgment, and insight into people. Although she is experienced in business and is an equal voice in ownership and governance issues, she regrets never receiving the education accorded her brothers and feels this as a handicap. As the family member who keeps the siblings functioning as a team, she is seen as the natural successor to her mother. Rita is married to Bob and they have six children. Bob is an independent entrepreneur and has never worked at the company.

Stefano Lombardi, age forty-five, the head of the Real Estate Division, buys and leases land for the company's new markets. Trained as an accountant, he is also deeply involved in managing the company's finances and in developing computerized systems for Lombardi

Enterprises. To his brothers and sister, Stefano seems happiest when crunching numbers and playing with the latest high-tech gadgetry. He is less talkative in groups than his siblings and tends to be uncomfortable expressing emotion. But privately he is just as articulate as his siblings, and can rise to the occasion to make an eloquent speech. He is highly reputed in the real estate field and teaches a course on real estate at San Francisco State University. He is married to Caroline with whom he has five children. Caroline has an MBA and also works in the purchasing department with Rita.

Frank Lombardi, age forty-three, the youngest sibling, was in charge of the Trucking Division, a business that lasted for five years but was recently closed because of heavy losses. Like his father, Frank Lombardi is charming and entrepreneurial by instinct, a good salesman who enjoys socializing with customers and suppliers. He's probably not as good a manager, however, and the failure of the Trucking Division has posed a serious test for the cohesion of the sibling team.

Frank is an adventurous sort who engages in a variety of outdoor sports from mountain climbing to scuba diving. He regularly runs marathons around the world. Frank aspires to move into a leadership position in the mainstream of the business, but he will have to work hard to prove to his siblings that he has learned from the trucking failure and can make a strong future contribution to Lombardi Enterprises. Frank is married to Susan, an accomplished poet and fiction writer who has at times worked for the family company. Frank and Susan have six children. He is very affectionate with his six children and regrets that his job often takes him away from home and family.

Lombardi Enterprises is thus a sweeping canvas, with both vivid and subtle colorations. The first transition from the founder generation was completed in roughly the late 1970s; the future ownership arrangements, however, are not yet clear. Together, the five siblings own 55 percent of the stock, divided equally, and they will eventually inherit their father's 35 percent (10% has been distributed to employees). How stock will be divided in the third generation has not been fully determined.

The second and third generations, moreover, will have to reach agreement on what the future structure of the company will look like. Will the twenty-five cousins be able to develop the same sort of arrangement that has worked so far for their parents? Can structures be developed to accommodate the ambitions of the different branches, including those of the nonparticipating shareholders? Can the cousins in the business learn to harmonize their interests and work as a team?

Or would too much complexity at this stage actually jeopardize the family's wealth and legacy? Should the family prune the shareholder tree and concentrate power in the hands of a few cousins who can then function, like their parents, as a partnership? Would it be simpler to return to one-person rule?

To understand the Lombardis' options and the planning that remains to be done, we must look closely at the family's values. Then we have to examine how Paul Jr. rose to the head of Lombardi Enterprises and how the partnership has evolved.

An Accident Leads to the First Succession

As often happens in family businesses, the succession was precipitated by an unforeseen event. During the summer of 1977, Paul Sr. was swimming at a beach in Northern California. Caught in an eddy, he was dragged down and nearly drowned. He spent almost half a year recuperating in a hospital. Fortunately, at about the time of the accident, Paul Jr. was returning from New York where he had spent two years in a mid-career training program with a large supermarket chain. Prior to that, he had been in charge of Lombardi's Market Division for five years. Now, with his father absent, the son was suddenly called on to make decisions affecting the whole company.

Proving the dictum that power is seized and not given, Paul Jr. not only filled the leadership vacuum but in a short time began to lead the company into new ventures. The son expanded the company's investments in real estate. Realizing that the company's fleet of trucks, used to transport produce to markets, was idle much of the time, he created a small Trucking Division and put his youngest brother, Frank, in charge. When Robert, the COO of the Markets Division, became restless, Paul Jr. created a separate division out of the company's winery in Sonoma, which was booming, and put Robert in charge. That satisfied Robert, who had always chafed at having to take orders from his older brother. His new position gave Robert more autonomy and also left him more time to pursue his political ambitions.

While Paul Jr. was beginning to assert his leadership, the father was recovering from the depression that followed his accident. Upon returning to the company in 1980, Paul Sr. was confronted with undeniable evidence that his children were not only managing the company quite capably but increasing profits. The father acknowledged that Paul Jr. had already become a dominant force in Lombardi

Enterprises. He occasionally asserted his influence by complaining about something the siblings were doing, vetoing a project, or setting limits on what the sibling partners could do. He also held on to the titles of chairman and CEO, which at times irked Paul Jr., who saw his father's title as symbolizing to outsiders Paul Sr.'s continuing dominance in the company. Five years after his near-drowning, however, the patriarch announced his retirement and formally turned over the CEO's job to Paul Jr.

It would be a mistake to conclude that this succession was entirely unplanned, however. Whether consciously or not, Paul and Anna Lombardi cherished the hope that the five children would eventually work together to build a dynastic company. Early on, as in many business families, they had developed a set of assumptions about their children's capabilities and their respective future roles in the business. They had, moreover, nurtured a spirit of collaboration among the siblings.

As the oldest sibling, Paul Jr. had been carefully groomed for a leadership role. But the Lombardis also placed a great deal of emphasis on education and training for *all* their children. The five siblings had jobs in the company from their earliest years. The sons were encouraged to go to the best schools and to seek training outside the business that would be helpful to Lombardi Enterprises. The family encouraged and paid for Frank and Stefano to spend a sabbatical year (with their families) at MIT's prestigious Sloan Fellowship program in Boston.

Although Paul Jr. was well prepared for the role he assumed, his father had never explicitly stated that the oldest son was his designated successor. Even after his accident, Paul Sr. had a choice: Instead of accepting the collaborative partnership system that was developing, he could have anointed Paul Jr. as his sole successor and then proceeded to help the son establish his authority. By sticking with the controlling-owner form, the family would have kept decision making simple and unified, thereby maintaining long-established habits of governance. If any of his children were resentful, he could have assuaged their feelings by giving them some stock or helping them establish businesses of their own outside the company.

With five smart and ambitious children all in the business, however, Paul Lombardi chose to develop a style of management at Lombardi Enterprises that was different in crucial respects from his own. The partnership structure was, in fact, what he and Anna had had in mind all along. Recognizing that the new generation had, in effect, taken over, the patriarch began distributing equal numbers of shares to the five siblings, and he put his stamp of approval on the new management style that was already evolving.

Evolution of the Sibling Structure

With his great energies, Paul Jr. has built the business significantly—its revenues have increased by about 150 percent since 1982—and he feels that his achievements justify his authority. Paul Jr.'s siblings recognize his accomplishments as a manager and are willing to follow his leadership on many important issues. Over time a delicate balance has evolved that allows Paul Jr. sufficient latitude to lead the company, while keeping him keenly aware of the need to consult with his siblings on major decisions. The creation of this sibling partnership is the group's most notable achievement, and Paul Jr.'s willingness to adapt to leading a team has allowed a workable system to emerge.

Under Paul Jr.'s direction, Lombardi Enterprises grew in response to economic opportunities. The subtle interaction of economic forces with the ambitions of the siblings shaped the organizational structure and the way authority was delegated. Clearly, for example, the winery was becoming a big business, needing specialized attention that the Markets Division was not equipped to give it. So it made sense to spin it off as a separate enterprise. But Paul Jr. also wanted a COO in the Markets Division who wasn't always challenging his managerial prerogatives, as Robert did. Creating a new division provided a perfect opportunity for Paul Jr. to get Robert out of his hair and let the second-oldest brother do his own thing; it also allowed Paul to hire a new COO.

The spouses of the three brothers have proven their value to the business. Paul Jr.'s wife, Teresa, was hired first, as chief buyer in the Imports Division headed by Rita. Later, the wives of Robert, Stefano, and Frank became buyers in the Import Division as well. What may look like nepotism was actually a boon to the company. All of the spouses are well-educated, well-traveled women with fine taste, who have had more exposure to trade shows and product markets around the world than most other employees. They have brought exquisite products to Lombardi stores and, like other family members, have reaped the rewards.

The organizational solutions have been well suited to the emotional needs of this family. The Lombardis spend much of their lives in one another's company. There are struggles and rivalries in this family, of course—absence of conflict among such a high-powered group would be a worrisome sign. While the Lombardis occasionally scream and yell at each other, they manage to patch up their differences and continue enjoying their close relationships. If anything, the members have to work at avoiding total submersion in family life and establishing unique personal identities.

The daughters-in-law generally get along well in the Imports Division, for example, but were a little envious of Teresa, who as Paul Jr.'s wife, reigned for years as "queen bee" among buyers. The pecking order among the buyers changed, however, after Caroline, Stefano's wife, took time off to study for an MBA at a top school in California. She came back with a lot of ideas for new products and pricing strategies, which greatly enhanced her influence in the department. Not long after, Teresa left the department to lead the Lombardi family foundation, and Caroline replaced her as head buyer.

Although Paul Jr. is the acknowledged first-among-equals, his power to make decisions is far more circumscribed than was that of his father, who ruled the company for twenty-five years. Along with older, non-family managers in the firm, the siblings had to unlearn many of the ways that they learned in their early training under their father. The scope of Paul Jr.'s authority was defined largely by an ad hoc, trial and error process. When he made a decision on his own and his siblings felt he should have consulted them first, they let him know he had exceeded his authority; he would then know that he must consult with them next time a similar issue arose. When he made a decision and afterward heard no protest from his siblings, he concluded that he had operated within his authority.

Only in recent years have the partners openly discussed and made more explicit the boundaries of the oldest brother's decision-making authority. They have agreed to let the CEO make decisions on any expenditure of money below a certain amount or on ventures that do not commit the company for longer than two years. The partners now meet weekly to discuss major issues facing the enterprise. Paul Jr. knows that on matters of major importance to the company—acquisition of a new business that involves risk, injection of capital into an existing operation, an issue having to do with governance of the corporation—he needs the consent of his sister and brothers.

Of course, reaching a consensus on major decisions usually takes time. That is often a handicap in volatile markets when decisions must be made quickly to take advantage of opportunities or prevent disasters. The Lombardi siblings have reached an understanding that gives Paul Jr. enough flexibility to act decisively when necessary; he may get his knuckles rapped later on if his siblings disagree with his judgment, but he nevertheless will take the lead in time-critical situations.

Although he often bridles at the restraints on him, Paul Jr. has learned to appreciate that consulting with his siblings often improves the quality of decisions. The Lombardis all bring different training, experience, and competencies to the table. The group often sees facets of an issue and possible ramifications of a decision that an individual might overlook. The system is not unlike that of Japanese companies: It takes a while to hammer out a consensus, but once it is achieved, the partners are likely to support it and move forward to implement it wholeheartedly.

Inherent Risks in the Sibling System

Lombardi Enterprises is fortunate to have enough major businesses so that each sibling has a domain in which to express his or her talents and leadership. There are inherent risks in this system of multiple leadership, however. Senior managers loyal to the old controlling owner may see opportunities to play one sibling off against another, as may customers, suppliers, and even employees. The Lombardis have run into the problem numerous times; now they are in the habit of checking with one another when they hear, second-hand from a non-family member, about something one of them has supposedly promised or decided.

A more fundamental threat comes from too much decentralization of authority and too little accountability. The Lombardis confronted this problem in 1993 when a team of management consultants did a thorough financial audit of the company's business units and found that while some were very profitable, others were marginal at best, bleeding badly needed capital. Unless the company made some crucial decisions on paring the unprofitable businesses, its cash flow would be severely impaired and its future growth placed in jeopardy. Much of the difficulty could be traced to the autonomy enjoyed by the various divisions—a system founded on the need to preserve sibling harmony. When Paul Sr. was still a powerful presence in the company, he had vetoed any investment by his offspring that he considered too risky and or promised too low a return. In recent years, however, the investments have been made by the divisional leaders—many of whom were siblings—without taking into account company wide priorities, return on investment, and opportunity costs.

The consultants' report led to a major restructuring of Lombardi Enterprises that exposed contradictions between family and business interests. The cost-cutting program called for the company to drop several enterprises that weren't making money. Several of these businesses were entrepreneurial pet projects of one or another sibling. They were not about to give up these ventures without a fight. Fortunately, however, data assembled by the consultants was convincing enough to assure them that the choice of businesses to be closed was based strictly on economic considerations and not favoritism.

The restructuring confronted the siblings with one of the biggest challenges to their ability to lead as a team. One of the businesses to be closed was the Trucking Division, which had been bleeding capital from the company. The division had won trucking contracts with several large manufacturers, only to lose them later because of careless handling of orders, late deliveries, and equipment breakdowns. The failures were directly attributable to Frank's lack of attention to management; with his talent for sales, he built up accounts, but then was not able to satisfy his customers. When the consultants strongly recommended against any further efforts to salvage the division, the siblings faced a critical question: What was to be Frank's future with the family company? Clearly, if Frank had been an executive in another company, he might have faced dismissal. Frank had to pay his dues for failing in his assignment; he could neither deny responsibility for the losses, nor make a strong case for continuing the investment in the Trucking Division. But firing him from Lombardi Enterprises might have seriously undermined family relationships.

His siblings were very conscious that this decision would set a precedent for similar situations that might occur in the future. Whatever they decided, they had to speak with one voice. They prepared a memo informing Frank that they could not offer him another line management position, but that if he wished to stay with the company, a position would be found for him at headquarters. Frank seemed to find these conditions fair. He decided to work on his own for a year or two as a sales consultant and then consider moving back into some role in the company. Meanwhile, he continues to sit on the boards of some Lombardi businesses.

Acknowledging Each Sibling's Contribution

In collectively managed businesses, the partners constantly struggle to maintain a balance between family harmony on the one hand and the need for coherent leadership and expedient decision making on the other. Such a structure can work only when the siblings can draw on a well of affection and trust in one another. The teamwork essential to maintaining family collaboration and managerial effectiveness in sibling partnerships is built on each sibling's respect for the others' opinions, needs, and perspectives. In the Lombardis' case, it has depended over the years on the support the parents have given the second-generation partners. Anna, the mother, long functioned as the linchpin of the family culture, the parental authority who averted outbreaks of destructive competition. More and more, as Anna Lombardi became older, Rita Lombardi began to assume this function, oiling the springs and gears of family relationships. Like many middle children, Rita functions as a kind of internal consultant to family members, trusted by all. Still, as the head of one division of the company and the mother of five children who aspire to managerial positions, her motives might be suspect in a crunch. To supplement Anna's support, the siblings have to find ways to strengthen their trust in one another.

They are slowly learning to openly express their appreciation for one another's efforts. With their natural rivalries, many siblings are inclined to be grudging in their compliments for their brothers and sisters. Even though a compliment is about the cheapest thing they can give each other, they are often stingy in their praise. All of the Lombardis work long hours and can point to achievements that have benefited the whole group. Recently, they have tried to acknowledge one another's performance more often and more generously, by saying things like: "That was a job well done," or, "I really appreciate the time and effort you put into that job." Such gestures may seem modest, but they can go a long way towards reducing feelings of rivalry and building the trust on which future cooperation depends.

Despite his self-confidence and bullish persistence, Paul Jr. was particularly in need of recognition for all he has done in expanding the business. His father, like every founder of a successful business, has always been honored as the family hero. Second-generation leaders, even those who function as heads of partnerships, crave similar heroic status. Before succession in the second generation could achieve closure, Paul Jr.'s contribution to the business had to be fully acknowledged. His brothers and sister gradually came around to conceding the importance of doing that. In family meetings, they acknowledged, first, that he had been running the business for fifteen years, and, second, that he had been responsible for much of the company's growth.

It was equally important for the company to convey the same image of Paul Jr.'s accomplishments to the outside world. For although his powers are restricted internally as the head of a partnership, he needed to have sufficient stature in the outside world to be able to deal effectively with a public that continues to have a monocratic bias. The company's banker, for example, usually wants to know whose word is law within the company. The family therefore held public events at which some of the members talked about the company's early years and the spirit of the founder. Then they introduced Paul Jr. as the current leader, and he spoke at length about the company's recent accomplishments and its goals for the future.

When issues do threaten to divide the siblings, the partners must find ways to sustain a collaborative relationship that will be so important in the future. Such an issue arose when Robert requested a leave of absence—with pay—for six months so that he could devote full time to his first session in the state legislature. Without his salary, he argued, he and his wife would have to make sacrifices in their lifestyle while serving in the legislature. He also noted that his high visibility as a state legislator would enhance the company's reputation.

Paul Jr. resisted, feeling that paying a family member for not working—no matter how proud they all were of Robert's election—violated standards of good managerial practice. Successful family companies the size of Lombardi Enterprises are often determined to stick to business-first rules and to avoid any suggestion that family members are judged by different standards. Indeed, this is the prevailing wisdom among professionals in the field. But in sibling partnerships, too-strict adherence to business-first rules can create ill feelings that eventually make teamwork impossible. On some occasions, the rules must be compromised for the sake of preserving sibling harmony. In fact, the Lombardis did just that. They agreed to let Robert continue sitting on the boards of a few Lombardi subsidiaries, in return for which he would receive a somewhat reduced salary.

Paul Jr.'s brothers and sisters have also done much to assuage his fears that one of them might try to hasten his retirement and replace him. With his vastly increased responsibilities for a growing company,

Paul Jr. decided in 1989 to relinquish his position as head of the Markets Division and concentrate on his CEO duties. He scheduled a retreat for the family to discuss who should replace him in the division, and for weeks he worried that one of his siblings might lobby for the job as a first step toward challenging his leadership.

When the retreat was finally held, he was surprised—and greatly relieved—when none of the four asked for the job. The other siblings evidently had no intention of intruding into Paul Jr.'s territory. Instead, the siblings decided to promote a qualified non-family professional manager to head the important Markets Division. (Later Paul Jr. told me of a dream that he had had the night after the retreat. He dreamt that he was held up outside his house by several men wearing stocking masks who ordered him to raise his hands. When he did as they demanded, however, the men dropped their guns, abruptly turned around, and ran. Paul Jr. did not make the connection between his dream and the events at the retreat until I pointed it out to him; it suggests his anxieties prior to the meeting and his profound feelings of relief when it was over.)

The Next Generation: A Greater Range of Choices

For the first succession, the parents over the years fostered a leadership arrangement and culture for Lombardi Enterprises that was different from the one Paul Sr. had created. For the next transition, the sibling partners who have succeeded him face an even more complicated range of choices.

The partners could choose to clone the present leadership form, giving each sibling who wants it a turn as the first-among-equals. In this way, they could probably keep the leadership in the hands of the second generation for another ten years or more. But none of the siblings had sought Paul Jr.'s job as head of the Markets Division, which would have positioned that person to take over the leadership of the whole company. Perhaps none of the four wanted to take over the CEO's job in the shadow of a formidable leader like their oldest brother. Perhaps the other four siblings simply felt they would make a more unique mark on the company by growing their own divisions.

In fact, when the partners discussed the question of who would head the Markets Division, they talked about succession to the CEO's job as well. They decided that the next change in leadership should take place when members of the third generation are prepared to take charge of Lombardi Enterprises. That still leaves open the question of whether the cousins should recycle the same structure or adopt a different governance system in the next generation. There are already signs that the sibling partners are strongly inclined to attempt to clone their own structure in the next generation. For example, just as they own equal numbers of shares in the company, they lean toward dividing the stock equally among the cousins. When ownership is divided among twenty-five cousins, however, the business must deal with many more issues than when it is divided only five ways. With more owners, there are more voices—and needs—that must be accommodated. How many nonparticipating stockholders is the family willing to tolerate? And if the Lombardis decide to concentrate the stock in a few hands, to prune the stockholder tree, how will this affect relationships in the family?

Other issues will inevitably arise in businesses that try to continue to divide stock equally in the cousins' generation. The Lombardi siblings are fortunate in that they have about the same number of offspring. In many families such symmetry is lacking, and that complicates ownership arrangements in the cousin generations. For example, in another third-generation company that I've worked with, one of the brothers has a single child while three other brothers each have three or four. If stock in the third generation is divided equally among the four families (instead of giving equal shares to each cousin), one cousin will own a fourth of the stock, which will give him much more influence than any of his cousins. If the cousins in the other branches cannot speak with one voice, their families will have even less influence on decision making in the company.

The Lombardi cousins must confront issues faced by many growing family businesses in this generation. Because they have grown up in different households and, in some cases, different communities, they do not know each other nearly as well as their parents know one another. While the oldest sibling partners can remember the years when their parents were struggling, the cousins have known only affluence.

Because of their numbers, not all the cousins will be able to hold top management positions; there isn't enough room at the top. The success of a sibling partnership depends heavily on developing mechanisms to ensure cooperation among the partners; in the third generation, when many family members want to participate, continued success depends on institutionalizing structures to ensure professional management. The process of choosing a leader in the third generation thus becomes more complicated than it was in the second generation. In addition, each of the sibling partners in the second generation often wants to make sure that his or her branch of the family is represented in top management. Already the Lombardi brothers and sisters are beginning to worry that Paul Jr. may be pushing his son Jamie ahead too fast in order to position him to be the eventual successor. Jamie Lombardi, age thirty-three, is the oldest of the cousins in management.

The entry of the oldest cousins into the company has already created a number of tricky issues for the family. Often members of the third generation reflect—and are inescapably constrained by—the tensions among the second-generation leaders. For example, one of Paul Jr.'s daughters, Susanna, who has an oenology degree as well as an MBA, has risen to the position of director of marketing in the winery, and therefore reports to her uncle Robert. In this position, Susanna is concerned about divided loyalties. In casual conversations, her father sometimes asks her about financial difficulties encountered at the winery, which puts her on the spot. She wants to give her father her assessment, but if she reveals too much information about the winery—information that might more appropriately come from the division—she risks disloyalty to Robert. Is Susanna to be considered a representative of her branch of the family? Or is she her own woman and loyal to her division? This kind of triangulation illustrates how managerial and family considerations become subtly entangled in cousin companies.

These are the realities of third-generation transitions that the Lombardis have gradually begun to understand. If the five sibling partners attempt to install a workable consortium structure in the next generation, they will have to set up mechanisms for selecting and grooming the few cousins who would work as a leadership team. But this is by no means the only possible choice. The Lombardis could decide that too much complexity might undermine the business, and that it's better to return to a single owner form. This alternative would be particularly attractive if the system were cash rich and could afford a buyout of others and if one of the cousins eventually emerges as an outstanding leader, head and shoulders above his or her contemporaries. Or the family might feel that choosing only a few to lead will create bitter feelings and divide the five families. They might therefore decide to go further down the road to professionalizing the business by hiring top managerial talent to take over the major executive positions, an option given some impetus when a non-family manager was appointed head of the Markets Division.

Whatever the family's choice, a strong collaborative foundation must be cemented in the second generation in order to prepare for a smooth transition to the third. The process will be complicated by the spread in ages of the siblings and their offspring. With each succeeding generation, the span in ages grows wider—with profound implications for leadership in the business. At this point in the Lombardis' history, for example, Jamie, Paul Jr.'s oldest son, is already working in a managerial position. The youngest daughter of Frank, the youngest in the sibling generation, is only ten and will have to wait many years before she can aspire to a managerial position. Obviously, in third-generation families with such a large age span, the oldest cousins will get the first shot at top positions. The youngest cousins will get their turn to lead last—if at all. This could upset the balance of power among the families and cause tension.

Indeed, some of the cousins are almost contemporaries of Frank. This closeness in ages can sometimes strengthen ties between the two generations: Frank, for example, is close to his nephew Jamie, who is in the Imports Division. But it can also aggravate tensions between the generations. One of Paul Jr.'s daughters, Rosemary, married a man named Richard who was given a job in Frank's Trucking Division before the family decided to close that business. Frank felt the husband's work was not up to par and fired him. The fact that Richard was only four years younger than Frank and tended, as a contemporary, to treat his boss as a generational peer may have contributed to the tension between the two. Frank felt Richard did not give him the proper respect and often stepped out of line. By firing him without consulting Paul Jr. or his other siblings, however, Frank caused an uproar in the family that lasted for several weeks.

The older third-generation family members are eager to take their place in management, to demonstrate their commitment to the company's tradition of professionalism. When the partners met to discuss the criteria for admitting members of the third generation to the business, the elder Lombardis decided that a college degree and one year's experience outside the business should be the minimum requirements. When the cousins themselves met to discuss the same question, they recommended much tougher hurdles: an MBA plus five years' experience outside the business.

The hard reality is that not all those who want to make careers in the company and aspire to the top positions on the ladder will be able to get what they want. That is why many families with the resources of the Lombardis encourage their younger members to start new enterprises of their own. Usually the drive to create new businesses enjoys high esteem in these families. The Lombardis celebrate their deeply rooted entrepreneurial ethic and tradition of industriousness. (In addition to serving as CEO of the family company, Paul Jr. has his own travel agency in Sacramento; naturally, many of his customers are employees of Lombardi Enterprises!)

Since new businesses will fuel future growth, families want to keep the entrepreneurial flame alive in succeeding generations. One way the Lombardis are doing that is by setting up a venture capital fund for members of the third generation who want to establish their own businesses. A family committee screens applications for funds. One cousin has received support to open an art gallery in San Francisco, another has launched a greeting card company with assistance from the fund, and a third has become a distributor of exercise equipment.

The negotiations over who will lead the next generation, and what type of structure is needed to govern a clan with many shareholders, will be more complicated. The Lombardis have set up a family council made up of representatives from each branch. The council brings together members of the second and third generations to discuss family values and goals. It sets policy for the holding company on major family and shareholder issues such as the criteria for employment of relatives and provisions for buying out shareholders who want cash.

In such situations, it is often advisable to let the outside directors alone choose the next CEO, subject only to a veto by the family council. The precise arrangement for managing Lombardi Enterprises in the future, however, must be left to the cousins themselves to decide. Much of the decision will turn on the preferences and relative talents and competencies of the cousins, on whether the families can agree on who is most qualified to lead, and, not least, on the needs of the business when the transition is to take place.

Since the transition from the first to the second generation in Lombardi Enterprises was not planned, but rather was improvised by Paul Jr. in response to unforeseen events, the third generation does not have a model of succession to go by. They *do* have a model for governing the company as a sibling partnership. But they would be well advised not to automatically assume that what worked for their parents will work for them.

Future Strains on the Partnership

The restructuring of Lombardi Enterprises has been notably successful. The closing of unprofitable businesses and the investments in new,
more promising ventures have resulted in dramatic improvements to
the balance sheet. The sibling partners have taken the first steps in
professionalizing the company and formalizing structures that will permit effective governance in the third generation. They are planning to
organize a board for the holding company with three independent
directors on it. They have hired a non-family senior controller, a
strong manager who is modernizing the company's accounting systems
and also helping to structure the agenda of the partners' weekly meetings. And they have established a family office to help manage their
wealth.

The sibling partnership is in its mature stage, but even so it must
cope with new strains. The senior Lombardis are infirm and need
constant medical supervision. The burden of managing their care has
fallen mostly on Rita, as the only daughter, although the other siblings
and their spouses help when they can. At this stage of their lives, the
siblings are keenly aware that when both parents are gone, collaboration in their partnership will be more important than ever, but perhaps more difficult to achieve. Rita will surely have a critical role in
filling the vacuum. But all members of the group have had to remind
themselves to make an extra effort to avoid expressing their rivalries
too freely.

The parents' medical condition also poses immediate financial
issues for the company itself. Although now far removed from
Lombardi Enterprises, the elder Lombardis retain control of important business-related assets, such as real estate, which have been used
as collateral for some company ventures. The sibling partners realize
that their lack of control of this other family wealth can profoundly
affect the relationships among them and even the operation of the
business. While not wanting to show any disrespect, they would like to
persuade the parents to turn over those assets to them now—before
death. But they do not know how to broach the subject with the ailing
parents.

This case history illustrates that the standard model for succession
in a controlling owner business, when applied to the complexities of
transitions into sibling or cousin companies, leaves out important data
and can therefore result in misleading diagnoses and inappropriate
prescriptions. Lombardi Enterprises demonstrates that a sibling part-

nership can work; collective leadership is not doomed to implode from internal dissension, as some experts have insisted. Nevertheless, the family's experience also shows the importance in each generation of re-examining the assumptions from the past and developing new leadership structures suited to emerging family needs and changing business circumstances.

Finally, the case shows that in some companies families may have to cope with overlapping generational transitions. At Lombardi Enterprises, as we have seen, an unpredictable event removed Paul Sr. from the company for several months, during which time Paul Jr. and his siblings began to take charge. When Paul Sr. returned to the business, he retained the title of chairman and continued to be a strong influence, but his power faded as the next generation demonstrated that it could run the business. At the same time, the siblings' children began to enter the company, and the siblings started to think through some of the issues the cousins would have to face in the third generation.

As we shall discuss in the chapters ahead, at each point in the generational transition the leaders will have a range of choices. As in the Lombardi family, the old leaders may still be around while the new leaders are consolidating their control, and even as that process is going on, another generation may be moving into place and preparing to take over sometime in the future. The Lombardi siblings have been able to juggle these two transitions with the playfulness and tolerance of contradiction that is characteristic of many strong business families, celebrating the founder's contribution even as he was being phased out of power, and maneuvering to gain advantage in the company for their own children even while laying the groundwork for a new, collaborative structure in the next generation.

PART II

Shared Dreams and Succession Planning

CHAPTER 4

Family Dreams:
The Genesis of Succession

IF succession is a journey, the beacon that provides a direction is the Shared Dream. The Shared Dream is a collective vision of the future that inspires family members to engage in the hard work of planning and to do whatever is necessary to maintain their collaboration and achieve their goals. It shapes the choices made at every point in the succession journey, from the company's strategic plan, to the selection of future leaders, to the type of leadership structure it will adopt in the next generation.

The general management literature has tended to assume that "vision" is something that can be imposed on a company from above, a tool in the leader's kit that can be pulled out when needed to inspire people and stuffed away when the job is done (as when former President Bush referred to "the vision thing").[1] Or else it is regarded as an abstract, woolly concept that is of little use when making practical, hard-nosed business decisions (as when Louis Gerstner proclaimed that "vision" was not what he needed to turn around IBM).

In family companies, Shared Dreams are highly personal and must grow from within, often over a period of years. The Shared Dream emerges from the family's fundamental values and aspirations. It defines who they are, who they want to be, what kind of enterprise they wish to build, and how they wish to be perceived by the world. Many German family companies, for example, are driven by an image of their company as being on the leading edge of engineering in their industries. Other companies such as Motorola, Gore Associates, and Nordstrom take pride in an organizational culture that is widely admired. Generations of families in the newspaper business have found common motivation in adherence to high journalistic standards and their contributions to the democratic process.

The Shared Dream often contains rich imagery, conveying a sense of excitement. Sometimes it expresses the family's formula for success. Often it has a religious inspiration or stresses a social mission beyond profit making. It would be hard to imagine a new generation of leaders at the Huntsman Chemical Co. who did not share the Mormon way of life and the desire to continue Jon and Karen Huntsman's devotion to various philanthropies. Or a new generation of the Reichmann family of Canada whose business principles were not guided by orthodox Jewish law and custom.

A Dream is not to be confused with a set of goals. Goals are much more specific and concrete than Dreams. While clear goals can certainly be motivating, they are generally shorter-lived from a psychological standpoint. Dreams provide the broader psychological context within which sets of specific goals can be organized, prioritized, and invested with excitement. They work at a deeper emotional level, and are thus often associated with mythic symbols that have personal significance for individuals. In heroic imagery, Dreams are about the war to be won, while goals are about the battles to be fought. Dreams have the power to sustain excitement throughout people's lifetimes, and to guide their fundamental choices of career, marriage, and lifestyle. Above all, the Shared Dream endows the family enterprise with *meaning*—it conveys a profound explanation for why continuing the business is important to the family.

Such a vision is not easy to create. It is forged through an ongoing conversation in which each of the members links his or her individual Dreams with some larger vision worthy of the family's best efforts. It may take years for family members to articulate their individual Dreams. For many it takes considerable effort to share their Dreams openly with other family members, which is the first step toward a consensus on a vision of the future. Whatever time it takes will usually be worth the effort. For success or failure in passing on the business and continuing it as a viable enterprise depends on the family's ability to create such a common vision.

The concept of a Dream[2] that drives entrepreneurial parents to aspire to build a business and pass it on to their children is frequently mentioned in the family business literature but rarely developed or rigorously defined. As I define it in this book, the Shared Dream builds on the ideas of Daniel Levinson, an authority on the psychology of adult development, whose work stresses the notion of a Dream in the lives of individuals. For Levinson, the Dream is a vision of the kind of life an individual wishes to lead that shapes his or her goals, expectations, and choices at every stage of the life cycle. The vision shapes a life structure that at every stage defines an individual's view of his or her social roles in the world, including relationships to others, the groups that are invested with significance, and career ambitions. "We are the product of our choices," Sartre once said. The critical choices made over a lifetime reflect the guiding force that shapes the life structure—the Dream. At key points in the maturation process, the Dream must be revised and revitalized to meet both the changing psychological needs and the external realities of different age periods. In his classic book *Seasons of a Man's Life*, which reported the results of in-depth research on the life trajectories of forty men, Levinson described some of the qualities of the individual Dream:

It has the quality of a vision, an imagined possibility that generates excitement and vitality. At the start it is poorly articulated and only tenuously connected to reality, although it may contain concrete images such as winning the Nobel Prize or making the all-star team. It may take a dramatic form, as in the myth of the hero: the great artist, business tycoon, athletic or intellectual superstar performing magnificent feats and receiving special honors. It may take mundane forms that are yet inspiring and sustaining: an excellent craftsman, the husband-father in a certain kind of family, the highly respected member of one's community.[3]

For Levinson the Dream is a "transitional phenomena" that develops in early adulthood and serves as an essential vehicle to explore and adapt to the various possibilities that adult life offers. Levinson originally developed the concept of the Dream after reading the work of D. W. Winnicott, a prominent psychoanalyst.[4] According to Winnicott, a child in a transitional period imagines various possibilities of his or her self and world in the future—"he enacts these imaginings in daydreams, play and other make-believe explorations." Levinson, like Winnicott, saw the Dream as a hybrid of fantasy and reality which stimulates the construction of future scenarios that are sufficiently anchored on what can actually be accomplished as to facilitate the mental experimentation necessary for career and life planning, and also are sufficiently infused with fantasy as to playfully stimulate creativity and excitement.

Adult development theory focuses primarily on the unfolding lives of individuals. Levinson acknowledged that the Dream is shaped to some extent by the social context, but he did not explore the process by which that happens. While the management literature speaks of vision as a requirement of leadership, no full-bodied theory has come forth to describe how that vision is conceived and developed, and why it is able to connect with the aspirations of large numbers of people in a business enterprise for whom it becomes a motivating force. Schein, for example, discusses many of the organizational processes through which leaders, and particularly founders, instill their vision in the cultures of the organizations that they build.[5] However, Schein takes the vision and how it came to be as givens. He does not explore the relationship between the private lives of these leaders and their visions. In the context of family enterprises, this relationship is inescapable. The leader's personal aspirations and his or her vision for the business are sometimes virtually indistinguishable.

The idea of a collective vision that drives a business enterprise is suggested, but not developed, in the work of other social scientists. Shapiro and Sokol, for example, imply that whether an entrepreneurial activity goes forward or not depends more on "exposure to those near oneself"—including role models and sources of moral and financial support within the circle of family and friends—than on exposure to models of great success. They also state that "the family, particularly the father or mother, plays the most powerful role in establishing the desirability and credibility of entrepreneurial action for an individual."[6] David Reiss, a prominent family theorist and researcher, describes the social mechanism underlying this process. Reiss discusses at length the formation of "shared constructs" and "family paradigms" as a set of framing assumptions about the nature of the world that shapes the members' relationships with their social environment. According to Reiss, these assumptions operate at a basic psychological level, drawing their power from the family's past experience in coping with adversity. In short, paradigms result from the accumulated learning of the family as a result of overcoming grave crises in the past.[7]

In business families, stories about the establishment of an enterprise that represent a family's ability to triumph in the face of adversity are likely to draw younger family members directly into the business, or inspire them to found their own businesses. Parents who hope to see a business passed on to the next generation can build on this by talking with their children about their hopes and dreams for the future. In fact, Reiss's work suggests that the process of mutually elaborating a shared construct of the future (or Dream), in a setting where "each member accords to the others the power of independent regard," can be an engrossing and tremendously moving experience for all.[8]

For a workable Shared Dream to emerge, the individual Dreams of family members must overlap substantially; otherwise, there may not be enough common ground on which to build a satisfactory future scenario. The Shared Dream is not the sum total of the individual Dreams of family members. Rather, it encompasses only the portion of each individual's Dream that he or she is willing to invest in a common cause such as the continuity of a family enterprise. Obviously the broader that common ground, the greater the possibility for effective collaboration. Family members may differ significantly in the degree to which they hook their aspirations to a collective vision for the business. The Dream of one sibling who aspires to a career position in the management of the family business may overlap substantially with the Shared Dream; the Dreams of other brothers and sisters who contribute as shareholders and or members of the board of the family office are likely to overlap less. Both the individual's Dream and the Shared Dream are dynamic, evolving in concert with individual life cycles. The amount of overlap for individuals in the system may change as they grow older. That is why the Shared Dream, like an individual's Dream, must be periodically checked against reality and renegotiated in order to maintain its excitement and momentum. The planning process will move forward most rapidly—with high levels of excitement—during those phases when the Dreams of the generations overlap the most.

How the Shared Dream Is Woven

A Shared Dream emerges through a "visioning process"—a continuing, open-ended discussion through which family members clarify their aspirations and expectations about the future, to themselves and to one another. Through this process, they assess the degree to which their dreams are congruent and feasible. How well the Dreams of the generations will mesh depends in large measure on the coherence of the parents' Dreams, and on the clarity and sensitivity with which they are able to express a Dream for the family as a whole that the members can more or less share. A balance between individual Dreams and the

Shared Dream is essential to the psychological well-being of all family members as well as to the harmony of the enterprise. The ability to strike this balance requires a degree of individuation and personal maturity on the part of each family member.

Ideally, as we will see, these discussions begin early in the life of a business family, when members of the next generation are young. Indeed, I believe that members of the younger generation are more inclined to connect their individual Dreams to the Shared Dream when an open dialogue about these aspirations begins early in their lives and they feel free to pursue their individual Dream even if it leads to a career outside the business.

Children are born into an intricate fabric already woven by the parents. As they grow, they must decide whether they can weave their individual Dreams into the family pattern—or must untangle their threads from the tapestry and look for different patterns that seem more promising. To them, the family business is seldom a neutral entity; it is a force in shaping their sense of who they are and what they want in their lives. On the one hand, the business can be a vehicle that makes their Dreams happen. On the other, it can be a barrier that blocks the fulfillment of their own Dream. They may choose to enter it enthusiastically, or they may wish to select entirely different careers. Whatever their choice, the business is likely to be a powerful influence on their developing ideas about themselves and the world.

Paradoxically, the younger family members must break away from the family in order to reconnect with it. A successful family business may, indeed, actually retard the process of individuation. In some families, the natural impulses of children to mature and develop evoke a deep anxiety in the family. Instead of encouraging them to become separate and fully mature adults, a family may try to draw them ever more tightly into the family tapestry. By the same token, the young may be enticed to take advantage of access to the money and power that the business offers before they have developed a sense of their own aspirations and psychological needs. As Minuchin has noted about his experiences with business families:

Issues of autonomy to which all families have to attend are prolonged, so that the usual conflicts that occur between children and parents in typical American families continue to be played out much later in life. Children in these families struggle until quite late with the question of "Am I myself, or am I the son or daughter of my parents?" Learning to differentiate—to understand the psychological difference between their issues and their parents—is often a central concern.[9]

When children who work in the business feel they must sacrifice too much of their own Dreams, they may become unhappy and frustrated. Subordinating their own identities and career aspirations to their parents' Dreams leads to a profound sense of self-betrayal. There are many sad cases of individuals who have succumbed to family obligation, trading in their individual Dreams for roles as custodians of the family company for which they have little passion or commitment.[10] Usually both the individuals and the businesses suffer.

People who are constantly disappointed with their efforts to achieve their Dreams may suppress their disappointment to avoid facing the pain. Some invest enormous amounts of psychic energy in keeping their Dreams secret, fearing that the modesty or simplicity of their Dreams will subject them to embarrassment. In a hard-driving entrepreneurial family, for instance, the young person who aspires to a peaceful life as a painter of landscapes may believe that his ambition, if not carefully hidden, will be ridiculed by other family members. For others, the Dream may be kept hidden not because it is too modest but because it is suffocatingly grandiose. For many entrepreneurs the gap between their lofty aspirations and their actual accomplishments may be too painful to acknowledge.

Successors to family businesses who have been forced to bury their true aspirations are unlikely to become inspiring leaders. Without a well-developed Dream, they are unable to convey a vision to managers and employees that will motivate them to move mountains for the family business. They are vacillating and unsure when confronted with major decisions.

Women in business families—and, indeed, in society at large—often must overcome many obstacles to developing a powerful Dream for themselves. Gilligan's interviews with girls before the age of puberty, for example, show that many have powerful Dreams of what they want to do with their lives; after puberty, however, these dreams seem to shrivel and even disappear.[11] Regrettably, young women often do not have a supportive social and psychological environment that encourages them to effectively experiment and construct a Dream for their lives. In many families daughters are given the message from an early age that they are expected to devote their lives to taking care of others and are thus not free to develop and pursue their own aspirations.[12]

Not all business owners have a Dream, I have found. Why some do, while others do not, is one of the critical questions that might be profitably explored in future research. I believe that some people do not develop a Dream because they are not encouraged to do so early in their lives—or are actively discouraged from doing so. The Dreams of young people carry the excitement and energy that comes from exploring a world that is "so various, so beautiful, so new."[13] Later in life, the Dreams of people who have never experienced that high-voltage charge can barely be detected because the current is so weak.[14]

A Shared Dream that is forged early in the lives of a young business family may be more powerful than one built through a visioning process later on. It seems clear, however, that without such a Dream, business owners will be not be highly motivated to do the hard work of planning for a succession. Instead, they may be more inclined to either keep the business in a prolonged holding pattern that leads to stagnation and failure or, if a tempting offer comes along, to sell the business. The latter decision can be the source of enduring disappointment for members of the next generation. A 1993 study of 400 children of family business owners who had sold their companies during the 1980s showed that about one-fourth of them had made efforts to buy back the business. Although these offspring may have supported the sale in the first instance, the study found that they had deep regrets later on. "They didn't understand how powerfully their identities were tied to the company," said one family business consultant who commented on the study for the *Wall Street Journal*. "It represented their heritage and legacy, not just a pile of assets."[15] These young scions had managed to develop a Dream for the family business, but too late. Perhaps these families had never developed a Shared Dream, and so were more willing to let go of the business.

Dreams of the Three Basic Business Forms

We saw earlier that the decision to recycle a current business form or adopt a new one has important implications for the succession process. I believe the process is driven by a powerful emotional undercurrent. It is rare for the process to be entirely calculated, rational, or instrumental, as it is frequently depicted in "how-to" books. The rational elements of these decisions are entangled and embedded in a web of emotional and contextual factors that play an important role in determining the business form that finally emerges. Human beings so often

appear to muddle through major life decisions without much awareness of what they are choosing and, most important, without a full realization that a choice is actually being made. Paradoxically, the choice is
sometimes not to choose at all; then the decision about a future business form is made by default.

Typically, business families don't start to pay attention to issues
of succession until the incumbent family leaders are nearing retirement age. By this time, however, much has already happened that nar-
rows the range of feasible options. The number of children, their genders, and their ages, are the givens around which any plan must be
organized. Their interests, attitudes, and competencies have in large
measure become clear. Accidents and other unforeseen tragedies may
have taken their toll. The texture of family relationships has also been
established in the family's evolving story line. For example, a sibling
partnership is not a likely option when the adult children do not get
along or have chosen to pursue independent careers outside the family company.

The family and business conditions that are present when succession planning begins provide the *context* within which the planning
process takes place. This complex amalgamation of nature, nurture,
and circumstance is always unique to each family. It reflects the family's history and distinct identity as a group, and embodies many life
choices that family members have made—either explicitly or by default.
In any family business, the experiences of the family, their values, and
their capabilities and traditions of communicating openly with one
another have a great deal to do with whether the family can develop a
Shared Dream that will provide a foundation for continuity.

My interviews with family business owners and their spouses suggest there are certain recurring themes in the developmental vision of
those individuals who see the family business as a vehicle for the fulfillment of their Dreams. These themes typically include both broadly
defined scenarios as well as detailed images of settings, structures, and
people. To some extent these images are romanticized, in that they are
idealized scenarios for the future.

For founding entrepreneurs, the Dream can be of themselves as
the leaders of family dynasties commanding great power and wealth. It
may portray the businesses as the vehicle for accomplishing great feats,
such as a dramatic breakthrough in technology. Other business owners
might imagine themselves to be exemplary providers and protectors
of their families for generations to come. Yet others might see their
family companies as means of becoming great philanthropists who

gain a significant leadership position in the community. For entrepreneurs, the Dream gives meaning to their work and family lives. It is why they persevere in the face of the many challenges and vicissitudes involved in creating a business. It is the wellspring of the creativity they need to adapt to continuously changing circumstances.

In some sense, realizing elements of the Dream in the business may be somewhat easier than doing so in the family. In the business, the entrepreneur typically has direct control over resources; he or she has the power to hire and fire and can command a degree of compliance from others with regard to the requirements of his or her Dream. Whether or not the Dream can actually be achieved, of course, depends upon the marketplace and the economic fortunes of the business. At home, however, the entrepreneur is only one of a number of critical actors shaping the behavior and expectations of the children. The others, of course, include his or her spouse, grandparents, aunts, uncles, in-laws, and the children themselves. In the family, the entrepreneur may not have direct control over resources, and he or she certainly does not have the power to hire or fire. If the Dream includes other family members, these are apt to be less subject to direction than employees.

In business families with a traditional division of gender roles, mothers are often the guardians of the collective Dream in a family. Their Dream often provides the glue that gives cohesion and a sense of belonging to other members of the family. It frequently emphasizes the perpetuation of family harmony through involvement in the business. In a large third-generation European company that I studied, the wife of the founder continued to exert considerable influence well into her old age. During one annual shareholder meetings, the ninety-five-year-old matriarch, in her wheelchair, addressed the group of thirty-six descendants and their spouses. She spoke eloquently of the importance of family and of the innumerable sacrifices made by previous generations. She recalled her husband's efforts to treat suppliers and customers with fairness and respect. She described his insistence on honoring all commitments and on repaying all his debts, even in the most dire circumstances, including two devastating world wars. She urged the younger generation to preserve the family's good name, reminding them of the founder's dying message to his children: "I do not leave you much money, but I do leave you a reputable name—use it wisely. It is your most precious asset." She exhorted the family members to continue to treat the business as a business, but also to remember that "your most important resources go home to their families every night."

Finally, she warned her loved ones against displaying their wealth ostentatiously, which would "only stir up envy and resentment."

When she was through, the whole group burst into applause and stood in tribute. Not only did her presentation serve to rekindle the family's enthusiasm for their values and legacy, it also highlighted the underlying themes of the Shared Dream—"to preserve and enhance the legacy of the family." Her vision provided unity, cohesion, and a sense of purpose to this complex multigenerational family enterprise.

But mothers who have never held a formal position in the company can also become bitter at what they feel is a lack of recognition. Some seek to fulfill their own Dreams through a favorite child who becomes a rising star and triumphs in the company. Once in a position of authority, the successful son or daughter is expected to give the mother the recognition she feels entitled to for her contribution to the family business.

Some picture of the future business form is usually embedded in the parents' Dream. Although it may be ill defined at first, over the years it assumes a more distinct shape, supported by the imagery in family stories and traditions. For example, the Dream for a controlling owner business form celebrates the one child who fulfills the parents' expectations and is able to embrace the parental legacy and expand upon it. In his surprisingly candid memoir, *Father, Son & Company*, Thomas Watson, Jr., recounts his father's ambitions for him at IBM. Tom Watson, Sr., who was not the founder of the company but had put it on the map, wanted his son to build IBM into an even greater colossus and thereby extend the father's accomplishment. Interestingly, one of the things that enabled Tom Jr. to leave the company and retire was the sense that he had fulfilled his father's Dream. When he ended his tenure the company was twice as big as the one his father had built. The fact that Tom Jr. had accomplished that much was evidence to him that he had, indeed, fulfilled his obligation towards his father.[16]

The Dream of the controlling owner business form encourages the parent to develop a special kind of mentoring relationship with a son or daughter. If a master-apprentice relationship is established, the parent's Dream may shift away from egocentric concerns and toward a genuine interest in the development of the heir. Through his identification with his son or daughter, the father can envision a kind of immortality in which his life's work is continued into the future by his own flesh and blood. The child, in turn, is expected to respond to the parent's expectations and measure up to the demands of the task by carrying out the parent's mandate in a successful way. For instance, an entrepreneur's

Dream may involve a specific vision of the business under the leadership of his eldest son or daughter. The Dream of the controlling owner form is closely associated with the monocratic notion that an ideal organization should have one—and only one—ultimate leader. This ideal, as I have indicated, is frequently used to justify the rule of primogeniture as the criterion for selecting the successor.

The Dream of the sibling partnership, in contrast, involves the notion of having not just a successful company but also a collaborative family. The vision here is of the children walking hand-in-hand into the future, thriving and carrying on family traditions long after the parents are gone. The sibling partnership evokes archetypal images of a band of fraternal leaders who have replaced patriarchal authority with a system based on equality. It is the imagery from which the French Revolution derived much of its powerful emotional appeal.[17] To achieve this Dream, members of the sibling group must care for one another, nurture one another, and harness the spirit of the family through the family enterprise. The kind of commitment needed is captured in the phrase of the Three Musketeers, "One for all and all for one."

This Dream conveys the conviction that family solidarity is important to business success. The parents achieve the satisfaction of fulfilling their mission as *parents* as well as business owners. By making the children equal partners who share in the fruits of the enterprise, they hope to achieve fairness and harmony in the family. The vision also implies that, in addition to being able to work together well, the siblings are able to collaborate in order to ensure their mutual protection. By circling the wagons, the children protect themselves against the vicissitudes of life and provide for their collective security. The underlying values in this case are egalitarian, with the emphasis on the development of teamwork and on the synergies that result from collaboration. There are many legendary sibling teams that vividly capture the imagery of a fraternal partnership, including the Wright brothers in engineering, the Mayo brothers in medicine and science, and, in business, the Bass brothers, the Bloomingdales, the Nordstroms, Nieman-Marcus, the Reichmanns in Canada, and the Puig brothers in Europe. In each of these cases great accomplishments are attributed in large measure to the sibling partnership itself—the underlying message being that no sibling acting alone could have ever accomplished comparable success.

The Dream of the cousin consortium is typically associated with families that have accumulated great wealth. This vision involves an extension of the sibling partnership to a broader network or clan of

cousins with a common lineage, ancestral symbols, stories, and traditions. As for Biblical tribes, the Dream becomes the binding force for
an extended group of families that trace their roots to the founders of
the company and their heroic accomplishments. (Interestingly, many
business families see their history as commencing with the founding of
the business and show little interest in all that went before.) In this
larger family community, the cousins are sustained by a network of relatives upon whom they can call in time of trouble for help and support.
The organizational vision associated with the Dream of a cousin consortium typically involves not just a large complex enterprise, but an
elaborate governance structure as well. This structure offers a number
of alternative possibilities for the involvement of cousins in such activities as the corporate board, the family council, or the family's philanthropic foundation. As Marcus has indicated, these complex governance structures often acquire a life of their own and become powerful
unifying entities that hold together dynastic families.[18] Examples of
legendary cousin companies that have survived the test of time include
the Rothschilds in Europe, the Cargill-MacMillans in the United
States, and the Mogi clan of the Kikkoman Company in Japan.

The three basic family business forms therefore are not just different types of family businesses; they are basic and distinct components of Shared Dreams. These three forms of family business function
as archetypal constructs (or paradigms, in Reiss's terms) that are commonly used by the members of business families to organize their
assumptions and aspirations—a "gestalt," if you will—about the kind
of family business they want in the future. At any given juncture in the
development of a business family, the members may hold different
Dreams about the future of the enterprise; one may aspire to recycle
the company as a controlling owner business, while others may wish
for the company to become a sibling partnership. In some families the
discussion of differences in Dreams becomes part of an ongoing debate
in the family. In other families, the differences are buried and become
the source of bitter conflicts that stifle the capacity to articulate a vision
of the future. In most successful business families, however, these differences are ultimately resolved and a coherent Shared Dream
emerges. In that Shared Dream one of the three business forms is
defined as the ideal that guides the process of generational change.

When multiple siblings and cousins are involved in a succession,
planning obviously reaches new levels of complexity. The Dreams of
many more individuals must be considered and synchronized into a collective Dream. The spread of ages among the successors can also be a

profoundly important factor. Siblings who are far apart in age will be at different stages in the life cycle, and timing will thus be a determinant of the family's willingness to come to agreement on a succession plan. The problem becomes even more complicated in the cousins' generation. Expectations are likely to be far more diverse among cousins, who have usually grown up in different households, some perhaps in cities or even countries distant from the source of the family's wealth. The age spread is apt to be even wider among cousins than among siblings, and the connection to the Shared Dream and legacy more tenuous. In these more complex systems, synchronizing the Dreams of the cousins in leadership roles becomes essential, since they will play a key role in articulating and promoting a Shared Dream to the other members of the extended family. The amount of time, energy, and resources that must be invested in developing a Shared Dream for a cousin consortium is thus much greater than in simpler systems. The process necessary to articulate a Shared Dream is considerably more elaborate, involving the creation of a "steering committee" made up of carefully selected leaders from critical family constituencies who actively work to define an "imagined possibility" for the system and to recruit the support of the rest of the family for the vision.

One Founder's Succession Dream

Whether the incumbent leader's Dream assumes a controlling owner business, a sibling partnership, or a cousin consortium will have a major impact on the kind of system that can ultimately be realized. The leader's Dream also shapes the style of parenting that his or her offspring receive, and thus, over time, influences the juniors in their expectations from and attitudes toward the business as well as the skills they choose to develop.

Consider a first-generation European family company.[19] The founder had built an impressive precision-tool business after World War II with his wife. The couple had four children—three daughters and a son—but the father's Dream was to turn over the company one day to the son alone. He hoped that the son would become the engineer that he had once aspired to be but did not become. He discouraged his three daughters from pursuing postgraduate education, but was thrilled when the son chose to study for a master's in engineering.

From a succession standpoint, the founder was extremely committed to the concept of a controlling owner form. His Dream influenced not just how he structured his company (positioning himself at the center of every decision), it also affected the way he dealt with his family. The eldest daughter and her father were very close, and she worked in the company for seven years, but her father never considered her a serious candidate for a managerial position. She was heartbroken and bitter at all the attention that he seemed to focus on her younger brother. Eventually she married and left the company.

The second daughter wished to become a nurse, but her father felt that was an unsuitable occupation and he discouraged her from it, insisting that she study business instead. After completing the technical education in business that her father required, she began nurse's training, but married and quickly became pregnant, leaving the work world. The son, the couple's third child, took more than ten years to finish his education, and repeatedly turned down his father's invitations to come to work at the company. The youngest daughter, an ambitious student, studied business and economics and wanted to go to a top-flight business school in America. Her father, however, felt that she needed no more education, and insisted that she come to work in the family company right after college. She eventually won her father's approval, working with him as his assistant at headquarters and traveling with him on sales trips. The father reluctantly began to realize that his youngest daughter was the only one he could rely on to fulfill his controlling owner dream for the business.

When the father became ill, the company's board (which included his wife and youngest daughter, as well as two outside directors) persuaded him to hire an experienced outsider as general manager. At this time the youngest daughter was put in charge of finance and administration. It was now evident that the father was grooming her to succeed him. For example, he put her in control of the trust that owned the company stock. Interestingly, whenever she suggested involving her siblings on discussions of business issues, her father would say, "Why do you want to complicate things by including the rest of the family. If you're in charge, *you* make the decision—don't ever share power."

After two years, the father fired the general manager, and the company was reorganized with the former chief engineer heading up technical operations and the daughter put in charge of the commercial and marketing sides of the business. When she pushed to have the company become more responsive to its customers and less driven by the technical designers, her ideas brought her into conflict with her father and the other board members.

Shortly after the reorganization, the son, now age thirty-five, finally finished his master's degree in engineering and, for the first time, became interested in working at the company. While the daughter was away on a vacation, the father signed an employment contract with his son. He informed the daughter about it only after she returned. Now, after ten years working side-by-side with the daughter, his attitude toward her suddenly began to change. He became increasingly argumentative with her, continuously challenging and belittling her ideas. At one point he even told her angrily that if she was unhappy with how he ran his company, she should leave. After some consideration, the daughter confronted the board of directors with a choice: Either they confirm her authority and agree on clear rules and responsibilities for everyone, or she would resign for the sake of family harmony.

The parents, the two older sisters, and the brother held a meeting without the youngest daughter to discuss the situation. Shortly thereafter, the father died suddenly. The daughter was still on the board of directors and was the principal trustee for her father's estate. After a confrontation with the board and much discussion within the family, she decided to take a leave of absence and let her brother manage the business.

It did not take long for the brother to realize that he did not have the experience and skills to run the business effectively, and he invited his younger sister to return. The two of them agreed to try to operate the company together. Her marketing and administrative skills as well as her 10 years of experience, coupled with his technical capability, helped them become a good team. They had to invent a number of creative solutions to problems of status and authority. Instead of having either one of them occupy the father's office, for example, they decided to share an office space and to work at a circular table to symbolize their collaborative stance.

The brother-and-sister pair were quite successful in running the business together for some time. However, the non-family board members and many of the senior executives soon begun to make the daughter's life difficult and to raise concerns about the viability of a partnership with "two bosses." After three years of working together, each of them began to feel that he or she could, in fact, run the business alone. Despite their success as a leadership team—or perhaps even because of it—the wear and tear of constantly having to confront others' expectations and beliefs took a toll, especially on the sister, who continually felt she had to justify her presence. After much soul-searching, the sister decided to leave the company for good, and she encouraged her brother to consolidate the stock of the business. The brother took on considerable debt to buy out his sisters and mother. Unfortunately, the company, now heavily leveraged and without the younger sister's business acumen, ran into serious difficulties and eventually had to be sold.

This story illustrates the longevity and far-reaching power of an entrepreneur's Dream. The father held onto his Dream tightly. As a result, he totally disregarded the talents and ambitions of his eldest daughter, and began to groom the youngest daughter for leadership only after it appeared his son would never finish school and join the business. Then, when the son finally became available, the father pushed his faithful and very talented daughter aside. His insistence on continuing the controlling owner structure inevitably produced an environment that could not support a sibling partnership—despite considerable evidence that the son and daughter working together brought much more skill and experience to the business than could either sibling alone. In spite of everything, the son and daughter managed the business successfully as a sibling partnership for three years. But without a strong motivating Dream to continue as a partnership, the team broke up and the family had to cash in its success. When asked what she felt had led to the ultimate sale of the business, the younger sister said:

Unfortunately, my family never learned to talk openly about our aspirations. So when we had to figure out what we would do in the future, we had a terrible time breaking past the idea of what we thought our father would have wanted. . . . Perhaps, if my brother and I had learned to collaborate earlier, if the concept of a leadership team had been sold to the employees, the board and to the rest of the family by my father, we could have had a much better chance of working together well. . . . As it was, it became too difficult for me. . . . I knew I did not want to become a bitter 45-year-old woman . . . so I decided to go and ultimately my brother had to sell.[19]

Reworking the Dream

As this case suggests, virtually all of the major questions that must be resolved in succession planning depend upon an understanding of the Dreams of the generation that is passing the torch and those of the generation that is receiving it. These Dreams shape the organizational context within which the succession occurs and they determine how children are either encouraged or discouraged about entering the business, as well as how they are groomed as successors.

The archetypal Dreams that shape the future of a business can be very resistant to change, but their substance is not static over a lifetime. Levinson believed that the Dream is reworked during certain key transitional periods in the life cycle. This is part of an intermittent process that combines periods of stability, in which the key elements do not change, with transitional periods, in which certain aspects of the Dream may be altered to bring them more in line with reality and the individual's internal needs.

An individual constantly mediates between the requirements of his or her Dream and the opportunities and constraints presented by life itself. Whenever an individual's life begins to drift away from the Dream, it creates tension within. This tension accumulates during periods of stability and becomes the fuel for change during the transition periods. The transition periods are typically age-specific. In the mid-thirties a person is concerned with achieving position and power. The early forties are the midpoint of life and are thus a time of reappraisal in which people may suddenly, unpredictably, seem to lose their bearings. They may lose interest in their work, launch new careers, divorce and remarry, and generally behave in ways that seem bizarre to friends and family. In their early fifties, adults slow down and take more interest in mentoring the young.

Changes in circumstances in the business can create tensions that compel revisions in the family's Dream. A father whose Dream involves passing the business to his oldest son may become concerned if he begins to feel that his son is neither interested in running the company nor capable of it. The more the son strays from the father's expectations, the more the father may want to redouble his efforts to bring the son into line with the requirements of his Dream. Changing the Dream is never easy. It requires considerable maturity and courage, and it must be undertaken at the right time. Too often Dreams aren't reconsidered until it's too late. For example, the father may hold on to the wish to pass the company to his son despite considerable evidence of his son's ineptitude. Unable to surrender his Dream, the father ignores the lack of fit between his son's capabilities and the leadership requirements of the business, and may proceed to structure a succession that is doomed from the start. Ironically, the father's unswerving commitment to his Dream sets the stage for his ultimate disappointment. Individual and family Dreams can blind key decision makers to the absence of critical conditions for a successful leadership transition or prevent them from exploring the full range of feasible options open to them and to their systems in the future.

In this chapter I have argued that if the succession process is to be planned effectively, the family must come together around a clear and engaging definition of the future scenario toward which they intend to move the system. This shared vision is intertwined with the Dreams that the individuals in the family have for themselves and their future together in the business, but a Shared Dream must also be revised in accordance with changing circumstances in the family and the business. In the following chapter we will look more closely at the visioning process itself and at the kinds of activities families can engage in to articulate their individual Dreams and forge a Shared Dream.

CHAPTER 5

Working with Dreams

W HEN a family embarks upon a visioning process, they run the risk that long-buried feelings may bubble to the surface. Sometimes the inability to address and clarify old issues can thwart the succession process. The endless bickering that occurs in some family businesses often masks underlying resentments involving buried Dreams. These hidden aspirations play themselves out in other arenas, distorting judgment on major business questions and sometimes doing great damage to the company. The son who argues with a father over whether an older manager should be fired, brothers and sisters who clash over opening new markets or developing new technologies—all may be expressing anger that has little to do with the merits of the case at hand, but instead reflects deep regrets over paths not taken in their lives. Many of those who wanted to pursue careers in other fields, but instead entered the family business, will blame their frustrations on their parents, rather than taking responsibility for making their own choices.

The difficulty of initiating meaningful conversations is compounded by the tensions arising from succession issues. The approach of the time for generational change tends to heighten the levels of stress and reduce the levels of tolerance. Senior family members are faced with questions about their mortality and the need to turn over control of the enterprise they have spent their lives building, as well as other family resources, to the younger generation. As parents worry about becoming irrelevant, their children are often impatient to take charge of the business. It is not unusual for communication to break down as those in power deny the need to turn over control, and those who desire more power deny their impatience.

Can families learn to talk openly about these things and lead themselves through a process of developing a Shared Dream? In some cases, they can; and in others, probably not. With help and encouragement, many families can mobilize the courage and acquire the skills necessary to develop and articulate a vision that can carry them through a succession process.

Commentators in the family business field do not give much emphasis to the obstacles to effective visioning. Even Ward, who offers the most elaborate and realistic description of how families can develop a vision of the future, tends to downplay the actual difficulties in the process. He alerts us to the fact that working out a family vision is a "demanding process" that "requires each family member to freely discuss his or her plans." But he is optimistic that "most families have inherent strengths that will help carry out this planning process." Other authors tend to make similarly optimistic assumptions about the capacity of families to withstand the strains of continuity planning.[1] Unintentionally, the family business field may encourage families to believe that the process will be easier than it is. Worse, professionals interested in helping business families may also develop inflated expectations of what can actually be accomplished, thereby setting the families and themselves up for failure.

Nevertheless, it is crucial for families who anticipate passing their companies on to the next generation to try to envision their future. Without a Shared Dream, a destination for succession, they cannot plan sensibly. The most productive way to define a feasible destination is to undertake the often difficult tasks of unearthing, articulating, and sharing their individual Dreams in order to decide whether or not it makes sense to pursue a Shared Dream.

In this chapter, I will review a number of case histories that illustrate some of the ways that family members' individual and collective Dreams shape the unfolding dramas of succession, paying particular attention to the ways in which the compatibility or incompatibility of Dreams can affect the process. In some of these cases, we'll see that families were able to adjust their Shared Dreams in ways that moved the family and the business forward—though at times in a different direction than the incumbent leadership may have anticipated. In other cases, family members were not able to make such adjustments, and they reached less promising outcomes. This chapter also describes some techniques for encouraging families to engage in discussions about their individual Dreams and to formulate their Shared Dream.

Families vary considerably in the extent to which the Dreams of the parents are compatible. In some families, the Dream of one parent is highly congruent with and reinforces that of the other. This congruency is, in fact, part of the foundation on which the parents' marital relationship is built. As we saw in the Lombardi case, the Dream of both parents was to leave behind a thriving sibling partnership as their joint legacy. Through the years, the founder and his wife wove the fundamental elements of that Dream into their approach to parenting. From the time when the children were very young, the parents supported and encouraged opportunities for collaboration and nurtured a sense of equality among the siblings. They heightened their children's awareness of their interdependence and the extent to which their future ability to survive life's adversities would depend on collaboration and mutual assistance. The fact that this vision was consistent—and shared—increased its power and influence.

The parents presented their children with a coherent worldview anchored on a consistent set of values and expectations and they practiced what they preached. Both senior Lombardi, for example, went to great lengths to get along with their own siblings and in-laws, thus providing a model for their children. As already noted, this does not mean that there are no conflicts or tensions in the junior generation today. The pushes and pulls among the five Lombardi siblings, however, take place within the context of a shared vision of the future that can be found in any healthy, enterprising family.

However, many families have Dreams that are less congruent than the Lombardis'. When the parents' Dreams are incompatible, this sets the stage for myriad difficulties, including conflicts among the Dreams of the offspring. In fact, incongruent Dreams are one of the leading factors explaining why so many successions fall apart.

A Couple's Incongruent Dreams

Our first case history concerns a family in which the children grew up hearing powerfully different messages from their two parents. I worked with this family for a number of years. After a diagnostic process during which I interviewed each of the members, it became evident that their system was approaching a generational transition without much of a Shared Dream. The parents had stayed together forty years and raised two sons and two daughters in spite of having very different aspirations for the future of their family and a long history of marital conflict.

At the time I met them, the juniors ranged in age from twenty-one to thirty-two years. The father, a leading European industrialist who had built a multibillion-dollar chemical manufacturing company, was the quintessential founder: proud, hard working, and exercising authority and power with great ease. A chemist by training, he enjoyed an especially close relationship with his oldest son, who also studied chemistry and earned an MBA from a top university. None of his other children had studied hard sciences. One daughter was an economist, the other studied art, and the youngest son specialized in business administration and marketing.

When describing his Dream, the father quickly pointed out that he did not believe in shared leadership. Ultimately, his Dream was to pass the company on to his oldest son, the only one who, in his eyes, had what it took to be a leader. This oldest son held a senior management position; he was the only sibling who had been allowed to work in the company. The father, who characterized himself as a loner, had a complicated history with his family of origin. He was not on speaking terms with his two brothers. The mother, on the other hand, was a gregarious woman who was particularly fond of her siblings, and got together with them on a weekly basis.

The mother had always resented the preferential treatment she felt the father had given their eldest son, which she believed had deeply divided the children and been destructive to the family. Her Dream was to see all of their offspring collaborating and looking after one another's interests. Ideally, all of them would be in management and share ownership as equal partners. She described the deep sense of shame that she felt every time someone asked her why the other three children did not work in the family business. Over the years she had invested a tremendous amount of herself in helping her husband build the business, and she felt that she had a right to a voice in how the future would be determined.

Needless to say, this was a family in conflict. The father's commitment to monocracy, coupled with his preferential treatment of the oldest son, violated the mother's ideals of fraternal equality and collaboration. The siblings had been caught in an intense rivalry since childhood. The sisters were particularly resentful of the father's favored treatment of the oldest brother; they felt they had not received similar encouragement and opportunities. When the father pointed out that the brother had earned his right to be the successor through hard work and sacrifice, the sisters felt he was simply siding with the brother—a view that was usually endorsed by the mother.

One of the consequences of the parents' mismatched Dreams was that the siblings themselves disagreed about the future scenario. The oldest son, while willing to collaborate with his siblings, shared his father's view that he should be the leader of the business. Along with the mother, the other siblings felt that they should all be equal partners. Although they were, in fact, less suited to the business than the eldest brother—in part because they have been kept out of it—they nevertheless felt entitled to the same authority as the brother in determining the company's destiny. Under such circumstances difficult choices had to be faced.

The family engaged in a visioning process that ultimately allowed the parents to express their Dreams more openly to each other and to understand the fundamental incongruence between those Dreams. Facing this basic conflict late in their lives, when so many choices and compromises had already been made, took courage. As the process unfolded, it became increasingly evident to this couple that until this issue was addressed, continuity planning could simply not go forward.

After many difficult conversations, the wife became more appreciative of the economic and social risks for the family of implementing the fraternal partnership of her Dream. She acknowledged that at this juncture it was unlikely that her children would ever learn to collaborate to the degree necessary to make a sibling partnership work successfully. She also understood that her oldest son was the only one among the siblings with a proven record of managerial excellence. Moreover, she came to accept the fact that her son's success was not simply the result of his father's favoritism, but had in large measure been earned by him.

The father, on the other hand, acquired a better understanding of the needs and concerns of his wife and his other children. For one thing, he understood that promoting his oldest son without even explaining his reasons to the rest of the family would fuel the rivalries among his children and would be destructive to the family in the long term. In one meeting, the father talked in detail about the oldest son's career path in the company; it quickly became evident to the siblings and the mother that there was much they did not know about how hard the oldest son had worked to achieve his high standing among senior executives. As a result of the discussions in the family, the father also moved to diversify his assets through the creation of a family office that would afford his other children a more equitable distribution of the parents' wealth.

The final plan called for the oldest son to inherit voting control of the family business and one-half of the nonvoting stock. The remaining half was to be divided equally among the other three children, who agreed to sign a buyout agreement that spelled out the conditions through which they could sell their stock back to the company if they so preferred. In addition, the other children were given a sizable share of nonbusiness assets owned by the family in order to compensate for the smaller share of business stock they would receive. The father also created a generous investment fund that would guarantee his wife's financial independence.

It took a number of sessions to identify and work through the fundamental incongruence of this couple's Dreams. There were separate meetings with the husband and wife, meetings with the couple, meetings with the siblings alone, and meetings with the entire family. Only then did the family start making progress designing and implementing the more technical aspects of the continuity plan.

Incongruent Sibling Dreams

The story of one second-generation partnership contrasts sharply with that of the Lombardi in chapter 3, and shows how a generational transition can be gridlocked because the individual Dreams *of the partners* remain undiscussed.

Two brothers seven years apart in age managed as copresidents a retail chain they had inherited from their father. The older brother looked after the retail end of the business, including purchasing and sales; the younger brother was in charge of administration and finance. For years their relationship had been riddled with tension—most of it unexpressed—and they had avoided any discussion of a continuity plan. The younger brother had three sons, two of whom were interested in joining the company. The older brother had two married daughters who were not interested in the firm, but the husband of one of them was interested in joining it.

During individual interviews, the two brothers revealed their entirely different scenarios for the future. The central element of the younger brother's Dream had always been to manage the company on his own, just as their father had done. He had always assumed that his older brother would tire of the work; since the older brother did not have any sons, the younger brother expected eventually to buy his shares at a reasonable price. Over the years, he had "put up" with his older brother because he did not have much choice—their father had divided the stock equally between the two. The younger brother had also assumed that after he had led the company for a number of years, his sons would succeed him. He had been very effective in conveying his Dream to his sons, who, consequently, had planned their college and graduate school educations around the assumption that the family business would one day be theirs.

The older brother, however, was not about to let this happen. A basic element of his Dream was to outperform his brother so convincingly that no doubt would remain in anyone's mind about which of the two "had really built the business." He deeply resented what he called his younger brother's "greediness," and he was determined to stay involved with the company "until the very end." What is more, the older brother felt that his son-in-law, who was interested in the business, was more qualified than either of his nephews to take over the business eventually. At every opportunity, he encouraged his son-in-law to consider a career in the company.

The son-in-law, an executive in a large corporation, was intrigued by the idea of owning a smaller business. As a result of his father-in-law's invitations, he decided that he would have a better chance of learning the business and becoming involved with it if he were to live nearby. He applied for, and was granted, a transfer from his fast-track job at his company's headquarters to a less promising position at a branch office in the town where the family business was located. That was ten years ago. Unfortunately, the father-in-law was unable to deliver on the son-in-law's Dream, because his younger brother refused "on principle" to allow in-laws to hold senior management positions in the family company.

Much of this conflict festered under the surface since the brothers had never attempted to talk to each other about how their personal aspirations and Dreams influenced their scenarios for the future. The very fact that they each suspected that their Dreams were incompatible blocked them from ever confronting the issue in an open and constructive manner.

The visioning process created a vehicle for them to have this conversation. Over the course of several meetings, the two brothers worked up the courage to level with each other in a way that cleared a path towards reconciliation and problem solving. Ultimately, the older brother realized the futility of trying to exceed his younger brother. Over the years he had focused so much on outperforming the younger brother that he had neglected many other unfulfilled facets of his Dream. In fact, the rivalry and competition had worn him down. He did not want to continue working so hard at the business. The discussions of his Dream sharpened his awareness of his wish to become a philanthropist; since childhood he had loved the ballet but had been discouraged by his father from getting involved with the performing arts. As part of the negotiation that followed, a buyout agreement was worked out that afforded the older brother the financial independence necessary to pursue these aspirations. He established a prominent foundation and is actively collaborating with his sons-in-law on a very successful new venture.

The younger brother is busy mentoring his two sons to take over the family business and hopes that they will avoid the difficulties he and his older brother encountered because they had not dared to discuss their Dreams.

The Tyranny of a Dream

When families openly discuss their aspirations, they often realize that their Dreams do not yet connect, or that the Dreams of some members connect while those of others do not. Or they may discover that their Dreams can never really connect, and that they do not belong in business together.

One entrepreneur invented highly sophisticated software for computer networks and created a $20 million business. Still, he was not satisfied. His Dream had always been to build a much larger, multidivisional enterprise. So although he would have liked to turn over the business to his daughter as his successor, he also wanted to manage it personally until it became a major corporation that was consistently profitable. When that happened, he believed he would finally get credit for being a truly innovative pioneer in the industry. The father was clinging to this aspiration even though he was in his seventies and had been diagnosed as having a terminal illness.

Nancy, his daughter, greatly admired her father, and like him, was independent and ambitious. She went to work for a Fortune 500 company after receiving her MBA from a top-flight business school and became phenomenally successful in their financial services division, earning a six-figure salary after a few short years. Although she had joined a big company to prove herself, she believed that she could earn a lot more money running her own business, and her Dream was to work alongside her dad. Her father, for his part, had indicated many times that he wanted her to come into the business and eventually take it over.

Both the father and daughter were thrilled during the early visioning sessions at the prospect of their working together. The father had involved her in his work from an early age, had taught her everything about computers, and taken her to industry conventions.

However, during the visioning process—and the negotiations over the terms of her entry into the business—her father's true ambitions were revealed. The scales dropped from Nancy's eyes when she discovered the deep contradictions in *his* Dream.

In negotiating the financial details of her entrance into the business, Nancy felt her father was stubbornly refusing to recognize all that she would be giving up in leaving her corporate job. The terms of his succession plan would make her responsible for the financial welfare of her mother and a handicapped younger brother, who would each own a third of the stock in the business along with Nancy. The family had no other major source of income apart from the business. To establish control, Nancy would have to buy out her mother and brother. In addition, she would be responsible for paying off the company's debt. The father also wanted to establish a board with outsiders on it to oversee Nancy, although he had never felt a board would be useful for him.

Nancy told her father, in so many words: "You brought me up believing that some day the business would be mine. Now you pull this stuff?" She believed her father was asking her to take care of his unfinished business of providing for his heirs while managing a business that might still be heavily in debt when he died. Although her father managed to maintain a good paternal relationship with her, he privately accused her of being "greedy."

This father's stance was a clear example of what Levinson characterized as "enslavement" to the Dream. Despite the approach of death, the father could not let go of his lifelong aspirations for his own glory for the sake of the survival of the business. The visioning process helped to reveal to Nancy the strength of her father's attachment to his own Dream and his extreme reluctance to change his goal dramatically at this stage in his life, despite his changed circumstances. In view of the situation, she chose to remain in her corporate position. Her father had no clear-cut candidate to succeed him in the business at this time.

No matter how solid the foundation for succession appears, this case illustrates it can crumble when the time comes to pass the torch if the family members realize that their Dreams are not compatible or not anchored on what can be accomplished given the constraints facing the company.

Clarifying Values

Engaging in a visioning process forced one young man from a well-known business family to confront his own values and see clearly how they differed from those of his father. The family business is a foundry which specializes in high-precision castings for arms for the military. The son was very much a product of the 1960s—politically liberal and very committed to the peace movement.

When the family met for the first time to discuss the future of the company, the father described details of the company's various military products. While the son had known that the company produced arms for the military, he did not know much about the specific weapons made in its plants or about the customers for them. When he heard the details, he knew the family company was no place for him. It was clear to him for the first time that his own values—and the Dream to which he aspired—made it impossible for him to have anything to do with the company. Instead, he chose to pursue an academic career.

The visioning process brought the values conflict to light in a forceful way that helped him realize his need to make a decision. Although the choice greatly disappointed his father, the son's early decision at least allowed the company ample time to develop an alternative succession plan. The father installed an employee stock ownership plan under which his shares would be acquired in stages, and he would remain CEO until the company was wholly owned by the ESOP.

Discussing a company's future is an educational process for the next generation. It serves the important function of giving children a clearer, more accurate picture of the day-to-day responsibilities of running a business, which helps them clarify their own values and career choices. It also serves to correct misunderstandings the children may have about the goals and values of the company, and about the parents themselves.

Often parents have talked very little to their children about what goes on at the office. The younger family members may overestimate or underestimate the size of the business; they may be completely in the dark about how profitable—or unprofitable—the company is.

When the real details were disclosed at one family's visioning session, a younger family member exclaimed:

My God, I thought this was a much larger business. . . . We have been pumping it up in the family for years and it turns out profits have been falling and there are not too many resources to pass around. I was planning my career on the assumption that this business was going to be here for a long time, when, in fact, it may not be.

Likewise, spouses of owners are often confronted with the reality that the entrepreneur has invested all of the couple's resources in the business and they do not have enough to retire on. Surprise, as a lawyer once told me, is the enemy in estate planning. Spouses are sometimes shocked at financial details revealed after an entrepreneur's death. They may learn, for example, that the family home has been offered as collateral on business loans. Suddenly, they become aware that in order to maintain their standard of living into old age, they will be dependent upon their children's success in the business.

Talking about the future of the company may reveal some of the darker aspects of the business, as well as the frailties of the parents. The children may learn that employees have not always been fairly treated, that managers have allowed plant wastewater to pollute the local water supply, or that parents have routinely engaged in tax evasion. Likewise, parents may become keenly aware that their children expect wealth without having to work too hard to get it, or that they expect to be promoted to president without first learning the business. When discussing future scenarios, information is sometimes revealed that surprises and even shocks the seniors or juniors and heightens a generational clash in values.

Talking openly about Dreams gives family members opportunities to reconsider and adjust their own aspirations in light of more accurate information. The process can drive children away from the business, but it can also unleash a new spirit of cooperation. A great burden is lifted from the shoulders of the young when entry into the business is seen not as an obligation, but as one among several career options. Paradoxically, the freedom to choose may actually cause them to look more favorably on careers in the family business. And when young people enter the family company wholeheartedly, it increases the likelihood that they will be successful.

For many families, visioning is thus a powerful experience that encourages older and younger members to reconnect as adults.

Clearly, talking about their aspirations, disappointments, and wishes can lead to new forms of bonding. Because of their long history together, all families approach generational transitions with heavy baggage of preconceived ideas about one another. Continuity planning provides opportunities to make these ideas explicit, to challenge and discuss differing interpretations of events and behaviors, and to understand the ways in which these various perceptions help or hinder family members' efforts to achieve their aspirations.

Reality-Checking a Dream

The second-generation owner of a large insurance company in Mexico was a generous but controlling father who had always expected that his three children would someday run the business together. He was the sort of parent who, when his children returned from college during the 1960s, could not accept their long hair and shabby clothing as a passing generational statement and, instead, constantly criticized them for it.

The oldest brother, a superb athlete, dropped out of college to join the company. His sister, an academic star who spoke several languages fluently, graduated from a top-flight business school; she came into the business a few years later as a marketer. The youngest son was gentle and kind, but had been hampered in many activities by a learning disability; he worked in the firm for several years in different positions, without much success.

The three siblings found themselves unable to get along in the business. The oldest, the general manager, frequently saw his decisions undermined by the father, who on occasion even ridiculed the son's ideas before senior managers. In like fashion, the oldest brother would not involve his extremely bright and better educated sister in policy decisions, and he exhibited impatience with the mistakes of the younger brother. Realizing that the younger son was unable to cope with his brother's attacks, the father set the young man up in a building supplies franchise. But that business failed, losing millions of dollars for the insurance company—money that the oldest son had been planning to invest in new facilities.

The situation had reached the boiling point when I was called upon by the father. My initial assessment was that any succession plan involving a partnership of the three siblings had only the barest chance of working—not because of economics but because of the conflicts in their relationships. Nevertheless, the father was willing to risk dissapointment and asked me to work with the siblings to develop a partnership. The siblings also wanted to give a partnership a chance, and pledged to do their best to make it work. Upon my urging, to help manage the transition, the father agreed to set up a board with experienced independent directors.

In their visioning sessions, some of the underlying causes of the family's distress emerged. The three siblings revealed aspirations in clear conflict with the roles they had been asked to play in the company. The oldest brother, who had spent some time on an agrarian commune in Northern California, really loved the outdoors and had always wanted to have his own farm; above all, he wanted to be his own boss. The sister had hoped to study architecture, but her father had persuaded her to go to business school instead; her skillful renderings of the work of famous architects covered her office walls. As for the youngest son, he had hoped to become a teacher and help others who suffered from handicaps similar to his own. Despite their early aspirations, the siblings had knuckled under to their demanding father and accepted the roles carved out for them. They all wanted to please him, but were not sure they ever could. One hopeful sign was that, despite their past clashes, they appeared to care for one another. They all said they wanted to remain on good terms with their siblings.

Unfortunately, the oldest brother did not surround himself with capable senior managers and advisers. An economic crisis in the country, combined with some costly mistakes by him, brought the company to the brink of disaster. It became clear that if the company was to survive, the older brother would have to be replaced as general manager. With my support, the board convinced the father to do so. A professional non-family manager turned the company around. Two years ago, with the further help of the board, the company was divided between the older brother and his sister, with other provisions made for the youngest brother. Each of the older siblings preferred to be his and her own boss, rather than remain as partners. The transition was accomplished amicably, and the entire family is happier today than in the past. The older siblings felt that it made sense for them to go back or train for the careers that might have been their first choices as younger people; fortunately, their lives as business owners have permitted them to pursue aspects of their original interests as avocations. In so doing they have found a way of reconnecting to unfulfilled elements of their Dreams.

This family's story shows the great costs involved when members of the younger generation feel they have not been able to freely select their careers. The older brother took pride in being anointed by the father as "first among equals." But, more deeply, he resented having been obliged to join the company before getting a chance to try his hand at farming. Likewise, his sister and younger brother regretted having been forced to abandon their career Dreams. Instead of confronting their father on these issues, they fought with each other. At times their conflicts led to a paralysis over major decisions.

The siblings' inability to pursue their own Dreams was not just based on fear of their father's criticism or loss of his love. In too many families, the promise of affluence and all that goes with it is a powerful temptation for the children. It tends to deter them from asserting their independence, especially when the parents use money in a manipulative way. Since the father controlled all the wealth in this family, it would have been risky for his offspring to confront him. It was a lot safer for the siblings to vent their frustrations by fighting with each other. Ultimately, the fact that this family agreed to divide their company will serve them well.

Parents can be so wedded to their Dreams that they are blind to what is happening in their family system. One of the most important functions of visioning is to test the Dream against reality. The parents have to get rid of illusions from the past and face the reality that the family they desired may well not be the family they have. Such re-evaluation is not easy. When parents are so committed to their Dreams that they hang onto them by denying reality, it often takes a trusted neutral outsider who weighs the evidence carefully to convey the message that they will be putting the business (and ultimately the family) at risk if they carry out their desired scenario.

Visioning Exercises

The work of visioning must proceed in building-block fashion, starting with the individual Dreams of the family members. Clarifying individual Dreams first is critical because they are the essential raw material from which a Shared Dream is constructed. All too frequently professionals get families to focus on the technical aspects of continuity planning (such as strategic, succession, and estate planning) before helping the members to articulate their personal Dreams and to examine the degree of congruency among these aspirations. However, until these Dreams are made explicit and worked through, until their full implications for the future are explored by the family, the best laid plans will lack the motivational force necessary for their implementation.

Members of a business family may vary considerably in the extent to which they have well-formulated Dreams. It is often the case that members of the junior generation have not made psychological contact with such fundamental questions as "What do I really want to do with my life?"; "Do I want to stay involved as a shareholder or employee of this company?"; "If I don't work in the business, what will I do?"; or "How do I envision the family, the business, and the ownership of this system in the future?"

The early work of visioning must therefore focus on helping individuals to articulate what they want for themselves and their families. As I have argued, trouble arises when young people feel pressured to enter a career they are not sure they want, in order to please their parents. One of the most important accomplishments of a visioning process therefore is to convey to members of the next generation that they are free to choose their own paths. During subsequent sessions, the Dreams of the individual members can be considered with reference to the challenges and opportunities that their family company offers.

Given the deep emotional roots that Dreams have in the individual psyche, it is often helpful to begin the work of visioning by engaging in activities that are playful and symbolic. Such activities can help family members get in touch with those aspects of their Dreams that may not be fully conscious but hold the most emotional resonance. When these unconscious wellsprings of desire can be tapped, they frequently provide the excitement and vitality needed to inspire sustained commitment.

Over the years I have experimented with a number of different kinds of activities designed to help business families articulate some of the hidden elements of their Dreams. One such activity involves having individual family members make collages using crayons, markers, magazine cutouts, and other materials that can be used to depict the ideal life to which they aspire. Once each individual completes his or her collage, each member of the family has an opportunity to describe his or her creative depiction of their Dream to the rest of the family. After each member has a turn describing their collage to the others, family members are asked to arrange their individual renditions into a collective family mural—forming a mosaic of the individual Dreams. When the mural is assembled, family members are asked to identify some of the common themes that run across the individual collages, and to comment on the extent to which the ideas, symbols, values, and themes described by the group capture some of the unique characteristics of the family as a whole. The issues and ideas generated through this process are documented and ultimately used as raw material for future work on visioning.

Naturally, there is a certain amount of preparation that needs to be done before a family engages in an exercise of this kind. The participants should first have some understanding of the concept of the Dream, and of its importance for continuity and the succession process. In order to stimulate the imaginations of family members, facilitators might tell anecdotes about the kinds of choices that have been made by individuals in other business families. The objective here is to widen the range of imagined possibilities for the different kinds of ownership, family, and management roles that individuals can play in a family enterprise. It may also be necessary to work with the family in order to create a climate of trust, and to defuse the resistance some may have to engaging in a playful activity the relevance of which they may not see at first. Once the exercise gets going, even the staunchest and most hard-driving of entrepreneurs ultimately suspend disbelief and get involved in the creative process.

The next step in the visioning process involves working with the ideas and issues that have been generated through the collage in order to begin constructing a more detailed description of the individual and Shared Dreams that can be used for the purposes of succession and continuity planning. To help them articulate their Dreams in more detail, I ask family members to write an imaginary newspaper article that depicts themselves, their family, and their business five or ten years in the future. In addition, they are given a set of questions (see Table 5-1) that invites them to describe in considerable detail how the business, the family, and the ownership will look in the future. They are also asked to provide a detailed account of the various roles they envision themselves and others playing in the future scenario.

Writing these articles offers family members an opportunity to articulate their own personal wish lists for themselves and for the family enterprise. The individual articles are then shared with all family members in preparation for a meeting in which each person will get to say more about his or her imagined future, and to explore together the ways in which the individual future scenarios are or are not consistent with one another.

Doing this work does not guarantee that a Shared Dream will, in fact, emerge. As some of the cases above suggest, the family may realize that continuing the family business no longer makes sense, or that it makes more sense for some family members to stay involved than for others. The key is to structure the process so that all imagined possibilities and their implications for the future can be freely discussed.

In conjunction with these kinds of exercises, families often find it helpful to make contact with other business families who have successfully completed a transfer of leadership to the next generation. This is particularly important for those families contemplating evolutionary successions, because they will be venturing into uncharted waters. A family currently in the controlling-owner stage can learn a great deal by visiting with a family that has been successfully operating as a sibling partnership. Similarly, a sibling partnership contemplating moving to a cousin consortium can gain a great deal of insight from a family with such a structure already in place. These visits allow family members to understand the challenges and rewards of operating in the new business form, and to gain a fuller appreciation for the range of possible roles that different members of the family could play in the future.

The Lombardis' Article Writing

In 1993 I asked the Lombardis to do the newspaper article writing exercise described above. Each family member was assigned the task of writing an article for the *Wall Street Journal* in the year 2003 describing their family and their company as they would like it to be at that time. Their "articles" would then be used as the basis of further visioning discussions.

A picture of how Lombardi Enterprises would be governed in the third generation had already begun to emerge before the five children in the second generation were grown. The founder, Paul Sr., had conveyed his wish for a business dynasty to his offspring through his words as well as through such actions as engaging them in exciting projects at the office from an early age. His adult children were determined to further the dynastic Dream. The five sibling partners hoped their children would all be active in the enterprise. However, their initial discussions suggested that they wanted to re-create a structure similar to their own, with each family in the third generation choosing a leader to serve in a five-cousin partnership. Later discussions convinced the Lombardis that trying to clone their own system in a third generation would be unwise. A new governance structure would be required, and the cousins would have to be trained for their roles in it. But much

Table 5-1   Thought Starter Questions

Write in the present tense placing yourself in the future, as if *your Dream for yourself and your family business has actually been realized. Assume a five-to-ten-year time frame.*

Personal	• What activities have energized your growth and development as a person up to now?
	• What are you passionately devoted to?
	• What balance have you achieved among work, family, and leisure?
	• What roles do you personally play in the family enterprise (e.g., management, family governance, family foundation, shareholder, board, mentoring)?
	• In what ways (if any) has the family enterprise helped you realize your aspirations?
	• In what ways (if any) has your family helped you realize your aspirations?
	• What have you given to yourself?
	• What have you given to your family?
	• What have you given to your community?
	• How would you like to be remembered?
The Family	• What is the age distribution in your family (add five to ten years to everyone's ages)?
	• What kind of family do you have (describe the texture of relationships)?
	• What makes your family successful as a family?
	• Who leads the family? How is that leadership exercised?
	• What values and principles hold your family together?
	• How committed are the members of the family to staying together in business?
	• What has the family done to pass those values on to the next generation?
	• What has your family done to nurture the development of the young?
	• What has the family done to look after its older members?
	• What has your family done to enhance its capacity to communicate?
	• How does the family handle conflict?
	• What does the family do for recreation?
	• What educational efforts does the family engage in?
The Business	• What strategy has the business followed over the past five to ten years?
	• Who leads the business?

Table 5-1 *(Continued)*

	• What particular talents and skills does the leader (or leaders) of the business have? • How has the leader (or leaders) been able to realize the company's strategic mandate? • How is the senior management team composed? • What is the mix of family and non-family executives? • How was the succession process handled? • What are the outgoing seniors doing now? • Are they retired? If so, do they retain any relationship to the company? • How influential are they still in determining what goes on at the company? • Who monitors the performance of the new leadership? • To whom is the new leadership accountable? • Who determines the compensation of senior executives? • What is the new leadership doing to ensure the development of the next generation?
Ownership and Governance	• How are shares divided among family members? • How is control divided among family members? • Is your system a controlling owner company, a sibling partnership, or a cousins consortium? • Describe the ownership structure. How does it work? Is the stock in trusts? If so, what is the relationship like between trustees and beneficiaries? • What governance structures exist to coordinate and monitor the activities of your family enterprise? • Is there a board of directors? • How is the board of directors composed? How well does the board work? • Is there a family council? • How is the family council composed? How well does the family council work? • What policies has the family adopted to manage the interface of family and business issues? • How have these policies been adopted? How effective have they been? Who enforces them? • How are shareholders organized? • Is there a dividend policy? If so, who determines it? • What has been done to educate shareholders about their rights and responsibilities? Describe some of the educational efforts. • Is there a stock redemption mechanism? If so how does it work?

work remained to be done before family members could come together and support a coherent mutual vision of the future.

In their articles the Lombardis all wrote about a company that had continued to grow through the years and become internationally known for its leading-edge management and use of sophisticated technology. Robert Lombardi's article conveyed a sense of wonder at how a small family business had burgeoned into a model $2 billion retail empire. Lombardi Enterprises, he wrote, had grown while pursuing "a balance of efficiency and equity" and while striving to meet the needs of their employees and the communities in which they operated. Paul Jr., the oldest brother and CEO, saw the company continuing to open markets across the country and anticipated the development of much larger stores; he also imagined the company expanding into Mexico and Canada with the assistance of joint venture partners. Stefano Lombardi imagined Lombardi Enterprises becoming a very large, publicly traded company that included a new credit card business. Rita Lombardi reported that in the year 2003 almost all family members, including in-laws, were working in the company's various enterprises. Her article devoted a lot of attention to family concerns, raising questions about how the five siblings would get along after their parents had passed from the scene. The Lombardis' reputation as an exemplary family for their service to state and local communities had grown over the years. The articles pointed to the strong family tradition that continued to be the root of the company's success.

In addition, the siblings described changes in their individual roles and in the organizational structure of Lombardi Enterprises. They saw the company, or the larger divisions, going public, with majority control remaining in family hands. Paul Jr. saw himself as chairman of a holding company that embraced all of the family enterprises. The sibling partners pictured themselves withdrawing from day-to-day management and assuming governance roles in order to let third-generation leaders take charge of operations. All wanted to devote more time to enjoying their wealth, families, and hobbies and interests. Worried about his heart condition, Paul Jr. saw himself giving up some of his burdens in order to "smell the roses" and to nurture the travel agency and the public relations firms he had started as separate ventures. Similarly, Stefano, shaken by the sudden death of a friend, was looking forward to taking life a little easier and spending more time with his family.

As might be expected, the articles all reflected the personal as well as the business aspirations of the Lombardis. Paul Jr.'s article began with a description of a banquet, attended by various government and business luminaries, at which he was honored for his outstanding leadership. Frank Lombardi, who was in his forties and wrestling with mid-life career issues—a year before his dismissal—saw himself as head of the Markets Division and a possible successor to Paul Jr. as chairman of the company. Robert imagined himself as a likely next governor of California. Rita Lombardi quoted herself in her article as wishing to go back to school to pursue the business education that, unlike her brothers, she had never received.

The question of who would lead the anticipated cousin consortium—and how the new leader would be chosen—remained up in the air at the time of the article-writing exercise. Unwilling to raise the hackles of his siblings on the succession issue (although he was understood to be grooming two candidates for the top spot—a non-family executive as well as his oldest son), Paul Jr. refrained from mentioning who would be CEO in the year 2003. In fact, at this point, none of the five siblings wanted to speculate, even playfully, about leaders for the next generation. During this early visioning, they did not want to be viewed as pushing their own children for leadership positions; nor were they willing to risk the displeasure of their siblings by passing judgment on the qualifications of their siblings' children.

While lacking details on who would lead the company in the next generation—a political hot potato—the articles did serve to concentrate the partners' attention on the future. The family was building on a foundation of cooperation laid long ago and strengthened over the years through the atmosphere of openness encouraged by the parents. This visioning process strengthened the Lombardis' resolve to move forward and thrash out a plan for succession. The specifics would be left for later. There was still time to gather more evidence about the capabilities of the cousins, reach a consensus on the best qualified, and decide which names would appear at the top of future organizational charts.

The restructuring recommended by strategic business consultants in 1994 put the visioning process on hold. The sibling partners of Lombardi Enterprises—and particularly Paul Jr.—became increasingly absorbed in the work of re-evaluating their businesses and shedding those that had proven unprofitable or insufficiently profitable. Several of these businesses had been maintained over the years because they were pet projects of one sibling or another. The need to close some of them down brought latent rivalries within the group to the surface once again. At one session, the rest of the partners accused Paul Jr. of pushing them too hard, of being unappreciative of their contributions, of wanting to run the company himself and get rid of them. Paul Jr. was depressed. He felt exhausted from the demands of the restructuring process, and resentful because he was no longer certain of the scope of his decision-making autonomy. The family was on the verge of despair at this session, and afterward, Paul Jr.'s wife, Teresa, sent me a fax describing the effects on Paul's morale. "What good are all these family meetings," she asked, "if they produce only pain?"

In my response I reminded her: "The purpose of all this is to protect your legacy and to secure the futures of your children." Later, when I met with Teresa, she spoke of the challenges they both faced with Paul's approaching retirement. Paul Jr. had taken on the leadership of the business, but not of the family, she confided. He still felt very insecure and in need of reassurance. Deep in his heart, he felt that, his many achievements notwithstanding, he had never become as great a man as his father.

Rekindling the Dream

This crisis in the Lombardis' cohesion suggested that the siblings had lost sight of their Shared Dream. Their commitment to continuity had weakened because of the pressures of restructuring, and because of their realization—from the work with their strategic consultants—that family considerations had distorted their business decision making, leading to poor economic results.

Most such business problems in a company, caught early enough, are fixable. Problems in a family are not usually resolved so easily. Unless the Shared Dream retains its excitement and vitality, unless the partners remain tightly bound by their mutual commitment, a company can readily come apart. The Lombardis' plight suggests that the Shared Dream must be periodically rekindled, especially when the business is under threat from internal or external forces. This rekindling can be accomplished through further work on the Shared Dream, as well as through enacting rituals and reviving symbols that remind the family members of the values and traditions that hold them together.

At our next session, I suggested to the siblings that there might be a deeper psychological reason for their seeming collapse of unity. The physical and mental decline of their elderly parents was a reminder that they would soon be alone and fully responsible for the future of the company. They themselves were also older now. Perhaps hearing a distant bell tolling for them, the siblings were hesitating to take the final steps in becoming independent adults—which would be to finish and carry forward their own, fully formed vision of the future. Instead, they were still clinging to parts of their parents' Dream, partly out of respect, but also to avoid facing their own mortality.

The siblings' inability to move forward was evident in their unwillingness to face crucial ownership issues. The parents still held 60 percent of the shares in the company, while the siblings shared a total of 40 percent. The five partners *believed* their parents' wills divided the stock equally among them, but they couldn't be sure unless the wills were opened. The lawyers would have allowed them access, but they felt that looking at the wills before the parents died would be disrespectful, and they were reluctant to do it. The enemy here was the silence about what the wills contained. Knowing how the stock would be allocated was crucial for resolving governance issues. Without knowing the ownership structure, the partners could not proceed to set up a holding company structure for the next generation. After many conversations, they met with the lawyers and forged a legally binding agreement that guaranteed an equal distribution of their inheritance among them regardless of the stipulations in their parents' wills.

At their next session, the five partners confronted the need to refurbish their Shared Dream. They shared one over-arching ambition: They all wanted to do right by their children. Further, they felt accountable to their children. This was the "hook" on which organizational change could be hung.

Family members in the second and third generations watched an interview with the founder, videotaped a few years earlier, in which Paul Sr. described his experiences and his beliefs. The seniors and juniors then broke up into separate groups for further discussion. The twenty-seven cousins were divided into smaller subgroups to discuss what help they wanted from the seniors in planning their careers. At the same time, the seniors met to discuss what help they could, and should, provide. After the juniors reported on the substance of their discussions, there was a long pause, and the meeting seemed to move on to other business. Then one of the juniors exclaimed, "Wait a minute, the seniors haven't reported yet!" This incident dramatized the fact that the juniors were watching their parents' behavior closely. Ultimately, the seniors realized, they were going to be *judged* by the next generation on how well they had prepared the juniors for their careers and how well they had planned the leadership transition and future governance of the enterprise.

The Lombardis' family business continues to thrive to this day. They have designed and implemented an elaborate governance structure that includes an independent board of directors, a family council, and a shareholders assembly (these structures will be discussed in detail in chapter 12). They have also selected a non-family executive who has succeeded Paul Jr. to be CEO of Lombardi Enterprises (Paul Jr. is now chairman of the board) and to help mentor the next generation of Lombardi cousins into leadership roles in the future.

Visioning in a Cousin Company

In third- and fourth-generation cousin companies, the visioning process is usually far more complicated. Many people and several family branches are usually involved when enterprises have reached this stage. In these large clans, discussions of the future no longer take place around the dinner table. More formal forums must be set up so that different members of each generation and branch of the family can express their needs and their views. A process must be established to hammer out a vision for company and to enlist support for it. If an outside facilitator is brought in, that person has to take a more directive role in structuring the visioning process.

A Canadian enterprise that has some 200 cousins in the fifth generation illustrates the complexity of these tasks. Although the family had come through three successful generational transitions in leadership, it was becoming clear that the enterprise had grown far too large to be managed by the existing structure. The company had started as a successful brewery, but had expanded into a conglomerate. It was organized as a loose confederation; each of the business units was dominated by one of the seven branches of the family, with little in the way of a coordinated corporate strategy. Overseeing this far-flung organization was a board that was like a family council, on which one member represented each of the seven branches. Board members rotated every three years, and often the representatives were cousins who had virtually no knowledge of the businesses and who were generally reluctant to impose discipline on inept family managers.

The company was in trouble because of mismanagement of some of its businesses and competition from larger multinational companies that had entered the Canadian market. While I was working with the family on management and succession issues, a team of other consultants did a complete analysis of the financial position of the various divisions. Their report concluded that the shareholders' return on investment could be increased significantly with a restructuring that would rid the company of weaker businesses and channel resources into the more profitable ones. It was clear that this company had to make sweeping changes, and the visioning process would have to play a vital role in defining alternative future scenarios.

An appeal to history and tradition can be a powerful unifying force in such circumstances. The Dreams that hold together multi-generational companies are often embedded in their history and traditions. Although time-honored ways of doing things can sometimes pose formidable obstacles to change, tradition is also the glue that prevents things from coming apart in times of conflict. At the height of the crisis, one of the aunts rose before a critical meeting and suggested a prayer "to thank God for our family and to celebrate who we are." The psychological force of their family tradition was palpable in the boardroom, acknowledged by all as they bowed their heads in prayer.

With so many fourth- and fifth-generation members, it becomes impractical to have a full-scale discussion of everyone's individual hopes and expectations, although individual Dreams are obviously still important. In large multigenerational companies it is essential to take a more collective approach to visioning, focusing on the expectations and interests of the generational groups and family branches, rather than individual Dreams alone.

In this case, members from each branch were interviewed to get a sense of their individual Dreams. Then groups of seniors and juniors met to discuss their expectations for themselves and for the company. Those two groups then reported their views to a task force set up to frame a vision for the company and present career options for the cousins.

In early visioning sessions, the elders placed strong emphasis on conveying family traditions to the young through stories, symbols, and clan events. They talked about a proud tradition of perseverance—evident in the company's well-known motto, "Persistence Pays." And they reminded the group of an event that had gravely threatened the enterprise: During a period of labor unrest in their province, beer makers were threatened with violence and sabotage. While other brewers sold their plants or moved away, this family decided to tough out the crisis in order to protect their assets and the jobs of their employees. These heroic stories inspired young family members to carry on the legacy.

When the juniors met as a group, they criticized the elders for being set in their ways and not moving fast enough to make needed changes. Well aware of the consultants' financial report, they saw the company's difficulties as threatening to rob them of their turn at the helm and their legacy to their children. When the juniors and seniors met together, shareholders in both generations complained that their equity was being eroded by management's inaction and protection of the seniors heading the weaker business units. The juniors also complained that the older men controlled the top jobs in the company, and that well-educated men and women of their own generation had limited opportunities.

Beckhard has described three elements that must be present before major change in large organizations such as this conglomerate can be accomplished. First, members of an organization must experience strong dissatisfaction with the status quo, and they must recognize that without major changes the pain will continue or even get worse. Second, there must be a clearly defined alternative that is engaging enough to mobilize the process of change—here is where articulating a Shared Dream is critical for change. And third, members of the organization need to see clearly the concrete steps that can bring about the desired change. Only when they can envision what will happen and how their lives will be improved will they overcome the natural resistance to change.[2]

To cope with this painful moment in their history, the Canadian family explored several alternatives during the visioning process. They thoroughly weighed the idea of breaking the company into smaller businesses that could be run by different leaders of the family. Their discussion helped the family understand that such a breakup could not be accomplished overnight. It might take three or four years before each of the individual businesses was strong enough to "float on its own bottom," and before various legal and financial steps taken to separate them could be completed. Ultimately, however, the family rejected the breakup alternative because it would cause emotional bruises among them that might never heal.

The consultants' financial data provided the "discontent" needed to move the system. The evidence that a restructuring could enhance shareholders' ROI by as much as 60 percent was a powerful incentive for all. A coalition of family leaders supported the appointment of a new CEO to lead the transformation. The man they proposed was an experienced family executive in his fifties who was commanding and comfortable with power yet very patient and accommodating of the family members' varied concerns.

Although opposed to the restructuring, heads of the weaker businesses were loath to speak against it. With all family members over eighteen voting, the family approved the new executive team by a margin of seventy to two. Afterward, family members were ecstatic at having taken this major step forward and anxious to get on with developing their restructuring plan. Members of both generations spoke about their commitment to each other, and the seniors pledged to do their best to coach the juniors to become their successors.

The task force thrashed out a new organizational structure. To manage an enterprise and family of this size required a professional board; three independent directors were appointed to the seven-member board. In addition, the families needed an institutional way to continue the visioning process, so that the changing needs and aspirations of the different groups could be discussed. A family council was set up to ensure that members of each family branch and each new generation (some of whom also sit on the board) will have a voice in setting the goals of the enterprise. The task force also recommended a number of steps to develop more options for the cousins. They proposed a scholarship fund so that young family members could study at the best business and professional schools. They urged that the company establish an internal market to buy back stock so that cousins who wished to cash in their shares could do so easily. And they proposed setting up a family foundation for those who wished to pursue philanthropic activities. These options were presented at a meeting of the two-hundred cousins and heartily endorsed by the group. Through the visioning process, the family as a whole achieved the unity and shared commitment that are necessary to get them through the rough spots and increase the chances of success.

The process of surfacing individual and shared Dreams, nurturing and developing them, is hard, challenging work. Facilitators of these discussions must challenge the members to exhume and revive long-forgotten or fragmented aspirations. Even in families that encourage such aspirations, talking about them openly can be difficult. The work of investigating and sharing Dreams presents opportunities for enriching relationships among family members as well as for developing a vision for the business that can inspire creativity and cooperation. The family business field would do well to develop additional techniques for stimulating such discussions and making them easier for families to have on a regular basis. Continuity planning must by necessity help to build a family's capacity to engage in the visioning work described here.

After a Shared Dream comes into focus, it must be continually reassessed and recharged by the family to fit changing circumstances.

The process of adapting the Dream to reality proceeds by fits and starts, becoming more pressing at critical junctures in the lives of family members. The dynamic cognitive process is akin to what Piaget, in the context of children's development, called "assimilation and accommodation." Often, however, a family does not fully understand the implications of its choice of a leadership structure. When moving to a new structure in the next generation, they lack mental maps of the terrain—and tend to underestimate the challenges of making that structure work. The next chapter will attempt to define the conditions required for successfully installing a controlling owner, sibling partner, or cousin consortium system.

CHAPTER 6

Assessing the Feasibility of the Dream

I have argued that agreement on a Shared Dream is an essential first step in planning for succession, and that this Dream usually envisions a future business form. The future business form may be only vaguely defined at first, and it may or may not equate with the realities of the family and the business as both evolve over time. The Dream must be continually reassessed and, if necessary, reworked, to conform with new information about the business and about the family. Families also need to recognize that the three basic family business forms—the controlling-owner business, the sibling partnership, and the cousin consortium—call for very different approaches to the exercise of leadership and authority. Families that decide to change their business form face a great challenge because their experience has not taught them how to make the new form work, nor to assess whether a given business form is feasible for their family. Even when a family "recycles" its business form, the next generation will inevitably face changed circumstances. Every family must be able to look ahead and picture how its leadership and governance structures will work when, for example, more of its heirs are involved in the business, or the economic environment changes dramatically, or products reach the mature stages of their life cycles.

The cognitive leap that is required for succession planning cannot be overstated. I am often struck by the misperceptions some families have about the paths they have chosen. When I explain the pros and cons of the choices they have made, they sometimes hear only those elements I describe that fit with their Dream. Their apparent lack of soul-searching about the challenges posed by their choices does not bode well for the succession.

The objective of this chapter is to depict the conditions required for successful adoption of each of the three types of business form: controlling owner, sibling partnership, and cousin consortium. My purpose is to lay out the practical problems that must be resolved in order to succeed at adopting one or another of these leadership structures and to dispel the illusions that families sometimes have when they are moving to a structure with which they have had little or no experience. In many such cases, the ideal can be achieved only with hard work and with specific kinds of training, and then perhaps only imperfectly.

Challenges of the Controlling Owner Form

The choice of a single leader risks abuse of power and can set up a "horse race." The distinctive feature of the controlling owner business is that authority rests ultimately on the shoulders of a single leader. In a CO-to-CO recycle, one and only one member of the next generation will emerge as the dominant leader and principal owner. By design, its success ultimately depends on the capabilities of the chosen leader. Paradoxically, one of the greatest advantages of the CO form—monolithic decision making—is also its biggest drawback. Instead of spreading the risk with a sibling partnership, the family bets the store and the family fortune on the leadership talent, business acumen, and emotional maturity of one person. A poor choice can have grave consequences. When parents choose one leader, there is the risk that love can cloud their judgment: A parent's attachment to a particular son or daughter can dictate the choice of a successor who, on the basis of his or her track record, is not a leader or even competent in business.

Since families who choose the CO form concentrate their stock in that person's hands, moreover, there is also the risk of abuse of power. The concentration of power in one family member's hands is a particular risk in family businesses because of its potential for disrupting family relationships. The successor who controls the family's most important asset can easily slip into a parental role, which can be bitterly resented by his or her contemporaries. Consider how brothers and sisters must feel when, instead of going to the parents to request a loan, they must go to the sibling who has risen to CO in the business.

When the CO form is the structure of choice for the future, the senior generation faces two difficult questions: Who will the leader be? And how will the rest of the family respond to this choice? The decision is obviously not difficult when only one member of the next generation stands out as clearly acceptable to all. When a group of equally talented siblings all aspire to be leaders, however, there is the risk that the choice of the CO structure will set up a competitive horse race, a winner-take-all struggle that could be destructive to family relationships and even to the business. Positions in the business tend to carry great prestige and power in the family. The need to elevate one sibling or cousin over another may aggravate rivalries that have been simmering beneath the surface. The more ambiguity there is surrounding the choice and the longer it is put off, the fiercer the competition may become. This puts considerable pressure on the business owner, who is not likely to want make a choice until the candidates have been tested over time, under varying circumstances, and one of them emerges as demonstrably the best qualified.

Parents cannot wait passively for this to happen on its own. One of the challenges for those who favor the CO form is to create opportunities for potential successors to demonstrate their mettle, to prove that their leadership will be in the interests of all and will bring economic benefits to all. But some parents shy away from exposing their offspring to real jobs—jobs with clearly delineated responsibilities and accountabilities. The more enmeshed the family,[1] the more protective the parents tend to be. I have encountered countless successor candidates who have been given hollow jobs such as "assistant to the vice president" and never get the chance to prove their real worth to their seniors, their peers, or to themselves.

As we will see, sometimes the reasons for this unwillingness to set up real tests lie beneath awareness. Thus some entrepreneurs avoid making a choice, stretching out the period of ambiguity and heating up the "horse race" among the candidates. Even in more functional families, parents may not be willing to favor one child over others, no matter how superior his or her demonstrated motivation and competence. If they really believe in the CO form as optimal for their future, they need to be prepared to create conditions that will make the choice of one leader possible, even at the risk of some family tension. When the final selection is made, it is more likely to be viewed as a result of parental favoritism if the reasons for the choice remain ambiguous and unsupported by a record of excellence.

A strong parent-successor relationship is crucial for the CO-to-CO recycle. The success of a CO-to-CO recycle depends to a great extent on the quality of the relationship between the outgoing and the incoming leaders. This type of one-to-one succession is very personal. During the transition period, the two people will be constantly dealing with heated issues at the office. The incoming leader will invariably be compared with the predecessor along a host of dimensions, including leadership style, managerial effectiveness, quantitative ability, and people skills. Feelings of rivalry will surface. Tensions will rise.

Since the chances of success are often enhanced when the outgoing and incoming leaders have a good relationship, researchers have sought to isolate the factors that influence the strength of this critical bond. In one in-depth study, I compared ten business families who had successfully negotiated the transition with ten others who had failed at it. Through a series of interviews, I assessed such factors as the amount of time the controlling owner had devoted to preparing the successor, how well the two got along at home and office, and whether the successor had worked outside the business. I found that by far the most important determinant of success was whether the senior leader and the new leader enjoyed a relationship beyond the work setting.[2]

In eight out of the ten businesses that were successful in carrying out the transition, the old and new leaders had shared activities outside the business that brought them close together. For many it was active involvement in a sport or hobby.[3] In companies that failed, however, the relationship between the principals tended to be of poor quality. In none of these companies did the parent and successor have some outside activity that excited them both and in which they participated together.

The power of this bond is illustrated by a father and son who became business partners late in life after both had succeeded at other careers. Robert Pamplin, Sr., had been president of the Georgia Pacific Company during twenty years of the lumber and natural resources conglomerate's most dramatic growth. His son, Robert Jr., was a highly successful investor before joining with his father to form R. B. Pamplin Corporation in Portland, Oregon, in 1976. R. B. Pamplin Corporation owns fourteen textile mills and a concrete and asphalt company, and is the largest privately held company in Oregon. Writing in the *Wall Street Journal*, Robert Jr. described the early development of

mutual interests that helped make their father-son partnership emi-
nently successful:

Perhaps the main reason my father and I work together so well is that we
like each other and have fun together. He made it a point to take me hunt-
ing and fishing in the swamps of the South when I was just six years old.
Some of my earliest memories of Dad are ones of listening to stories by
lantern light, sleeping in a shack, catching fish and eating squirrel stew.[4]

Such shared experiences do not necessarily mean that a quality relationship will continue to exist or that a successful CO-to-CO succession
is guaranteed. Other variables can affect the transition. Memories of this
sort do, however, provide a foundation for the relationship and for
acceptance of the parent as a mentor. When parent and successor can
continue to connect around an activity both enjoy, that connection does
a great deal to ease the emotional strains of the transfer of power.

*The creation of minority shareholders can lead to disappointment and
conflict for the new CO.* Many parents desire a CO structure for the
future, but want to leave all their children some stock, whether or not
they work in the business. Sometimes the parents are forced to create
minority shareholders (or to split the shares into voting and preferred
stock) because the bulk of the family's wealth is invested in the business.
In such cases, the new controlling owner inherits a hybrid structure in
which he or she has de facto control while remaining responsible for
the economic well-being of the other siblings, who often become
shareholders by default.

The consequences of this arrangement can be profound, since the
creation of this significant group of stakeholders forces a degree of
interdependence on siblings (or cousins) that they may not be able or
willing to sustain. Those family members who inherit the minority
shares may have much of their wealth tied up in a business over which
they have little or no control. Their dependence on the success of the
new CO often generates resentment and conflict, particularly when
this ownership arrangement is forced on siblings and/or cousins.

In first-generation companies, both the successor and the predecessor typically have little experience dealing with minority shareholders. Doing so can be especially challenging for those successors who
follow in the footsteps of a strong CO founder and who naively expect
to exercise their authority with no encumbrances. In these situations
successors tend to view family shareholders not as investors interested

in the success of the business but as intruders who continuously make financial demands and interfere with their ability to run the company.

In one family company I studied, the parents clearly wished to retain the advantages of the CO structure but chose to divide the stock equally among their children. After the parents' deaths, the son who was appointed the next controlling owner complained bitterly about having to "carry" his four siblings:

Everyone always understood that I was the one who would inherit the family business. I worked in it for well over twenty years. I made considerable sacrifices and ultimately achieved the respect of all employees. My parents led me to believe that I would get the company with no strings attached. However, shortly before their deaths, they came to feel that not giving my siblings significant amounts of stock would be unfair to them. Unbeknown to me, they changed their will, leaving me with voting control but giving them approximately equal amounts of shares in the business. What good is having control if every decision I make turns into a huge family drama? I feel like an ox pulling the rest of the family along. The irony of it all is that they thought that this arrangement would minimize conflict among us.

Here we see an unworkable compromise between the parents' Dream for a CO structure and their need to be "fair" in estate planning. They aspired to continue the CO form and had identified a highly capable successor but, through poor planning, they had painted themselves into a corner. This case was particularly difficult because after establishing certain expectations with the successor, the parents altered the structure of ownership without telling their children. The successor always thought he would have the same freedom to govern the business that his father had enjoyed. The realization that he now had to take the needs and concerns of his siblings into account flew in the face of the CO Dream.

As minority shareholders increasingly assert their rights in the courts,[5] the ideal of the independent entrepreneur, accountable to no one, is rapidly becoming a fantasy. For single successors whose Dream has always been "Someday the business will be mine," inheriting a crew of unwanted shareholders requires a considerable adjustment. Moreover, the very notion of complete independence without accountability, which is often the fantasy underlying the appeal of the controlling owner form, is far removed from the realities of modern-day leadership. This expectation can create considerable disappointment among CO successors who crave autonomy and independence.

When there are minority shareholders, resources should be set aside in case a buyout becomes necessary. Minority shareholders, too, may become dissatisfied, feeling that their assets are locked into a company which, in their view, offers them inadequate returns and little voice in major decisions. Thus it is advisable that families moving toward a CO structure with minority owners set up the ground rules and financial mechanisms necessary for buying out dissatisfied shareholders. In the absence of a buyout agreement and a stock redemption fund, the "pruning of the shareholder tree" which often occurs may well put a severe strain on both the family and the company.[6]

Buyouts require capital planning and must be carefully structured to prevent lasting resentments in the family. Although the business is sometimes a risky investment, it usually is regarded as having the potential for expansion—particularly if the new CO is an effective leader. When the CO buys out his or her siblings to consolidate control, the arrangement must therefore take into account not only the company's present value, but also its future growth potential. If the business does not grow after the buyout, the siblings are usually thankful for having been able to get their money out in order to invest it in more secure or lucrative assets. If the business takes off following the buyout, the siblings may be left with a lingering belief that the CO shortchanged them. One way to prevent this resentment from festering is to include a provision in the buyout agreement that would give them some added compensation depending on the company's future performance.

Challenges of the Sibling Partnership

Partnerships that are formed as a last resort—to preserve family unity—are likely to fail. Sibling partnerships are difficult to manage because the natural competitiveness of brothers and sisters often carries over in adulthood. I've seen some shrewd and accomplished business leaders in their sixties and seventies still argue with their siblings over such things as who sits at the head of the table, who has the most glamorous office, or who has the best-looking spouse and the smartest children. A sibling partner once gently admonished me because my memos often listed his brother's name first. Even in the healthiest families, the pressures of working together day after day, year after year, can turn up the heat in these rivalries and strain personal relationships.

Ironically, business owners will often make their children partners in the next generation precisely in order to avoid having to choose one as the leader, thereby aggravating deep-seated rivalries. Family systems theorists have described a scale of intensity in the relationships of families ranging from "disengaged" (those in which the members are highly autonomous) to "enmeshed" (those in which the members' lives are wrapped up in one another). Functional families fall somewhere in between the poles of this spectrum. It is the enmeshed families who, when their unity is threatened, are likeliest to make a reactive choice of a sibling partnership.

Bowen and other family systems theorists have described a pattern of behavior in enmeshed families that can lead to this result. Some of the members, when they begin to feel suffocated by too much closeness, look for ways to assert independence. They may withhold information from other managers about their department's sales or the deals they have made—information that is vital to the functioning of the company. Or they may assert their need for independence by fighting with siblings or parents over business issues, or engaging in publicly embarrassing activities. This behavior only intensifies other family members' determination to preserve unity and prevent too much differentiation in the group. The seniors may try to impose a partnership in the ill-conceived hope that it will reverse the centrifugal forces that threaten to pull the family apart.[7] Instead of being driven by a Shared Dream, succession decisions are driven by a need to avoid conflicts. Such reactive partnerships do not have good prospects. Sooner or later, a structure based on negative motivation will crumble under pressure.

The toughest call: Are the siblings capable of collaborating? Many parents who own companies aspire to succeed both as business owners and as parents. As one measure of their effectiveness as parents, they wish to see their offspring working together harmoniously as a team. Often the result of this ambition is that they downplay evidence that some (or all) of their offspring have never gotten along well, and that a partnership among them has little hope of succeeding.

In their extensive study of sibling relationships, Bank and Kahn suggest that sibling rivalries can take radically different paths in adulthood:

For some siblings, aggression and rivalry are an attempt to maim or humiliate; one may live a part or all of one's life knowing that the presence of a brother or a sister makes one physically or emotionally unsafe. At this extreme, to spend time with a sibling is to enter enemy territory, emotionally charged with murderous tension. At another extreme lies conflicts that are neither humiliating nor crippling but instead become part of a creative and interesting dialectic that strengthens the relationship. These brothers and sisters can laugh about their ancient wars, deflect a sibling's attack, and, in the process, grow wiser and more mature.[8]

At the heart of most sibling rivalries is a process of social comparison. Adult siblings continually compare one another along a number of critical dimensions, including achievement (e.g., who has the most money, the higher rank, or most awards); sexuality (e.g., who is the most attractive, whose spouse is most desirable); social relations (e.g., who is the most outgoing, charming, charismatic). In a business, this social comparison can take many forms. It is not unusual for two brothers who have been in business together a long time to compete over whose department is most efficient or productive, or to try to outsmart each other in meetings with their managers. Siblings in business are also exceedingly attentive to each other's salaries and perks, continuously monitoring how the rewards are being distributed among them. Underlying this preoccupation is the ever-present fear that one of them may get more or take advantage of the other.

A critical challenge for parents is to assess whether their children's rivalries are too deeply entrenched to preclude any possibility of collaboration. This is not an easy judgment to make, especially for parents who want desperately to believe that their children love each other and will be able to hammer out their differences. To prevent wishful thinking from clouding their judgment, parents should solicit the views of others who know the children well—family members, outside board members, trusted advisers—as to whether they will be able to function successfully as partners.

For a partnership to work, there must be evidence of strong commitment to collaboration and an even distribution of complementary skills and talents. Numerous companies that have functioned as CO businesses in the first generation consider moving to the sibling partnership in the second. Frequently, as we have pointed out, neither the controlling owners nor their families realize the fundamental structural changes that this move entails.

Successfully negotiating the transition to a sibling partnership requires a rather uncommon set of conditions. First and foremost, seniors must assess whether the partners-to-be have robust and congenial fraternal relationships. Second, there must be evidence that siblings are ready to face a common future, that they have a Shared Dream and that they are willing to invest the time and energy needed to forge viable work relationships.

As obvious as it sounds, some parents do not understand that without some agreement on goals and mission, a partnership may well flounder. The siblings must be willing to share the credit for the enterprise's successes and the blame for its failures. No matter how the work is divided, they must allow all to have a voice in major decisions and facilitate compromise when they disagree.

The goal of interdependence that characterizes effective sibling partnerships has fundamental consequences for behavior, requiring the partners to truly appreciate and celebrate one another's triumphs. The spirit was summed up by social psychologist Morton Deutsch: "Your win is his win; his loss, your loss." To make a team, the partners have to work at comparable levels. Yet each usually brings unique skills to the team which, when combined with the others' skills, create synergies that raise the partners' overall level of performance.[9]

In some families the preference for an egalitarian partnership grows out of a long-standing commitment to family collaboration and teamwork. One gets the feeling in families like the Lombardis that the business is important not just for making money but as a place where they can do what they enjoy most, which is working together. These families encourage their children to develop their unique individual identities and talent from the early years, while at the same time instilling a deep ethic of cooperation. Collaboration in these families is viewed as the key to the survival of individual family members as well as their common enterprise.

The psychological literature on group performance shows that the most successful teams have little redundancy and much complementarity in the skills and experience of their members.[10] The principle is little understood in companies where managers purposely put together teams made up of people with similar experience and backgrounds, hoping they will work better together because of what they have in common. Much of the literature on team building is pertinent to sibling partnerships, but sibling teams do have a number of qualities that make them unique as performance units. The knowledge of one's brothers and sisters that comes from growing up in the same household—an awareness and appreciation of one another's goals, attitudes, and reactions to specific circumstances—can lead to synergies and decisiveness in managing a business together. When this shared history is blended with a common sense of purpose and complementary skills, the mixture can be phenomenally powerful.[11]

Success, however, depends heavily on whether the talents and skills of the siblings are fairly evenly distributed and whether each is willing to accept the role for which he or she is best suited. There is evidence that differentiation in skills, and even in personalities, grows naturally in families as a result of intragroup competition for what is often experienced as a scarce resource—notably parental attention.[12] In many effective sibling teams, there is one partner who is good with numbers and excels at quantitative tasks, another who is gregarious by nature and loves to be involved in sales and marketing, and a third who is a gifted strategist always thinking two or three moves ahead. If one sibling cannot perform his or her function competently, the others may have to step in. When workloads and levels of effort are unevenly distributed, feelings of resentment may erupt (along with demands for differentials in compensation). Likewise, the partnership will be severely strained if one sibling aspires to a position for which the others do not believe that person is qualified.

One of the strengths of the Lombardis' partnership is that each sibling is well aware of the skills of the others, and together they strive to organize in ways that allow them to harness their natural strengths. Sibling partners in general must not only recognize and honor each others' talents, but have little desire to compete with the others in their areas of competence. The challenge for both seniors and juniors is to correctly assess, whether such a critical balance and mutual appreciation of talents exists, and whether each of the potential partners has some insight into his or her own limitations. Once again, no easy task.

Harmony requires a clear division of labor and agreement on titles. Effective sibling partnerships typically have an explicit (although not rigid) division of labor, so that each of the partners can enjoy a degree of autonomy in his or her specific area. In a multidivisional business, for example, each sibling may be in charge of a division or profit center. In a functional organization, the siblings may lead separate departments, such as sales and marketing, research and development, or manufacturing. Almost invariably, sibling partners get into trouble when the boundaries of their authority are not clear or one begins to intrude on another's turf. There is always the risk in such a setting that rivalries will be expressed as a fierce competition between divisions or departments. Even where rivalries are not intense, siblings can become myopic, focusing on their own separate fiefdoms and losing sight of their common objectives.

Although a division of labor well anchored in a complementarily of skills is desirable, the group must also coordinate key activities, including strategy, allocation of capital, and tax planning. Some workable balance needs to be found between individual expression and the collective interests of the whole organization.

Whatever the division of labor, titles will always be a sensitive issue, particularly in a sibling system based on more or less equal ownership. The challenge in these partnerships is to come up with titles that convey equality among the partners and yet have some meaning to subordinates and outsiders who deal with them.

Sibling partners must find ways to manage conflict in their business relationships. In long-lasting partnerships, I have observed an astonishing diversity of conflict-management strategies. These strategies are often unorthodox from a management standpoint and imbued with the culture and folklore of the families that invent them. Usually, there is an aversion to voting as a means of resolving issues, since that may leave the minority unhappy. More typically, partnerships place a strong emphasis on consensus as the ideal in reaching major decisions. The partners agree to debate an issue for as long as it takes to arrive at a workable solution that all are willing to live with—even if some still feel the solution is less than perfect.

The Lombardis have a strong commitment to consensus. Every week the five siblings meet to discuss anything that might produce conflict. Whenever discussion arises about one of their children's responsibilities, pay, or performance, the parent is allowed to state his or her opinion at the meeting but must then leave the room and let the rest of the group decide the matter. The system works, the Lombardis have told me, because of a certain reciprocity over time. The siblings all know that as long they are fair in their judgment of the others' children, their children can expect fair treatment.

Two Chilean brothers who inherited a sizable family business from their father had been encouraged by him before his death to follow a simple procedure when they disagreed. The father had a trusted business associate living in Switzerland, a man of great experience and judgment. On those few occasions when the brothers could not agree, they were to call the father's friend in Switzerland to mediate. They follow the procedure to this day. Each brother gets on the phone and argues for his point of view. The Swiss gentleman, now in his eighties, then says:

"Frederick is right," or "George is right." The brothers abide by his ruling, and that ends the disagreement. Most importantly, they have called the father's friend only three times in thirty years of working together.

Some sibling partnerships make very creative use of non-family managers or a senior adviser to help them resolve their differences. Typically, this person is considerably older than the siblings, has an established reputation inside and outside the business, and enjoys the trust of all. He or she may even assume a quasi-parental role. In some European companies, the *consigliere* (as he is called in Italy) is a senior manager who has been a trusted adviser to two or three generations of family leaders and often serves as a mediator.

Other siblings develop a process that I call management by triangulation. Under a tacit arrangement, each of the partners has a non-family manager who is closely allied with his or her interests and viewpoint. The siblings meet frequently—daily in some cases—in a committee that includes their designated representatives. Whenever a partner does not agree with another, he questions, or attacks, not his brother or sister but the sibling's non-family subordinate. Similarly, when the partners want to introduce a new proposal that may be controversial, they may do it through their representatives, which allows them to avoid arguments and save face if the others vehemently disagree with the idea. Although the sibling teams that I have interviewed about this arrangement frequently admit it is somewhat cumbersome, and certainly unorthodox from a managerial point of view, they insist that it works for them.[13]

Four brothers in the Midwest inherited a large meatpacking business thirty-five years ago. On his deathbed, their father said to them: "You are each inheriting a quarter of the shares of this business. Strive to reach consensus whenever you can. However, it is very likely that there will be times when the four of you will not agree." He then produced a bolo tie with a silver and turquoise amulet that he kept under his pillow and said: "I will assign this amulet to one of you at random. And in those instances when you cannot reach consensus, the one who has the amulet should be given the right to the last word." The father paused and then said: "There is a catch, however. Whenever the authority of the amulet is invoked to settle an issue, the one imposing his will on the others must forgo the amulet and wait a turn before he is eligible to have it again."

The brothers, who instantly adopted the system, swear by it. In thirty-five years the amulet has gone around twice and the brothers have managed to grow a highly successful billion-dollar company.

Among the many reasons why this system seems to work so well for them are these key ones: The brothers were able to evoke the father's memory and willing to abide by his proposal and, from a practical standpoint, the system encourages the brother who wears the amulet to push for consensus unless he feels so strongly about an issue that he is willing to forgo his right to the last word.

In another sibling partnership I studied, the siblings adopted a process that they referred to as "car time." This highly successful $500 million company is owned by five siblings—two brothers and a sister who are in senior management roles, and two brothers who are passive shareholders. When the siblings were growing up, the family went on extended driving vacations in their station wagon during the summer months. Ever since, the siblings have associated being in the car with an opportunity for heated debate and for thrashing through a conflict until consensus is reached. To this day, whenever the three siblings in management cannot agree on an important issue, they hop into the car and drive around until they work through their differences.

Obviously, I am not suggesting that these mechanisms can easily be imported into any family. On the contrary, they often reflect the unique experience, identity, and culture of each individual family. Over the years, however, I have seen enough of these conflict management arrangements to conclude that the particular mechanism is not as important as the existence of a pre-established dispute-resolution process that the family is willing to accept. The specific mechanisms work in most cases because they openly acknowledge that disagreements are inevitable and because they promote a sense of fair play and equity over time.

Finally, in successful sibling partnerships a sense of humor often plays a crucial role in smoothing tensions that grow out of the underlying competitive dynamics. As Freedman and others have noted, persisting childhood rivalries can become quite destructive in a business setting when re-enacted sub rosa.[14] These tensions can be defused, however, if siblings understand that mature adults sometimes act like children and if they can put their rivalries in perspective. Humor is one way brothers and sisters make a point in a nonthreatening way when a sibling's behavior provokes or offends. Indeed, the ability to talk freely and laugh about these rivalries is one of the clearest signs that siblings will be able to manage them in a partnership.

Relationships with in-laws must be managed effectively. The role that some in-laws play in aggravating tensions between family members who work together in a business is well known—and often joked about.

In-laws are said to be a mirror reflecting the state of relationships between family members at the office, but they can also be creators of conflict. The consequences of ignoring or mistreating in-laws can be especially serious in family companies managed by siblings. When the siblings bring their grievances home from work, their spouses can become so incensed that they carry on the argument until it escalates into a family feud. The feud may continue among the spouses long after the sibling partners themselves have forgotten it.

Some in-laws realize how destructive such behavior can be and actually play a constructive role in oiling the gears of a partnership. In one instance the wives of two brothers working in a business made a pact: The two women agreed that if one of their husbands complained about a wrong done him at the office by his brother, the wife would not allow herself to be drawn into a triangle. Rather than egging him on or taking up his cause with other family members, she would urge her husband to take up his grievance directly with the brother. If one of the brothers griped about rewards received by his brother but not given to him, the wife would reassure him that rewards balance out over time and he would eventually receive his. These wives actively discouraged conversation between the husbands that involved social comparisons—about salaries, possessions, status in the community, the achievements of their children. On numerous occasions they stuck together and intervened to cool the fires of a dispute.

Sibling partners must find ways to enlist the loyalty and support of in-laws. For example, by looking for opportunities to involve the in-laws in the articulation of their Shared Dream, sibling partners can create a sense of inclusion and thus heighten the in-laws' commitment to the success of the sibling partnership. Also, the involvement of in-laws in a family council can assure spouses that they are full-fledged family members whose opinions are valued. When encouraged to participate in family discussions, in-laws learn to appreciate the owning family's values and traditions. They also become more educated about ownership and governance issues that are likely to affect their children's future, in which they have a legitimate interest.

The emergence of a lead sibling—a "primus inter pares"—poses strains that must be handled by the group. When leadership ability is not evenly distributed among the team members, one sibling may emerge as the most powerful of the group. While all remain equal owners, one partner thus carries more authority and is recognized as "primus inter pares." Typically, this situation arises because the company needs one person to speak for it in business circles or the community or because one sibling is far superior to the others in business skills and leadership ability.

The Steinberg family built a multibillion-dollar supermarket and real estate empire in Canada out of a small grocery store founded by the mother. Sam Steinberg, one of four brothers in the second generation, was a dynamic entrepreneur whose talents, unfortunately, far surpassed those of his siblings. He virtually "carried" his brothers all their lives while building one of the largest enterprises in the country. His daughter, Mitzi, recalled with distaste that he dictated the brothers' every move: "When he said sit, they sat down; lie down, they lay down."[15] No doubt this dictatorial style planted seeds of resentment that contributed to the downfall and sale of a very successful family enterprise.

A first-among-equals must earn his or her authority and continually justify it.[16] The would-be leader must find ways to demonstrate his competence or expertise to the others. This process is often complicated; the aspiring leader may be tested by his partners over a long period of time. First, the lead sibling must offer clear proof that the others will benefit economically from his or her leadership (engineering the turnaround of a faltering division might be one such proof). Second, the leader must consistently demonstrate a commitment to the Shared Dream and the overall objectives of the group rather than a personal agenda. To accomplish this, he or she must be sensitive to the other siblings' needs and views on key issues. Third, the lead sibling must show he or she can be trusted not to abuse his or her power. The leader who begins to assume a parental role will be quickly brought back to the reality by the others and, if the lesson is not learned, will lose legitimacy.

Finally, the lead sibling must always be conscious of the need to share the spotlight and the glory of the enterprise's achievements with his or her partners. The message that should go forth, to the community and to the company's stakeholders, is: "I may be the leader, but I could never accomplish anything without the support and contribution of my equal partners." In short, the lead sibling establishes his or her legitimacy by demonstrating not only managerial competence but generosity of spirit.

The question of which partner speaks to the media when the occasion arises can become a sensitive issue. Usually, one of the more gregarious and articulate partners is chosen for this role, but that person may be taken to task if he seems to speak for himself rather than for the group. Interviewed by a major newspaper, one of three brothers who are partners took all the credit for the phenomenal growth of their family company. The other two partners were furious. The message that came back to the brother who had stepped out of line was: "Don't you ever do that again."

The partners must take steps to counteract divide-and-conquer strategies, as well as the bias against shared leadership. Inevitably, some employees and outsiders will pursue their own personal agendas by exploiting differences of opinion between the sibling partners. This is a risk in any governance structure that relies on multiple leadership, but it is a particular challenge for siblings, whose rivalries may lie just beneath the surface. Consider, for example, the case of an employee who wants to run his department his own way and is constantly stirring up arguments between the two brother-partners on other issues so they do not have time to interfere in his bailiwick. Clients, suppliers, and other business associates can play this same game. In one company the problem was so prevalent that one frequently heard line had become a family joke: "Oh, but your brother offered me a much better deal!"

Siblings who are loyal to one another are well aware of the risks of this divide-and-conquer strategy and adopt strict rules to counteract it. For example, they may agree to consult regularly on all major issues and present a united front when they have reached a decision. They may agree never to fight in front of employees or in public. The sibling partners in one company fired a senior manager who had repeatedly worked behind the scenes to divide them for his own benefit. The dismissal sent a powerful signal to the rest of the organization that such behavior would not be tolerated.

Sibling partners must also deal with outsiders who view their co-leadership arrangement as a fundamental weakness. Bankers, suppliers, and clients want to know, "Who is the boss?" They fear that shared leadership will be vacillating leadership, uncertain and lacking in accountability. Siblings who have adopted such a system must therefore be prepared to "sell it" to outsiders. They must show that they are committed to making the system work, and have adopted norms and rules to break deadlocks and ensure it will work effectively in times of stress as well as normal times.

One company that is skeptical about sibling partnerships is Caterpillar Inc., most of whose sixty or so dealerships in North America are family owned and run by a single CO. Although siblings in some Caterpillar families would like to run the business as a team, the company insists that in its relations with dealers—as the director of North

American operations once told me—it must be able " to look into only one pair of eyeballs." Two brothers in one dealership, hinting at their dissatisfaction with the policy, joked that they might be able to satisfy it if each covered one eye during meetings with Caterpillar management.

Seniors should not let tax and estate planning issues dictate the choice of a sibling partnership. George E. Marcus, an anthropologist who writes about dynastic families, has suggested that tax and estate planning structures can take on a life of their own. Often this happens because a powerful group of professionals has invested a large amount of time setting up these structures for the company and has a strong stake in continuing to orchestrate them. Ironically, the family's equity and wealth, which they have worked many years to build up, ends up dictating business structure and family relationships.[17]

Problems begin when parents divide up the stock in the company among their offspring as the path of least resistance. The thinking here is that an equal division of the company's assets is clean and simple to implement. At the same time, however, it often means the company is boxed into a partnership form of leadership. The choice becomes a way for the parents to avoid having to determine which of their children is best qualified to run the business.

Larger family companies may be organized as a collection of many interrelated businesses, the ownership of which is embedded in a complex web of trusts and holding companies. The lawyers have set it up this way, quite rationally, in order to minimize inheritance tax liabilities. Often they have given little thought to how this elaborate ownership structure will affect succession and the future leadership structure. The task of disentangling these trusts and holding companies for the purpose of achieving an optimal distribution of assets in the next generation then becomes prohibitively complex. The family thus chooses a sibling partnership not because of a Shared Dream that they believe is the best system for their family and business, but out of fear of wrestling with ownership arrangements that have been set up for tax reasons.

The Challenges of the Cousin Consortium

Institutional structures need to be put in place to manage the complexities of a cousin company. The Dream of the cousin consortium tends to be associated with families that have enjoyed considerable success in business and accumulated great wealth. Wealth and the size of the business are important because below a certain threshold of resources a cousin consortium usually cannot be sustained. This is particularly so when there are several branches of the family and large numbers of cousins depending upon the business for their livelihoods.

Siblings who have enjoyed a successful working relationship over the years tend to want to re-create that same leadership structure in their children's generation. They look for the same sets of talents and skills in their offspring that will permit a division of labor similar to theirs, and they expect the same informal methods of communication and decision making to work for the next generation as it worked for them. What the siblings don't always appreciate is that the harmony and collaboration they were able to achieve is relatively rare. Having been brought up together, they benefited enormously from a shared experience and understanding of one another's values and attitudes that may or may not be present in their children's generation. Usually they don't fully understand how difficult it will be to recreate their system under the radically changed circumstances in the third generation.

A major new reality is the growth in the number of shareholders who are not involved in management. The need to respect the rights of minority shareholders—and keep them happy—introduces a new level of complexity into a family business that is often poorly understood and managed. The team spirit that characterized the sibling generation cannot be relied upon to manage differences among forty-five cousins who are managers and/or owners. While in the past many decisions may have been made on an informal basis—by siblings intimately familiar with one another's preferences and views—now structures like a board with outsiders on it may become critical for resolving major issues. Likewise, a forum where shareholders can discuss ownership issues, and another in which family members can express their legitimate rights and further their common legacy, become much more important.

The challenge at this stage is to contain entropy by putting institutional structures in place to manage it, while also finding ways to enhance the unity and commitment of the family through a celebration of the history and values that bind the branches in a common legacy. The culture of the family company must move toward more explicit goals, policies, procedures, formal forums, and written constitutions. The business now requires more formal structure, and people must be trained to function within it.

The greater the complexity of the organization at this stage, the more time, energy, and resources have to be invested in setting up these structures. Yet seniors who have worked well together as sibling partners tend to regard such structures as unnecessary and overly bureaucratic.

The new system needs to maintain a balance of power among the branches. Of the many challenges that confront cousin consortiums, maintaining a balance of power among the various branches is unquestionably the most important. Each branch, for example, may wish to have at least one member of the family represented in top management. This may not be acceptable to the rest of the family if a position cannot be found for the person, or if he or she is not qualified.

It is not uncommon to find family companies that in the fourth generation have more than 100 cousin-shareholders, each owning a small fraction of the company. Although the owners think of themselves as an extended family with a common heritage and identity, the business at this stage resembles a publicly traded company in many respects. Unlike the publicly traded firm, however, the family enterprise often does not have clear boundaries between management and ownership, and this adds to the complexity of decision making.

The distribution of cousins across the various branches is probably the most significant determinant of whether a workable balance of power can be achieved. Trouble begins when there are more heirs in one branch than another—which is likely to be the case in large families.

Consider the example of a second-generation European company owned equally by four brothers. The brothers plan to divide the stock equally among their children and to establish a cousin consortium in the next generation. For thirty years the brothers have grown accustomed to having an equal voice in the company's policies and decisions. But in considering their future options, the brothers must wrestle with a different reality: The oldest brother has five children; two work in the company and three do not. The second brother has only one son, who heads the marketing department. The third brother has four children, two working in the business and two not. And the youngest brother has five children, all of whom are still in school.

The fact that the second brother's son stands to inherit one-fourth of the company's stock has already increased this cousin's influence in the system significantly. While family relationships generally remain cordial, a subtle hierarchy has developed among members of the next generation. The other cousins tend to defer to the views and wishes of the second brother's son. Fortunately, the "lead cousin" happens to be a very competent individual who as head of the marketing division quadrupled the company's sales. He has earned credibility among both family and non-family senior managers and is positioned to be the next CEO. But he also has a strong commitment to the family and is unlikely to abuse his advantageous position. Nevertheless, the other cousins privately worry that he might do so.

Another family business has been governed by five sibling part-ners in the second generation. Four of the brothers each had two to five children. The third brother had no children at all. When this brother died at the ripe old age of ninety-three, he left all of his stock to the children of one of his younger brothers, with whom he had a close relationship. Suddenly the younger brother's branch, which had only two children and had always been ignored by the rest of the fam-ily, acquired a controlling share of the company. In the transition from the third to the fourth generation, the two cousins from the younger brother's branch emerged as powerful leaders of the system—even though they were among the youngest in their generation.

This unequal distribution of children is fairly typical of family companies that have reached the cousin stage. It poses a fundamental dilemma for the parents: whether to maintain a distribution of stock by stirpes or to reallocate shares so that each of the cousins controls an equal amount of stock—as their parents did in the previous generation.

Each option poses significant challenges. If a family chooses to preserve the stirpes structure, that will establish an unequal distribu-tion of stock and give some cousins more influence than others. On the other hand, if the ownership is divided equally among the cousins through a buyout process the branches with the most children will acquire a larger amount of stock and the influence of their branch will grow proportionately.

The resolution of this dilemma is not simple and often depends on the degree of trust that exists among the branches. When trust is lacking, the branch with the fewest children will naturally be reluctant to give up shares for the sake of equality among the cousins. The nego-tiation of this issue is so tricky that more often than not, the seniors decide to allocate shares by stirpes because that is the easiest way: It does not require the seniors to negotiate a buyout.

But adoption of the stirpes option requires a much different gov-ernance structure from the one the seniors were used to. The unequal distribution of stock changes the rules of the game in the manage-ment of the business and calls for creation of forums to promote agreement on major issues and minimize conflict. One of the biggest risks in a business that has been led by siblings is that they will attempt to recreate in the next generation not just their leadership structure but their ownership structure as well. Thus if four siblings decided to pass their stock to their offspring in four separate trusts, this arrangement will perpetuate a mindset that views the family as divided into four stirpes. It may lead eventually to pressures for representation of each of the four stirpes in management or on the board—which may mean that people who are less than qualified are appointed to prominent positions.

At this business stage, the cousins must learn to think of themselves as one family rather than four. The archetype that is most conducive to this mind set is that of a clan rather than an extended family. The greater differentiation of the family in the third generation requires a new integration. Before they can be welded into a single entity, the cousins and their parents must fully appreciate the extent of their differentiation and must design leadership and governance structures appropriate to the new conditions.

The seniors must be able to openly discuss—and assess—one another's children. Many third-generation family businesses end up as cousin consortiums because that seems to be the natural next step in the progression from a sibling partnership. As in transitions from CO to sibling partnership, the sibling partners in the second generation may divide the company stock equally among the cousins, hoping to avoid conflict. They thus choose the cousin consortium structure by default, without realizing what they are getting into. What the seniors are usually trying to avoid in these transitions are arguments over which of their children are most able and most deserving of assuming leadership roles in the next generation.

Few topics are more sensitive and likely to fuel ancient rivalries among brothers and sisters than the worthiness of their respective children. The problem is compounded when there are a limited number of jobs available in top management and many capable cousins who aspire to that level of responsibility. Realizing that hard choices will have to be made, the older generation anticipates conflict between the partners—and prefers to avoid the subject. Each sibling may then make plans for passing his own stock to his children without consulting the other partners on an overall ownership plan for the business. For example, one sibling may leave his shares in a trust in order to force his children to vote with one voice. Another may transfer shares to each of his children. Still another may create a holding company for her children alone.

This kind of uncoordinated planning is untenable if the company is to continue as one enterprise. The seniors must have forums in which the ownership and governance issues are confronted and procedures worked out for appraising, selecting, and training successors.

Both family managers and passive shareholders must be trained to respect their different roles and responsibilities. Senior managers of cousin consortiums often look upon passive shareholders as greedy nuisances, and regard paying dividends as charity rather than a management obligation. While shareholders do sometimes make excessive demands, and often fail to appreciate the issues management must wrestle with, keeping them happy is not just a matter of charity. If unhappy shareholders insist on being bought out, management may have to go outside the company for capital—which is usually costly.

Typically, cousins who work in the company are highly committed to its success. Their careers—and egos—are invested in it, and they can feel passionately about continuing the business as a family legacy. In contrast, cousins who are not involved with management may lose interest in the family company over time and become uneasy about having their equity tied up in it. Often passive shareholders complain about being "rich on paper and poor in cash." A lack of mutual appreciation and communication between the "ins" and the "outs," moreover, leads to a polarization between the two blocs. The cousins in management tend to undervalue the financial contribution of their nonparticipating cousins, who want to be treated as serious investors. The managers may also ignore the family shareholders' requests for a voice in major policy decisions. For their part, the passive shareholders sometimes assume they have a right to intervene in day-to-day decisions that are the prerogative of management.

The different perspectives of the two groups collide most often in discussions of dividend policy. The cousins in management want to reinvest the resources available to the company in order to achieve further growth, while the shareholders demand a higher return on their investment. The managers tend to view dividends as a wasteful "milking" of the business, while the passive shareholders frequently point out that the managers do not depend on dividends to maintain their living standards but enjoy substantial salaries and bonuses along with perks. Very often the shareholders feel they have many of the burdens of wealth (such as tax and fiduciary liabilities) without any of the privileges. They frequently envy their cousins in management, whose lavish lifestyles, they may assume, can only be a result of taking advantage of their control of the company.

Cousin companies are plagued by these conflicts, which are inherent in the different vantage points of managers and shareholders. While each side is justified in its position at times, conflict can be avoided only when both groups are clear on the boundaries between their respective roles and responsibilities. This is particularly so for passive shareholders, who are usually given little instruction in the needs of the business and their obligations as shareholders.

The distinction between cousins in and out of management also has important family consequences. In larger family enterprises the economics of the system often result in a growing income (and life-style) gap between shareholder cousins who hold senior executive positions (and thus earn substantial salaries and bonuses) and shareholder cousins out of management. Learning to avoid invidious comparisons and to accept these disparities as inevitable by-products of the different institutional roles that cousins hold is one of the important challenges at this stage.

Since the business is the family's most important asset, in both a psychological and an economic sense, the cousins in senior management positions tend to evolve into leadership roles in the family as well. For example, important family gatherings such as Christmas, Passover, or Thanksgiving dinners are likely to be held in the homes of those cousins who are leaders in the business. At these events, cousins who work together in the company inevitably gravitate toward one another. Whenever the conversation turns to business, cousins who are not in management feel excluded from the "inner set."

All this emphasizes that families moving toward a cousin consortium must find ways to narrow the gap in understanding between owner-managers and shareholders by setting up appropriate integrative mechanisms and educational programs. So, for example, family-controlled companies must learn to manage their shareholder relations in ways much like those used by top corporate executives in public companies. They must be acquainted with the legal rights of minority shareholders and honor them in a professional way; they have to keep shareholders informed about issues in the company with periodic reports, develop explicit dividend policies, and organize shareholder meetings.

Likewise, shareholders who lack business experience must be given some minimal instruction in such basics as how to read a balance sheet in order to be in a position to assess management's policies and performance. They must understand their rights and economic interest, but they must respect the managers' superior knowledge and experience and give them free rein to make decisions necessary for the health of the company.

To avoid friction among the branches, ways need to be found to prevent the disillusionment of the youngest cousins. At any given time, the ages of the various cousins determines who is in the pool of eligible candidates for top management positions. Almost invariably, the children of the oldest sibling in the second generation are the first to enter the family company and to rise to managerial jobs. The children of the second sibling come next, and so on down the line. By the time the youngest sibling's children are old enough to be considered, there may be too many cousins already in the company and no openings left at the top. The youngest cousins may end up in operations that are tangential to the main business, such as a smaller subsidiary or a regional office.

Younger family members who find the path to top management blocked can cause long-lasting divisions in the family. Creating opportunities for them is one of the biggest challenges of the large cousin consortium. Typically, these younger cousins feel shut out of the power and reward structure of the business, even though they control, like their older cousins in management, equal amounts of stock. Their disadvantages tend to become compounded over time; with no one to speak for them in top management, later generations of their branch may be overlooked in the competition for positions.

Gender issues also play a role in determining the balance of power among branches. Often women are excluded from management positions in the second generation, even when they own equal shares of stock. The exclusion of daughters in the second generation is a precedent that tends to get passed down to the third. If female cousins do not participate in management, they may become further removed psychologically from the system, which can aggravate tensions between the family managers and passive shareholders. Moreover, because of combined age and gender biases, the youngest daughter in one branch may have not any chance to gain a top management position.

Generally speaking, the branches that have direct involvement in the management of the company have the most influence over the allocation of the family's assets. So the systematic exclusion of the members of one branch creates an imbalance that further threatens harmony in both the family and the business.

In this chapter I have noted the various challenges facing families moving toward one or another of the three basic governance structures. I have pointed out that one of the fundamental problems in planning for succession is the assumption that leadership styles and structures that worked well under one form of leadership will also be successful under a new form. As both the seniors and the juniors assimilate new information that helps to answer these types of questions, the mental maps in their heads shaped by their Dream may undergo subtle alterations. The Dream itself—and the future business form that is envisioned—may have to be revised to accommodate new information about what may or may not be feasible.

A defined future for the family emerges only gradually, at a pace determined by the maturation of the members; it has to be patiently negotiated, often over years. The process is open-ended and continuing, but that does not mean the family should delay the tough choices that must be made in a succession. As the biological clock continues to tick and the time for a leadership transition approaches, the process may have to be condensed and accelerated. The next section of the book is concerned with the main tasks that must be accomplished in a transfer of leadership and how an understanding of the psychology of human development can help family members manage these tasks at every stage in the evolution of the business.

PART III

Human Development and the Timing of Succession

CHAPTER 7

Developing Successors:
The First Steps

TIME is the engine that drives succession in family companies. Gradually and inexorably, the aging process moves the individual family members and the business through various stages. If all goes well, the working out of a Shared Dream, the mentoring of the juniors, and the retirement planning of the elders will ultimately bring about a generational change and the establishment of a new leadership. The older that seniors and juniors get, the closer they come to the transition and the more energy they must devote to completing the various tasks associated with succession. Whether the process is smooth or jumpy, fraught with tension or relatively harmonious, will depend on the quality of family relationships.

The idea that people's psychological needs and perspectives differ according to where they are on an age spectrum would seem to be a matter of common sense. Yet family business owners seldom appreciate how powerfully—and predictably—the pressures of the various phases of the maturation process shape their own personal concerns and those of the relatives with whom they work. Typically, differences of opinion among relatives are inappropriately attributed to personality characteristics rather than to structural factors such as age or gender.

Just as the maturation of an individual unfolds in well-documented stages, business families evolve in a predictable sequence in which the relative ages of the participants have a major effect on the quality of relationships and the capacity of the junior and senior generations to work together. In a family business, the developmental perspective can pave the way for better communication between generations and encourage families to develop effective, non-blaming ways of resolving life's inevitable conflicts. By anticipating the psychological pressures that accompany each stage of life, moreover, families can put structures and policies in place to help their members deal with them constructively.

These next five chapters of the book will view the timing of succession against the background of the evolution of the business family—that is, the aging and growth of the individual members through time. The major tasks to be accomplished will be viewed through the prism of our knowledge of human development and maturation over the life cycle. Researchers have defined four stages in the evolution of a family business, each of which presents distinctive challenges and psychological issues for members who are active in the business as well as for their spouses and children.[1] We summarize them in Figure 7-1.

During the first phase—Young Business Families—one or both parents are working hard building a company or consolidating their leadership in an existing company. The parents are usually between thirty-five and forty years old and their children are eighteen or under. The multiple demands on the working parent make this a stressful period. While establishing his or her authority in the business, the young adult must also build a strong, lasting marital relationship and learn to be an effective parent. As we will see later in this chapter, even at this stage parents can do much to convey to children the challenges and joys of working in a family company.

The central preoccupation of business couples at this stage is achieving success in business and, by so doing, earning credibility and stature in the community. These young adults are moving from being junior members of their world to becoming legitimate senior members with authority to "speak with one's own voice"—often not an easy task for successors in family companies.

In the Mid-Life and Managing Entry stage, the children are in college or about to graduate and are ready to do some serious thinking about their future careers. As we will see, they are full of book learning and eager to demonstrate, to themselves and others, that they are capable adults. Their parents, in their late thirties to early fifties, may be preoccupied with personal issues associated with the mid-life transition. This can be a turbulent period in which increasing awareness of their aging and mortality triggers self-doubt and a loss of

Figure 7-1 The Four Developmental Stages of Business Families

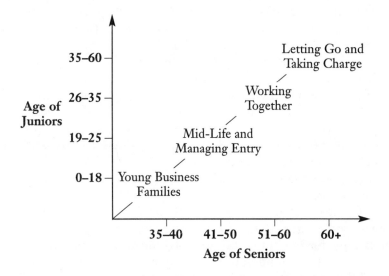

confidence. Having established their leadership in the business, they are questioning their Dreams. They are asking whether it has all been worth it, whether the business payoff has been worth the sacrifices. This introspection and self-questioning can make it difficult for them to evaluate their offspring clearly and coach those who choose to enter the business.

In the Working Together phase, the parents are between fifty and sixty years old. If they have resolved the insistent questions posed by the mid-life transition, they have reached calmer waters. They are now truly able to do the mentoring needed to prepare their offspring for leadership. If they have failed to find answers to the acute questions of mid-life the consequences for succession and continuity could be grave. The Working Together stage may be the last opportunity the parents will have to instill in their children the skills, values, and attitudes necessary for family business continuity.

At this point the juniors are in their late twenties or thirties and are trying to establish themselves within the family company as credible successors. The young family members realize that the time for experimenting is mostly over. They feel a need to get serious about life, to commit themselves to some career path and deepen their knowledge of what is required to be a success on that path. If their experience thus far in the company has not been fulfilling, they may decide that the family business is not for them; they still have time to pursue other opportunities outside the business. If their experience in the family company has been positive—if they believe they can realize their Dream in it—they will re-commit to it and think seriously about what is a realizable career progression within the family business.

The Letting Go stage poses the final test for seniors. Will they finally step aside and let their successors, who by this time may be in their forties and waiting anxiously in the wings, take command of the company? This phase is perhaps the most difficult of all because our society tends to celebrate youth and achievement and pays little homage to the wisdom of elders. Many business leaders who have devoted their lives to building a business regard retirement with terror; even the most enlightened leaders can develop resistances that are difficult to counter.

Of course, not all families fit neatly into the four basic phases in a business family's growth that I have described. The age spread between generations, for one thing, can vary significantly, leading to a lack of synchrony in the evolution of the family business. Some parents have their children late in life, others early. There are blended families in which the children of successive marriages participate, and the age span of the members is thus broader. In some systems, members are moving through the stages of family development together, while in others the age spread is such that the members are always at different stages. Indeed, this is one of the ways to distinguish the developmental stage of a family company. The family in a controlling owner company, for example, typically moves through these developmental stages together. In sibling partnerships, on the other hand, the spread of ages is broader and thus the system may have members going through at least two developmental stages concurrently. Finally, one of the fundamental challenges that confront cousin consortiums is that the age spread is so wide that there is a full spectrum of developmental issues and needs that must be attended to at the same time. Some cousins may be facing the challenges of entering the business, for example, while much older cousins who are in leadership positions are wrestling with issues of aging and letting go.

In Western societies, institutions are generally under the control of people in their late forties to mid-sixties. A man or woman who is older than eighty and still in executive command of an organization may therefore be perceived as an anachronism. Likewise, people in their twenties who are given responsibility for others two or three times their age may be distrusted and have difficulty establishing their authority. These biases are not coincidental; they have some support in biology and in experience. The demands of a CEO's job, for example, may be beyond the stamina of an eighty-year-old. Similarly, the twenty-year-old may not have acquired all the experience necessary to an effective leader.

A developmental perspective can help us understand the fit between our individual needs and the demands of the roles that our social systems thrust upon us. The intellectual foundation upon which this model is built has deep roots in Western thought, particularly in the discipline of developmental psychology. This body of thought emphasizes that the human life cycle can be understood as a process that moves predictably through a series of discrete stages, each posing a set of dilemmas that grow out of the interaction of nature and nurture. The individual must resolve the dilemmas at each stage in order to successfully negotiate that stage and move on to the next. Over a lifespan, a unique individual thus emerges from the interplay of biological, psychological, and social forces.

Extending this developmental approach, Erik Erikson[2] provided an eight-stage theory of human maturation that covered the entire life cycle from childhood to old age. For the infant, the chief task is to develop a fundamental sense of trust in the world. For the teenager, the major challenge is to establish a unique identity. In old age, the individual has to take stock of his or her life and achieve a sense of integrity. Erikson pictured a gradual and continuous process, demanding at every juncture the resolution of two conflicting tendencies. Each stage poses a unique dialectical tension, which, if not resolved at that time of life, persists into the next stage. In the absence of a nurturing environment, for example, the baby grows up without a sense of trust that those around him will meet his needs. Thus, the child moves on to the next stage lacking confidence to meet the new dilemmas that must be resolved. Likewise, the fifty-year-old who is still preoccupied with building up his or her own achievements and devotes little attention to coaching and mentoring the next generation may develop a sense of failure for not fulfilling a fundamental need at that stage of life.

Daniel Levinson[3] builds on Erikson's dialectical approach but sees the process as occurring in a more discontinuous, stop-start fashion.[4] In Levinson's developmental theory, the life cycle is driven not by events in the individual's environment but by the predictable temporal pressures attendant to biological aging and the maturation process. Levinson proposed that at each stage of life, the individual constructs a pattern of relationships, a "life structure," which provides stability. With each passing year, however, as the individual approaches a new stage, the pressures mount on that structure. At certain key transition points the individual is compelled to reconsider significant aspects of his life and perhaps to make major changes in his marriage, his career, or his relationships to his children. These periods of transition are also opportunities to reassess the Dream—the person's expectations about what he or she will accomplish in life and what he or she will settle for.

Although there have been some attempts to assess the implications of developmental theory for family systems, few investigators have applied the theory to the particular realities of business families. A notable exception is the work of Davis and Taguiri,[5] who studied the influence of life-cycle stages on the quality of father-son work relationships. Davis and Taguiri surveyed eighty-nine father-son pairs who worked together in business. They found that father-son relationships are not stable over a lifetime but vary according to the developmental issues faced by parent and child during a given period of their lives. Their research suggested that the developmental needs of a father and a son are less likely to be compatible when the father is in his early to mid-forties and the son is in his late teens or early twenties. Levinson's study of men showed that in their forties they are typically struggling with a mid-life transition that forces them to question what they have done with their lives and what they want to do with the time remaining to them. Davis and Taguiri concluded from their research that men of that age may be too preoccupied with themselves to begin preparing their children to enter the business effectively. By the same token, the teenage son of a father in his forties is still struggling with the process of separation from his family, working hard to create conditions that make him want to leave the family. The youth may not be ready to think about his future career. The same father and son may well have an easier time working with each other ten years later, when the father has reached his fifties and the son his late twenties. By this time the father has entered middle adulthood and is seeking meaningful mentoring relationships; the son is likely to have worked through the issues associated with establishing a separate identity and is more inclined to welcome his father's offer of mentoring.

The Davis-Taguiri study recasts the generic and more static formulation of adult development theory into a dynamic intergenerational framework. The two researchers were the first to stress the importance for succession of "life-cycle intersect," showing how the relative ages of participants in a family business could affect the chances of completing the necessary tasks at every juncture of the process. Davis and Taguiri studied only fathers and sons, but the basic assumptions—that intergenerational relationships will vary with age in predictable ways—likely apply as well to fathers and daughters, mothers and daughters, or mothers and sons. Unfortunately there is not yet any cross-gender life-stage research to deepen our understanding of these possibilities in the context of work relationships.

Levinson did a study of women, *Seasons of a Woman's Life*, for which he and his associates conducted in-depth interviews with forty-five middle-aged women who were academics, full-time homemakers, or executives in the corporate-financial world. The book concluded that "Women and men go through the same sequence of periods in adult life structure development, and at the same ages." But Levinson also argued that perceptions of opportunities by both males and females, and the decisions they make, are profoundly influenced by "gender splitting"—that is, by "the rigid division between female and male, masculine and feminine, in all aspects of human life."[6]

While Levinson believed that the timing and sequence of life stages and of key transitional periods are quite similar across the genders, Carol Gilligan, a psychologist at Harvard, has suggested that the developmental issues for women may well differ significantly at each life stage. For example, in early adulthood men are still preoccupied with individuation and separation, while women at the same stage are concerned with the often conflicting issues posed by the need for separation, on the one hand, and the development of intimacy, on the other. From the different dynamics of separation and attachment in their gender identity formation through the divergence of identity and intimacy that marks their experience in the adolescent years, male and female voices typically speak of the importance of different truths, the former of the role of separation as it defines and empowers the self, the latter of the ongoing process of attachment that creates and sustains the human community.[7]

Gilligan's research also suggests that most women do have Dreams similar to those of men. But women in our society have not generally been encouraged to pursue career Dreams. The message they have received from their elders has usually been: "Don't get too enthusiastic about what you want to accomplish in life, because when you are older you will have to take care of a lot of people—your husband, your children, perhaps even your aging parents." Instead of developing their Dreams, women, under the weight of these burdens, may follow what Levinson called a "script," a predictable behavioral routine that drains passion and vitality from the pursuit of one's Dream.[8]

Gender splitting, in the form of expectations of family and society, still pushes women more than men into the role of caretakers, not only in their families but often in their careers as well. The ticking of the biological clock creates pressures to have children during the very years when young adults are also seeking to establish the foundation of their careers. While many young men are encouraged from the earliest age to pursue a heroic Dream outside of the family, young women, even when they have career Dreams, must continuously wrestle with the countervailing pull of traditional homemaker and caretaking roles. From raising their children to caring for elderly parents, many women find they are primary caregivers throughout their lives—often at the expense of realizing their other "imagined possibilities." This, in fact, is one of the most significant conclusions of Levinson's study of women.

Despite the paucity of developmental research on gender differences, the model advanced here is useful in understanding the underlying forces likely to affect business families by virtue of the difference in ages between the incoming and outgoing generations and, in sibling partnerships and cousin consortiums, the distribution in ages among members of the various generations that simultaneously coexist in the system. Such is the potential power of these ideas that just knowing the ages of the men and women in a particular business family is often enough to anticipate the types of issues they are likely to be facing at a given stage in their lives.

Policies and governance structures in a business can either help members of both junior and senior generations to master the challenges appropriate for their stage of life—or they can retard the process. When they retard the process, the natural rhythms of generational transition may be thwarted, producing much individual frustration and unhappiness as well as threats to the stability and continuity of the business. Developmental psychology thus offers a useful heuristic for understanding the tasks that must be accomplished at each stage of the succession continuum. It also provides essential background for determining the timeline for planning. Above all, it drives home the essential point that succession planning is not an event but a lifelong process that involves the whole family.

Sowing the Seeds of a Shared Dream

For years, Nan-b and Philippe de Gaspé Beaubien, owners of a communications firm in Canada, threw the annual employee Christmas party at their home. From the time their children were young, they served drinks and canapes and mixed easily with the staff; all now hold prominent positions in Telemedia, Inc. When the Huntsman Chemical Company acquired the polystyrene division of Shell Oil, Jon Huntsman had to persuade the 185 workers to go with his company rather than find new jobs with Shell. Huntsman threw a picnic for the workers at which several of his nine children circulated among the guests, helping to sell them on staying with Huntsman; 184 of the 185 eventually chose to stay.

These contacts with the activities of the company accomplish a number of things: First, they show the children that business is not just hard work but can also be fun. Second, they introduce members of the next generation to what the business is all about—its products, its customers, its essential functions and routines. Third, from contact with senior executives, children observe the professionalism necessary in business; they come to know and appreciate the accomplishments and knowledge of the people who lead the company.

Whether or not they ultimately join the family business, children in these years can learn much about their special place in the world—and their special responsibilities. They come to understand that they are members of a family whose forebears have achieved something unique, who have built an enterprise that benefits many other people and is frequently in the limelight. They learn about family traditions and values. The idea is ingrained that because of this tradition they will be held to high standards of conduct in their community.

Parents have to achieve a delicate balance in conveying these values. While kindling enthusiasm for the business, they have to avoid the kinds of guilt-ridden messages that will only squelch enthusiasm, such as "I'm doing this all for you" and "Some day this will all be yours." Many parents do not realize that without free choice, there can be no genuine commitment.

What can families do to increase the likelihood that the members can work together toward common goals in their business? One is to create an environment in which children will feel free to talk about their aspirations. In these conversations, which can be formal or informal, parents can communicate the substance of their Dream to the children through their words and behavior—especially their excitement, enthusiasm, and passion. Parents have a responsibility to foster the development of their children's character, but the question of how best to accomplish that poses a thorny dilemma. On the one hand, they are aware that children need freedom to explore the world and find their own paths and that too much parental involvement can become a burden and interfere with healthy development.[9] On the other hand, parents are expected to guide their children's choices, to steer them in the "right" direction, and to influence their expectations of the future. Through complex verbal and nonverbal communication, rewards and punishments and, most important, through their own behavior and choices, parents send powerful signals to their children.

Blended into these messages are projections of the parent's own aspirations and fears. Hence parents typically wish to pass on to their children the positive elements of their life experiences and to spare them from the pain and disappointments that they may have suffered themselves. When parents try too hard to influence their children's aspirations and interests, their efforts often backfire. Many parents exhibit disapproval of the aspirations of young children whose Dreams are not yet fixed and may be expected to change many times before they reach maturity. The boy or girl who expresses interest in a career as a paleontologist after seeing the movie *Jurassic Park*, for example, should be encouraged to read about the subject and visit museums and even project sites with the parents to see what paleontologists do and how they work. It is never too soon for parents to demonstrate that they respect the career aspirations of their children and will continue to do so. Above all, children must feel that they are free to choose their own Dreams. Parents who are too judgmental, who attempt to control their children's behavior by heaping scorn and ridicule on expressions of the children's deepest aspirations, can be particularly destructive.

The father of Ted Turner of Turner Broadcasting provided a notorious example of the judgmental parent who sought to impose his views on his son through ridicule. Ed Turner, a driven entrepreneur who built a billboard advertising company in the South, was an alcoholic given to severe mood swings. According to one biographer, he loved his son dearly but also hoped to goad the boy to greatness. He had sent his son to an Ivy League college to gain the sophistication the father felt was needed for a business career. When Ted Turner informed his father that he planned to major in classics, he received this letter in reply:

There is no question but this type of useless information will distinguish you, set you apart from the doers of the world. If I leave you enough money, you can retire to an ivory tower and contemplate for the rest of your days the influence that the hieroglyphics of prehistoric man had upon the writings of William Faulkner. . . . It isn't really important what I think. It's important what you wish to do with your life. I just wish I could see that the influence of these oddball professors and the ivory towers were developing you into the kind of man we can both be proud of. I am quite sure that we both will be pleased and delighted when I introduce you to some friend of mine and say, "This is my son. He speaks Greek." [10]

Such communications are bound to be devastating to young people, and are apt to incite them to rebel against the parent's influence. To expose his father's narrow attitude toward the classics, Ted had Ed Turner's letter published, anonymously, in the college newspaper; young Ted was already a defiant son by the time he had reached college. The brilliant and dynamic son took over the family business after his father committed suicide in 1963. He lived up to his father's expectations for him by building a global news and entertainment company, but he was tormented by the same mood swings that had plagued his father. [11] His father's scorn could easily have defeated a young person of lesser talents.

Children are very attentive to the contradictions between parents' words and their deeds. The parents' behavior is likely to make a stronger impression than their expressed beliefs and values. [12] For example, how parents behave toward their own siblings can have a strong influence on how their children respond to one another. How a father treats his parents has a powerful effect on how his children treat him. A young person's choice of career is invariably influenced by the child's reading of whether the parents have found their work lives satisfying as well as by the degree of success that the parents have achieved. Consider the father who returns home every evening exhausted, complaining bitterly about how badly he has gotten along with his relatives at work. The parents may express the explicit message that the children are welcome in the family business; the children, however, will be receiving an entirely different message: Stay away unless you want to be miserable like your father.

In some families, the clash of powerful and contradictory messages from parents can entrap children in a double-bind—a paradoxical form of communication that is relatively common in families and, in extreme cases, is associated with serious family dysfunction. [13] For example, many families glorify the qualities of a founder who has succeeded by asserting his independence, going off on his own and establishing his own company despite opposition from others. Yet the children may be urged from their early years to join the already established family business. When they do, they may find that they have to subordinate their own ideas and aspirations to those of their parents. Yet, to succeed by the family model, they would have to reject their parents, refuse to join the family business, and establish their own successful enterprises. There is no right course available to them.

When the children are growing up, however, many positive lessons can be conveyed in the context of the business. The head of a well-known retail chain tells a story about when his daughter was ten years old and visiting the family's main store on a Saturday morning. The daughter was playing on the floor of her father's office while her father held a meeting with senior managers around a conference table in his office. They were working on a thorny problem. It seems that space was limited and the store did not have enough checkout counters to prevent long lines and delays for customers leaving the store. The daughter overheard the discussion and, during a coffee break, suggested a solution to her father: "Why not try to put two employees and two cash registers at each checkout counter? I was in a store with Mom recently that managed to put two registers in the space of one. . . . I know it can be done!" To her father's astonishment, the girl proceeded to draw on a piece of paper the design of an alternative arrangement. After the break, the father had the daughter tell the executives, who agreed that the girl's suggestion was the answer to the problem. Within two weeks the front end of the store was redesigned using the daughter's idea, which proved to be a success. Naturally, the girl could not wait to get to the store each day after school to see how her idea was being implemented.

For the daughter in this story, the decision sent a powerful message: Ideas for improving the store will be taken seriously no matter what their source. More than that, the message was that the family business was a place where she could make a difference and where her Dreams could be fulfilled. The daughter is now the CEO of the family company and performing exceptionally well. Children are experts in fun. When parents are able convey excitement for what they *do*, children pay attention.

I interviewed three siblings who own and manage a remarkably successful business that was started by their parents. I asked them why the three of them had been interested in working together in the first place, and to what they attributed their ability to collaborate so effectively. In particular, what had their parents done to encourage this? The older brother said the following:

Our parents never forced us into anything. On the contrary, they always encouraged us to pursue our own dreams and interests. However, it was very clear from the beginning that the two of them loved what they did—their enthusiasm was contagious! For example, my father would frequently seek our opinion on experiments that he would do to satisfy his customers. After listening to us, he would implement our ideas and subsequently tell us how things turned out. We understood early that business could actually be a great deal of fun.

His sister added:

[Our parents] always shared their excitement and at the same time they gave us *lots* and *lots* of *choice* to be who we wanted to be. In fact, I was the only one of us who studied business administration in college.

Parents have found a variety of ways of sparking enthusiasm in members of the next generation for careers in the family business. But these parents also teach their offspring respect for professionalism, and they demand the standards of performance without which a business will not be viable. Without professionalism, motivated children will not be adequately prepared to carry on the business. But when families stress only professionalism, children may not see the family company as a place where they can satisfy their deepest aspirations. The result in the third generation is often an abundance of passive shareholders and a shortage of real leaders.

Managing Entry

As the analysis above suggests, families that do a good job preparing young family members to enter the family business have usually paid a great deal of attention to the children's dreams and developmental needs. An environment has been established in which family members can comfortably discuss career choices and the future of the business. By the time they reach college, the young people have a fairly accurate understanding of the opportunities, the satisfactions, and the potential risks of getting involved with the business. The parents have encouraged them to "think big," to expect much of themselves and to become the best people they possibly can, whether through the family business or other career paths they may be considering.

Young adults in their early twenties, experience the world as both exhilarating and potentially threatening. As we've noted, they are eager to explore multiple possibilities—without committing fully to any. To use Erik Erikson's metaphor, young adults at this stage view life as an amusement park in which they can't wait to try out all the rides. Bringing the children into the family business at this stage can be premature. It can needlessly retard not just their psychological development but also their substantive understanding of the workplace.

The young person's anxieties about being viewed as a beneficiary of nepotism can rapidly erode his or her self-esteem and unnecessarily heighten the sense of awkwardness associated with the transition from adolescence to the adult world. Under this pressure, the young family member may, in fact, make more mistakes than he or she would in a similar job at another company. These early work blunders can not only be costly to the business but to the person's self-confidence and career development. Among non-family employees, they may encourage a generalized expectation of the successor's incompetence, which, in time, becomes a self-fulfilling prophecy. The young family member is not trusted with significant responsibility and given opportunities to test his or her capabilities and to learn. Over the years I have encountered many sons and daughters who were labeled dismal failures in their family's company, and yet have flourished in an alternative work setting after leaving the business—much to their own surprise as well as that of others.

To the young person starting out in a business career, candid feedback from coworkers and supervisors is absolutely essential to correcting mistakes and improving job performance. Not surprisingly, in a family business, a young family member starting out is not likely to get high-quality feedback. In the words of one young family business heir: "People either love you too much and constantly sing your praises no matter what you do; or they hate you and continuously disapprove of your work. . . . It is very hard to figure out how I am, in fact, doing."

For parents, too, the decision to invite the offspring into the family company may be riddled with complications that are often not fully examined at the time of the invitation. The years the incumbent leaders spent securing a foothold in the family business may have left them little time to spend with their spouses and children. The nagging feeling that they have missed out on the children's growing-up years can prevent them from seeing their children as independent adults. This may lead to an ill-conceived attempt to reconnect with grown offspring by pressuring them to join the family business.

Consider the case of an extraordinarily gifted young man who excelled in a number of subjects, including math and science, but was passionately interested in the visual arts. In college this young man wanted to major in painting, but his father, arguing that he could never make a living as an artist, persuaded him to study economics, which would be a better background for working in the family business. Likewise, when the son was considering job offers after graduation, a similar struggle ensued. Seeking a compromise between his own desire for an artistic career and his father's wish for him to make a career in the family business, the son accepted a position restoring paintings with a leading art auction house. Again the father objected, arguing that the son needed an MBA. Once again, the son acquiesced in his father's wishes. He graduated with honors from a prestigious business school and entered the family company as vice-president of a key division.

Much to his father's disappointment—and his own—this very talented man has failed in practically every assignment he has ever undertaken. He has, moreover, caused substantial losses for the company. Through his record of failures, the son has punished his father for robbing him of his Dream and, at the same time, expiated his own guilt for his frequent arguments with the father. At the age of forty, the son still looks at his early paintings and sketches from time to time and wonders what would have become of his life if he had followed his earlier ambitions to be an artist.

Like this man's father, business owners may, with the best of intentions, attempt to shape their children's educational choices in order to ensure that the new generation will be capable of carrying out the family legacy. Typically, the more prestigious the family business, the more pressure is exerted on the children to pursue an education that will be of value to the business. After college, there may be invitations to join the family company, often accompanied by the promise of financial rewards that border on bribes.

Business owners who are over forty have already encountered the turbulent developmental issues associated with the mid-life transition. If they have not worked through these issues, they may have a much harder time disentangling their own psychological needs from those of their offspring. At this time of life parents often begin to pin their hopes on members of the next generation to accomplish their unfulfilled Dreams. Feeling particularly vulnerable and self-critical themselves, they become, by extension, critical of the performance of their offspring. Levinson elucidates this psychological dynamic:

[At mid-life when the parent's aging] weighs heavily upon him, [the off-spring's] exuberant vitality is more likely to arouse his envy and resentment than his delight and forbearance. . . . If he feels he has lost or betrayed his own Dream, he may find it hard to give his wholehearted support and bless-ing to the Dreams of young adults. When his offspring show signs of failure or confusion in pursuing their adult goals, he is afraid that their lives will turn out as badly as his own. Yet when they do well, he may resent their suc-cess. Anxiety and guilt may undermine his efforts to be helpful and lead him instead to be nagging and vindictive.[14]

Given the developmental needs of both parent and child, the best solution at this stage of life is the one often recommended to the off-spring of a business family for many different reasons: It is best for the potential successor to work outside the family company for a few years. K. H. Rogal explains:

While an independence-seeking twenty-two year old may have difficulty getting along with a reputation-building forty-year-old parent, the passage of time is likely to bring the developmental needs of the two in concert. In this case, the heir would be well served to spend a few years working outside the family environment, with the understanding that joining the firm later is a probable outcome. This precludes conflict over the youth's need to keep options open and develop adult life structures.[15]

Setting Entry Requirements

Explicit policies are essential for regulating the entry of young family members into the company. Ideally, these policies are developed before the first of the offspring are knocking at the door of the business. More and more companies insist that before joining the family business, the children must work outside of it for three to five years in order to establish their credibility as professionals and as managers of organiza-tions in which their family affiliation is of no consequence. Success in the outside world does not necessarily guarantee that these heirs will subsequently be offered a position in the family business; on the con-trary, it may be only one of several criteria that need to be met before a family member will be considered for a job.

There are a number of advantages to exposing young people to other companies early in their careers. Business families are often enmeshed in the intricate web of their own traditions and lose sight of important technological and managerial developments in the wider business world. These families get an added benefit when they encourage their children to seek employment in companies that are bigger, more sophisticated in management techniques, and more advanced technologically than theirs. Some families insist that members of the next generation find employment in a related industry. This is a relatively common requirement in companies in which a leader's credibility depends on being able to demonstrate an in-depth understanding of technical processes and products. Often the offspring do return to the family company, bringing with them know-how and experience needed to carry out necessary innovations.[16]

From a developmental standpoint, the most important benefit of working outside the family business is that it increases the likelihood that potential successors will get accurate performance feedback. Outside the safety net of the family business, they learn from their mistakes and develop an appreciation for the work ethic. Moreover, they gain a better perspective on the value of money and their own comparative worth as employees in the marketplace, which helps them to develop more realistic expectations of the kinds of rewards they might be entitled to if they enter the family business. The juniors' compensation in family firms is rarely pegged to market rates.[17] One of the advantages of requiring young family members to work outside the business for a few years is that this provides some benchmark with which to determine their salaries when they enter the family business.

When families adopt specific policies to regulate the entry and exit of relatives, they must also pay careful attention to the process by which these policies are adopted. The imposition of strict rules may generate resentment, especially if the later entrants feel they are being held to a tougher standard than older siblings or cousins who entered before the rules were adopted. For this reason, the juniors should be encouraged to buy into the process by participating in both the formulation and administration of the rules.

By adopting a strict policy that excludes family members from employment unless they have leadership potential, families protect themselves against charges of nepotism. Drawing this line, however, does not mean abandoning those members who are average or poor performers. On the contrary, owners of these companies often go out of their way to help family members who cannot meet the company's standards to establish themselves in the outside world, such help is usually provided through the family rather than the business. Likewise, the family should do everything it can to help those whose performance does not measure up to the expected performance levels after joining the business. If they continue to fall short of expectations, however, there is no alternative to letting them go. Many families anticipate such a scenario and adopt a policy to deal with it. Typically, the policy will provide that if a family member is not performing at an optimal level two years after the date of employment, he or she will be asked to leave the family company. How "optimal performance" is defined varies from family to family. But it usually refers to a level of performance comparable to what a person who aspires to rise to a senior management position is normally expected to achieve.

Carefully drawn standards and a system for collecting performance data are essential to ensuring that every family member is fairly evaluated and given a maximum chance of achieving a position consistent with his or her talent, interests, and work ethic. Some business owners express concern that too many formal rules and overly bureaucratic structures may drive the new generation away from the family company. In my experience such concerns are not warranted, particularly in families that involve the children in the development of hiring and firing policies that will affect them. When discussions of these issues start relatively early in the development of the family and convey the importance of professionalism, parents are often surprised to find that members of the next generation themselves tend to favor adoption of stringent rules for employment of family members.

Of course, some younger people may feel intimidated by the high performance standards required and may avoid seeking jobs in the family business as a result. Families that set high standards would rather turn away those who, for whatever reasons, do not want to face up to the challenge, than lose competent young people who might reject the family company precisely because management does not do an adequate job of distinguishing between competent and incompetent managers.

Attitudes of the Entrants

If parents have done their job in the early years, their offspring will enter the company with an attitude of humility and a proper respect for the company hierarchy. Young people often have an inflated view of their capabilities when they enter the company. Parents need to thoroughly brief them on the difficult line they will have to walk in their first years and how their behavior will be interpreted by others. There should be a clear "psychological contract"[18] that makes explicit both what the juniors can expect and what the company will expect of them.

Family leaders need to show an appreciation for what the young adults already know and will bring with them to the company, the implicit message being: "You are talented young people who have something to offer. Your innovative ideas are welcomed and we will give you room to experiment and grow." Even though they are members of the owning family, they will make mistakes; they cannot be expected to be perfect. However, they should be reminded that they have to honor the experience and professionalism of non-family employees who have been doing their jobs for years. The behavior of young family members should convey that they are willing to learn, that they are secure enough to take honest criticism, and that they want to be treated like any other employee at their level in the organization.

Many potential successors feel insecure when entering the business and try to compensate for it by exaggerating their own experience and skills. Other employees will perceive this as arrogance. A young family member who acts like an owner rather than a new employee —of whatever rank—will inevitably be resented. Nothing undermines a successor more, for example, than pulling rank and going behind the back of a supervisor to change a decision or obtain preferential treatment.

The young heirs should get the message that, yes, they are special. As family members, they will have opportunities for growth and be privy to information that other employees do not routinely get. The opposite side of the coin is that they will have to prove themselves like everyone else in the company. While their pay may be modest and pegged to market rates at the start, as family members they can expect to be well rewarded in the long run if they succeed, eventually with stock ownership. They should know from the start, however, that there are no guarantees they will get to the top. This is part of the explicit "contract." From the time they arrive in the company, young family members should understand—and accept—that this risk is part of the deal. Indeed, if they really have the right stuff, they will insist on jobs with real accountability that will give them the chance to demonstrate their worth.

Where in the company a young entrant begins working should, of course, depend on prior training, interests, and capabilities. Some care should be taken to fit the person to the right starting position. A daughter with an MBA from Wharton and three years' experience at

Morgan Stanley probably shouldn't be left too long in a warehouse job loading trucks, even if it helps her to demonstrate humility and learn the business "from the ground up." Likewise, it would be unwise to make a son who never finished high school a vice president and pay him a high salary when he arrives at the company. Whatever the young man's potential, it would send a warning signal to everyone else in the company that nepotism is a threat.

Experience suggests that family members are frequently either underqualified or overqualified for their first jobs in the family company. Parents' assessments of their own sons' and daughters' capabilities are often notoriously extreme—they tend to either underrate or overrate their offspring. In designing career development programs for young family members, companies are well advised to place them in jobs with accountability for specific measurable results. These jobs should be challenging but commensurate with the juniors' skills and level of maturity.

Once young family members are inside the company, they are entitled to some sense of what their career paths might be. How long will they spend in their initial position? How will their objectives be determined and, if they meet them, where will they go next? What chance will they have to get line management experience as well as opportunities to become familiar with different divisions?

Here again, timing is critical. The company leaders should examine the organizational chart and, noting the ages of senior managers, determine what positions might be opening up through normal turnover that will give young family members real responsibility. Certain positions might be earmarked as absolutely essential to affording successors the broad-gauged experience they will need to lead the business. The company's likely strategic direction should also be considered in designing their career paths. If the strategy is to expand abroad, for example, any family member who aspires to a leadership position should probably learn what it's like to work in another country.

The Role of Non-Family Senior Managers

When the time comes for the offspring to enter the business, parents must concern themselves with the practical implications of the event for the rest of the company. For senior managers who have always enjoyed a special relationship with the owner, the hiring of a son or daughter may be perceived as a threat. If nothing else, the arrival of the heir threatens to weaken the special ties managers have enjoyed with the owner. For all the mythology surrounding entrepreneurship, successful businesses are not built by a single, heroic individual. Rather, they are usually a collective achievement, requiring the talents and energies of a number of key people around the incumbent leader-owner. Over time, these veteran managers come to feel a sense of psychological ownership of the business. The presence of the owner's son or daughter serves as a powerful reminder to these trusted managers of who does, in fact, own the company. It creates a perception—real or imagined—that in the long run family members will receive special treatment when the time comes to determine who will be eligible for the top jobs in the company.

In some family companies, the employees' commitment to the family is so strong that the entry of younger family members is welcomed as a sign of family continuity and stability—provided, of course, that the new members are viewed as competent. In other companies, however, the entry into the business of unseasoned young family members can trigger the departure of key executives. The cooperation of these non-family executives is vital to the training and development of the young potential successor. Unless reassured of their importance to the incumbent leader and to the firm, the senior staff may not give their wholehearted support to the succession process and may, indeed, set themselves up as competitors with the younger generation for leadership positions.

Family companies that manage the entry process effectively often select a group of senior non-family mangers to assist with the development and early training of the young family members. In the best cases, these trusted non-family mangers are past the mid-life transition themselves and are willing to coach the entry and early development of the juniors, greatly facilitating the process by which these children incorporate themselves into the family company.

Again, we are here talking only about the entry process; in the next chapter we will discuss the role that senior managers can play in the later mentoring that takes place. In both phases, experienced non-family managers have an opportunity to shape the values and attitudes of those who will own and possibly lead the family enterprise some day. One of the biggest challenges for successors is to develop working relationships with a number of key non-family executives. The relationship is in the personal interest of the senior managers as well. It allows them to demonstrate to the firm's future leaders their own value as indispensable managerial resources whose judgment the juniors must learn to respect.

The senior managers who are selected to guide the young family members in the early stages should know from the start what is expected of them: The coaching of the young entrants is an important part of their job responsibilities. The future of the business depends upon it, and they will be evaluated and rewarded, in part, on how effectively they perform this function. Most important, the company leaders have to create a climate in which it is okay for the senior managers to tell their young mentees the truth about their performance. The family leaders have to convey the message with conviction and sincerity and make sure they stick to it in their subsequent actions. All it takes to undermine the career development program is for the owner to criticize a senior manager for an honest assessment of a son or daughter's performance.

Some senior managers are, of course, likely to view the assignment as the first step in their eventual outplacement from the company. This is more of a threat in smaller companies, which have fewer positions at the top. To defuse this fear, the family leaders need to reassure managers who are chosen to train family members that they will not lose their jobs as a result. Indeed, it should be part of every executive's normal responsibilities to groom potential successors for their positions; that is just prudent management policy. Senior executives who are not routinely training "understudies" who can step into their position—whether a family member or not—are not doing an essential part of their jobs and are putting the company's continuity at risk. At the same time, it should be clear to senior managers that any effort to sabotage the careers of their young tutees will not be tolerated.

Family Tensions at the Entry Stage

The entry of a son or daughter into the family firm may arouse profound emotions in the parent. The owner may be genuinely joyful at having the children with him or her at the office every day and happy at the prospect that the business will one day be carried on by them. Indeed, it is the feeling of pride and satisfaction that comes from watching one's own children mature and blossom professionally that helps the senior generation to make the sacrifices necessary to ensure the continuity of the business into the next generation.

But the arrival of potential successors may also be experienced as the first step in the parent's inevitable decline. This vague fear may be heightened when a very capable young heir comes in brimming with ideas for change. As one successor put it:

The heir often arrives enthusiastically brandishing new tools and techniques that may expose weaknesses of the top executive. In the daily interchange of ideas, the heir may pass judgment on the parent's decisions—a discomfiting position for all but the most secure parents.[19]

The entry of the offspring into the parent's work world may change the dynamics of the family as well. Before, the rest of the family may have had only a minimal interest in "the place where Dad (or Mom) works." Now, because of the involvement of another family member—a son or daughter—everyone takes a keener interest, including the owner's spouse. The business owner may welcome the opportunity to share work experiences with family members and educate them in this critical aspect of his or her life. Indeed, this participation strengthens the Shared Dream that provides the foundation for succession and continuity. However, the family's new-found interest may feel intrusive to the owner. Suddenly, the business owner feels more exposed to loved ones and hence more vulnerable to their criticisms—not just at the office but at home. Typically, the entry of the offspring broadens the range of perspectives on business issues that are available to the family. Events in the business are now discussed not just from the vantage point of the business owner but from that of the working offspring as well. No longer is the business owner the sole conduit of information about the business in family discussions. Now he or she is forced to deal with another set of perceptions and voices. In families that have traditionally maintained a fairly tight separation between business and family, these changes may acquire an even greater significance. The move almost certainly complicates family life.

The entry of one child into the business may also stir up rivalries among siblings. The sequence in which children get involved with the family business is still often determined by birth order. Even in families that do not expressly adhere to the rule of primogeniture, the first-born is often the first to join the business, which elevates the oldest child in the family social hierarchy, confirming—or introducing—in the minds of the other siblings worries about parental favoritism.

First-borns in the business establish an early claim over certain opportunities and resources. They get "first dibs" on a limited number of interesting entry-level positions, and because they are able to accumulate the most work experience and seniority, they often move up the organizational hierarchy more rapidly than siblings who enter later on. However, the first to enter the family business may become a "guinea pig" if the family has not yet learned to manage the steps in the entry process effectively. At what level in the organization should the offspring come in? What jobs are and are not suitable for a family greenhorn? What is an appropriate level of responsibility and compensation? How can performance be measured and effective feedback provided? Which of the senior managers can supervise and perhaps even mentor the offspring? The handling of these all-important issues will set important precedents for how family members will be incorporated into the business in the future. The first to enter the business may stumble from the family's lack of experience in dealing with such matters. By the time other siblings are ready to join the business, the family is likely to have worked out the "dos and don'ts." Later-borns may be envious of the first sibling to enter the company, and worried that there will be fewer opportunities for them, but by the time they enter the business the rules for hiring and performance by relatives should have been clarified, and a process worked out for managing their career development.

For those who may be considering other careers, the entry of the first sibling is, in a way, a boon. With one child in the business, the parents may be satisfied that the legacy will eventually be passed on. They are therefore likely to bring less pressure on the other children to come in. The other siblings may thus feel free to explore their career options in and out of the family business without the added burden of the fear that they will disappoint the parents.

Sibling and Cousin Consortiums

Managing the entry process is more complicated for the leaders of sibling partnerships and cousin consortiums because they usually have to evaluate and groom many more candidates. At this stage in the evolution of a business, a comprehensive plan for screening, training, and evaluating candidates for positions in the company is a necessity.

One large family enterprise that has devoted considerable thought and energy to such a program provides an interesting example of how the entry process can be structured. Recognizing that many of the current family leaders of the company will retire or consider retiring in the next ten to fifteen years, the third-generation shareholders have developed an Accelerated Leadership Development Program. The program has two streams, one for family members seeking leadership positions and another for non-family employees who aspire to such positions. The program for family members is designed both to help them decide if they really want a career with the company and for the company to train and evaluate them. In the first phase of the leadership program, they are hired under contract as temporary employees and put through their paces in 142 weeks of work experience. The program exposes them to every phase of the business, from physical labor on the factory floor to desk jobs in the accounting, public relations, and safety departments, in both the operating companies and the family holding companies. Supervisors are assigned to guide them and their performance is documented.

The family defines the mission of the accelerated program as follows:

To ensure that members of the Fourth Generation—and other designated individuals with high potential—are provided with opportunities to develop and acquire, in an expeditious manner, the knowledge and skills needed to allow them to achieve their full potential and, where appropriate, to become future leaders of the Company.

The manual for the program spells out its goals:

Each member shall gain a full appreciation for their heritage.

Each member shall recognize the importance that the family places on work that is meaningful, as well as physically and mentally demanding.

Each member shall, through first-hand experience, require a realistic impression of the diverse nature of the Company and the affiliated family companies.

Each member shall, through exposure to numerous leaders, mentors, coaches and counsellors, gain an appreciation of what it takes to lead an organization in a highly competitive environment.

Each member shall recognize that the knowledge gained during Phase I represents only a fraction of the knowledge they will need to become proficient in any given discipline or function, and that acquiring in-depth knowledge within a given field is a long-term process that typically requires total immersion for an extended period of time.

Such an elaborate program prevents personal bias and branch politics from creeping into the evaluation of the candidates' work and the final determination of which ones will be offered jobs. The screening of candidates in sibling and cousin companies is complex—and political. The inherent potential for sibling conflict over hiring one another's offspring is further magnified when there are many talented and capable cousins interested in jobs but not many positions for them in upper echelons of the company. Some sibling partners deal with the problem by adopting rather extreme measures, either closing the door entirely— deciding that none of the cousins will be offered jobs—or by opening the door to all the job seekers in the expectation that the best and brightest will eventually rise to the top and the others will fall back.

Obviously, the size of the company and the number of capable offspring in the next generation are crucial data to consider in determining whether either of these two extreme solutions is necessary. Siblings who have a history of working well together rarely choose either extreme. Instead, they usually try to avoid problems by agreeing on some sort of formal rules for evaluating one another's children, and, most important, by enlisting outsiders in the process.

For example, some sibling partnerships manage this potentially volatile issue by developing a formal assessment committee. The committee may be made up of outside board members or two or three trusted external advisers. The assessment committee is often expected to make recommendations to the siblings on whether one or another of the cousins shows promise as a business leader. In order to be effective, the assessment committee must work discreetly with both seniors and juniors. The juniors must be able to trust that the committee members will make a concerted effort to be impartial in their judgment and prudent about protecting the privacy of the juniors. Such a committee cannot be effective if the juniors perceive that it is simply a surveillance network for their parents. For their part, though, the juniors must understand that the committee may occasionally have to share some information with the parents about them; otherwise, the seniors may not have enough information to evaluate the juniors for jobs. Thus committee members need to strike a balance in handling information that is helpful to both generations.

Further, the role of the committee should be broader than simply assessment. In some sibling and cousin companies the committee members themselves serve as mentors to young family employees, helping them lay out career paths in the business, introducing them to the company culture, recommending further education and training, and giving them continuing feedback on performance.

The need for formal systems for assessing the performance of successors is particularly acute in the companies that have numerous family aspirants for jobs. A few of the largest family companies have set up computerized systems for tracking the progress of younger family members according to measurable performance goals. This is especially helpful in older companies in which several branches of the family have ownership interests. In these companies, decisions about which cousins will be offered jobs and which will not usually have a political tinge. In addition to choosing on the basis of performance, assessment committees must be concerned about whether the various branches of the family are adequately represented by cousins in business and/or in governance roles. In order to accommodate as many young people as possible at this stage, cousin companies must also develop a range of other opportunities for those who are not offered positions in management. Participation on company boards of directors, family councils, boards of family foundations—all afford young people opportunities to get experience and remain connected with the family legacy even though they are not involved with management. Care must be taken to match the interests and skills of the cousins and the demands associated with particular roles. Some family companies, for example, set up a specific training program for those cousins who may be interested in running for the board of directors in order to provide the necessary skills for responsible board membership.

The development of a venture capital fund for young family members who want to become entrepreneurs is another option that has been successfully used by many family companies. Successful family businesses are about creating wealth, and one of the best ways to expand a family's wealth—as well as create more career options—is to provide capital for building new businesses. If successful, these ventures may eventually create business synergies with the family company. Indeed, some companies set up the fund as part of a holding company structure that enables various family entrepreneurial ventures to share staff and resources with the parent company. The venture fund caters to the young person's need for independence and differentiation from family. The process is also educational in itself. What better way to learn how to develop a business plan, to make hiring and firing decisions, to deal with banks and suppliers, to manage inventories, and so on, than to grow one's own company?

The families that manage venture funds for young members most effectively are discriminating in the loans they make. They use standard business criteria for evaluating loan applications and they have rules for financial reporting and repayment. They also make certain that the ventures do not interfere with the juniors' completion of formal education. One young scion who was given capital from such a fund was so successful in business that he neglected his college studies. When word got back to the parents about his poor academic record, the venture fund instituted a strict rule denying loans to young family members who did not keep up their school grades.

Once young family members in all types of systems have gone through the neophyte phase in the family business, they must deepen their commitment. They have now usually reached their thirties and have had a chance to assess the realities of the workplace and measure their own effectiveness in it. To move into a leadership position, they must now take on major responsibilities. They must learn what it takes to become strategic leaders, responsible owners, and spokespeople for the family company. They are ready for mentoring.

CHAPTER 8

Mentoring

IN the world of the family business, mentoring has a particularly evocative meaning. It conjures up hallowed images of cross-generational collaboration between master and apprentice dating as far back as the medieval guilds. These images are at the very heart of the concept of a family business. Indeed, it is through successful mentoring that the knowledge and expertise accumulated by the seniors in a particular line of work, as well as family traditions and values, get passed to the next generation. This transfer of knowledge from parents to children makes family companies truly unique—it is one of their fundamental competitive advantages in the marketplace.

Developmentally, Davis and Taguiri's research[1] suggests, the "working together" phase offers optimal conditions for this process to occur. The parents at this stage are between fifty and sixty years of age and have negotiated the challenges of the mid-life transition. The offspring, in their late twenties and thirties, are seriously committed to careers in the business. Both generations are ready to get down to the tasks of mentoring, if they haven't already. Much of what happens at this stage will determine whether or not the business will be passed down to future generations.

Many family business owners choose not to mentor their own children, fearing that it may jeopardize the parent-child relationship. No matter what the level of parental involvement, mentoring in a family business cannot be done by parents alone. In larger companies, mentoring is part of a systematic effort involving senior executives and even board members that exposes young successors to a range of skills and experiences that prepare them for leadership.[2]

In this chapter I will describe the roles of different types of mentors and review mentoring systems that have been used successfully in a number of family businesses. I will examine the qualities needed by senior executives and professional advisers chosen as mentors in family companies and how teams of mentors are organized. Next I will consider the importance of a company's future strategy in the design of a mentoring plan. I will end with some thoughts on the complications that parents face in mentoring their own offspring in a family business and whether love and mutual respect can survive the turbulent emotions often unleashed in this relationship.

While mentors often play a quasi-parental role vis-à-vis their mentees, the fact that mentors are typically *not* a parent is assumed to be one of the inherent advantages of the relationship. For instance, under the master-apprentice system in the Middle Ages, many families sent their sons to learn the trade under the tutelage of a master to whom they were not related. Many of the guilds prohibited children from becoming apprentices to their own parents. Similar restrictions exist to this day in some professions such as medicine.[3] Large corporations tend to discourage people from working directly with close relatives and probably would oppose a mentoring relationship between family members for the same reasons. The underlying assumption here is that the absence of a familial tie will help both the mentor and the mentee to understand and honor each other's needs more effectively. Mentoring by a non-parent is assumed to be desirable not only because it is unencumbered by the emotional baggage inherent in the parent-child relationship, but also because mentors are usually transitional figures while the child-parent bond is presumably for life.

Mentoring in the fullest sense involves much more than guidance, assistance, or sponsorship of a young person's career by a more experienced and accomplished senior. It can be a profoundly emotional experience that shakes the young adult into a realization of his or her Dream, builds confidence in his or her capacity to achieve the Dream, and creates the conditions necessary for the young person to enter the world of seniors as a full-fledged adult. Indeed, it may be that the deepest mentoring relationships are accomplished when both parties choose each other freely instead of being "assigned" to each other.

The experience of Tom Watson, Jr., the late CEO of IBM, suggests that in some cases mentoring by a parent in a family business must be preceded—indeed, depends upon—a profoundly transforming mentor relationship with an adult that occurs outside the business. Watson never believed that he had what it took to succeed his father, Thomas Watson, Sr., as CEO until he served as personal pilot to Air Force General Follett Bradley during World War II. Under Follett, Watson experienced what it was like to work independently of his father. Follett helped Watson to believe in his own capabilities, authenticating his adulthood and encouraging the young Watson to return to IBM after the war.

When Watson first arrived at the company, he was surprised to find that he would not be working under his father's supervision but for the senior Watson's No. 2, Charley Kirk, a veteran executive and prodigious worker who had dozens of different responsibilities at IBM. Kirk, then in his forties, did his best to teach Watson, even though he himself had aspirations of succeeding the founder as CEO. Tom Jr. described his unique vantage point as Kirk's mentee:

He had a large desk in the office, and he simply told me to pull up a chair alongside. "I don't have time to explain everything I do," he said, "but you'll learn if you sit here and watch." That was where I perched every day for months, and whenever Kirk went to a meeting I'd go along. I saw practically everything he did. I learned how to make decisions. For Kirk was excellent at making them fast and making most of them right. Sitting by Kirk, I had as good a cross-section of IBM's problems as I could have gotten anywhere in the company. [4]

There are risks in assigning non-family executives to mentor young successors, as we will see. In Watson's case, the relationship with Kirk turned destructive when it became increasingly apparent that they were competitors for the top job at IBM. Young Watson demanded Kirk's removal, and not long after Kirk died of a heart attack. Some years later, after an embarrassing stint as a salesman, Watson began to work directly with his father, and, although their relationship was stormy, he had the confidence to stay the course and rise to leadership of the corporation.

Tailored to the Individual

Larger family companies that do a good job of mentoring usually have a formal, step-by-step process for developing the managerial and leadership skills of the individual successors. In smaller family companies, by contrast, this process takes place fairly informally, determined largely by the instincts and intuitive knowledge of the business owner. Whatever the company's size, a mentoring plan is ideally driven by the leaders' vision of a future strategy and structure.

Mentoring is personally tailored to the individual. Unlike training, it is concerned not just with teaching specific skills, but with giving the mentee a broad, comprehensive view of the whole business and its competitive environment. It focuses on instilling the kind of maturity in managing others and developing a vision for the business that is required of those who will ultimately own and lead the company. It is also the process by which the mentee, if he or she passes all the tests, earns the right to lead.

To be effective, the process must be negotiated with the successors right from the start, laying out specific jobs and competencies that must be mastered at each stage before the mentee can move on to the next stage. In this process, the mentee acquires basic conceptual and business skills in such areas as strategy, marketing, and budgeting, and learns to deal effectively with a variety of people who play different roles. When mentoring is successful, seniors and juniors are able to maintain mutual regard, while setting up real tests of a mentee's capabilities. Both mentor and mentee have a profound respect for information that enables the seniors to evaluate performance. Whenever possible, the mentee is assigned to jobs that generate objective data on performance.

Of course, the ingredients of leadership are not all easy to quantify. There is an ongoing discussion in the field of organizational theory about how managerial performance can—and should—be measured. But many companies have been able to develop clear criteria to hold mentees accountable for their performance in various kinds of roles. Typically, mentees are assessed on key variables such as profit margins in the unit that they are assigned to manage; output of a production unit; turnover of employees in their department; sales goals; cost and inventory efficiencies. An ongoing feedback process is established so that both mentor and mentee trust the validity of the information being gathered and used to shape the learning process.

Although all of this may sound obvious, family companies frequently ignore the need for accurate and reliable data. Either little data is systematically gathered on the offspring's progress, or the data that is gathered is so susceptible to subjective interpretation that it is practically useless to further learning. In the best mentoring relationships, the mentor plays a critical role in helping the junior reflect on his or her experience. However, when the mentoring is being done by a parent it is more likely that, out of protectiveness, the parent will try to soften the impact of the lessons that the offspring need to digest. As one entrepreneur who effectively mentored his son told me: "The secret of my mentoring relationship with my son revolves around the Biblical saying that 'The truth shall set you free.' I invariably get into trouble whenever I have tried to shelter my son from the consequences of his own decisions."

We have seen how Tom Watson, Jr., learned the ropes at IBM by observing a veteran decision maker at work. This type of direct behavioral modeling is age-old and in smaller companies it is the primary vehicle through which the seniors convey their expertise and knowledge to the next generation. The offspring are given opportunities, over a period of time, to watch the parent making major business decisions, managing employees, and dealing with customers, business associates, and financial institutions.

One owner of a family insurance firm allowed his son to work by his side and even encouraged the son to listen to his phone conversations in order to learn how to talk to customers. This father also took the son along to meetings with customers and bankers and introduced him to his professional network within the industry. Some people were at first uneasy having the inexperienced young man present at the meetings. However, as the son attained a deeper understanding of the clients' needs, he began to participate in the meetings and brought added value. The clients then became a lot more comfortable with him; they appreciated his contributions and even seemed pleased to be participating in the father's mentoring of his successor.

Modeling is particularly important in service industries, in which personal relationships are critical. Modeling also takes place in larger firms. It is vital in teaching business negotiation skills. In one second-generation company the owner-manger, who takes considerable pride in his ability to put together complex financial deals, explained to me that deal-making—in his opinion the most essential part of his leadership role—is far too complex to be reduced to a concrete series of tasks:

The only way for my daughter ever to comprehend what it is that I do in bringing about successful deals for our company is to sit with me and watch me perform this complex operation over and over again. After a deal is done, she and I sit together for an extensive period of time and dissect the process in order to make sure that she understands the logic behind why I chose to go down one particular path instead of another.

By reflecting on these experiences with his daughter, this business owner has been able to convey to her a fundamental sense of both the strategies that he uses in action and the values and ethical principles that guide his leadership of the business. Over time, as new deals have come up, the father has gradually shifted from being the primary deal maker to being mostly an adviser to the daughter, who conducts most of the negotiations.

Mentoring for the Future

Modeling, however, has significant limitations. First, a real leader cannot be created simply through observation and imitation of the behavior of experienced elders. At a certain point in the mentoring process, after the mentee has absorbed many of the fundamentals, those with a strong sense of self are likely to want to develop their own leadership style. If the parent insists that there is one and only one way to lead, the offspring may lose interest, thereby jeopardizing the process. Only when successors feel they are able to incorporate what they are learning into their own personalities and styles will they be able, ultimately, to perform to their fullest potential. Only then will their leadership have the authenticity and conviction necessary to win followers.

Second, successors must acquire the skills necessary to lead the business of the future, not the one that exists today. This means embracing new strategies and new technologies—maybe even new products—that will fundamentally change the way the business is managed. If the mentoring process concentrates on imparting skills and perspectives that may be obsolete, the succession will be flawed. In today's world, family companies—even smaller ones—have to anticipate changes in the competitive environment and be ready to alter their products and processes in order to respond effectively to market needs.

Nowhere has this been more evident than in Europe. With the consolidation of the European Community, many of the most prestigious family companies that for generations have enjoyed leadership positions in various market niches must now undergo a fundamental transformation in order to compete with giant multinationals in those markets. One dramatic example is a family-owned Italian leather-tanning company which responded to the challenge by giving up the niche it had long occupied and transforming its product line. The tanning business had been invaded by producers in developing countries with relatively low labor rates. Unable to compete internationally, the Italian company instead became a leading distributor of finished leather, inviting foreign producers as well as other Italian companies to sell through their channels—a classic case of, "If you can't beat 'em, join 'em." The company elders had the wisdom to realize that to succeed in its totally new market, members of the younger generation needed mentoring in entirely different skill sets than those they themselves had learned from previous generations. Because the seniors were able to anticipate these dramatic changes in the industry, the juniors, as part of the development program, gained experience with major distributors of finished leather in the United States and Asia.

Three Approaches to Mentoring

Other approaches to mentoring in family companies are more eclectic and involve a mixture of modeling, didactic, and experiential learning. The didactic elements of the mentoring process are tailored to the specific needs of the offspring and of the company. It is not unusual, for instance, for parents and offspring to attend seminars and to use the opportunity to learn new skills together. The experiential component is typically dealt with through the careful design of a career path that will give the offspring exposure to critical line and staff positions in the business over an extended period of time. The assignment to each successive position is contingent on the mentee's performance in the previous position. Progress is reviewed continuously and honestly by a mentor who oversees the process. (Of course, the risk in rotating potential successors through too many brief assignments is that they will never be in one position long enough to gain experience making big decisions.)

Providing real jobs with real accountability is easier in a large company than a smaller one, but it must be carefully planned and managed in order to avoid creating friction with senior managers. Particularly in larger companies, family owners must be respectful of hierarchy and formal procedures when assigning young family members to responsible roles. I've seen owners move senior managers out of their positions—even, in some cases, firing them—in order to give their offspring major roles. Such a policy can be highly destructive to the morale and integrity of any organization. There are a number of approaches to mentoring that provide opportunities for young family members without firing or demoting managers.

Rotation. This approach, described above, is probably the one that most companies adopt. The mentee works for a specified period in each of the company's departments, and receives mentoring in each from the senior person in charge of the department. For all the reasons mentioned above, a rotation plan will be limited in its benefits if the mentee does not have real responsibilities and is not expected to perform up to a measurable standard before moving on to the next department. In other words, mentees must be put in a position to make real decisions that carry the risk of possible failure.

Vertical loading of responsibilities.[5] This strategy involves "pushing down" to the mentee responsibility and authority that formerly were reserved for higher levels of management. For example, top managers of a manufacturing company usually receive a steady stream of data from the production line—the number of units produced, raw materials inventory, operations costs. But they are notoriously slow to interpret the data and return recommendations on corrective actions that need to be taken by line supervisors. A young successor who is assigned to supervise the assembly operation might therefore be made responsible for interpreting the data before it goes to top management and for implementing the changes that he or she deems appropriate. This would not only test his or her own ability to interpret and make critical production decisions, but would also probably speed up the process of interpreting the data and introducing efficiencies.

Special projects. In one company, the owner had built a highly effective executive team and was unable to offer his daughter an executive position that made sense in the short term. Instead, he decided to give her a leadership role in the development of a strategic plan for the company. In this role, the daughter was forced to interact with each of the senior executives for a sustained period. While at first the senior executives were rather skeptical, over time they became so enthusiastic about her leadership of this process that they proposed that the daughter head an ongoing task force to monitor the implementation and continuous review of strategic planning.

While performance is the ultimate measure of a potential successor's capabilities, special projects are sometimes important for what the mentees can learn from them rather than the objective results achieved. When the Caterpillar Co. decided in the 1980s to manufacture a small garden tractor to compete with John Deere's line, one dealer saw a perfect opportunity for his offspring to learn what it takes to start and run a business profitably. Caterpillar manufactures huge earth-moving equipment and none of the family members had experience with the new product for this market. So the parent turned over complete responsibilities for marketing the small tractor to members of the next generation. They had to study the market, open new showrooms, advertise the product, talk to customers, manage inventory. The product itself did not match Deere's and failed to find a market—mostly because of Caterpillar's inexperience at manufacturing small tractors— but this opportunity was an invaluable learning experience. This example supports the notion that objective data on results achieved by mentees must frequently take into account factors outside the mentees' control that may have compromised their performance. In other words, seniors must interpret the data in context.

Selection of Non-Family Mentors

From the point of view of the business as a whole, every senior executive must assume the responsibility for training their younger managers—family and non-family. In this way the concept of succession planning and of mentoring successors is not limited to the top job but is, instead, pushed down throughout the organization as an ongoing fundamental part of every senior manager's duty. Indeed, the development of future leaders is essential to the perpetuation of every institution, the organizational analog of individual generativity. The strongest argument for asking non-family managers to devote time and effort to the process is that mentoring is essential to continuity in the business. One business owner gathered his senior executives and presented the case this way:

You have a problem. Unless I am able to train my daughter effectively to take charge of this business the continuity of the business is uncertain. If there is no succession I will probably sell the company. But I also have a problem. Unless I am able to recruit your collaboration in helping me coach her, I stand a chance of losing or alienating my most valuable senior executives. What should we do about this?

Often the parents have no trouble enlisting the support of their executives. Owners of successful family companies usually surround themselves with loyal and capable professionals who tell them the truth and understand the importance of family in the company. It is not uncommon for non-family managers to regard it as an honor to mentor the owner's children; being selected for this role affirms their value to the company and the family and the security of their position. Mentors are chosen not just for their skills and expertise but for their personal qualities. They are highly trusted as people who are devoted to the company. They tend to be nurturing individuals, who take pleasure in teaching others. Usually, they have a good sense of the distinctive issues of managing a family business, or they seek some formal training in those issues.

Mentors have to feel secure enough about their own position in the company and their own capabilities not to be threatened by the up-and-coming successor for whose development they are responsible. This means not picking people whose careers have peaked and who are in dead-end jobs, and instead choosing executives who are still making important contributions and could, if ever replaced in the family company, find other equally good opportunities.

Talented and ambitious non-family managers such as Charley Kirk of IBM—no matter how well they understand the central place of the family—often see young family members as rivals for power and position. Because competition between mentor and mentee can seriously complicate the mentoring process, family companies that plan the process well avoid assigning the young people to non-family executives of the same age and generation. The non-family executives chosen as mentors are typically in a "bridge generation," approximately halfway in age between the younger generation members and the senior leaders. Thus, if the juniors are in their early thirties and the seniors in their seventies, the mentors are commonly in their fifties. At this age, non-family managers are at the pinnacle of their careers and are usually in touch with cutting-edge technologies and strategies being taught in the business schools. They have the vitality and enthusiasm that permits young people to relate to them as coaches and "big brothers." Yet they are old enough and secure enough in their positions not to regard the young family members as immediate rivals; they have reached the stage of life when generative concerns have become important to them.

How the older-generation leaders define the mentoring process and communicate it to others in the company is critical to recruiting help and support for the process. The family leaders must explain to those selected as mentors what skills they are expected to impart and what the criteria of success will be. Most important, the seniors make very clear that the juniors must be held to strict standards of performance, and their progress accurately reported to elder family members. In many companies with mentoring plans, of course, the process is not limited to junior members of the family but also includes non-family employees who aspire to positions in top management.

Mentors cannot be imposed on mentees. If a mentoring relationship is to succeed, the juniors have to be given some power to choose. In larger family companies, the family leaders may identify five or six senior executives from whom the next-generation members can select a mentor. The family leaders meet with the chosen mentors to explain the goals of the program and what is expected of them. From time to time, the mentoring group meets on their own to assess the progress of the mentees and how the program can be strengthened. The mentoring group has responsibility not only for teaching but for ensuring the proper climate in the company for mentee development. This may mean, for example, speaking up for them to top management to ensure that their accomplishments are recognized and they receive opportunities for promotion. It may mean quashing false rumors about people who might lose their jobs to make way for promotion of young heirs. The members of the mentoring group often become a support group for each other, exchanging ideas and at times addressing the owner with one voice to remove roadblocks to successor development.

Some family owners have gone outside the company to hire executives who will make good mentors in addition to handling other responsibilities. For example, the Beaubiens, owners of Telemedia Inc., recruited the former dean of one of Canada's best business schools to head their family office. This man had worked with students for many years. He had a reputation for understanding young people and the Beaubiens felt he would make a good mentor for their two sons and daughter in the company. The choice was not made by the parents alone, however. Their children were also involved in the process and had a tremendous amount of respect for the person who was selected.

The owner of one engineering firm in New Jersey recognized that he couldn't teach his son and designated heir all that the young man needed to know to succeed him. Dick Monsen of Monsen Engineering, whose company installs and services air-conditioning systems, was fifty-nine years old and expected to retire in ten years. He hired three outsiders as a mentoring team for his son, Eric. The novel mentoring program created for Eric was designed to shape him into a company president within a decade. While the son had talent in sales and marketing, he had never held a management position. He also lacked the technical sophistication of his father, who has an engineering degree from MIT.

The father hired a chief operating officer and a chief financial officer who were given specific responsibility for teaching Eric what he needed to know. As an incentive, the two executives were offered stock in the company, which gave them a long-run stake in seeing Eric succeed. "Does it ever occur to me that Eric had better do a good job?" asked the COO, Gene Savetierre. "Yes, I'm going to be collecting money from this company." In preparation for their role, both Savetierre and chief financial officer Joe Coyle made a point of educating themselves about basic family business issues through seminars and substantial reading. In addition, a consultant was brought in to serve as an executive coach for Eric and a member of the mentoring team.[6]

Mentoring Multiple Successors: Siblings and Cousins

While heightening awareness of the mentoring effort throughout the company, seniors must also avoid raising expectations that any of their offspring is guaranteed the top job. Mentoring takes place relatively early in the succession process, and it is therefore important to leave open the possibility that the potential successor or successors may not, in the final analysis, prove capable of leading the company. Paradoxically, for parents to be effective mentors, they must accept the possibility of failure. Without it, successors cannot establish their credibility and the mentoring process may be anchored on parental wishful thinking rather than the reality of the situation.

Parents have an obligation to communicate very clearly to potential successors the goals of the mentoring process, the yardsticks that will be used to measure their progress, and the duration of the process. The juniors need to have assurances that the process will not be drawn out and that if they pass all the tests in the prescribed areas, they will eventually be given leadership opportunities. Potential successors always face the risk that elders who are unwilling to relinquish power will keep "moving the goalposts," devising new tests and standards to justify remaining in control. If the mentoring process is unnecessarily drawn out, the mentees may become cynical and lose the incentive to continue.

Similar caveats apply to successors in companies moving toward sibling or cousin systems in the next generation. When there are several potential successor candidates, all can be groomed at approximately the same time without raising the expectations of any one of them. The same requirements for skill building, performance testing, and data gathering that apply to single-owner companies are central to the mentoring of future partners in these larger and more complex companies.

But the mentoring process in these systems must also be designed to foster collaboration between the partners-to-be. Indeed, the process should provide tests of whether all are capable of working together. In addition to evaluating each sibling's or cousin's performance in various job assignments, all should be evaluated on how well they work with the others to achieve common goals. If there is evidence that the group cannot work collaboratively, the seniors may want to rethink their future plan, perhaps dropping from it any of those who demonstrate during the mentoring period that they may not function well in the group—or pose an obstacle to achieving its goals.

When there are several successors who will be partners in the next generation, mentoring becomes a bigger project and it is even more essential to have a plan that guides the stages of the process. Some companies assign each sibling to a senior manager. Other companies employ the rotation system, with each department head serving as a mentor during the time the young person has an assignment in the department. Because siblings will tend to become somewhat specialized in skills, depending on their aptitudes and interests, they may gravitate to one department or another, or, in a larger business, to a particular division. The senior managers of these departments may therefore assume a larger role in their mentoring. In companies owned by partners, each offspring tends to be mentored by his or her parent and thus often specializes in the same areas as the parent.[7] This is not always desirable, for a number of reasons. First, the mentoring period should test the successors' aptitudes in a variety of skills and expose them to the full range of the company's activities. Second, aptitudes and interests don't necessarily run in families, and management will not be able to evaluate the candidate's capabilities if he or she is mentored only by the parent.

One potentially tricky situation occurs if the parent devotes more time to mentoring one sibling over the others. This appearance of favoritism can aggravate existing rivalries among siblings. However, it is often unavoidable if the parent has decided that one sibling will inevitably become "first among equals" in the partnership and therefore needs more attention from the parent in order to develop leadership and deal-making skills. In some larger companies I have seen, the parent gets around the favoritism issue by mentoring the siblings as a group, meeting with all of them together to provide instruction and engage in modeling behavior for the benefit of all.

Quite commonly in cousin consortiums potential successors are mentored by an uncle or an aunt. As we've seen in the Lombardi case, this situation can work when there is trust and affection among members of the extended family. But it also raises touchy psychological and political issues. Where interbranch rivalries exist, some family members may fear that aunts or uncles cannot act as impartial and dedicated mentors if their own children are also potential successors. At best they provide little help to the offspring of a sibling; at worst, they may actually hinder a young niece or nephew's career. For their part, aunts and uncles serving as mentors to offspring from another branch may be concerned that their young mentees may pass on inside information about their department's work to rival sibling partners in the senior generation.

Whoever does the mentoring, one of the most important tasks in building a sibling system is to strengthen the bond among the team members. This is done in some families by planning activities for the group that bring them closer together, such as sending them all to executive development programs where they spend two or three weeks learning together. Siblings are encouraged to engage in team activities, such as sailing together or going on an Outward Bound expedition or using similar opportunities to learn experientially how to cooperate under intense circumstances. They often establish regular weekly meetings or lunches at which they discuss among themselves how the mentoring is going; they may then give the seniors feedback on how the process is going and how it can be improved. Some companies design special projects that foster cooperation in the group. For example, the siblings may be given responsibility for developing an outside board for the company. Together, they spell out the qualifications for directors, recruit and interview candidates, and make recommendations to the seniors on the structure and composition of the board.

Besides all the other skills that must be mastered by successors in any family company, the cousins are trained to cope with the special requirements of businesses at this stage of development. They learn to function within complex governance structures such as boards and family councils, to be sensitive to the concerns of different branches of the family, and to manage shareholder and dividend policies. During the mentoring period, cousins who will be working together in top management may be asked to tackle group assignments (similar to those mentioned for siblings) that test their ability to work as a team and produce results. Some cousin companies send junior family members to examine the governance structures as well as shareholder and dividend policies in other businesses of comparable size—including public companies.

Mentoring by a Parent

In the final analysis there are many responsibilities in a family business that can only be effectively taught to the next generation by a senior parent or other closely related family members who hold leadership positions. As I have indicated, it is difficult to have a mentoring relationship between a parent and child. Under what conditions, then, might we expect parental mentoring to take place in a way that circumvents at least some of the potential difficulties associated with this complex overlap of roles? To explore this question we must first understand the differences between parenting and mentoring.

Parenting is invested with a great deal of emotionality. Mentoring, by contrast, is instrumental in the sense that it revolves around the transfer of a set of skills and expertise from the mentor to the mentee. For this to occur mentee and mentor must have mutual respect for each other's competence as well as a certain degree of psychological distance. In mentoring there is an insistence on measuring up to the stricter standards of the work world. The relationship is one of interdependence—not dependence. To be effective, the mentor cannot spoon-feed the mentee. Instead, the mentor's job is to create a learning context that will motivate the mentee to do what needs to be done. The young person being developed is actively involved in shaping the learning process. While there is an implicit differential in authority between mentor and mentee, the emphasis placed on self-initiated learning makes the relationship inherently less hierarchical. The mentor can help in setting conditions for learning and structuring choices, but ultimately it is the mentee who must make the choices and live with the consequences.

One of the important roles of a mentor in any business is to make certain that the interests of the individual mentee are congruent with those of the organization. Young successors-to-be are often tempted to pursue training and interests in the company that do not promise to contribute anything to the short- or long-term needs of the business. The mentor's job is to rein in the mentee and look for ways that the mentee can grow within the organization while making a contribution that is genuinely needed. As obvious as this sounds, it is difficult for a parent to maintain this firm posture with his or her child.

Consider one fairly common example: A father who was mentoring his son in a large family real estate company gave in to the son's desire to buy a fast-food franchise in order to learn more about business. The purchase of a fast-food franchise made little strategic sense for a real estate company, and whether the son could learn much of value to the business from it was questionable at best. But the father was eager to please his son and reluctantly agreed to invest in the franchise. The decision was based more on affection than a hard evaluation of whether or not the franchise would ultimately serve his son's developmental needs. Of course, both father and son may have had other motivations for pursuing the franchise arrangement. On a more unconscious level, for example, the father may well have wanted his son out of the core business, fearing that the young man would ultimately replace him. The son, for his part, may have been less interested in going into the food business than in getting out from under his father's shadow.

The franchise failed. Not only did the son learn little of value to the real estate business, his venture soaked up valuable resources from the family company. The father compromised his role as mentor by allowing love to interfere with his judgment about the potential risks that this deal would have for the son's development.

Parents' own early experiences will influence their willingness and capacity to mentor. Successful business owners have usually gotten considerable help from others along the way—from a spouse, a predecessor, or trusted senior managers who guided their development. As they get older, they are increasingly aware of a need to repay that debt and become a mentor to others. Their careers have usually reached a pinnacle, and the wish to mentor reinforces their sense of having "made it." Now it becomes important for the older person to see his or her ideas, philosophy, or unique approach to life passed on to the young. For the mentor, establishing a relationship with a talented young protégé who is pursuing a career in the same field becomes a rejuvenating experience that revives a sense of youth and playfulness. Levinson indicates the developmental importance of the experience:

Being a mentor with young adults is one of the most significant relationships available to a man in middle adulthood. The distinctive satisfaction of the mentor lies in furthering the development of young men and women—facilitating their efforts to form and live out their Dreams, to lead better lives according to their own values and abilities. Nurturing the development of children and adolescents is a major, age-appropriate function of early adulthood. It is the more elemental form of the parental impulse. During middle adulthood, a man can take a further step and nurture the development of young adults. Mentoring utilizes the parental impulse, but it is more complex and requires some degree of mid-life individuation. As he gains a stronger sense of self, and of his own continuing development in middle adulthood, a man is more able to foster the development of young adults.[8]

Most mentor-mentee relationships serve an important—often critical—function in the lives of both individuals for a defined period of time. Only rarely do they go on past the time when the mentee completes the mid-life transition:

The mentoring relationship lasts perhaps two or three years on the average, eight to ten at most. It may end when one man moves, changes jobs or dies. Sometimes it comes to a natural end and, after a cooling-off period, the pair form a warm but modest friendship. . . . Most often, however, an intense mentor relationship ends with strong conflict and bad feelings on both sides. The young man may have powerful feelings of bitterness, rancor, grief abandonment, liberation and rejuvenation. The sense of resonance is lost. The mentor he formerly loved and admired is now experienced as destructively critical and demanding, or as seeking to make one over in his own image rather than fostering one's individuality and independence. . . . The mentor, for his part, finds the young man inexplicably touchy, unreceptive to even the best counsel, irrationally rebellious and ungrateful. By the time they are through, there is generally some validity in each one's criticism of the other.[9]

One question that arises about parental mentoring in a family business is whether the parent-child bond can survive such turbulent emotions. Both parent and adult offspring will want the family relationship to survive the mentoring period in the business. Mentoring may place added strains on a parent-child relationship that is already problematic. But the risks of an explosive rupture when the mentoring period comes to an end may be exaggerated.

Kramm, who has studied mentoring relationships (although not parent-child pairs) has pointed out that how the separation phase of the mentoring relationship ends depends upon timing. If on the one hand the mentoring period goes on too long, either the mentor or the mentee is "likely to resent the other as the relationship becomes unresponsive to the individual's changing needs and concerns." On the other hand, if the two are separated prematurely, before their emotional needs have been satisfied, one or the other party will suffer feelings of loss, abandonment, and anger. Kramm's in-depth interviews with eighteen mentoring pairs in non-family organizations indicates that the relationship does not have to end with bitter feelings. On the contrary, mentors and mentees may remain friends long after the period of deep emotional involvement has concluded:

The separation phase is a period of loss, but it can be a period of excitement as well. If the separation is timely, the senior manager takes pride in seeing someone she helped move on to positions of greater responsibility. Great satisfaction comes from knowing that she helped a young manager learn critical skills, develop self-confidence, and advance in the organization. Similarly, the young manager feels a personal accomplishment in moving on and a positive challenge in operating effectively without the senior manager's close guidance.[10]

Whatever the risks, parents commonly do much of the mentoring of offspring in family businesses. In smaller family companies parental mentoring is practically unavoidable. In these systems unless the parent becomes actively involved in the training of the next generation, he or she is unlikely to have capable successors who will continue the business. Even in larger family companies that have capable non-family senior executives who can be enlisted as mentors, there are things that young potential successors must learn that only the parents can teach. For example, only a parent owner can guide a son or daughter in applying family values to day-to-day business practice, in managing sensitive issues of relations with non-family employees, and in understanding proper behavior for family members in the community.

How Parental Mentoring Ends

If parent and offspring can get beyond the psychological challenges associated with the working together stage—if the mentoring is proceeding well—the mentee will be learning the subtler aspects of the parent's philosophy and business savvy that will position him or her to contribute to the organization's future. The parent will gain the pleasure of seeing his or her offspring win the approval of others in the company and carry on some of the ideas and traditions that are part of the parent's legacy.

At some point in the relationship, however, the mentee will begin to articulate his or her own ideas about the company's future. If the mentee is a dynamic individual—in the image of the parent—he or she is bound to develop an original vision of the future. Very likely that vision is bound up with new technologies and approaches to management that are on the cutting edge of what the younger generation is learning in colleges and business schools. At this stage of life the parents are thinking of security, while the eager young are ready to take risks in order to make their own Dreams happen.

The mentoring relationship may then take a difficult turn. The potential for conflict over ideas and goals may become part of a power struggle between parent and offspring over the company's future. The mentor relationship is nearing an end. The mentee feels there is little more to be learned from the parent. The parent may feel that his or her position and legacy are threatened. If the mentee succeeds in gaining power, he or she may well change the company so fundamentally that it will no longer embody the values the parent cherishes.

These are the circumstances in which some mentoring relationships end in the disillusionment and bitterness described by Levinson. It happens in some cases of parental mentoring as well as in other mentoring relationships. In those business families that manage to avoid such a blowup, the mentoring relationship continues formally—by mutual consent—but without much further learning going on. That is, the mentee still honors the parent as mentor, paying dutiful respect to the elder's opinions and advice. In reality, however, the son or daughter understands that some of the parent's views are becoming dated and can no longer be relied on as a beacon for the company. The successor-to-be is now guided by his or her own vision and insights. Nevertheless, he continues to outwardly acknowledge the authority of the elder.

Underlying the process is an unspoken code in which both mentor and mentee understand each other's developmental needs but rarely talk about them. They may still clash occasionally, but they will battle only on selected, very sensitive issues. The outward forms of the mentoring ritual are preserved, but the inner reality has been transformed. To soften any tensions that arise from the de facto end of the mentoring process, both parent and offspring may reach out to the other in order to rediscover activities outside the business which they have enjoyed together in the past. They may continue to go fishing or collaborate in philanthropic or community activities. Once again, the pleasure of shared activities serves to keep the bond from loosening.

Naturally, this new stage of the relationship depends on the generosity that each is able to extend to the other—and an appreciation of the ironies of their shifting relationship. In one company, a son who had been mentored by his father had led the company through a tremendous growth spurt during this period. While his father gave him full credit for this accomplishment, the son publicly attributed most of the growth to his father's leadership.

Even though it calls for face-saving gestures by both generations, this post-mentoring ritual, which can go on for years, never seems to lose its authenticity or become hypocritical. The reason for this, I believe, is that it is based on genuine caring by both parent and successor. It stems from true generativity—a continuing celebration of their joint achievement during the mentoring phase.

CHAPTER 9

Anointment and Taking Charge

I N 1986, Frederick Wang, the oldest of two sons of Dr. An Wang, was named president of Wang Laboratories Inc. Fred Wang was thirty-six years old, had a bachelor's degree in mathematics from Brown University, and had worked at Wang Labs in various jobs since joining the company in 1972. While he was liked and respected by his peers, he would probably not have been offered the presidency had he not been An Wang's oldest son. Fred Wang took charge of the company, moreover, at an especially perilous time in its history, providing a perfect illustration of how circumstances can greatly decrease the odds that a leadership transition will "take."

The company was one of the premier computer giants of its time, with sales well in excess of $2 billion a year and a work force of over 30,000 employees. But Wang had gradually been losing market share. By the mid-1980s the company was entering a crucial phase in its development. Competition in the market for personal computers and other desktop products such as calculators was becoming increasingly stiff. It was clear that An Wang's successor would face a formidable challenge in repositioning the company to regain its leadership in the rapidly growing personal computer field.

Some analysts regarded Fred Wang as an impatient, contentious, and overbearing manager who would have a difficult time commanding the respect that his father had earned among engineers, scientists, and managers, let alone the outside directors. Press reports from that time suggest that Fred was promoted prematurely because his sick and aging father could no longer keep up with the stress from the crisis that the company was undergoing. Even before Fred was nominated to succeed his father, board members had expressed doubts about the son:

For years they had been quite concerned about Fred. Members of the board of directors had worried that Fred did not have the experience, the judgment—the overall heft—to lead the company. Ever since the middle of the 1980s, outside directors had made repeated efforts to persuade the Doctor to bring in a professional manager; to give Fred an impressive title if need be, but to avoid placing the young man in operational control of this sprawling, worldwide corporation in the thick of the most competitive industry on earth. The outside directors had beseeched the Doctor to find the smartest, most experienced person available to run the company. An Wang would not yield. To the directors he said: "He is my son. He can do it."[1]

Fred Wang could not do it. He was unable to reverse the company's decline, and in 1989 his father was forced to fire him. He was replaced by a senior non-family manager, who promptly restructured the company and took it in an entirely new strategic direction. By the early 1990s, however, Wang Laboratories had dwindled to a fraction of its former size. In return for an infusion of cash of $100 million from IBM—the company that An Wang had once vowed to overtake—the company agreed to sell its customers IBM equipment.

It would be unfair to conclude that the downfall of Wang Laboratories was entirely due to Fred's premature promotion to the top job. However, the evidence certainly suggests that it was a mistake of cosmic proportions to promote a relatively young and inexperienced family member to the presidency at such a critical juncture in the company's history. An Wang is not the only business founder who made an unwise choice of a successor. Other family companies, once household names—Schwinn bicycles, Steinway pianos, Steinberg's—have fallen by the wayside in part because of successors who did not have the right stuff. By and large, family companies pay too little attention to developing systematic methods of testing and evaluating successors before they are given major responsibility for the company.

This chapter will examine the most important tasks to be accomplished during the taking-charge phase of a successor's development. During this phase, designated successors are usually between thirty-five and forty years old; they are now committed to careers in the business. We will consider first the developmental challenges they face at this stage of their lives and why rigorous tests and assessments of their leadership are essential to establishing their authority in the business and credibility with major stakeholders. Second, we will examine some of the challenges of preparing a team of siblings or cousins to take charge of a family company. Finally, we will discuss how a transition in leadership should be planned and announced in the company as well as the testing and intrigues the new leader can expect to face after an initial honeymoon phase.

Developmental Challenges

Adults in their thirties are transitioning out of what Levinson refers to as the "novice phase" of early adulthood and entering the "settling-down" period. This is the time of life when they seek to secure a presence and an identity in the adult world. The individual has already forged a Dream and may have made some fundamental life choices regarding occupation and marriage. The key issue typically is not so much "What is my Dream?" but "How do I make my Dream a reality?"

For designated successors in a family business, the challenge is to secure their claim to leadership of the company. Having committed themselves to the company, they are eager to get on with the realization of their Dream through it. Nevertheless, some of them are continually nagged by doubts. The most capable young leaders are still keenly aware of other attractive career options open to them. They wrestle with such questions as: "Will I be allowed to show what I can do?" "Will I be able to control my own destiny and that of the company?" At this stage the potential successor must establish his or her credibility with the seniors, but, at the same time, assert his or her independence. Levinson points out the built-in dilemma posed by these conflicting needs:

On the one hand, a man [in his thirties] wants to be more independent, more true to himself and less vulnerable to pressures and blandishments from others. On the other hand, he seeks affirmation by society. Speaking with his own voice is important, even if no one listens—but he especially wants to be heard and respected and given the rewards that are his due. The wish for independence leads him to do what he alone considers most essential, regardless of consequences; the wish for affirmation makes him sensitive to the response of others and susceptible to their influence.[2]

The process by which a successor is "affirmed" is complex, since it depends not just on what he or she is able to accomplish by him- or herself; it requires the endorsement of the senior generation as well. It is one thing to establish oneself in the world at large, and quite another to do so under the ever-present shadow of parents and other family elders. Whether consciously or not, many seniors are reluctant to empower members of the next generation because doing so implies they eventually must move out of the way and turn over control to them. Consequently, many successors at this stage are unable to attain the degree of independence and legitimacy they seek.

In my work with family businesses I have met many men and women in their late thirties and early forties who are still treated as adolescents by their parents. Prolonged dependence of young adults on their parents can have serious psychological consequences. How can young adults feel like responsible adults and parents to their own children when they are continually made to feel like children themselves, as many are in a family company? The problem is compounded when, as often happens, the young person's parents are paying for some or all of his or her household expenses, including the food the family eats, the clothing that they wear, and the cost of the childrens' educations. Many would-be successors in this situation try to compensate for their insecurities by adorning themselves with the trappings of success, such as grand titles, expensive cars and clothing, and other conspicuous displays of wealth. Paradoxically, this behavior usually only further erodes the successor's authority in the eyes of his or her own family as well as among employees of the business.

At work, the need to "speak with their own voice" often motivates new leaders to quickly implement organizational changes. Necessary as these changes may be from a business standpoint, they are also driven by the young leaders' psychological need to position the company in a way that will enable them to fulfill their own ideas and aspirations. Changes in a family company's direction and strategy typically grow out of the young leaders' wish for more independence and autonomy, their yearning to put their own stamp on the business.

However, every new initiative will be evaluated against the backdrop of traditional ways and past obligations. Whether it's a major reorganization, a strategic shift, or an investment in a new technology, the previous leader and other senior members of the old team are likely to question every proposed change. They may even regard any departure from the status quo as personal criticism, as a reminder of the obsolescence of their ideas and methods. Opposition from the elders may blind the young leader to the potential shortcomings of the changes he or she is so eager to introduce. The successor-to-be may then undervalue the usefulness of particular individuals, strategies, and procedures simply because they are associated with the old regime.

One of the biggest challenges facing new leaders at this stage is to consolidate control of the organization while still honoring the achievements and perspectives of the previous leadership. In order to successfully negotiate the process of taking charge, young leaders must assemble a team of people who are loyal to them and who understand the direction they wish to take the company. That often requires the retirement of many of the senior family and non-family managers to whom the family may be deeply indebted for long years of service. Many of these older managers may have served as mentors to young successors when they were learning the ropes. The fact that most family companies do not have a mandatory retirement age further complicates this process. Young leaders must therefore learn a delicate balancing act if they are to succeed at taking charge: They must negotiate the exit of the old guard without establishing a reputation as being heartless or ungrateful.

Earning It: How Young Successors Prove Their Mettle

We have seen that to secure their leadership role, successors must be welcomed into what Levinson referred to as "the world of the seniors." To accomplish this, the successor must understand the subtle but critical distinction between power and authority. Power refers to a successor's capacity to influence the behavior of others. Authority, in contrast, refers to the successor's *right* to influence the behavior of others. At first glance the distinction may seem academic, but on closer scrutiny its significance becomes forcefully evident. Power is often derived from the simple fact that the successor happens to be a member of the owning family. As such, he or she is assumed to have a special connection to the ultimate bosses of the system and thus considerable influence over the behavior of others. Authority, unlike power, has to be earned. It flows from the bottom up, not from the top down. It depends in great measure on the willingness of the followers to ascribe competence, trustworthiness, and leadership ability to the successor. The more a successor relies on the power that flows from his or her connection to the family, the less authority he or she is likely to acquire. Attempting to exercise leadership without authority is always a rather risky proposition. As Machiavelli suggested, those who acquire power through privilege have to struggle greatly to retain it, whereas those who become rulers through hardship and toil experience great difficulty acquiring power but can then hold it with ease.[3]

Earning authority in the business requires visible accomplishments. While good schooling helps, it is only through repeated success meeting challenging objectives that successors earn the respect of those who will eventually be their followers. Dazzling titles, large offices, and conspicuous displays of wealth and power will not accomplish this.

Typically, successors prove their effectiveness by their actions in critical business situations—by turning a particular department around, by increasing the sales figures in significant ways, by developing and introducing a new product line, by penetrating a new market, by resolving a serious production problem or a crisis such as a labor strike or a serious financial entanglement. The best place for successors to develop—and demonstrate—their capabilities is in a line position rather than a staff job. Successors given responsibility for the financial results of a division or some other business unit can be measured by whether or not they deliver on their goals. By consistently achieving their financial goals, or even exceeding those targets, they provide visible evidence of their capacity for doing the same for the whole company.

The contrasting experiences of two cousins in a multinational beer company show why jobs that have measurable goals are critical to a successor's development. Herbert and Andrew Garth[4] are in their late thirties. Both have MBAs from prestigious universities and entered the family company at about the same time. Both are bright, motivated, and show aptitude for leadership. Herbert has been largely involved in staff work, helping to develop strategy and keeping the board of directors informed about policy decisions. Herbert has become a kind of alter ego to his father, the chairman of the company. He advises on complex financial, legal, and strategic issues that no one else at headquarters wants to handle. Although also based at headquarters, Andrew, by contrast, is in charge of a worldwide sales staff. In just five years, he has doubled foreign sales of the company's beer through an innovative global marketing campaign. Herbert is held in high esteem by senior managers, but Andrew has impressed everyone in the company as an executive who produces results—the kind of leader needed for the future growth of the business. While senior managers acknowledge that Herbert has a lot of raw talent, they find it difficult to describe what he actually does; some complain that in management meetings, he tends to offer theoretical solutions to real-world problems instead of volunteering to take on the problems and fix them.

As this example suggests, the kinds of jobs assigned to successors can determine whether they succeed or fail at dealing with the main issue at this life stage—which is to demonstrate their capabilities to themselves and other key persons in the company. As Goethe put it: "What you have inherited . . . you must earn to possess."

Affirmation from the Seniors

The blessing of the elders is also crucial for the new leaders to establish their authority. The managers and other employees need to know that proven, strong leaders in the older generation endorse the next generation's readiness to lead the company into the future. This validation is a process, not just an announcement to the company and the media (although that may help at the appropriate time). The anointment process is carried out over an extended period, although not an indefinite one—it usually lasts three to five years. During this time the seniors must provide concrete evidence to stakeholders of the successor's maturity and accomplishments. By so doing, they convey their trust in the successor's judgment and confidence in his or her ability to lead.

The elders have to step aside at appropriate times and delegate important tasks to the successors, at the risk of costly mistakes that might have grave consequences for the company and, perhaps, for the economic security of the elders themselves. I am not arguing for recklessness, or for devising impossible assignments for potential successors who may not yet be ready to handle them. However, it is also reckless to wait until successors are in the pilot's seat before their teachers determine whether they know how to fly. In effective successions, there are no surprises. The successors and their team need to be battle-tested before the leadership transfer takes place; afterward, they will have to face challenges alone, when the seniors may no longer be around to give advice.

So some risks are necessary to a successor's development. But will seniors be willing to take them if their wealth and retirement income are not secure? A bungled succession can place in jeopardy wealth that has taken years to accumulate. Many older business owners who have their wealth tied up in the family company do not realize how quickly it can be wiped out as a result of a successors' mistakes. They place their own personal assets at risk unnecessarily, by, for example, offering their homes as collateral for loans to finance the successor's new ventures or expansion plans for the family business. One reason some business owners don't realize the risks is the feeling of invulnerability that comes from having had everything they have touched turn to gold. So what can ever go wrong? Another reason they'll take big chances on their children is out of a sense of parental obligation.

Nevertheless, experience shows that to take charge successfully, juniors must learn to live with the consequences of their decisions. To merit the rewards of high office, they first have to accept some of the responsibilities and risks inherent in top-level positions. Older business owners who have taken steps to diversify their investment portfolios and to safeguard their retirement income will feel better about extending such opportunities to their successors. This raises complex questions about the relationship between retirement planning and succession planning, which I will take up later. For now, suffice it to say that unless the seniors do an adequate job of providing for their own financial security, they will not be insulated from the effects of poor decisions by their successors. They will therefore be less willing to step aside and create conditions that will ultimately foster the empowerment of the juniors.[5]

The Biggest Challenge: Creating a Vision

Even when successors pass all the tests and demonstrate exceptional competence, they may not have done enough to establish their claim to leadership. True leaders offer a vision of the future that inspires employees and shareholders and gives the company a meaningful direction. The vision articulated by the successor builds on the foundation of the family's Shared Dream and defines values that profoundly influence the company's culture, its strategy, its choice of products, and its relationships to key stakeholders.

At this stage of life, many young leaders are focusing their efforts on consolidating their power base, not on creating a new vision to guide the company. To succeed, however, they must walk at least a few steps ahead of their followers and keep the big questions constantly in mind: "Who are we? Where are we going and why?" As we saw in chapter 4, developing and articulating such a vision is not an easy process. It takes time; it takes effort. The vision must convey both respect for what has come before and the expectation of exciting change. The new leader exhibits an understanding of the conditions that the family business will face in the future and proposes new and innovative management responses. By imparting a new direction and new sense of purpose, successors and their team revitalize the company and earn their place in the world of the seniors.

Clearly, the process I have described goes beyond the rather contrived definition of a vision that one finds in many how-to books on management. In principle, I am certainly not opposed to spelling out a vision in a formal "statement." But writing it down on paper is not enough to achieve the successor's purposes. Successors must take every opportunity to inform the critical stakeholders—the family, the shareholders, the senior managers, key employees—of the direction they intend to take. The successor must make the case with conviction and passion for why this direction makes sense and why it will carry the company to new heights of accomplishment. Otherwise, people will see it as an artifice and will be skeptical of the successor's authenticity as a leader. This is one of the fundamental reasons why the previous leadership cannot just hand a vision of the future to the new leadership. It has to be articulated by those who will have the challenge of carrying it out.

During this phase the succession process looks very much like a relay race. To maximize the team's performance, the runner with the baton must not slow down before placing it in the next runner's hand. Likewise, the next runner must start running before being handed the baton and then take off at full speed. After passing the baton, however, the first runner steps out of the way and allows the next team member to take charge of the team's effort. Each has a role to play. However, the burden of seeing that the transition takes place without missing a beat falls disproportionately on the shoulders of the runner taking the hand-off. For unless the successor takes off with a burst of speed, the team will lose time and his or her leadership will not be seen as legitimate.

More often than not, however, the emphasis is on establishing the successor's credibility within the business—that is, with the company's managers and employees, its key customers, suppliers, and bankers. While it is necessary for successors to demonstrate their ability to manage and build the business, that is not sufficient to ensure their success as leaders of a family company. In order for successors to emerge triumphant from the anointment process, their leadership has to be strongly endorsed by the family and by the principal shareholders. This is one of the unique aspects of succession in a family enterprise. Successors must show by their actions that they understand they are ultimately accountable to the shareholder group, including those who do not work in the company. They need to demonstrate that they will keep the shareholders informed of the company's goals and plans and will attend to their need for dividends and their desire for a voice in determining governance policies.

Likewise, they must celebrate the family and the value, past and present, that other family members have brought to the enterprise. By virtue of their leadership of the company, successors can have a dramatic impact on the economic well-being of other family members. They thus become ipso facto leaders (though often not the only leaders) in the family. By advising a relative's children in their careers, for example, or using their contacts to help family members, or providing opportunities for them within the company, successors show they will promote the aspirations of individual family members and not just their own interests and those of the business. They may also instruct nonparticipating family members about the benefits of having a business in the family and, when appropriate, seek their advice in solving shareholder and governance issues. They do whatever they can to relieve the pressures on the families of members working in the business. By their participation in forums such as family councils, they show that they respect the family's right to be heard on certain issues affecting the business and its governance.

Siblings and Cousins: Realizing Aspirations Through the Team

In both sibling and cousin companies, successors often have to function as members of a team. While this is particularly true of those companies in which all (or most) siblings and cousins will be directly involved with the management of the business, collaboration is also essential in those systems in which some of the siblings or cousin owners choose not to go into the business. In either case, they must continue to learn how to adjust their individual Dreams to the Shared Dream, even after they have made their commitment to collaborate as shareholders. Sibling or cousin partners continue to confront situations in which their individual aspirations have to be subordinated to the collective effort. Negotiating the tension between individual and collective demands takes an unusual set of qualities.

Five siblings who inherited a shoe manufacturing firm provide a good example. After the father's death, the mother strongly supported the idea of the five working together in the business. The siblings had always enjoyed a close relationship and felt that they could make a partnership arrangement work. About five years into the experiment, however, the youngest brother, then in his mid-thirties, began to have serious doubts. What he had admired most about his father was his independence, the freedom to make his own decisions; his father had been "master of his fate." Believing he could not realize his own Dream in the partnership, the son sold his shares and left the company to start his own business. The decision was painful because he felt that he was betraying his siblings as well as the family Dream. In addition, it was clear that his net worth would have grown far more rapidly if he had left his assets in the family business rather than starting his new venture. In his own colorful words, he preferred to be "the head of a mouse rather than the tail of a lion."

Siblings who choose to stay together reach a different conclusion. They conclude that the benefits of familial collaboration—the fun of working with brothers and sisters, the payoff from pooling assets, and the satisfaction of building a legacy for their children—outweigh the sacrifices of individual autonomy that are often necessary in a partnership. (In practice, many siblings give too little attention to estimating the economic benefits of staying in a partnership as opposed to starting their own business.)

To enter the world of seniors, each sibling in a partnership still has to establish credibility as a manager in the business and as a caring relative in the family—but with a difference. It is more important for the partners to convey a collective presence to stakeholders and the community, a sense that the whole is greater than the sum of the parts. Therein lies the secret of successful sibling partnerships, and the answer to skeptics who consider such arrangements unworkable.

Siblings convey a collective presence in a variety of ways, such as showing they are willing to make compromises with their own ego needs in order to work as part of a team in the long run. Often a cooperative bond is forged from their very need to establish a united front vis-à-vis the previous generation. This is a common development in family companies founded by a prototypical charismatic entrepreneur: The siblings band together to counteract the powerful authority inherent in the figure of the founder.

Empowering a team as a defense against a powerful parent may work as a survival strategy, but by itself it is unlikely to inspire a sibling partnership to do the hard work involved in running a business. The sibling team must consider what will happen after the parent dies. Their partnership will rest on a shaky foundation if it is built by a reactive process rather than a proactive one. The partners must substitute a more positive Shared Dream for the bonds that welded them together against a common "enemy." Otherwise, the partnership will almost surely come undone.

To establish the authority of the team, each partner also must perform in a way that enhances the perceived competency of the group as a whole. This does not necessarily mean that all of them have to be outstanding performers or leaders. It does mean all must be viewed, at a minimum, as competent or "good enough" performers.

Consider the distribution of talents in one sibling partnership made up of three brothers and a sister. Each sibling owns a fourth of the stock and all are involved in managerial roles in the family business founded by their father. The two older brothers are extraordinary performers and wonderfully caring family members. Not surprisingly, they have risen to the top, one becoming chairman and the other CEO. The sister is not a strong manager, but as a financial expert her advice is regularly sought and valued by the two leading brothers. Over the years she has made a large contribution to the business. The third brother, however, is a continuing liability to the partnership. Even though he holds the title of marketing director, he has never taken his responsibilities seriously. He consistently comes to work late and leaves early. He cannot make decisions and seldom follows through on the work he agrees to do. It is clear to everyone that, were he not a sibling, he wouldn't even be employed by the company. By condoning his poor performance, the other siblings undermine acceptance of their whole team. Senior non-family employees begin to question whether the partners have the backbone and commitment to demand equally high standards of family and non-family employees alike. Along with outside business associates, the senior employees wonder whether the shared leadership arrangement will really work.

Another barrier to sibling cooperation is raised when some brothers and sisters feel that the parents have always favored one of them over the others. In such families the "favorite child" faces a challenge requiring consummate diplomacy. The sibling who appears to have been favored must make a major gesture to defuse any lingering jealousies among his or her brothers and sisters. He or she can earn their trust for example, by demonstrating an eagerness to redress their wrongs. One way favored siblings commonly establish their bona fides with the team is to side with their brothers and sisters on issues involving conflict with the parent. In such situations, the favored sibling risks his or her own well-being but conveys a commitment to the sibling group as a whole.

In a cousin consortium, the promotions of next-generation members into the upper echelons of management may very well involve a rearrangement of coalitions among various family branches. While the amount of stock owned by each branch ultimately determines the balance of power in a cousin system, representation in the leadership is also an important yardstick of influence. Other things being relatively equal, the branch with the most members in senior management will have the most influence over the economic resources of the family. As in sibling partnerships, managerial ability alone is not sufficient to establish the authority of successors in a cousin consortium. Unless successors earn the trust of the various branches and are willing to constructively manage the political dynamics of the system, they will face many obstacles to establishing their authority during the take-charge phase.

The process of taking charge in a cousin consortium is usually much longer and considerably more political than in other systems. Lead cousins must demonstrate that they will look after the interests of *all* the branches. The transition can be less difficult, however, if the company has a board of directors with experienced outsiders that guides the development of the future leaders and ultimately empowers them.

The obstacles to entry into the seniors' world can be even more formidable when the consortium has a comparatively large group of elders who can validate or undermine the successors' authority. For instance, if one branch is dominated by elderly cousins who are passive shareholders, they are likely to want the company to pay generous dividends, and they will favor successors who express support for such a policy.

The politics of the process are not just driven by economics, however. Multigenerational cousin consortiums can be prisoners of their past. Ancient grievances can continue to roil the waters. If a forebear in one branch once betrayed a cousin in another, descendants of the wronged cousin may mistrust successors from the other branch for generations. One example is the complex case of a sixth-generation, multibillion-dollar European company entirely owned by sixty-seven shareholder cousins. The company was originally established by three brothers. They created a dynasty with three basic stirpes—branch A, branch B, and branch C. For three generations, most of the effective leaders came from branch A, descendants of the oldest founding brother. After the death of the president from that branch in the 1920s, however, leadership of the company shifted to two cousins from branch B, who had the support of the cousins in branch C. This change in the power balance created a rift between branch A and branch B. The cousins from branch A were so distressed, in fact, that they tried to sell a significant part of their holdings to a multinational competitor—unsuccessfully. The other two branches viewed this as an act of disloyalty and betrayal.

More recently, when the lead cousins from branches B and C were about to retire, the most qualified successor, as fate would have it, was in branch A. He held an MBA from a top-flight university and had an exemplary record as a leader and manager both inside and outside the family company. While all the senior cousins agreed that he was the best candidate, the cousins from branch B were reluctant to endorse his candidacy. Needless to say, the successor felt that he was being judged unfairly because of something that had happened a generation ago. He was not finally accepted as the successor until, on his own initiative, he stood up at a shareholders meeting and passionately vowed to redress any wrongs that his ancestors may have committed against the cousins in branch B. His pledge was the critical event that cemented his authority and paved the way for his entry into the world of the senior cousins.

Rising to leadership in a cousin consortium thus requires a willingness to manage a very complex group of shareholders. The most effective successors in cousin companies embrace this part of their job wholeheartedly and often invest as much time dealing with governance issues as with managing the business.

The Selection Process:
Who Ultimately Decides?

Whatever future leadership structure is envisioned, somebody must decide how the people who will serve in it will be selected. Many incumbent CEOs assume that they must make the choice by themselves. This is not always advisable, because they may tend to choose only those who are similar to them in managerial style or who agree

with their objectives. What the company needs for its future development, in fact, may be quite different.

Should the ultimate choice be left to the board as a whole, which
presumably has impartial outsiders, or a committee of the board?
Should the family council have a role, and, if so, what should it be?
Should members of the next generation who are active in the business
make the decision, since they are the ones who must make it work?

Sometimes it may be preferable to leave the choice to the juniors
rather than the seniors, because they are the ones who will have to live
with it into the future. But that option carries obvious risks. Unless the
juniors are quite mature, accommodating, and realistic about their respective strengths and weaknesses, letting them choose a successor could
aggravate rivalries and turn the choice into a destructive horse race.

The best way to avoid the complications and risks of letting either
the current or future leaders make the choice entirely on their own is
to involve other stakeholders in the decision. In some companies a
committee of outside board members is charged with nominating the
successor, but the family shareholders have to approve the nominee. In
other companies, a succession task force is established to supervise the
development of candidates and to make a nomination, which, again,
usually has to be ratified by the board or the whole shareholder group.
The task force, as we've indicated, is usually made up of trusted senior
managers, family members who may not work in the company but are
thoroughly acquainted with it, and, sometimes, an outside consultant.
In larger family companies, a senior human resources person plays a
key role because he or she usually has substantive knowledge of the
successor candidates' performance histories and of how the succession
process should be handled.

Whoever ends up making the choice, the leaders must be both
open and discreet in the way they go about doing it. On the one hand,
the process used to arrive at the choice must be transparent, so that the
successor candidates—as well as other stakeholders—do not feel it has
been arbitrary; the process acquires legitimacy when everyone sees that
it is being conducted in a fair, rigorous, and orderly manner. On the
other hand, the group making the decision must be careful to protect
the privacy of the candidates, whose character and strengths and weaknesses they examine under a microscope. Not doing so may stimulate
arguments in the family and company over the relative merits of the
candidates and trigger unnecessary competitiveness among the candidates and their supporters. Arguments of this sort undermine the
integrity of the process.

Deciding on Titles

During the selection process, the question of titles is sure to come up, especially if the company is to be led by a more or less egalitarian team. The issues surrounding the choice of titles must be resolved before the transfer goes forward.

Titles are important mostly for what they represent to the outside world. They have value in defining roles and responsibilities, but they also pose risks of conflict. Because they confer prestige within both the company and the family, they can incite jealousies not only among siblings and cousins but among spouses and family branches. Some of the fiercest succession battles are fought over titles and what they connote to different people.

Like other businesses, family companies choose titles that they believe will establish the function and authority of their officers in the eyes of the various stakeholders. But the meaning of titles is mostly in the eyes of the beholders. In some family businesses, the title of chairman is held by a retiring or retired patriarch or matriarch who no longer has much power in the running of the company. The chairman's role may include few, if any, responsibilities, especially in a family company lacking a board of directors. Sometimes, the chairman may even be a relative who has never had a significant role in the company but has been given an important title, perhaps even a salary, to enhance the person's self-esteem and keep him or her out of the managers' hair. As in many large public corporations, however, the chairman of a family company often is the dominant figure in the organization by virtue of status and the fact that he or she may control a majority of the voting shares. As the patriarch or matriarch, the chairman, moreover, is usually the most influential member of the family.

When two siblings are to become equal partners, the question of who is to be called chairman and who CEO or president raises an issue because a president or CEO is usually thought of as reporting to the chairman. In a sibling team structure, this can be a particular problem for the younger siblings who are reluctant to be seen as taking orders from or enjoying less prestige than an older brother or sister, as well as for status-conscious spouses, who do not wish to take second place publicly to the chairman's spouse. It can be an even greater problem when a younger sibling holds the title of chairman on a management team that includes older brothers and sisters.

I always try to disabuse these families of the notion that the chairman is "the boss," pointing out that in companies that have boards, the president and CEO do not report to the chairman but to the board as a whole. This seems to relieve at least some of the anxiety that equal partners feel about the prospect of treating the chairman as "the boss."

The chairman looks upward toward a critical constituency—the shareholders—and leads the board in shaping the organization's policies and strategic direction. While the board is responsible for overseeing management of the company, the CEO or president looks both outward toward the business environment and downward into the organization; he or she is responsible for implementing the mandates of the board and managing the business day to day. In some family companies, the president and chief executive officer are one and the same person, but in others there is both a CEO and a president, with the former usually subordinate to the latter. In large companies, public and private, titles offer clues to the future succession in leaders. When one individual is dominant, the person may hold all three titles of chairman, president, and CEO. When an anointed successor is almost ready to shoulder greater responsibilities, he or she may be given the title of CEO, with the senior leader retaining the chairman and president titles. In time, the successor may then become both CEO and president. At this point the senior member retains the chairman title, signaling that he or she is on the way out. Finally, the leadership transfer occurs when the younger leader assumes all three titles. With a new generation of successors, the cycle begins anew.

Many people (and some government regulators) see an inherent conflict of interest in having the same individual serve as chairman and CEO because the chairman leads the board that is responsible for overseeing the activities of the CEO. Indeed, in Germany and Scandinavian countries tough corporate governance laws prohibit the chairman of the board from also serving as CEO. In the United Kingdom, the managing director who is akin to the CEO of a company usually serves on its board, but the board has a separate chairman. Boards in both the United Kingdom and Spain tend to act less like boards in the United States than like executive committees that meet frequently and participate in management decisions. In Spain, the chief operating executive is not the president, but a "consejero delegado" appointed by the board to supervise operations. Titles in many countries are geared to what is most familiar to suppliers and customers. For example, a Spanish company that does much of its business in the United States uses the titles of chairman and CEO for its two top officers because these terms are most easily understood by American customers.

As I've indicated, family companies moving toward a leadership team sometimes rotate the title of president between partners, appoint copresidents, or establish a chief executive office with multiple leaders. These approaches to titles, usually the result of a compromise, have mixed effects. The notion of, say, two partners serving alternate terms as president maintains the appearance of the standard hierarchical management structure: There is only one president at any given time. In fact, anyone close to the organization—and the partners themselves—recognizes that the president's powers are circumscribed by the nature of the system. Each partner knows that during his or her tenure, decisions cannot be made unilaterally. The views and preferences of the other partner must be honored; otherwise, the other partner will simply reverse the first one's policies during his or her turn as president.

Outside the company, the idea of having two or more copresidents or a chief executive team may still be perceived as "oddball," and perhaps even as an indicator of a lack of internal cohesion and direction in policy. Communicating an uncommon leadership arrangement, such as copresidencies, requires unusual symbolic steps. For example, I often advise clients moving toward a sibling partnership to remodel their offices to symbolize the equality on which their collaboration rests. When two siblings became copresidents of a European company that had long been dominated by a single parent-owner, they decided to leave the former president's office unoccupied. Instead, on the floor below, they built adjoining offices of approximately equal size, connected by a boardroom furnished with a round board table—so that during meetings no single individual would seem to have a superior position at the head. Afterward, when I visited the company, the brothers proudly took me on a tour of the remodeled offices, explaining that the new design had had a more profound effect in conveying the nature of their partnership than any of the speeches they had made.

Far too much emotion is invested in issues surrounding titles in family businesses. Too many family business owners think of titles as set in concrete, when they really can be quite plastic and vary with circumstances. In my experience, most people associated with a business understand who the ultimate authorities are, regardless of titles. They are the people who know how to get things done, who have authority because they have earned it, and who are usually natural leaders secure in the knowledge of their competence. Still, titles in family companies often convey subtle hierarchies and shades of meaning in both the business and the family. To promote collaboration among multiple leaders, they must be attended to.

Establishing a Timetable and Making
the Announcement

Assuming that the successors have passed all the tests and demonstrated their ability to lead, the next task is to develop a timetable that breaks the transition into a concrete sequence of steps, with a beginning, a middle, and an end. A clear timetable helps people organize their work schedules and business dealings and adjust their expectations to the requirements of the new era. In many family companies, a lot of the top management responsibilities have already been assumed by the successor by the time the choice is officially announced. More typically, responsibilities are transferred on a schedule that phases out the old leader's responsibilities gradually. The incoming and outgoing leaders determine just how long this process takes. It should not happen overnight, but neither should it be unnecessarily prolonged. Between six months and a year is the average timetable in family companies.

After a schedule is established, the seniors and juniors must stick to it. Otherwise, questions may arise about whether the process is being taken seriously—for example, whether the seniors are engaging in a delaying action calculated to maintain their control. The seniors should have a plan for their retirement (we will talk about this more in chapter 11), and negotiations for any stock transfers that will be part of the leadership transition should be drawing to a close. The leaders in both generations must be concerned about departures from the timetable that are not caused by unforeseen developments such as a major business crisis. They must be vigilant in identifying delays that are due to resistances to the change.

Even as the successor prepares to take charge, the company should put a contingency plan in place in case he or she is incapacitated by an accident or sudden illness. The unexpected death of a successor is rare. Because it would pose a grave threat to the business, however, the possibility should be considered from the perspectives of family, ownership, and management, and the company should run through a drill to plan its responses.[6]

The question of how to convey the news of the succession to the family, the company, and the world at large requires some thought. Of course, in some companies the choice has been assumed for some time, and the public announcement, if one is made, is a mere formality. When several candidates have been in contention, however, the announcement must be managed skillfully and diplomatically. How the announcement is framed, the explanations and justifications for the choice, and the timing—including when different constituencies get the news—can either help or undermine the new leader's authority and the success of the transition that is about to occur.

Some business owners choose to make the transition quietly, without any kind of official or public announcement. This is probably a mistake, because outsiders may interpret this as reflecting some embarrassment or deviousness in the choice. Making no announcement tends to downplay the importance of the transition and may even suggest that the seniors are not really planning to step aside. Obviously, this is not the way to inspire confidence in the successor and establish his or her credibility and authority.

The choice of the new leadership should get a strong endorsement from the board and the family leaders before any public announcement is made. The family leaders should also inform the rest of the family shareholders before any public announcement is made; indeed, one reason for informing the shareholders first is to discuss ground rules for preventing leaks to the press. Senior managers should be informed as soon as possible after the family, because their support will also be critical in the transition. They will play a key role in disseminating the news and explaining the rationale for the choice.

The announcement to family and key stakeholders should include some detail on how and why particular choices were made. In addition to evidence that the best person possible has been selected, it should include a sense of the new leader's vision and the direction in which he or she plans to take the company. The message also needs to emphasize the strong endorsement of the choice of successor by the company leaders and the board of directors.

The core message should be consistent, but it may have to be customized for different constituencies. The challenge for those preparing the announcement is to anticipate the concerns that each stakeholder group will have and to address them in a thoughtful way. For example, the announcement to the family needs to convey a sense of pride and emphasize that the successor will look after the concerns of the family and not just the business. The announcement to the financial community might stress the successor's plan for creating shareholder value through new investments or a strategy for increasing the company's market share. If the company's stock is publicly traded, the potential effects of the choice on share prices has to be addressed. For all constituencies, the announcement might explain considerations important to the future of the company, such as the fit between the business strategy and the successor's qualifications, and between the family's values and the successor's. The companywide announcement should convey a strong sense of direction and a feeling of renewal that will rally support and create excitement about the future.

The more the change in leadership departs from tradition, the more detailed the explanation needs to be. In particular, if a change in structure is involved, employees will want to know what that means for them, who they will report to, what any new titles mean, and what role, if any, the outgoing leaders will have. For example, if the company is now to be led by a team of siblings, how will the leaders divide responsibilities among them, where will major business decisions be made, and how will they be implemented?

Less detail is needed in releasing the news to the broader public. The message for the larger community should stress the qualifications of the successor and his or her commitment to the legacy of the previous generations, to preserving jobs, and to continuing the company's philanthropic contributions to local organizations, and so on.

Many family companies also choose to organize a formal event to publicly announce the choice of successor and make the leadership transfer official. Typically, these events include a description of the selection process; an explanation for why the successor is the most desirable choice; a farewell statement by the retiring seniors; and a statement by the new leadership that describes their gratitude to the seniors, their appreciation of the traditions and values of the family business, and their vision for the system in the future. If carefully staged, announcement events can be very important opportunities to legitimize the leadership change and help all members of the organization understand, adjust to, and accept the transition to a new era. They help convey that the leadership has acted responsibly in looking after the continuity of the system. From the standpoint of the organization's culture, the symbolic and emotional impact of such "rites of passage" should not be underestimated.

The Aftermath of the Transition

Inevitably, the announcement will leave some disappointment in its wake. The leaders must pay attention to assuaging the feelings of other strong candidates (and their families) who aspired to the position. Their contributions and their importance to the future of the company should be acknowledged. Just as in the aftermath of a political election, there is a need to bind up any wounds from the selection process and come together to create a new future. This might, in fact, be a time to renegotiate the terms of the disappointed candidates' roles in the business, providing them with new opportunities that are both face-saving and professionally challenging.

There is a risk that "consolation prizes" offered to disappointed candidates will compromise the effectiveness of the company's management and governance structures, however. Disappointed candidates are sometimes given titles that sound as if they have more responsibility and influence than they do. Others are put on key committees despite a lack of qualifications. Some disappointed candidates are even invited to serve on the board where they can become a disruptive force if they have major policy disagreements with the new leadership. Peace is always highly prized in a family company, especially after a succession contest that leaves some scars. But it should not be peace at any price. Inevitably, some disappointed candidates will leave the company. If that happens, the new leader and his team must simply regroup and find competent replacements.

Whatever hurt feelings are left in the wake of the selection process, the announcement of a change in leadership is usually followed by a celebration and sense of renewal in the company. This is especially true when the leader is recognized as exceptionally talented and qualified to lead the enterprise into a brighter future. During this period, everyone is cooperative and the anxieties prevalent during the transition process begin to dissipate. The honeymoon does not last. Inevitably, the system needs to test the new leadership. Once the anxieties have calmed down, the successor is besieged with requests for special favors or attacked by those dissatisfied with his or her policies.

Dr. Roy W. Menninger described such a period of testing that followed his assumption of the presidency of the Menninger Foundation in 1967. The famed clinic in Topeka, Kansas, one of the premier centers in the country for the treatment of mental illness, had been operated as a family business. Roy Menninger, a psychiatrist with little training as a manager, had been chosen to succeed two powerful and esteemed figures, his uncle Dr. Karl Menninger and his father Dr. Will Menninger. Although well liked compared with his tyrannical uncle, the new president discovered that his former colleagues on the staff were not only deferential toward him, they seemed intimidated to the point of not being willing to speak up at meetings. There followed a procession of "fawning yeasayers" offering support but really seeking special favors from the new leader. This honeymoon ended with a more virulent phase:

The paranoia and scapegoating that were prominent in the organizational culture was soon turned against me—though by a devious route. I had always been known as a "nice guy," so it was difficult to attack me openly. For this reason, the anger, fear, and suspicion went underground. An unpleasant atmosphere of backbiting, name-calling, and petty, unjustified criticism of one's previously close colleagues became flagrant. When intense competitive struggles broke out between departments over such things as staffing and budget allocations, the blame was—to use the jargon of our profession—displaced upwardly. It was all my—"their"—fault.[7]

In this atmosphere, Roy Menninger found himself becoming cynical about people's motivations. It fed his insecurities about whether, as president, he could ever match the accomplishments of his famous forebears.

Successors need to be forewarned that their actions will be questioned and their authority tested by those around them. Otherwise, they may perceive opposition as a sign of lack of confidence in their leadership or an omen of failure. This perception may lead to self-doubt or, worse, feelings of anger that tempt successors to lash back at their critics.

Often a contentious issue arises that forces the new leadership to make a choice that will please some people and make others unhappy. This is what happened in one large multinational manufacturing company when two cousins took over the helm from a member of one branch of the family. The election of the two cousins was greeted with acclaim by the entire clan, which included a number of cousin-owners who were not active in the company. The cousins were very conciliatory on most issues, until one branch of the family began to lobby for a fundamental change in the structure of the board. The leaders of this branch argued that because they had more members than the others, they were entitled to more representation on the board. The other branches countered that the basis for allocating seats had always been the number of shares owned by each branch, not the number of people in each.

When the issue came to a head, the two cousins were forced to exercise their power for the first time as the new leaders. Drawing a line in the sand, they declared that the board would not be restructured. The decision angered the branch that had been lobbying for a change, but ultimately the tensions faded and everyone in the family breathed a sigh of relief.

In this period of testing, the new leaders must be willing to hold their ground, to show a determination to pursue their objectives, and to indicate limits on how far they can be pushed by critics. This forceful response is particularly important when the new leaders are charged with leading the company in a new direction requiring major organizational adjustments. Effective leaders cannot please all the people all the time. The testing that often follows the honeymoon period may be designed to assess whether the new leader has what it takes to make the hard decisions endemic to any organization. Psychologically, it may be the very method by which the group of followers eases its fears and reassures itself that the system has in fact made a wise choice.

CHAPTER 10

A More Systematic Selection Process

As the tenure of an incumbent leader draws to a close, the various formal and informal stakeholders become increasingly aware of how high the stakes are in the process that is about to begin. The relative rarity of the succession in a family company (an average of once every 20.6 years according to one study) increases the likelihood that people will view it as a once-in-a-lifetime opportunity to advance their careers and increase the benefits they derive from their direct or indirect involvement with the company.[1] This does not necessarily heighten the determination of many families to exercise caution and use rigorous procedures in selecting successors. On the contrary, the momentousness of the choice often simply raises anxiety levels or deepens resistances to developing an explicit succession plan.

The owners' own assumptions and biases may also come to the fore as the time for change approaches unless systematic procedures are laid out to evaluate the candidates and make the final choice. It is well documented that leaders are inclined to pick successors who replicate their own qualities.[2] This tendency is often enhanced when the selection process involves the incumbent leader's own children and close relatives. In family businesses the selection process is further complicated by the family's assumptions about their own uniqueness—their special mission and legacy, their dynastic ambitions, and their identification with certain personality traits and management styles that have

223

brought past successes. These biases make it difficult for incumbent leaders to consider the needs of the system as they go about the task of selecting the future leadership.

Authorities on succession planning tend to agree that the selection of future leaders must be driven not by the needs of the organization as it is today, but as it will be in the future; otherwise the system may fail to meet changing competitive needs.[3] Like all dynamic systems, businesses are constantly evolving. The leadership needs of a fast-growing company are quite different from those of a mature, multidivisional company. Henry Ford, An Wang, and Canada's Sam Steinberg are prime examples of visionary entrepreneurs who ultimately failed as managers. Conversely, many individuals who may have been very successful managers of large, highly professionalized organizations are incapable of entrepreneurship.

Many business owners have bought into the notion, widespread in business schools, that someone trained in general management can successfully lead any type of business. In family businesses this assumption is particularly risky because these systems are often so steeped in tradition and inwardly focused that they can be notoriously slow to respond to important market changes that threaten the viability of their products and services.

This chapter examines how a company goes about defining the pool of candidates for top leadership positions, evaluating the candidates, and making the final selections. First, I will analyze the psychological and political factors, including a family's dynastic expectations, that often bias the process and result in a poor choice of successors. Second, I will describe the various ways companies attempt to minimize bias as well as the influence of political and emotional factors in assessing future leaders. The core of this discussion will be a description of steps in strategic selection by which the leadership attempts to align the skills and abilities of successors with the future business needs. Third, I will look at how the needs of the family owners shape the organizational criteria for selecting the leaders and the need in some companies to consider the combined strengths and weaknesses of the top leadership team and not just a single leader. Finally, I'll discuss the primary considerations in deciding whether to include non-family executives and/or outsiders in the pool of candidates.

For purposes of this chapter, I will assume that the incumbent leaders in a family company see a leadership transition as both necessary and inevitable, that the family has articulated a Shared Dream and committed itself to a particular family business form for the next generation, and that a pool of family and non-family candidates has been identified from either formal or informal discussions. Now the organization must get down to the business of making hard choices about who is best qualified to lead and under what kind of system.

Dynastic Ambitions Cloud Judgment

Very often the lack of rigor in selecting successors is a result of an attitude in family companies that puts the family's legacy ahead of business needs. Usually, these families have strong dynastic expectations—the leaders are committed to building an enterprise that will last far into the future and bring ever increasing wealth, prestige, and power to their descendants. We can conjecture that dynastic ambitions led An Wang to inflate estimates of his son Fred's competence and to ignore any criticisms of the son's managerial experience and leadership capabilities. Indeed, published reports on how An Wang reacted to anyone's disapproval of Fred suggest that he interpreted such criticisms not as commentaries on Fred's capabilities but as attacks on his family. If highly professional companies the size of Wang Laboratories do not put rigorous procedures in place for selecting successors, it is not surprising that small and medium-sized family firms do not see the need for them either. Yet succession of unqualified heirs poses an even greater threat to continuity in smaller businesses.

By the time a generational transition approaches, the leadership's assumptions about how the process will take place may be clear. Over time, signals will come from top management about the criteria that will be used to select the future leadership, particularly whether or not non-family as well as family executives will be considered. If a highly competent non-family executive is promoted to a position of significant responsibility or is publicly recognized for his or her accomplishments, then other non-family mangers become more hopeful about their chances for reaching the top slots. On the other hand, if all or almost all significant positions of authority are assigned to members of the family, senior non-family managers will conclude that they will be shut out of the leadership selection process. Then they may consider moving to other organizations where their chances for advancement will be more promising.

The behavioral cues to dynastic ambitions are not always easy to interpret. This is particularly true when a family is ambivalent about the extent to which family or business considerations should drive the selection process. It is quite common, for instance, for a business owner to one day raise the hopes of a non-family manager for promotion by openly acknowledging his or her contributions, only to turn around the next day and dash those hopes through unwarranted criticism (or elaborate praise of a family heir competing for the same position).

The greater the ambiguity surrounding how the selection process will be managed, the more people will tend to assume that blood rather than business acumen and performance will ultimately determine the choice of leaders. Similarly, the greater the ambiguity in the family itself about how the selection process will be handled, the more the members will assume that factors such as parental favoritism or sibling position will drive the choice.

Dynastic expectations can be measured along a hypothetical continuum. At one extreme are families who deeply believe that leadership and business talent are built into their genes. This notion—that the family has produced heroic business leaders in the past and will do so again in succeeding generations—is often an integral part of a narcissistic sense of specialness and invulnerability in their psychology. Given this belief system, if such a family reaches the passing-the-baton stage without at least one qualified family candidate, the members experience an embarrassing loss of face.

At the other end of the continuum are business families who do not adhere to the view that leadership of the business must be passed down to a family heir. Indeed, the very notion of dynasty runs directly counter to deeply held values regarding self-reliance and individual achievement in these families. They attribute the heroic accomplishments of the founders to a unique blend of talent, perseverance, circumstance, and sheer luck that is unlikely to reoccur among the descendants, and they regard nepotism as a threat to the long-term efficiency and viability of the enterprise. As a result, younger family members are discouraged from seeking positions in senior management and, in some cases, are even prevented from doing so by company policy.

Unlike An Wang, Ken Olsen, the founder of Digital Equipment Corporation (DEC), strongly believed that Digital was his business, not the family's. Accounts of the development of Digital suggest that even though Olsen's brother Stan worked at the company for a number of years, he was not encouraged by Ken to make a career at DEC. Quite the contrary, he was encouraged to stay away after he left management. Ken Olsen invited no other members of the family to join the company. [4]

We've already mentioned the Dorrances of Campbell Soup as a prime example of a family that years ago chose to rely on non-family management to run the company. An example well known in European circles is the Spanish multinational Roca Radiodores, a producer of bathroom fixtures for four generations. With the number of cousins in the family growing, an uncle in management pushed through a policy whereby family members would no longer be considered for management positions. Nevertheless, the Roca family, with some sixty shareholders, is still active in company events and promotes its values and traditions as a unifying force in the company's culture.

If a family's dynastic ambitions powerfully influence the process of selection, the intrigues that often surround the choice also test the rationality of the selection process. Various stakeholders will be watchful as the time of transition nears. When it becomes clear that the selection process is moving forward, some will begin to press for their own agenda and their own candidates.

The political and emotional forces aroused in the final stage of passing the torch are illustrated by the experiences of a fourth-generation cousin company. The seventy-three-year-old uncle who had been president and CEO for the past twenty-seven years was at long last seriously contemplating retirement. As he solicited advice from various constituencies, he became increasingly aware that his imminent departure might unleash complex political dynamics that would put the stability of this billion-dollar enterprise at risk. His conversations with family managers revealed a relatively intense struggle between his own son and two other cousins, who felt that the time had come to pass the leadership of the company to their branch of the extended shareholding family. When he talked with senior non-family managers, the suggestion was made that perhaps the best course in the firm's history would be to turn over all executive functions to non-family professionals. Nonparticipating family shareholders saw in the succession a unique opportunity to increase the number of passive family shareholders on the board of directors. Their agenda, clearly, was to gain support for a more equitable dividend policy and give the cousins in their branch greater access to senior executive positions. Perplexed and disappointed by the intensity of the politicking in the company, the uncle decided to postpone selecting a successor.

When the final selection of the new leader is left to a collision of interests and personalities, the result is often either no choice—the decision is put off until the senior leader dies—or a poor choice. The lack of rigorous selection procedures leads to the succession of a family member who is not prepared—and sometimes not motivated—to take on the role, or one whose vision and experience is not congruent with the organization's future needs and strategy.

Identifying Leadership Requirements

The choice of a new leadership must be solidly grounded in the company's best assessment of the organization's future and competitive position. The first step is to envision a strategic scenario for the business for a time when the incumbent leadership generation is no longer in control of either ownership or management. The second step involves deriving specific leadership profiles from the strategic scenarios. The fundamental question at this stage is: What skills and qualifications will be needed in order to respond effectively to the opportunities and challenges likely to be confronting the organization in the future?

To develop such a scenario, the company must constantly monitor the changing economic and competitive climate. The incumbent leaders can then draw up a list of the qualities of the ideal successor or successors. The list will, of course, describe essential core competencies, such as leadership ability, knowledge of the company's industry and processes, and planning and communication skills. It must also take account of the company's special situation and strategic direction. If a major downsizing is contemplated, for example, the chosen successors must have demonstrated willingness to take tough decisions when necessary for the well being of the organization. Successors who want too much to be liked—as many do who are anxious to differentiate themselves from hard-nosed parents—would not be the best choice in these circumstances. If the company is under fire from government and the media for its environmental impact, the situation requires leaders who are experienced in public relations, politically astute, and accustomed to negotiating with government agencies. If the company is planning to develop new products and services, it will need someone with entrepreneurial ideas and energy at the top.

Drawing up such a list may underline the complexity of the tasks facing the company. For example, large multidivisional companies with a wide array of products facing different market conditions may conclude that a single leader is unlikely to have the range of skills needed to manage all of them competently. In these circumstances, they may begin to think about organizing a leadership team of individuals who together have the diverse skills and experience that are required.

One of the most useful approaches for thinking about strategic selection in the business was developed by Gerstein and Reisman. Although their framework was originally developed for non-family companies, the underlying logic is equally applicable to family businesses. Table 10-1 summarizes seven common situations that dictate a company's strategy at a given point in its history. Each alternative has a set of characteristic issues or challenges associated with it. Hence, for example, startups are usually characterized by high financial risk and endless workloads, while divestitures are often a response to a weak competitive position, morale problems, and skill shortages.

Table 10-2 offers us a useful summary of the major job thrusts and leadership characteristics associated with each of the seven strategic situations Gerstein and Reisman identified.

Of course, few business situations fit neatly into any one of these categories. In fact, larger family companies typically are organized as holding companies with a portfolio of businesses which may have varied strategies and thus fall into different categories. In such companies it is particularly important to approach the selection process with an awareness of the variety of strategic scenarios a given system faces, and its corresponding leadership needs.

Developing an Ideal Profile

Occasionally, business owners are uneasy about the essential elements of strategic selection. A number of techniques can be used to help business owners feel more at home with the process. Some senior leaders hold brainstorming sessions in which they make lists of adjectives describing the kind of person or persons most likely to meet the challenges posed by a strategic scenario. Another technique is to anchor the discussion around a set of practical questions designed to stimulate thinking about the type of leadership that will be needed in the future.[5] (This is particularly important for those who will select successors in smaller family companies, who may be less familiar with the process of strategic selection.) Questions include:

- What are the strategic challenges facing this leader in the family, the ownership and in the business in the coming six months? Year? Two or three years?

(Continues on p. 231.)

Table 10-1   Characteristics of Various Strategic Scenarios

Strategic Situation	Key Characteristics
1. Startup	• High financial risk • Limited management team cohesiveness • No organization, systems, or procedures in place • Endless workload: multiple priorities • Generally insufficient resources to satisfy all demands • Limited relationship with suppliers, customers, and environment
2. Turnaround	• Time pressure for "results": need rapid assessment and decision making • Poor results, but business is worth saving • Weak competitive position • Eroded morale: low esteem and cohesion • Inadequate systems: weak or bureaucratic infrastructure • Strained relationships with suppliers, customers, and environment • Lack of appropriate leadership: period of neglect • Limited resources: skills shortages; some incompetent personnel
3. Extract profit and rationalize existing business	• "Controlled" financial risk • Unattractive industry in long term: possible need to invest selectively, but major new investments not likely to be worthwhile • Internal organizational stability • Moderate-to-high managerial/technical competence • Adequate systems and administrative infrastructure • Good relationships with suppliers, customers, and environment
4. Dynamic growth in existing business	• Moderate-to-high financial risk • New markets, products, technology • Multiple demands and conflicting priorities • Rapidly expanding organization in certain sectors • Inadequate managerial/technical/financial resources to meet all demands • Unequal growth across sectors of organization • Likely shifting between doing current work and building support systems for the future

Table 10-1 *(Continued)*

Strategic Situation	Key Characteristics
5. Redeployment of efforts in existing business	• Low to moderate short-term risk; high long-term risk • Resistance to change: excess bureaucracy in some sections • High mismatch between some skill sets, technology, and people relative to needs created by redefined strategy • Likelihood of lack of previous strategic planning; high operational orientation in executive team
6. Liquidation/ divestiture of poorly performing business	• Weak competitive position, unattractive industry, or both • Likely continuance of poor returns • Possible morale problems and skills shortages • Little opportunity for turnaround or redeployment due to unsatisfactory "payback" • Need to cut losses and make tough decisions
7. New acquisitions	• Acquisitions may be classified into one of the above situations • Pressure on new management ambivalent/defensive about change • Fundamental need to integrate acquired company with parent at some levels

(Continued from p. 229.)
- How would you know or begin to suspect within the first three months whether your choice was going to be successful? What would be some of the key indicators?
- Who are the people and roles that this person needs to interact with? What specific things does each of the appointing authorities want from this leader? What conflicts might there be with him or her?
- What behaviors, attitudes, and skills are required to be effective in relating to each of the major stakeholder groups (e.g., family, shareholders, senior manager, the board, clients, suppliers, financial community).

(Continues on p. 234.)

Table 10-2   Leadership Characteristics for Strategic Scenarios

Situation	Major Job Thrusts	Special Characteristics of Ideal Candidates
1. Startup	• Creating a vision for the business • Establishing core technical and marketing expertise • Building a management team	• Vision of a finished business • Hands-on orientation: a "doer" • In-depth knowledge in critical technical areas • Organizing ability • Staffing skills • Team-building capabilities • Personal magnetism: charisma • Broad knowledge of all key functions
2. Turnaround	• Rapid, accurate problem diagnosis • Fixing short-term and ultimately, long-term problems	• "Take-charge" orientation: strong leader • Strong analytical and diagnostic skills, especially financial • Excellent business strategist • High energy level • Risk taker • Handles pressure well • Good crisis management skills • Good negotiator
3. Extract profit and rationalize existing business	• Efficiency • Stability • Succession • Sensing signs of change	• Technically knowledgeable: "knows the business" • Sensitive to changes: "ear to the ground" • Anticipates problems: "problem finder" • Strong administrative skills • Oriented to "systems" • Strong "relationship orientation" • Recognizes need for management succession and development • Oriented to getting out the most: efficiency, not growth
4. Dynamic growth in existing business	• Increasing market share in key sectors	• Excellent strategic and financial planning skills • Clear vision of the future

Table 10-2   *(Continued)*

Situation	Major Job Thrusts	Special Characteristics of Ideal Candidates
	• Managing rapid change • Building long-term health with clear vision of the future	• Ability to balance priorities, e.g., stability and growth • Organizational and team-building skills • Good crisis management skills • Moderate–high risk taker • High energy level • Excellent staffing skills
5. Redeployment of efforts in existing business	• Establishing effectiveness in limited business sphere • Managing change • Supporting the "dispossessed"	• Good politician/manager of change • Highly persuasive: high "inter-personal influence" • Moderate risk taker • Highly supportive, sensitive to people: not a "bull in a china shop" • Excellent "systems thinker": understands how complex systems work • Good organizing and executive staffing skills
6. Liquidation/ divestiture of poorly performing business	• Cutting losses • Making tough decisions • Making best deal	• "Callousness": tough-minded—willing to be the bad guy • Highly analytical about cost/benefits—does not easily accept status quo • Risk taker • Not glory seeking: willing to do dirty jobs; does not want glamour • Wants to be respected, not necessarily liked
7. New acquisitions	• Integration • Establishing sources of information and control	• Analytical ability • Relationship-building skills • Interpersonal influence • Good communication skills • Personal magnetism—some basis to establish "instant credibility"

(Continued from p. 231.)

- What are the day-to-day tasks and responsibilities? What particular skills would add value? Which skills would be essential?
- What skills and past experiences does the leader need in order to work effectively?
- What are the typical daily, weekly, monthly, and yearly activities of the job?
- What are key adjectives that would describe the ideal candidate?
- If you had to pick only five of these to capture this person's essential qualities, what would they be?

Defining Organizational Needs

While envisioning a future business strategy is necessary to the selection process in any organization, it is not sufficient in a family enterprise. The future ownership and family circumstances likely to face successors must also be given great weight. The three-circle model (depicting the overlap of business, ownership, and family) is useful in defining the future scenario.[6] The fundamental premise of the model, as we have seen, is the systemic interdependence between family, ownership, and business issues in family companies.

The appointing authorities must continue to review the family business forms that they want in the next generation. I have developed a framework similar to Gerstein and Reisman's for the family and ownership needs of the organization. Table 10-3 summarizes some of the characteristics of ideal successor candidates for the three basic types of family business forms.

Other commentators have noted the interdependence in a family company of the owner's estate plan, the company's strategic plan, and the succession plan. Unless these three equations are solved simultaneously,[7] it is virtually impossible to anticipate the conflicting demands for resources that are likely to result from the generational transition. The total resources needed to pay estate taxes, revitalize the strategic position of the company, and finance the comfortable retirement of the parting seniors often exceed the capabilities of the system. Unless the potential financial strains are addressed, it will be difficult to forecast the circumstances that the successors will ultimately face. How can the successors be asked to revitalize the family business, for example, if all the financial resources necessary to carry out that mandate will be soaked up by estate taxes?

Table 10-3   Successor Candidates for Family Business Forms

Type of Future Family Business Form	Characteristics of Ideal Successor Candidates
Controlling Owner Business	• Strong entrepreneurial and leadership skills • Clear vision and commitment to personal Dream • Comfortable exercising leadership alone • Deep understanding of business • Unambivalent about "taking charge" • Capable of leading other family members • Well differentiated from predecessor • Comfortable being in the limelight • Charismatic
Sibling Partnership	• Strong sibling ties • Strong team leadership skills • Clear vision and commitment to *shared* Dream • Ability to work in groups and bring out the best in others • Strong communication skills • Good conflict management skills • Generosity of spirit—willingness to share glory • Comfortable with group rewards • Willingness and ability to coach weaker members • Patience and a sense of humor
Cousin Consortium	• Clear vision and a commitment to *shared* Dream • Strong communication skills • Ability to lead a strong group of non-family executives • Authority and credibility in the extended family • Ability to manage complex shareholder arrangements • Deep understanding of the needs of uninvolved family shareholders • Ability to develop and work within complex governance structures (boards and family councils)

The further away the leadership transition is in time, the more difficult it becomes to forecast what may actually happen in any given industry. In the best of cases, strategic planning in the company is already institutionalized as an ongoing activity so that when the leadership transition approaches, there will be considerable information available regarding the likely strategic challenges and opportunities in the foreseeable future. The longer the time frame of prediction, the more important it is to develop several plausible strategic scenarios and to think through the leadership implications of each.

The Choice of a Non-Family CEO

After defining the organizational and strategic needs of the company, the current leadership has two other critical choices to make. Will only family members be eligible as candidates, or will an outstanding non-family executive be considered? And if non-family executives will be included in the pool, do they have to come from within the company or will outsiders be considered?

Many companies turn to either an inside or outside non-family CEO as an interim choice until the family successors are old enough and qualified to run the company. Cargill, the giant commodities trading company, is an example of a generations-old family company that benefited from leadership by non-family presidents while younger family members were being groomed for management positions. Other families have decided on principle to keep family members out of management altogether. This school of thought argues that the only way to prevent family problems from destroying the business is to turn it over to non-family management.

As the time for a generational change approaches, pressures to seek a new leader outside the system often mount as a result of the fears and political intrigue that surround such transitions. Of course, by ruling out any involvement of their members in management, families do not automatically insulate their companies against their internal politics and family dynamics. The conflicts are simply bumped up to the governance level—for example, to the board—where different factions may battle over corporate policy and strategy. As we've noted, Campbell's Soup, whose stock is publicly traded, has suffered its share of internal squabbles among family shareholders even though family members are not in management.

Another reason that family companies sometimes go outside the business to hire a new CEO is that they anticipate a major change in strategic direction or a restructuring and believe that only an outsider will be capable of accomplishing it. Their logic is based on the common belief in corporate America that insiders are too tied to people in the organization and the culture to be able to implement any drastic departure from the status quo. For a family business, the decision to recruit an outsider will turn on how strongly the family feels about maintaining its distinctive culture and how much it needs new blood and new ideas in order to make a fundamental change in direction. But family companies take some risk when they choose an outsider on the basis of strategic considerations alone. Bringing in an outsider for the sake of preventing the family's internal politics from spilling over into the company may produce a new leader who is antagonistic to the family. To assuage their own anxieties, some families recruit an "Attila the Hun" to, in effect, save the company from themselves.

The owners of a multinational company in Europe, for example, faced a number of controversial and difficult decisions that they could not bring themselves to make, including the firing of a number of long-time staff. They brought in a tough non-family manager who was experienced in the politics of large public companies to do the dirty work for them. After the new CEO had cleaned house and tidied up the organization, however, he turned his skill at political maneuvering against the family itself. Ownership of the company was divided among three family branches, and the CEO played one off against the other to build his own power base.

This executive no doubt thought that what he was doing was good for the company. Indeed, what he did was based on his long experience as a professional manager in more corporate settings. He did not realize that by creating friction in the family, he was undermining the long-range continuity of family ownership. He was ultimately fired, and the family hired a new CEO with vastly different personal and professional qualifications, except for his demonstrated competence as a manager.

Many business owners who see pitfalls in family management overcompensate by recruiting non-family leadership that is insensitive to their concerns and dismissive of the important contribution made by the family to the success of the business. One non-family CEO who had been hired to take a family company in a new strategic direction actually attempted to purge the company not only of family influence but of its symbols and traditions. He cut all corporate funding for a foundation that was the basis for the family's community outreach program. He insisted that the family office be removed from the corporate headquarters where it had always been. The annual picnic was no longer held at the family mansion as it had been traditionally. And leaders of the family were no longer invited to participate in and speak at corporate functions and celebrations. Members of the family weren't the only ones who reacted negatively to this campaign. Non-family senior managers worried that the new CEO would turn the company into a corporate bureaucracy that lacked the heart and inclusive values of the family culture.

A non-family CEO must be sensitive to the needs of the owning family and able to work comfortably within its culture. Families that opt to go outside for a new CEO should seek a leader who will honor their values, wishes, and expectations while maintaining standards of professionalism that are essential to the success of the business. A non-family CEO should understand that he or she is accountable to the family shareholders and cannot ignore their voice. Indeed, it will be part of the CEO's mandate to help the family articulate a Shared Dream for the future and work toward achieving that Dream by every means possible. Non-family CEOs have to subordinate their own agenda to the family's. They must be willing and able to mentor the offspring of the owners. They need to be consultative leaders who regularly discuss critical issues with key family stakeholders and gain their support for all major decisions. Whoever is chosen needs to be able to strike a delicate balance. In their work with their management team, non-family CEOs must represent the interests and preferences of the family ownership. At the same time, in meetings with the family, they must support their managers and argue the case for professionalism, for maintaining high standards, in the company. They must even be willing, when necessary, to confront the family if they feel the family's actions may be harmful to the enterprise as a whole. Finally, in decisions on allocating resources, they must honor the family's financial expectations. But the non-family CEO should also appreciate the advantages of a family enterprise and keep the family's focus on long-run objectives rather than short-term profit opportunities.

Criteria for Team Leadership

In exploring the future needs of the system, the ideal leadership role should not be thought of as an isolated individual, even in a controlling-owner firm. A leader's strength invariably depends on the quality of the people around him or her, and effective management depends upon a configuration of skills in the top executive group. Hence, it is more productive to think about a profile of leadership skills and competencies that will be needed in order to manage future strategic challenges—and how they are distributed among the group of individuals who will share leadership responsibilities.

The idea of a leadership team becomes particularly critical when thinking about the selection of successors for a large, multifaceted family enterprise. The challenge of the selection process in such companies is to assemble a team of successors who as a group embody the full range of required skills and experience. Thinking about the succession transition in terms of a leadership constellation broadens the range of possibilities for resolving selection dilemmas considerably. Corning Inc. offers an interesting example of this. Founded in 1851, the specialty glass company that invented fiber optic cable has always been controlled by the Houghton family. The Houghtons have been actively involved with the management of the company for five generations, and they feel strongly that qualified family involvement in management has been good for the company. Because of their commitment to taking a long-term investment perspective, the company is able to invest significant amounts in research and development (more than twice the average for other businesses of it size). However, for the last sixty-five years the company has always tried to balance family and non-family membership in the top management team.

Working with only two titles, chairman and president, since 1930, a member of the Houghton family has held one title but a nonfamily member has held the other. In 1971, when it became time for providing for Amo [Amory] Houghton's successor, the company adopted the team mode, creating two vice chairmen. But the balance of power was stable, with two Houghtons and two nonfamily members. That team stayed in place for ten years until William H. Armistead [a nonfamily manager] retired, and two years later Jamie [James R. Houghton] put his new team in place consisting of six members in total, with only one active Houghton.[8]

Motorola Inc. is another example of an outstanding company that has developed a team leadership mode of operation combining family and non-family executives. Robert Galvin discarded the concept of a chief executive officer in favor of a chief executive office that has usually consisted of three individuals. The notion of shared leadership, which extends throughout the Motorola organization, provides opportunities for management development as well as protection against discontinuities in leadership. Thus, when George Fisher, a key member of the chief executive office, left Motorola to become CEO of Kodak, the company did not suffer disarray from his departure. Gary Tooker, age fifty-four, and Christopher Galvin, forty-three, simply took over his responsibilities.

The concept of the leadership constellation can also be used in situations in which a strategic scenario calls for a balance of power among different branches of an extensive shareholder system. In these cases, executive teams may be constituted to bring together an optimal configuration of skills among non-family executives and a group of highly talented family executives from different branches of the family.

In one large European company, for example, the leadership team is composed of a senior non-family executive and three cousins from different branches of an extended family. The non-family manager, who has worked with the cousins for more than ten years and commands considerable respect, serves as a coach and facilitator of the group. The three cousins are extraordinarily competent and have been carefully groomed to meet the challenges of the future. One cousin is the creative genius behind new product concepts—he has already launched three highly innovative products. Another cousin has developed the international sales network needed to compete effectively against the giants of their industry. The third cousin is the visionary strategist who is able to articulate the direction for the system and motivate the employees to do their best. The development and selection of this leadership team is regarded by the outgoing leaders as their single most significant accomplishment.

Gathering Data on the Candidates

The best predictor of future performance is past performance, says a maxim in psychology. There are several approaches to managing the next step in the selection process, which is to gather data on the various successor candidates and weigh their performance. A good place to start is with a historical review of the candidates' performance in the various positions they have held during their careers. This can be a difficult and frustrating task in small and mid-sized family companies which seldom keep reliable records of performance. These firms simply lack the human resources personnel to do a good job of collecting data, and often the information retrieved is fragmentary and of doubtful reliability.

When historical data is lacking, in-depth interviews with the candidates can sometimes yield valuable information. The interviews are particularly useful in assessing how objective candidates can be about where they have done well and where they have fallen short as leaders and managers. Over the years I have met a number of sophisticated family business owners who have modeled their approach to successor selection on one invented by Reginald Jones, when he was chairman and CEO of General Electric. At the time he developed the technique, GE had seven highly capable successor candidates from whom Jones wanted to select the best three to make up the executive team, as well as an overall leader of the team. He used the following method to gather data systematically and select his successor, Jack Welch, and members of the team:

Unannounced, a confidential session was held between him and each of the seven candidates. He posed the following dilemma: "you and I are in an airplane; it goes down, and neither of us survive. Who should be the next CEO?" This "really catches them cold," says Jones. It's amazing what is learned about the chemistry of the group when each one talks about the others for a few hours. Similar conversations were held with other senior officers about to retire, those "with whom I could talk openly" because they held no personal stake. And the Senior Vice President of Executive Management, "who was intimately familiar with all these people," provided input. All this was shared with the Management Development and Compensation Committee of the Board.

Three months later another conversation was held with each candidate. But this time they were prepared; notified in advance, they arrived with "sheafs and sheafs of notes." This time, however, "I don't make it but you do," Jones told them. "Now who do you pick? And who else should be in the Corporate Executive Office?" The top three candidates were chosen with this data contributing significantly to the decision. Then, after 14 months with those three attending all board meetings and working with the Corporate Executive Office, the number one man was chosen, Jack Welch. Specific criteria Jones used included: 1) choosing someone unlike himself, and 2) looking at the future environment demands his successor would face.[9]

One of the most original aspects of Jones's approach to selection was the extent to which he paid attention to the ability of the successor candidates to work effectively as a leadership team. While care must be taken in applying this approach to the specific circumstances of family companies, it can be very helpful in building teamwork among groups of siblings or cousins.

Consider the case of a business owner who was committed to passing the company to his three sons. The sons were all hard workers and strongly committed to the company's future, but the youngest son had consistently shown more leadership skills than the other two. The relationship among the sons was strong and cooperative. Although the father sensed that the older sons readily acquiesced to the leadership of the youngest, he worried that if he arbitrarily assigned the role of CEO to his youngest son, the others would interpret the decision as favoritism and resent it. On the other hand, while he was willing to experiment with a sibling partnership and had divided his stock equally among the three sons, he felt strongly that the most capable of the three should be formally recognized as the leader of the company.

After considerable soul-searching, the father adopted a consultative process using Jones's airplane interviews. As he talked with his two oldest sons, he was surprised to learn that they willingly recognized the youngest son's leadership skills. The interviews opened up discussion of the future leadership roles of each of the three, and the father was pleased when the older sons themselves suggested naming the youngest brother as their CEO. In this way the sibling partnership was launched as a first-among-equals. Having the older brothers actively participate in the selection process served to legitimate the younger son's leadership and authority.

Another approach to rating candidates' performance and capabilities is by means of structured questionnaires that elicit the views of supervisors, peers, and subordinates who have worked with each of them in various functions and projects. In some family companies, people throughout the system are too intimidated to discuss potential successors forthrightly with the top leader. In these situations, some business owners, often with the help of an outside facilitator, do a survey asking senior managers to rate the candidates—anonymously—on criteria that have been identified as crucial to the company's future. Some companies contract with outside firms to gather data on the candidates. Other companies send their younger managers to assessment centers, which use behavioral instruments and various situational tests to evaluate leadership skills. The drawback of using outsiders, however, is that these firms tend to employ rather standard leadership criteria, which may not reflect the specific needs of any given system.

These techniques are not mutually exclusive. Indeed, in the social sciences the use of multiple methods of gathering data is considered more reliable than use of any one method alone. Whatever technique is used, the process of collecting information on the candidates' track records, so that their respective performances may be compared and matched against the company's leadership requirements, is central to the selection process. If only scanty records have been kept, the incumbent leadership has to experiment with other methods. In order to limit the influence of subjective judgments on the final choice, they have to collect as much data on the candidates as they can in the time that remains before the transition is to take place.

Measuring the Candidates Against the Ideal

Let's assume that the senior leaders have compiled a record of performance for each of the candidates. The next step is to use the data to prepare a detailed description of each candidate's strengths and weaknesses—a performance profile—that can be matched against the list of criteria for the ideal successor. This will enable the seniors and juniors to identify weaknesses in each candidate's profile that can perhaps be remedied with further training or experience within the time remaining. A development plan or curriculum can be drawn up for each candidate that specifies developmental opportunities aimed at enhancing the candidate's skills in areas deemed to be critical for the business.

But what happens if the company has run out of time, if there is pressure to anoint a new leader soon and all of the potential successors need more experience or training? If no qualified successors are in sight, the company's only choice may be to go outside and conduct a search for a chief executive to serve for a period of time as a bridge manager until younger candidates are fully prepared to be leaders.

A case can be made, in fact, for doing an external search regardless of whether or not the company's internal candidates are ready. For one thing, the very process of interviewing outside candidates often helps to clarify the qualities the company needs in its leadership. For another, the search provides market-driven benchmarks of the leadership skills the company is seeking and how they should be compensated. In the final stages of the selection process, an external search gives the senior leaders an overview of how the candidates compare on the key qualities needed.

An Overview of the Selection Process

Figure 10-1 depicts my synthesis of the various elements in the selection process. While the diagram is broken up into discrete steps, it should be thought of as an ongoing process in which the appointing

Figure 10-1   The Successor Selection Process

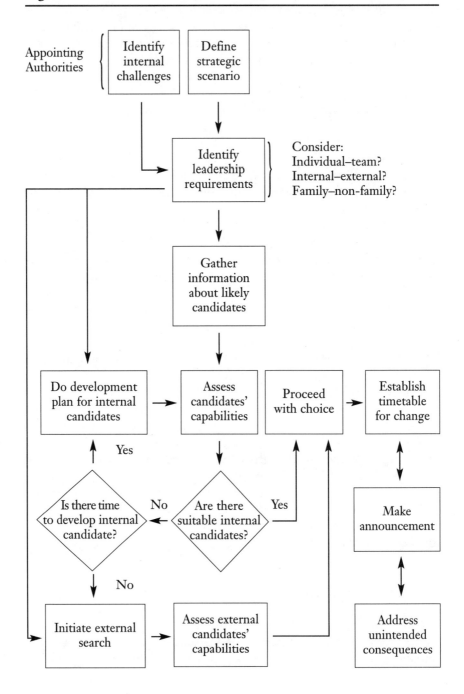

authorities (who will vary from one business to another) are continuously anticipating the leadership needs of the company, assessing the qualifications of the successor candidates to meet those needs, and providing opportunities for them to learn the required skills and prove their competence.

The chart is based on the experience of companies that have carried out one or another phase of the process effectively; not many companies have handled every phase equally well. How this process is applied will, of course, depend upon the available personnel and circumstances in each company. Further, it does not necessarily occur in a linear sequence. The process is dynamic, with some steps going on simultaneously and with a number of "feedback loops." So, for example, after identifying the requirements of leadership, the company proceeds to gather information about internal candidates, but at the same time it may initiate an external search to gather benchmarking data and assess the talent available outside the company. After assessing the internal candidates, some may be deemed suitable successors; the company can then proceed to refine the options and make a choice. If the leaders decide that none of those in the available pool are ready, they must then assess whether there is time to develop the internal candidates. If time is lacking, they may then embark on an external search.

In arguing for such a process, I do not mean to imply that strategic selection can supply all the answers to a company's future or even identify with certainty the best qualified people to be its leaders. The business of forecasting the future is always riddled with uncertainty and should be treated with caution. The hesitancy of some business owners to embrace the notion of strategic selection is not entirely without rational foundation. The strategic management literature in general has recently come under attack for assuming that the leaders of organizations have a level of mastery over their environments and their own organizations that is largely a fantasy.[10] Even in the most rationalized of organizations, the process of strategy formulation and implementation is always a messy affair. As Ward has indicated, "the actual choice of a business strategy is, and forever will be, more art than science."[11] This is particularly so with regard to the strategic selection of leaders in a family company, because so many managerial and familial factors come into play.

In the final analysis, the exercise of analyzing the opportunities and risks of a number of plausible scenarios for the future may be more important for its own sake than for the accuracy of the predictions that are made—as Eisenhower once said: "Plans are useless but planning is everything." Experience has taught me that thinking strategically about the selection of successors enhances the quality of the choices that are made. Top executive positions tend to be surrounded by a certain mystique. Business leaders routinely insist on a "good fit" when hiring individuals for jobs at lower levels of their organizations, but they tend to avoid the same approach when selecting top executives. Perhaps keenly aware of the complex array of tasks that leaders of family companies are asked to perform, they resist efforts to break down and analyze the specific skills that are needed, believing that those tasks are so multifarious and ambiguous as to defy analysis. Perhaps just as important psychologically, the process of dissecting the tasks a business owner is called upon to perform, and questioning the future relevance of those tasks, raises the incumbents' anxieties about their obsolescence and may, in their own eyes, undermine their heroic stature.

After going through the process of strategic selection, the appointing authorities sometimes do reach the sobering conclusion that their skills and management style may no longer be viable. A mature leadership, however, will realize that such a conclusion in no way demeans that style or their special contribution to the organization during their years at the helm. Indeed, the exercise of strategic selection often facilitates the constructive expression of the deeper emotional issues that succession planning can stir up in the incumbent leaders. Just as important, it can help to prevent those emotions from intruding decisively in the selection process and skewing peoples' judgments. As Gilmore has pointed out:

During leadership transitions, anxiety is often high, and the risk of distorted thinking is great. Groups [or families] can shift easily from grossly overrating a former leader to the reverse. It is particularly easy to fall prey to imagining a perfect candidate out there who in some magical way will address all the needs of the organization.[12]

By rigorously defining a variety of strategic scenarios for the organization's future, the appointing authorities develop a series of categories with which to assess the capabilities of successors and so avoid "magical thinking." If performed sensitively, this approach often lowers resistance to succession planning by making it easier for people in the system to discuss the future needs of the business. The process can also serve as an antidote to the misguided notion that a general manager can be brought in to deal with any particular set of circumstances.

Even more important, a strategically driven selection process helps those who are ultimately chosen as the new leaders to reach agreement on the goals and the future direction of the company and to cement their leadership and authority. An explicit understanding of why they—as opposed to other candidates—emerged as the chosen few helps to validate how much their unique talents and strengths are valued within the system. The process focuses their attention on the challenges they will be taking on and enhances their accountability for realizing an explicit strategic mandate. In other words, it spells out their marching orders.

CHAPTER 11

Letting Go

D URING the last years of succession planning, while a family company is developing and testing candidates for leadership in the next generation, another drama is unfolding. As the juniors rise to positions of major responsibility and prominence in the organization, the seniors become increasingly aware that their tenure as leaders is drawing to a close. Regardless of their particular mixture of genes, diet, and exercise, business leaders in their mid-sixties and seventies are showing inevitable signs of physical and mental decline. The prospect of an imminent generational changeover in leadership almost invariably unleashes powerful emotional undercurrents. This is the stuff of Shakespeare's *King Lear* and *Henry V*. Both are archetypal tales of succession that center on the fundamental issues of this timeless generational relay—Lear epitomizing the anxieties and indignities that lurk in the souls of departing monarchs, and Henry V depicting a process by which aspiring princes establish their credibility as effective leaders.

Family businesses make it possible for seniors to enjoy their tenure at the helm well beyond what is customary in non-family companies. Typically, family companies have no mandatory retirement age—at least not one that applies to executives from the family. For seniors, the freedom to set the pace of their departure is one of the benefits of owning a business. It allows them to customize the process of their retirement in a way that is consistent with their health and individual

249

preferences. When managed responsibly, this flexibility allows business owners to surrender their leadership with more dignity and even—for those who are most adaptable—to retain a constructive role in the company.

The passage of a successful business from one generation to another can be a joyful experience in which seniors and juniors share a sense of joint accomplishment and look forward to a satisfying future for their company and their families. The senior who resists planning his or her succession to the bitter end is by no means representative of the universe of family business owners. Although some leaders hang onto their businesses as if they were liferafts in the stormy seas of aging, many sail into retirement buoyed by exciting plans for activities they have waited years to do and looking forward to new challenges. Numerous business owners depart the field with honor and leave their companies in the hands of capable successors.

Nevertheless, the lack of a fixed retirement age in family businesses also makes the succession process more vulnerable to the darker side of the entrepreneurial personality. The many succession tragedies documented in the family business literature show that when left to their own devices, senior leaders often abuse their prerogative to manage their own retirement. The well-documented evidence of little or no succession planning in so many family businesses doubtless can be explained, in part, by natural and largely unconscious resistances of many business owners—even enlightened and sophisticated owners. While most analyses of this phenomenon emphasize the resistance of the individual aging leader, other powerful elements in the system often conspire to delay or undermine the planning process and the leader's departure.

A generational change threatens to deprive some spouses, for example, of prerogatives and functions in the company that they may have enjoyed for years. These roles may include anything from running a part of the business or managing the company's finances to helping employees with their family problems and organizing social activities for clients.[1] Consciously or not, spouses may support the owner's opposition to planning their departure for a number of reasons, not just loyalty.

The firm's senior managers, too, are confronted with difficult emotional issues. Many of them have probably enjoyed close personal ties with the owner for years; indeed, that may have been one of the reasons they stayed with the company for so long. In a generational transition, their status as members of the senior team—and perhaps even their jobs—may be in jeopardy. Even if their jobs aren't threatened, they may be inclined to hang onto their close, privileged position with the senior owner as long as they can and avoid having to trade it for a more formal relationship with a successor.

This tacit conspiracy to extend the tenure of the senior leader frustrates the generation that may have been waiting in the wings for some time,[2] and in highly competitive industries it can put the future of the whole enterprise in jeopardy. For at this stage the aging owner is often risk-averse—more concerned with protecting wealth than building it. As Ward has frequently noted, the products and ideas responsible for the success of the business may well have matured by this time. A new strategic focus may be necessary to revitalize the company and ensure its survival. Abundant research shows that non-family companies turn over leadership more frequently, in part, to renew the company's strategic direction. In family companies, the failure of aging leaders to adapt to changing markets and embrace innovative ideas can lead to stagnation and the eventual demise of their enterprises.[3]

Whether or not succession planning will occur depends, in the final analysis, on the will and courage of the senior leaders. While other stakeholders in the family business may resist planning, it will go forward if the seniors provide the leadership. In this chapter I will discuss why some leaders are more resistant than others. I will examine the profound psychological dilemma facing seniors at this stage of their lives and its powerful effect on the course of the leadership transfer. The resolution of this dilemma helps to explain why some are capable of letting go and managing their departures smoothly, while others are not. In addition, I will explore the powerful impact of the letting go process on the business, the family, and other critical stakeholders. In particular, I will look closely at the consequences for successors and their teams of each of four different exit "styles" that are typically exhibited by retiring seniors.

The Psychology of Leadership Departure

Business leaders in their mid-to-late sixties must come to terms with the fact that time is running out on the unrealized aspects of their Dreams. Inevitably, people of this age face the realization that much that they set out to do in their lives will be left undone. For those unable to free themselves from a grandiose Dream, time is experienced as a logarithmic progression on an old-fashioned slide rule, in which the distance between the numbers grows increasingly short. With every passing day, the master builder becomes more keenly aware that no matter how hard he works, he will never live to see the completion of his cathedral. Many driven entrepreneurs react to this painful realization by wanting to pack yet more activity into their allotted time. Ironically, some push themselves relentlessly to exhaustion, accelerating the very aging process that terrifies them.

Research has shown that people age at different rates and that the process can be significantly retarded by improvements in diet, increased exercise, and advances in medical technology.[4] Nevertheless, older people are coping with defective vision or hearing, heart disease, cancer, and other chronic ailments. The symptoms of loss of mental acuity from such degenerative brain diseases as senile dementia and Alzheimer's disease develop gradually and are difficult to detect. Like King Lear at his worst, some business owners are slowly transformed into caricatures of their former selves. In its extreme form, the psychological picture is

of a slow deterioration of personality and intellect because of impaired insight and judgment and the loss of affect. The progression of the condition is more painful to the beholder than to the person. Interests become restricted, outlook becomes rigid, conceptual thinking becomes more difficult. . . . Typically, affect is blunted and exaggerated . . . an obsessive person may become unbearably pedantic and rigid, or a social extrovert may become facile and inappropriately jocular.[5]

A poignant memoir in the *New Yorker* magazine dramatized the costly effects on a family and a company when an aging leader demonstrates bizarre symptoms and there are no provisions for his removal. The article traced the downfall of one of the country's oldest and largest frozen food companies, Seabrook Farms. Written by John Seabrook, a grandson of the founder, the article traced the decline of the company directly to the senility of his grandfather, C. F. Seabrook, who remained at the helm well into his eighties, long after he lost his capacity to lead. As early as his mid-fifties, C. F. had shown signs of what was then called "hardening of the arteries," experiencing "spells" in which he would sometimes show up in a clothing store wearing several layers of bathrobes. A stroke in 1941 shook C. F.'s confidence, but he remained firmly in charge of the company, battling his three sons for control, well into the 1950s. Seabrook Farms suffered a series of setbacks that were aggravated by C. F.'s incapacity and the leadership struggles at the top. Efforts by the family to have him declared mentally incompetent in court failed. C. F. Seabrook eventually disowned his sons and sold the company to spite his family.[6]

Not all business owners of advanced age fit this extreme portrait, of course. Still, even many of those who are in relatively good health no longer have the energy and drive and willingness to change that are essential qualities in some industries today. Business owners who have been in power for twenty years or more have accumulated a lifetime of experiences and ideas that may no longer be relevant in a rapidly changing business and economic climate. While it is not easy for anyone to know exactly when a CEO's business philosophy and skills have become "obsolete," the CEO himself is often the last person willing to entertain the possibility that he might no longer be the best person for the job.

The leader's realization that his or her talents and knowledge may be out of touch with changing business realities may come as a rude awakening. This is particularly a problem for entrepreneurs, whose frequently grandiose self-images helped give them the confidence they needed to succeed against all odds. The deeply ingrained conviction that they are masters of their fate is a critical ingredient of the entrepreneurs' relentless determination and success. Indeed, assumptions about the heroic nature of entrepreneurs—and thus about their immortality—are often central, unconscious tenets of the cultures of both their families and their businesses. These hidden assumptions provide the impetus for a system-wide denial of the leader's ultimate demise that conspires against thoughtful planning for the entrepreneur's departure and for the continuity of the family business under the leadership of the next generation.

With their prowess declining, men often become increasingly dependent on their wives. Some of the women turn into true matriarchs who, operating behind the scenes, determine the outcome of many successions. Spouses can either accelerate or delay the rate at which the business owner turns over the leadership role in the business. They can powerfully influence the business owner's assessment of the competencies of their children and, in so doing, alter the standing of one or another of the potential successors. Typically, the wives are younger than their husbands; after the business leader's death, they often become the critical decision makers upon whose wisdom—or lack of it—the survival of the system depends.

As we discussed in the Lombardi case, mothers can also play crucial roles in harmonizing the competitive dynamics among rival siblings. For many business families the death of the mother—rather than that of the all-too-dominant father—becomes the most traumatic hurdle to overcome during the process of generational change.

The Basic Dilemma of Late Adulthood

Whether or not family business owners nearing retirement age use this time in life constructively to secure the continuity of the organizations they have built depends in large measure upon their success in resolving a basic psychological dilemma described by Erik Erikson. Erikson maintained that people at this stage struggle to reconcile themselves with the broader significance of their lives. The fundamental dilemma of this era is an ongoing struggle between "a sense of despair" and "a sense of integrity." For many nearing retirement, the despair stems from a deeply felt disappointment over the lives they have led, a disappointment which, as Levinson pointed out, usually has some basis in reality but which may also contain a large portion of irrational self-accusation. According to Erikson, the sense of despair

expresses the feeling that time is short for any attempt to start another life and try out alternative roads to integrity. Such despair is often hidden behind a show of disgust, a misanthropy, or a chronic contemptuous displeasure with particular institutions and particular people—a disgust and displeasure which, where not allied with the vision of a superior life, only signify the individual's contempt of himself.[7]

The sense of integrity, on the other hand, is described by Erikson as deriving from a transcendent acceptance of one's place in the sequence of human generations:

It is the post-narcissistic love of the human ego—not of the self—as an experience which conveys some world order and spiritual sense, no matter how dearly paid for. It is the acceptance of one's one and only life cycle as something that had to be and that, by necessity, permitted of no substitutions: it thus means a new, a different love of one's parents.[8]

Erikson suggested that this sense of integrity finds expression through the wisdom that is accumulated from countless life experiences and from a fuller appreciation of the extent to which one is the product of a particular culture and a singular moment in the flow of human history:

Strength here takes the form of that detached yet active concern with life bounded by death, which we call wisdom in its many connotations from ripened "wits" to accumulated knowledge, mature judgment, and inclusive understanding. . . . The end of the cycle also evokes "ultimate concerns" for what chance man may have to transcend the limitations of his identity and his often tragic or bitterly tragicomic engagement in his one and only life.[9]

The fundamental tension described by Erikson suggests that business owners unable to overcome their sense of despair will be incapable of mobilizing the courage and internal resources necessary to relinquish their control over family and business decisions to the next generation. Their narcissism, this theory would predict, prevents them from appreciating and empathizing with the needs of their successors. They are incapable of viewing the next generation with the spirit of generativity that Erikson deemed essential to fulfillment in later life. So long as aging business owners remain preoccupied with the pursuit of their own heroic mission, thoughts about their physical decline and ultimate death can be kept at bay. The pursuit of the impossible Dream keeps the entrepreneur's system in tension and engaged in life.

From a succession standpoint, Erikson echoed Dostoevski's insight that death must first be reckoned with before the magnificence of life can be fully appreciated and embraced. It is through the very acceptance of their own mortality that business owners marshal the courage and energy needed to plan the continuity of their organizations. And, in so doing, they actually consolidate their legacy and their contribution to future generations—which, after all, is as close as any man or woman can come to immortality.

Four Styles of Departure

By invoking Erikson's analysis, I am not suggesting that seniors entering late adulthood must disengage from life and renounce further accomplishment. On the contrary, the sociological literature on retirement shows that for many seniors, the absence of meaningful work frequently accelerates the aging process. The question becomes whether seniors can find challenges that enable them to move on from leadership of their enterprises and give the next generation their opportunity to steer the ship.

To describe how different business leaders handle the psychological consequences of this transition, I will use the terms supplied by Jeffrey Sonnenfeld in his insightful book *The Hero's Farewell: What Happens When CEOs Retire*.[10] Using surveys of CEOs of both family and non-family companies, Sonnenfeld describes four styles of departure of retiring leaders. Two of the types, the "monarchs" and the "generals," are unable to surrender control of their companies in earnest. The other two types, the "ambassadors" and "governors," turn over control to successors and leave office gracefully and constructively.

Each style, in my experience, reflects a different manifestation of the inner Eriksonian drama. The ambassadors and governors are able to achieve a proactive, constructive resolution of this psychological dilemma, while monarchs and generals engage in a reactive struggle in which the despair-versus-integrity polarity may never be successfully resolved.

Contrary to Sonnenfield, who did not find any correlations between the exit styles of the four types and particular managerial styles, I have found in observing family companies that monarchs and generals tend to be more autocratic in managing, while ambassadors and governors are generally more consultative or democratic. These differences become important to the succession process because a leader's management style creates the organizational context in which succession is planned or isn't planned, moves forward or is resisted, is successfully completed or is stymied. It influences the kind of people the company hires, the rules and procedures it establishes for retirement, the training and evaluation of successor candidates, and the extent to which managers are encouraged to think independently and creatively. The importance of all of these actions looms larger as the transition approaches.

The monarchs fit a familiar stereotype: They refuse to let go and typically will not even consider planning their departures. The generals are as determined as monarchs to stay in power and retain control, but their strategies are more devious and subtle. They may actually embark on a succession plan while unconsciously plotting their eventual return to power—by, for example, installing an incompetent successor. Under Erikson's theory, we may assume that members of both groups have been unable to successfully compromise on their lifelong Dream and achieve a new level of acceptance in their "one and only life"—a sense of wholeness and inner peace. These business owners are fundamentally driven by anxiety. At a time in life when they could be enjoying the fruits of their successes, they are instead running from their fears; they continue to drive themselves hard in order to avoid the specter of obsolescence and death. They seem unable to fully appreciate their accomplishments and contributions to the lives of others.

The monarchs are often narcissistic personalities[11] who structure their environments in ways that foster dependency in both their families and their businesses. As they get older, they become even less willing to delegate authority and share information. They select managers and advisers who are not independent in viewpoint or behavior. They may also attempt to control every decision in the lives of family members, from their spouse's wardrobe to their children's choices of mates. In a relentless effort to get their way, they offer or withdraw family resources such as money, the use of vacation homes, automobiles, or stock or positions in the family business.

Characteristically, monarchs are unwilling to consider any type of planning for continuity. Their spouses and children, as well as their senior managers, are usually disinclined to raise questions about succession until the evidence of the owner's decline—and the risks to their own security and wealth—becomes abundantly clear. "Fueled by their compelling vision," Sonnenfeld writes, "monarchs rule until death, until forcible removal by palace revolts of the board or their subordinates, or until the firm is sold."[12] In some cases the health of aging monarchs is so fragile that people around them fear that to raise issue of retirement would upset them and jeopardize their lives. In the rare cases when a consultant is hired to jump-start a succession process, the aging owner will typically meet his or her arrival with suspicion, either turning his back on the consultation or actively sabotaging the process. Because the power to change the system and structure a succession plan is usually in the senior owner's hands, little can be accomplished without the person's involvement. But sometimes a near brush with death, either directly or vicariously through the loss of a business associate or dear friend, can mobilize a monarch to do something about succession.

In one family company I studied, a quintessential monarch, the founder of a real estate empire, made considerable progress in developing an effective estate and succession plan only after medical complications from minor surgery nearly killed him. During his two-month absence from the company, his oldest son flawlessly carried out a complex acquisition of a major competitor. When the founder returned to the business, the realization that he was no longer indispensable came as a shock. Seeing that his son was capable of extraordinarily effective leadership when given the opportunity, the father confessed to me:

My return to the business has been a bittersweet experience. On the one hand, I was very happy to see that my son, the senior management team, and the board functioned so effectively without me. On the other, I was depressed to realize that my son, the senior management team and the board functioned so effectively without me.

After years of resisting the advice of his lawyer, accountant, and consultant, he finally implemented critical elements of his much discussed, but always delayed, continuity plan. Prior to his illness, his estate plan divided the stock of the company approximately equally among his children. Unfortunately, the relationship among the siblings was plagued with rivalry and competition, and it was quite clear that the conditions for a sibling partnership simply did not exist. While in the hospital he thought hard about the complications that were likely to arise in the future were he not to leave control of the company squarely in the hands of his oldest son. Upon his return, the father restructured the estate plan in a way that would give the oldest son unequivocal control of the business. Shortly thereafter, however, the founder returned to power with more force and dynamism than before, displaying the typical monarch's resistance to ever abdicating the throne. His new estate plan, however, had significantly improved the likelihood that the business would continue after he is gone. Over time the father has turned his considerable energy to new projects both inside and outside the company that keep him engaged and out of the way of the son and his executive team. However, to this day he still cannot resist the urge to behave arbitrarily on some important matter in order to remind everyone who is really "the boss."

Potential successors to monarchs often fit the stereotype of the cowed, weak-willed heirs of empire builders. Lacking opportunities to develop their potential and rise in the family company, the best and the brightest choose to go elsewhere to pursue their careers. Those who are left behind are forced into secondary roles. Many are filled with rage at having given up their own Dreams for a life of dependency and powerlessness. Their sense that only the monarch's death will free them to pursue their own ambitions often fills them with guilt. Indeed, it is only after the monarch's death that some of them do, in fact, blossom. Frequently, however, it is too late by this time to repair the psychological damage to their self-esteem and to correct the dependency culture created by the monarch's autocratic rule.

For the spouses, on the other hand, the monarch's demise often offers an opportunity: They may carry on the monarch's Dream, if they have always been highly committed to it themselves, but with a different style. They often try desperately to repair some of the damage done to family relationships, by introducing a softer and more accommodating approach in both the company and the family. However, their efforts often run into trouble because one or another of the children tries to emulate the authoritarian style established by the deceased monarch. Many, nonetheless, use this time to groom successors who will be able to take over the company in the future.

Generals exhibit less frustration than monarchs at having to sacrifice the fulfillment of their Dream at this stage of their lives. They are more willing to surrender some of the prerogatives and trappings of power in order to preserve their authority. If they initiate a process to plan succession in the company, however, it is usually because they know that this is what is expected of great leaders. But they often install weak successors, or deprive them of the training and development opportunities they need in order to succeed, or insist on keeping senior managers loyal to them rather than letting the successors pick their own executive teams.

The leadership may actually be transferred to a successor—or successor team—while the general keeps a watchful eye on their performance. But the transfer may be timed to coincide with a crisis situation in the company that will make it harder for the new leadership to succeed. Like General de Gaulle in postwar French governments, the old leader then lies in wait for the opportunity to demonstrate the flaws and failures of the new leadership—and his or her own indispensability to the company. Riding to the rescue of the company, the general gains a sense of vindication by proving that those who may have forced his or her retirement were misguided, and that only he—or she—is capable of fulfilling the vision and doing the job as it should be done.

This is not to say that the general's strategy is consciously Machiavellian or evil. Indeed, the general's deeper motives may be kept from consciousness for good reason: A parent who pursues such a strategy in a family business would find it difficult to live with the guilt of plotting against his or her own children. Like monarchs, generals are fleeing from the threat of their own decline and demise. They fear that in surrendering the symbols and prerogatives of their positions their lives will be empty and meaningless. Unlike the monarchs, the generals send conflicting signals to those around them. By going through the motions of planning their exits, they raise hopes and expectations, only to dash them before any real change has occurred.

For would-be successors, the frustration and humiliation of having power given and then taken away by generals—sometimes repeatedly—can engender feelings of helplessness that erode the successor's effectiveness and initiative. They live in constant worry that the exiting generals will criticize their performance and undermine their authority. In many business families, this no-win situation leads to an escalating conflict between the generations, a polarization of the family, and bitter feelings that sometimes linger for generations.

Ambassadors Remain but Find New Roles

Unlike the monarchs and generals, the governors and ambassadors are psychologically able to achieve the sense of integration that is necessary to negotiate the challenges posed by advancing age. The ambassadors turn over managerial authority to their successors, but work out a continuing role for themselves as advisers or representatives of the family business. The governors are able to sever their ties with the family company entirely and move on to new challenges, such as starting another business, running for public office, or getting involved with a family foundation. Both types are able to overcome the disappointment at not having achieved all they may have wished for in life, and consequently become more adept at attending to the needs of the next generation. Instead of envying the vigor and prowess of the young—as the monarchs and generals are inclined to do—the governors and ambassadors take pride in their successors' development and achievements. They are able to see their own values and aspirations continued through the younger generation. At the same time, they understand that their successors are separate from them and, in order to succeed as leaders, must think and act for themselves.

The ambassadors and governors nurture independent thinking and growth, not just in their successors but in their employees as well. This quality significantly enhances their ability to delegate and to empower their subordinates. It also enables them to overcome fears of their own obsolescence and, instead, focus on productive activities they might pursue in retirement. Often the new activities are eagerly anticipated, not because they represent an extension of a grandiose Dream, but for their own sake, for their inherent interest, even for the very reason that they free the aging leader from a lifelong, obsessive need to achieve and excel. The spouses of ambassadors and governors, in my experience, tend to be supportive of their efforts to plan for the day when they will be free to pursue other activities and spend more time with their families. These spouses are often excited about the possibilities that retirement may offer for them as a couple.

Both types feel fundamentally satisfied with their contributions to the companies they have led. They differ, however, in the extent to which they still want to remain connected to it. The ambassadors wish to retain a connection to the company, but without longing to return to power. Under the best of circumstances, ambassadors retain the respect and authority that comes from being elder statesmen, without succumbing to the temptation to directly influence those now responsible for major decisions.

By this stage of their lives, ambassadors have usually completed the hands-on mentoring of their successors and are content to play an advisory role to the new leaders, perhaps with the title of chairman or simply as board members. (Actually, the choice of a dignified title for a departing ambassador can be quite intricate. Some are called chairman emeritus; in larger companies, they may become chairman of the executive committee of the board.) They may devote much of their time to outside activities, representing the company at ceremonial functions in the community or in philanthropic activities. Sometimes they are able to continue in an important nonmanagerial function in the company. For example, one founder of a company I studied was an engineer whose first love was research and development. He had invented the roller technology for processing raw steel into bars. In his mid-seventies, after turning over control of the company to his son, this former CEO returned to the R&D department—"to the bench"—where he continued to do research. By the time my study was over, he was eighty-three years old and had obtained five new patents for inventions that became leading products for the company.

The very presence of the ambassador may create some confusion among employees and other stakeholders and prevent successors from clearly establishing their own identities and agendas. In the best of cases, the successors have established their right to lead, beyond all doubt, by their own performance. However, departing leaders can do much to clarify their new roles as supporting players by open expressions of trust in the new leader and support for his or her management team—and by giving advice only when asked. They can also continue to serve as a bridge between the newer, younger leaders and members of the older generation outside the company who are still customers, business partners, or suppliers of the company. Symbolic gestures can also become important to clarifying the ambassador's new status within the company. For example, to emphasize that the successor is now in charge, the departing leader may vacate the executive suite and move his or her office to another floor or even a different location outside of the main business. The Polaroid board, wishing to honor founder Edwin Land's legacy—without his involvement in management—built him his own "castle on the Charles" in Cambridge, a good distance from headquarters.

Steve Bechtel, Sr., the former CEO of the worldwide family construction company, provides another example of an ambassador who seems to have clearly defined—and carefully observed—the boundaries of his role after turning over control to his son, Steve Jr., in 1960. The father, as chairman emeritus of the company, visited the company's customers and business associates around the world. His presence symbolized the importance the company accorded to a given venture or project. While the father would engage in exploratory discussions of business contracts with government officials or other potential clients on these trips, he would bow out when discussions reached a serious stage and turn the actual negotiations over to the successor and his team. This succession pattern worked well: Steve Jr. adapted it for the leadership transition to his son, Riley, in the late 1980s.

The key to the ambassador's new role is continued mutual trust between departing leader and successor. This is most likely to occur, my research indicates, when the two—usually parent and son or daughter—have had a longstanding high quality relationship. Ambassadors are able to maintain their positions and continue to contribute to the company so long as they do not use their authority and reputation in ways that are contrary to the objectives of the new management team. When the seniors continue to express their trust and support of the juniors, and the juniors respect the dignity of the elders and continue to pay homage to the seniors' past contributions, the company profits from the continued presence and counsel of the ambassadors.

Because many generals go through the motions of planning their succession, it takes a discerning eye to distinguish them from ambassadors. One of the most significant differences is that the generals tend to choose weaker, more dependent successors, while ambassadors are likely to select the strongest candidates. In addition, generals are likely to be a lot slower than ambassadors to transfer ownership control to their successors. While many owners retain voting control after transferring the majority of stock to the next generation, generals are inclined to hold on to the stock even after turning management of the company over to successors.

Another test of a retiring senior's true intentions may occur soon after the transfer of leadership. Since adversities of one sort or another are inevitable in business—economic downturns, the emergence of new competitors, a falloff in demand for a principal product—the successor is likely to confront a major challenge soon after taking control. When that happens, the predecessor's behavior will indicate whether he or she has truly renounced command of the company. Generals are likely to see the adversity facing their successor as an opportunity to reassert their power, and may take steps to undermine the successor, by indicating, for example, that the new leader is not competent to handle the challenge. The reaction of ambassadors is likely to be just the opposite. Instead of seeing adversity as an opportunity to jump back into the leadership role, they view it as a chance for the successor to demonstrate his or her mettle. They will convey their unwavering confidence in the successor's ability to handle the situation, and yet make themselves available to provide advice in the situation, should the successor request it. And if their advice is not sought, they are not angry or disappointed.

Governors Move to a New Playing Field

Of the four types, governors are the least concerned with the trappings of office and the least ambivalent about severing their ties with the family business. While they may still be eager to pursue unfulfilled aspects of their Dream, they move on to new playing fields in order to realize their unmet aspirations. It is interesting to note that Sonnenfeld's survey of family companies indicates that governors tended to come from larger companies with established boards of directors and active independent directors. In these companies, the succession process tends to be more institutionalized. These CEOs were generally less successful than other leaders in terms of their overall performance, but they had managed to turn things around in their organizations during the final two years of their tenure. This finding suggests that they were perhaps able to create a forgiving and supportive organizational context that permitted them to make a clean break with the company themselves.

In my experience, governors in family companies are typically driven by a wish to rekindle their own entrepreneurial spirit. Entrepreneurs to the core, they derive much more pleasure from the startup phase of business development than from managing a more mature enterprise. They love the energy and excitement of the formative years and may have even grown bored with the family business. It is not unusual to see governors nearing retirement team up with their children to create entirely new ventures. When this process is managed effectively it can result in a diversification of the family's assets and encourage the entrepreneurial spirit among family members. (Paul Lombardi, Sr., who, as we saw, preferred to "teach people to fish" rather than to give them a fish, in his later years joined his grandchildren in a number of successful business ventures.) Like some ambassadors, many governors choose to become very active in philanthropic circles and create their own foundations. Still others have gone into teaching, consulting, or politics. Some are very distinguished members of their communities or have national stature and accept government and ambassadorial posts. Many see such service as an opportunity to give back to their countries and to test themselves in a new and broader arena of influence.

David Rockefeller's departure from Chase Manhattan Bank is an example of how true governors go about planning their exit. After a long career at the bank—and contrary to the expectations of many—Rockefeller managed to turn over control to Willard Butcher, his longtime associate and chosen successor. Rockefeller had developed many external interests that facilitated his retirement as Chase's chairman. Following his departure, he became more active in the Rockefeller Brothers Fund and various other family enterprises. He did more philanthropic work with such organizations as the Museum of Modern Art in New York and with Harvard and Rockefeller Universities. He became involved in international activities with the Council on Foreign Relations, the Trilateral Commission, and the International Executive Service Corps (which he founded with the purpose of encouraging retired executives to serve in developing countries). He also devoted considerable attention to maintaining his family's unity and its economic and social vitality. In an interview on his retirement, Rockefeller commented:

For my own part, I seem to continue to be as busy as ever. Indeed, I have just returned from a trip to the Far East in which I was able to combine some pleasure with business. . . . Perhaps I have been more fortunate than some others in having these opportunities, but my retirement has been a very rich and rewarding experience. Certainly, any fears of sitting at an empty desk waiting for the phone to ring have proved unfounded.[13]

Organizational Complications

In his analysis of the various exit styles, Sonnenfeld rightly alerts us to the risks of viewing any given style as inherently good or bad for a business. In fact, the very leadership qualities that may serve the organization well during one period of its development may hinder business continuity at a later stage. The perseverance associated with monarchs and generals, their zealous commitment to the pursuit of a singular vision, is the fundamental driving force behind the growth of a business. When the time comes for them to move on from their company, however, those same qualities can become roadblocks to succession. Likewise, the psychological maturity and generosity of spirit that enables ambassadors to be effective mentors to the next generation can make it difficult for their successors to establish their own leadership and sense of direction. The difficulty here typically lies with the successors, who wrestle with feelings of betrayal and guilt if their management style or policies diverge from those of the former leader. This issue can come to a head, for example, if successors are forced to retire senior executives who have been loyal to the ambassador during his or her tenure.

Because of such complications, the process by which the next generation takes charge of the business is often prolonged. This drawn-out transition is risky in times of rapid environmental change that call for a fundamental rethinking of business strategy. In one company, the successors' hesitation to discontinue manufacture of the ambassadorial founder's favorite products, and their reluctance to launch new and more innovative product lines, cost the company significant losses in market share. When asked why it had taken them so long to reposition the product mix, one of the successors said: "Regardless of how much business sense it made, closing down the side of this company that was most associated with our father felt to us like slapping him in the face after all he has done for us." It was not until the ambassadorial founder himself started to voice his concerns about the company's loss of market share that the successors felt comfortable implementing the needed strategic changes.

As for governors, their very eagerness to sever their ties with the organization and pursue other endeavors can create problems for the family company. The sudden absence of the former leader may be experienced by the successors as an act of abandonment. Even a more gradual disengagement from the company may result in a neglect of the process by which authority is turned over to the next generation. It is not unusual, for example, for governors to underestimate the extent to which their wisdom, support, and coaching are essential to an effective handoff of leadership responsibilities.

Retirement styles also have significant consequences for the families of departing CEOs. Other things being equal, relationships in families of monarchs and generals tend to be considerably more complex and dysfunctional than those in families of ambassadors and governors. The hard-driving ambition of monarchs and generals often brings them into conflict with their loved ones during the transition period. Typically, they are not very interested in the Dreams, aspirations, and needs of the young, and they can often get into generational battles during the succession process that can have devastating consequences for family relationships. Those who do get around to selecting a successor sometimes do so only after reaching the terrifying conclusion that they may not live long enough to realize their lofty aspirations. When this occurs, they may seek out someone in their family to whom they can delegate the completion of their Dream. Paradoxically, they often want someone who resembles them, and, at the same time, will be subservient to their wishes.

The family dynamics that accompany the retirement of ambassadors and governors tend to be less problematic. Because these leaders are less driven by narcissism, they tend to be more empathetic to the needs of the younger generation and much more open to discussions about the leadership transition. A shared family Dream is born precisely out of open, ongoing discussions of family members' aspirations that start while children are young. More importantly, the families of ambassadors and governors are often better able to support their members as they embark in the pursuit of their Dreams in the family business or outside of it.

Nevertheless, ambassadors and governors stepping down from leadership of the business face some problems of adjustment. Turning over control of the business to their offspring requires an acceptance of the fact that their centrality in the family—up to now derived in part from their control of the family's principal source of income—will eventually come to an end. Over time, as the parents age, responsibility for organizing family gatherings—say, for Passover, Christmas, and Thanksgiving dinners—is taken over by their children. The elderly parents become honored guests. In many ambassadorial successions, the offspring deliberately delay their involvement with these functions so that the implicit hierarchy of the family is not altered abruptly, thus allowing the parents more time to make their adjustment into old age.

Retirement in Flocks: Cousins and Siblings

The problems of leadership succession and retirement associated with sibling partnerships and cousin consortiums are more complex because of the sheer numbers of leaders who may retire at once or within a short time frame. In sibling partnerships, the issues associated with leadership and ownership succession almost invariably increase the level of stress among the fraternal partners. It is not unusual for siblings who collaborated well over a lifetime to find themselves suddenly entangled in intense conflict over succession in the business. The timing as well as the terms of their departures are frequent bones of contention. Often their conflicts center on whether the siblings should retire sequentially over a period of years, thus giving each sibling a turn at the helm, or all together, thus accelerating the shift of power to the next generation.

In sequential retirements, the siblings who will relinquish their management responsibilities first (usually the older ones, but not always) tend to be mistrustful of what the others will do with the business when they gain command. Typically, the siblings who exit management remain involved as shareholders. They often feel the need to monitor the performance of the siblings left in control and second-guess their decisions. When departing siblings are bought out, they may still keep a close watch on the company's results because the payout process is often stretched over an extended period.

The retirement of some siblings can be tricky for another reason: It may leave a serious deficiency of skills at the senior level. Younger siblings, in particular, tend to underestimate the extent to which the success of the fraternal partnership stemmed from the overall mix of skills and experience that the siblings as a group brought to the leadership team. Those who stay involved in the management of the business sometimes feel a strong need to demonstrate that they can do a better job of managing the company by themselves—at times at the expense of the business. Drops in the performance of the business can lead to a crisis unless the siblings fill the void in functional skills that results when one or another partner retires. Such a crisis, moreover, may prod the departing siblings into coming back from retirement and set up an escalating conflict that paralyzes the succession process.

This dynamic is often compounded by the fears of the siblings who have left the company that those who remain may do something to take advantage of them. Some worry that the ones left behind will alter existing compensation arrangements and begin to take out more in salary and benefits than they did in the past. Others are concerned that the siblings in control will not share relevant information about what is happening in the business with them. In other words, those who leave must find ways of constructively negotiating the movement out of management and into roles as passive shareholders. An important part of that change requires developing the structures and the level of trust necessary to negotiate the boundaries between management and ownership.

Naturally, the individual plans of the sibling team members make an important difference in how a sequential succession unfolds. For example, a conflict between the siblings that stay involved and those who choose to retire may create just the kind of opportunity that a departing general needs to subvert the succession transition. If a lead sibling acts like a monarch or a general, he or she could jeopardize the succession planning process, unless, of course, the other siblings can exert sufficient pressure to enforce a planned departure.

When a group of sibling partners all retire together, the key issue is how to select their successors. As we have noted, the process of assessing the competence and capabilities of their children can rekindle old rivalries among sibling partners. Often the retiring siblings try to circumvent this potential conflict by instituting another shared leadership arrangement much like their own. However, the likelihood that such a recycled system can work in the cousins' generation is quite small. The relationships among cousins are typically quite different from those of the siblings, as we have argued, because of their wider array of needs and interests. Senior partners who handle the transition process most effectively often buy time by installing an interim non-family manager who can be a mentor for the cousins and make more impartial assessments of their individual capabilities.

A strategy for managing the retirement of the sibling partners is indispensable for the transition to succeed. In partnerships that manage the demands of this stage well, the seniors agree on a schedule for the succession well in advance. They may, for example, agree on a formal retirement age and make a commitment to monitor one another's retirement plans as the process unfolds. When siblings all leave at the same time, it is advisable to develop a retirement scenario that allows the siblings to continue their collaboration well into their retirement. Retirement projects such as the development of a family foundation, a family office to coordinate the family's wealth management, or alternative business ventures can be designed so as to retain the interest of all the retiring siblings. An additional advantage of doing this is that the siblings can continue giving one another support in adjusting to retirement—and they can monitor one another's behavior so that none of them makes an attempt to sabotage the succession.

For family companies that have reached the cousins phase, the letting go stage also raises both concerns and opportunities. On the one hand, these companies tend to be larger and more complex structures and consequently offer a broader range of elder statesmen roles for seniors to retire to. As I've noted, cousin consortiums are often made up of a group of operating companies which may or may not be strategically interrelated and which are owned jointly by a holding company controlled by the cousins. In these systems, cousins who have been active in management can play a constructive role not just on the holding company board but on the boards of the subsidiaries as well. Having a wider array of roles to choose from at the senior levels provides more flexibility in managing the process of letting go.

On the other hand, the succession process in cousin-owned and cousin-managed consortiums is vulnerable to the complex branch politics of the extended family. I've already described the two factors that determine how power is distributed among the cousins: Branches with fewer cousins, each owning more stock than cousins in branches whose shares are more fractionated, are in a powerful position, as are branches that have more members in senior executive roles than the others. Cousins in leadership roles have an influential role in shaping the career paths of junior family members, for example, and they often try to maintain the status quo by promoting younger members of their branch as potential successor candidates. Moreover, they resist succession planning in order to hang onto power long enough to nurture the development of junior cousins from their branch.

The retirement of those cousins in control of management becomes an opportunity for cousins in other branches to realign the balance of power in their favor. Branches that have been traditionally excluded from senior management try to seize the moment and push their candidates into top slots, arguing that it is "our turn" to manage the company. If these disenfranchised branches have been unable to produce qualified successors, however, they may well advocate hiring non-family managers for the top positions in order to weaken the traditional hold of the "in" branches. The branches on the outside looking in may also view the succession transition as an opportunity to correct managerial deficiencies that they had hesitated to raise when control rested in the hands of the leading branches. The "outs" can thus attempt to enhance their control during leadership transitions in two ways: by insisting on the involvement of cousins from their branch or by making the branches in power accountable through the adoption of more explicit and professional standards of managerial practice.

Just as in publicly held companies, the tenure in office of senior leaders in cousin consortiums is contingent on their ability to generate effective results for the business. Surprisingly, even these older companies do not usually have institutional ways of easing leaders into retirement. It is still rare to find large cousin companies in which the succession process has been adequately institutionalized and monitored. This makes the choice of future leaders in these companies even more vulnerable to political forces than it is in the larger, publicly traded non-family companies.

The Need for Clarity About Timing

Business families who manage succession effectively pay a great deal of attention to the timing of the process and make it explicit. The seniors and juniors negotiate step by step when and how the transfer of executive responsibilities will occur. Because people have to plan their work according to fixed dates, they focus their energies on delivering on their promises to one another. An agreed-upon retirement schedule also depersonalizes the exit process. It allows older siblings to move out of management without feeling as if they are being discriminated against. It can thus reduce the risk that destructive rivalries will be awakened.

Clarity about timing is important precisely because it encourages the seniors to be accountable and decreases the likelihood that they will, whether consciously or not, sabotage the process. The timing of succession will depend upon the exit styles of the aging leaders—and, indeed, on whether or not they are willing to depart at all. As we have seen, mobilizing a monarch to plan for succession is like pushing a rock uphill. So far neither social science research nor the experiences of family business practitioners have yielded creative solutions for preventing the rock from rolling downhill time and again. To put it bluntly, would-be successors to monarchs usually have only two options: They can either stay in the family business and wait until the leader dies, or they can leave and pursue their interests outside the family business.

An agreed-upon schedule for the transfer may prevent a general from leaving prematurely in the hope of returning triumphantly, like the knight in shining armor, to save the day at a later time. An explicit schedule enables the company to monitor the progress of the transition and hold a general's feet to the fire on the agreed withdrawal dates. In one company, the successor did everything he was asked in order to prepare himself to take charge of management, but his father, a general at heart, kept changing the terms of the transition. At one point the son complained:

I'm certainly willing to work hard to prepare myself to lead this company. However, it is disheartening to see that every time I score my father decides to change the rules of the game.

The situation did not change until an explicit schedule for the succession was negotiated and presented to the board of directors for their approval and monitoring.

Because they remain close to the company, ambassadors may be tempted to interfere with the new leadership. Often they get sucked back into management by the neediness of others who call upon them for their opinions and expertise. Here again, an agreed-upon schedule is indispensable to inform everyone of the timetable of the ambassador's retirement and, more important, to make clear the ground rules of his or her future role.

As for governors, it is essential to devote considerable thought to the timing of their departure, lest they be tempted to disengage from the family business prematurely. The development of a schedule can help ensure that the business will continue to benefit from the input of governors beyond their time as leaders of the company. Some family companies work out consulting contracts with parting governors in order to keep a formal connection with them. Some retain them as board or committee members. In all such arrangements, the role given to departing governors should have real substance. If it doesn't, they are likely to resent being forced to prolong their connection with the family company and may distance themselves psychologically from it.

Planning for Retirement

With the possible exception of true governors, most family business leaders do not have a clear vision of their lives in retirement. Aging business owners need to be encouraged to think seriously about what they will do once they step down from the top job.

The psychological literature shows significant individual differences in how people adjust to retirement. The vast majority of Americans look forward to retiring; in fact, only one-fifth of people ages sixty-five to seventy-four are still working at jobs. Studies show that most seniors are quite content to lay down their former responsibilities and enjoy a relatively leisurely life, many would resent being forced to remain "in the saddle" or maintain their former levels of activity.[14] The literature also suggests that aging adults who have been accustomed to lives filled with mental and social stimulation are not content to sit on the front porch and watch the passing traffic. Indeed, there is evidence that those who maintain former levels of stimulation stay healthy longer than that do retirees who disengage psychologically from work and social networks. Other research suggests that cognitive ability declines among those who are no longer called upon to handle complex tasks. Most people do, in fact, maintain their activity patterns after retirement. According to one text on human development, retirement has no noticeable effect on the size of retirees' social networks, the frequency of their social contacts, or their satisfaction with the social support they receive: "It appears that people in old age are satisfied in old age when they can achieve a good fit between their lifestyle and their individual needs, preferences and personality."[15]

They may enjoy opportunities to relax and pursue leisure activities at first, but sooner or later they will become restless. Researcher Robert Atchley has proposed that retirees go through three phases after leaving their careers. For a few months, they go through a honeymoon phase in which they partake of all the leisure activities they have been meaning to do for years and never had time for. They relish their newfound freedom and spend time playing golf or traveling with their spouses. Men who have been retired for thirteen to eighteen months, however, show some disenchantment with their new lifestyles; in this second phase of retirement, they are restless and no longer so optimistic about the future. The research literature identifies a third phase, however, in which men who had been retired for longer periods were relatively satisfied again.[16] Unfortunately, research on the retirement patterns of women in business careers has yet to be done.[17]

Our culture does not do a very good job of celebrating retiring leaders. Business owners who gather the courage to plan their exit often find that the world does not offer them a great deal of positive reinforcement. If anything, planning for one's departure is seen as a sign of weakness rather than as a manifestation of responsible leadership. A business owner I interviewed told me:

When I finally decided to do something about my succession in the business, the first thing I did was to tell my closest friends—all of them business owners like myself—and, much to my surprise, they each told me in their own distinct way that I was "nuts." One asked me whether I had gotten bad news from the doctor or something. . . . Another just came right out and said, "You're still young and vital. How can you abandon the troops so early in the game?" It took me a while to figure out that my willingness to attend to this issue, threatened them with their own succession and mortality issues.

Given these attitudes, it is not surprising that even those business owners who have done a superb job of planning their retirement feel self-conscious about their new status. On this issue perhaps more than any other, it is truly "lonely at the top." The very absence of a vocabulary for expressing and describing the experience is a serious hindrance to communication in business families that are facing a generational change. Often a good deal of the anxiety generated about retirement stems not from the major existential dilemmas it raises, but from relatively mundane questions about what life will actually be like in retirement, such as What will I use for an office? What title should I put on my business cards? Who will answer my phone? Attending to these concerns early in the leadership transition can often greatly facilitate the business owner's willingness to let go. Some business owners anticipate these issues well in advance of their retirement. Some hire a personal assistant to whom they can delegate many of the responsibilities for the management of their private affairs that may have been handled in the past by their corporate staff. Others establish their own private offices, complete with secretaries and staff, away from company headquarters.

Another concern of business owners contemplating retirement is that they will be ignored and ultimately forgotten when they step down. Typically, their lives have been so centered in running the family company that they do not appreciate the extent to which their skills are transferable to other activities. If encouraged to plan for a second career, they may reply that at their age it would be futile, if not ludicrous. Yet many business owners, like David Rockefeller, find themselves busier than ever in their retirement years. In my experience, business owners who are most successful in retirement have somehow managed to get back in touch with their Dreams and rekindle them in new roles and venues. For some, this may involve rediscovering aspects of their personality, such as an artistic sensibility, that have lain dormant. For others, the new roles may include work-related challenges such as serving on the boards of other companies or pursuing new business ventures. For many the process may include getting more involved in philanthropic activities and community work. Finally, for many business owners the incentive to retire is the opportunity it will give them to reconnect with spouses, children, and grandchildren.

There is some hope that retirement will no longer be regarded as a one-way ticket to oblivion. Aware of the need to learn about succession and retirement, some leaders have begun to form support groups with other business owners with whom they can compare experiences and learn. Over the past ten years many family business support and educational groups have sprung up throughout the country, usually as part of university-based outreach programs. Educational programs can help leaders of businesses to understand that they have an essential responsibility to the people who depend on them, and especially to the enterprise they have built, to plan their departure effectively. The best programs include opportunities to learn from others who have been through the experience themselves and can offer insights on how to manage the transition. These kinds of educational experiences can also help spouses and juniors understand the complex emotional issues faced by senior leaders planning their departure. This is particularly important because the heroic stature that leaders have acquired in their families and businesses often creates an aura of self-reliance and invulnerability about them. As the spouse of a prominent entrepreneur once told me:

My husband has always been the rock of Gibraltar for us. We have grown accustomed to his strength and confidence. It never really occurred to us that he could ever grow weaker, that he would ultimately depend on us for support. Frankly, after you've lived with Superman for forty years it is hard —and scary—to accept that he is actually human and frail like the rest of us.

For the followers in the company, the excessive idealization of a leader throughout his or her career comes home to roost when the boss begins to appear more vulnerable. At a deeper psychological level, they may suddenly feel abandoned, without a secure parental figure to take care of them. Or they may experience the leader's behavior as a profound betrayal, as if they have previously been living a lie. They may become punitive toward the departing leader, for example, by withholding offers of help and support at just the time when he or she needs them the most.

The lack of understanding of what the retiring leader is going through only strengthens the psychological resistances to succession planning. All too frequently spouses collude with the leader's resistance by letting their own fears of what life will be like after the leader's retirement take hold. The spouses have often taken part in the leader's Dream and, on his or her long climb to the pinnacle of entrepreneurial success, they have held the legs of the ladder steady. Many have forged their own identities as the spouse of a powerful business owner. They worry about their own loss of status when the leader surrenders his or her position.

Although educational programs can help enormously, such programs alone are certainly not enough to overcome the resistances associated with succession planning. As I have argued, families that manage succession effectively tend to frame the process so that the expectations regarding the timing of the leadership change are reasonably clear. Rather than steering into the unknown with no compass, these families lay out their course clearly and work at clarifying the length of time it will take for the generational transition to take place—that is, for the outgoing leaders to step aside and for the new leaders to consolidate their control over executive decisions, policies, and resources.

This chapter and the three previous ones have dealt with the planning of succession and the key issues and tasks faced by both generations during each stage. Now we will turn to the institutional structures that can determine success or failure. We will examine the unique requirements of the governance of a family company and how three key elements—the board, the shareholders' assembly, and the family council—are organized to ensure continuity.

PART IV

Governance for Continuity

CHAPTER 12

Governance Structures and Processes for Continuity

IN large and complex family business systems, ownership may be indirect and difficult to untangle. The family holdings are often tied up in trusts that have the effect of giving a few trustees ultimate authority over the company's destiny. In many cases, the structure is designed not only to reduce taxes but also to prevent family emotions from disrupting the management of the business. The lawyers for the principal owner purposely design the trusts and write a shareholders' agreement that will block any effort by dissident family members to challenge the principal's control.

This containment strategy is, in my view, basically wrong-headed. It usually reflects the principal owner's unwillingness to deal with the human side of running a family business—the messy emotions that come with the territory, especially in later generations when there are many more family members with varying interests and points of view. No matter how strong the legal dam erected by the principal owner, it is likely to give way under pressure from members of succeeding generations.

My view is that interests and emotions can be successfully managed, and that it is essential to do so in order to ensure continuity in a family business. Keeping the shareholders happy and committed to the business is good for both the business and the family. And the best way to accomplish that is to establish forums where the separate issues and

Figure 12-1 Governance Structure for Family Enterprise

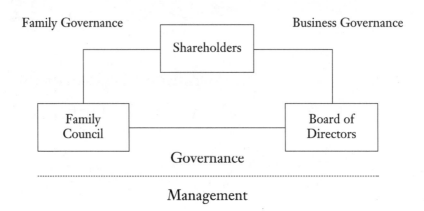

concerns of the business, the shareholders, and the family can be openly discussed and constructively managed.

This section of the book is about how those structures are designed in family companies that are well governed. Specifically, I will deal with the three pillars of family business governance: the board of directors, the shareholders' assembly, and the family council (see Figure 12-1).

What is governance and why is it so important for continuity? Governance usually refers to the ways in which a company organizes itself to do business within a legal framework of the society in which it operates and its own bylaws. In the context of public corporations, the concept is largely defined by the fiduciary responsibility of the board of directors to represent the interests of shareholders in overseeing the strategic direction and policies of the company as well as the decisions and performance of management. Even many leaders of family companies think of governance almost exclusively in these terms, ignoring the needs of both the family and the shareholders for separate forums in which to voice their concerns. As we will see, moreover, family shareholders themselves often fail to understand the critical distinction between business governance and business management.

Adrian Cadbury of Cadbury Schweppes, who was chairman of an influential commission on corporate governance in the United Kingdom, has written that governance is about "how to harness the power of corporations to the benefit of those they serve, without impeding their entrepreneurial drive."[1] This definition implies that companies have a moral and ethical responsibility to fulfill the needs of a multiplicity of stakeholders, including their employees and the communities where they do business. While family companies share this obligation, we will be concerned in this section of the book with governance of key stakeholders in the family company.

Governance structures in family companies must be designed to safeguard the long-term interests of family shareholders by ensuring the growth and continuity of the enterprise and promoting the family's harmony and welfare. This definition implies that both the business and the family are in need of governance. It also suggests a broad role for the board of directors in a family company.

While the responsibilities of directors of public corporations have been defined in volumes of statutes and case law over the years, there are few legal guidelines defining the particular responsibilities of directors of family companies. What, for example, is the fiduciary responsibility of a board in a family company for seeing that the owners prepare for a transfer of leadership to the next generation or do proper estate planning? Are the directors legally liable if a business loses much of its value after the death of a dominant leader who refused to plan adequately for his or her succession? Can they be blamed for going along with an owner who creates a partnership of his offspring in the next generation even though the successors are incapable of functioning as a team?

Whether they like it or not, independent outsiders on family business boards are often called upon to intervene in situations that are above and beyond the normal obligations of overseeing the direction and operation of the business. The shareholders they represent, moreover, differ in significant ways from the relatively anonymous mass of investors who buy stock in public companies but have virtually nothing to do with the companies they invest in.

Most family companies are undergoverned. If they have legal boards, they exist largely on paper and lack directors with independent voices whose experience and expertise can help the company significantly with key strategies. Although annual shareholder meetings are required by law, the meetings in many family businesses are usually pro forma events in which shareholders listen passively to briefings on corporate policies by top officers. Very few family businesses, moreover, understand that a family organization may be absolutely vital to the long-term health and continuity of the company.

Usually, the need for more governance arises from the stress and confusion that result from not attending to the greater complexities in a multigenerational business and family. Family members begin acting "strangely." Resentments and rivalries develop over jobs and inheritance among people who previously were friendly and predictable. This seemingly bizarre behavior may even be interpreted by some family members as symptoms of mental illness. Some family members begin to believe that the only solution is to sell the business, and, indeed, many businesses are sold under such circumstances.

What is often lacking in such situations is structure: The family needs a place to grapple with these tensions and learn to manage them. But the family council has a larger role than that: It is to visualize the future, to continually anticipate how the family will evolve, what its needs will be, and to what extent the business will be able to fulfill those needs. The council is a forum for lifelong learning, in which young potential successors develop enthusiasm for the business and learn the values of professionalism and stewardship that will be essential to fulfilling the Shared Dream. The council attempts to forge a consensus on the best leadership system for the future, help the family to adjust to the political changes brought about by the leadership transition, and may even help the board of directors develop ideal profiles for the type of leaders it wants in key positions such as chairman and CEO.

Governance has to be regarded as a way of life in family companies. The leaders not only have to know how to organize effective structures; they have to know how to use them. If governance structures are the engine of continuity for family companies, the ongoing education of family members in how to use these structures is the oil without which the engine cannot run.

This concluding section of the book will examine the importance of these structures and processes in preserving the stability and continuity of the business as well as in carrying out successful transitions in leadership. Both chapters in this section are largely concerned with older family companies facing the complexities that come with the growth of the business and the extended family. This chapter describes how each pillar of the governance—board, shareholders' assembly, and family council—is organized to function effectively. It summarizes the essential "carpentry" in building governance structures. The chapter considers the basic composition of each forum, the issues appropriate to each, how the members are chosen, how their meetings are organized, and the basic issues that they discuss.

Chapter 13 will look in greater depth at the vital contributions made by an active, independent board and by a family council. It will pay particular attention to the role of outside directors in helping the family owners to clarify their Dreams and develop successors, and to the role of the family council in articulating the values and traditions that they expect the business to embody. The chapter will also examine how the decisions and activities of the three governance structures are coordinated

While reading this section, it is important to distinguish governance structures from the business forms discussed throughout this book. Business forms—controlling owner, sibling partnership, and cousin consortium—refer to the distribution of power and authority in the business, which often is congruent with the ownership system. In controlling-owner companies, for example, the chief executive may be the principal or sole owner; the only structure that may be needed at this stage is a board with qualified, independent directors. But the separation between owners and managers and the development of different branches that is characteristic of later generations demands more structural elements. At the sibling partnership stage, both a family council and a board may be necessary or desirable. The cousin consortium, with its much more complex ownership structure, may require an effective forum for shareholders—a shareholders' assembly—as well as a board and family council. Finally, there is no perfect governance system for family companies. This section offers only a menu of possibilities that may make sense for a given company and family at one or another stage in its evolution.

To illustrate the boundary lines between major constituencies in a family business, I often ask business owners to imagine they own a company whose primary asset is a 747 airliner. As with any investment, the shareholders have a right to demand a certain level of return. They can also dictate the overall risk-reward ratio that management is obliged to pursue. They have a right to insist that the pilots flying the plane be competent and that the airliner is optimally maintained and serviced. Owners do not, however, have a right to enter the cockpit and fly the plane themselves (unless, of course, they are—at a minimum—licensed to fly 747s). Nor do they have the right to tell the pilot what buttons to push, what levers to pull, and how to read the dials. Flying the plane is the responsibility of pilots, because that is what they have been trained and hired to do.

There is a boundary that should not be crossed between the

Figure 12-2   The Family Business System

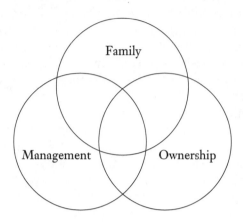

rights, privileges, and responsibilities of owners and the rights, privileges, and responsibilities of managers. That boundary is the cockpit door. If owners are entitled to their rights, they also have to understand their limitations. Even though owners are the ultimate authority in a privately held (or family controlled) company, they do not automatically have the right to run it.

Likewise, although the board of directors is the ultimate legal authority in any company, the board's prerogatives in a family business may, in practice, be severely constrained by the values and traditions of the owning family. The aircraft in our analogy can be used for many purposes: to fly passengers, to carry cargo long distances, to airlift food supplies to Bosnia for the United Nations. While the board is charged with determining the best uses of the aircraft in order to ensure investors an adequate return, it steps over the line if its strategy violates a value or principle that is considered sacred by the family. For example, if the family believes that its success has always been based on maintaining the highest safety standards, the board would be ill advised to embark on cost-cutting strategies that might jeopardize those standards.

Family businesses in their first years are usually small and can be managed fairly informally. If the company has a board, the people who sit on it are often the same family members who manage the company. The founding entrepreneur is usually the principal owner as well as the CEO who runs the business, and is often the dominant leader of the family by virtue of his or her control of the family's resources. In the early stages of the system, the family becomes accustomed to thinking of management and governance as the same function.

We have seen, however, that as an enterprise takes off and starts growing, and as the family gets older and the numbers of shareholders and potential shareholders multiply, the system comes under increasing strain. With the growth of the extended family comes the differentiation of interests among three groups—family members, shareholders, and participants in management (see Figure 12-2).

Unless the people in each group are educated to understand their separate rights and responsibilities, confusion gradually develops about the important differences between family and business issues, as well as between ownership and management. The symptoms of a lack of clear understanding of boundaries are readily apparent:

- The shareholders interfere too much in the day-to-day work of the managers; the managers withhold information from the board or act as if they are not accountable to the board.
- Family concerns such as employment of a relative or a member's behavior outside the business are constantly discussed at board meetings.
- At family social gatherings, conversations are dominated by talk of business decisions, sometimes making members who do not participate in the business feel left out and resentful.

Many family businesses maintain the same simple ownership structure from generation to generation—with a single controlling owner in charge. Other companies go down the path of greater complexity and accept the challenges of learning how to manage it. They anticipate the kinds of issues that are likely to arise and put in place structures and policies necessary for dealing with them constructively. The board of directors, the family council, and the shareholders' assembly each has a vital role to play in planning for the inevitable leadership transition when the whole system will be under considerable stress. Let us now examine how these three basic structures are organized, the rights, responsibilities, and privileges that go with their respective roles, and the boundaries between them.

The Shareholders' Assembly

Although family businesses have many stakeholders, the rights of the owners are paramount. The board of directors has legal responsibility for protecting their interests and carrying out their objectives, but the board needs the guidance of shareholders on ownership issues that fall within their discretion. Those issues concern how ownership is to be divided and structured to maintain family control. Among the types of issues that shareholders should address are:

- Is the company taking too many risks, putting shareholder capital in jeopardy?
- Is the company growing fast enough to assure shareholders of a larger return on their investment than they can earn elsewhere?
- Are top management positions in the hands of the most competent people?
- Is the board doing a good job of overseeing management and looking out for shareholder interests?
- Should the dividend policy be more conservative, or less?
- What plans does management have to address the liquidity needs of shareholders?
- What sacrifices will shareholders be called on to make next year?
- Can the company develop an internal market for shares or a redemption fund in case a shareholder wishes to cash in stock?
- Has the board discussed a plan to go public?
- Is any restructuring of ownership contemplated?
- Is management considering any acquisitions or divestitures of businesses in the near future?
- If shares of the family-controlled company are publicly traded, how will the behavior of family members affect stock value?

Shareholders need a forum that allows them to address these issues comprehensively. The annual meeting often does not do the job adequately, either because these matters are not easily addressed in one meeting a year or because the group is too large or too diverse to permit constructive debate. Most family companies, moreover, do not make good use of the annual meeting. The meeting tends to be purely informational, with board officers and top managers lecturing a passive audience about the results achieved in the previous year and plans for the next. Typically, any substantial ownership issues that arise are referred to committees, which then report to the next year's meeting of the full group—often called the stockholder assembly.

This assembly usually consists of all family shareholders who are over the age of twenty-one, but the composition varies considerably. Some assemblies include spouses as nonvoting members; others include younger adolescents, to educate them about shareholder matters early on.

As the family tree branches out, the shareholders often delegate ownership issues to a committee that represents them between assembly meetings. In companies where the family's stock is held in a trust, the legal authority to exercise shareholder rights rests with the trustees. In these systems, the shareholder assembly is made up of the beneficiaries of the trust that owns the company's stock. The trusts in some systems are paternalistic, intended to protect the beneficiaries from themselves. Such trusts are often controlled by non-family trustees appointed for life. In other, more inclusive and empowering trusts, the trustees are considered essentially representatives of the beneficiaries. In these systems, the beneficiaries elect some or all of the trustees, whose terms are staggered to ensure rotation.

Some families distinguish between shareholders who work in the company and those who do not. Ongoing responsibility over ownership issues is delegated to the family shareholders who are in senior management so are presumably better informed about the business.[2] One example is the Roundtable Assembly organized by the de Gaspé Beaubien family, owners of Telemedia, Inc., a large media company in Canada. Only holders of voting shares who work in the business are eligible for membership in the Assembly, and they must be elected by a vote of the members of the Roundtable. However, the Assembly may also elect highly capable cousins working outside the company as members, and even provide these talented individuals with financing, if necessary, to help them purchase stock so they can join the group. The Roundtable Assembly sets the rules of ownership in Gaspeau, the holding company for Telemedia, Inc., and conveys the views of the majority owners on a regular basis to the CEO and the board on everything from corporate strategy to family values.

Meetings of the shareholders' organization are the proper arena in which to raise broad questions about the board's and management's performance and plans. The board and management are obliged to search for solutions to the specific concerns raised at these meetings. The shareholders' assembly, moreover, is an excellent forum in which to perpetuate the strong spirit of family ownership that is essential for passing the business on to future generations. By training young stockholders to play an active role in protecting their investment, it can build commitment to the family legacy. There are, of course, issues that do not fall in the domain of ownership and are more appropriately discussed in other forums. The shareholders' assembly is the wrong place, for example, to discuss such family matters as requirements for family members seeking jobs in the company or the estate plans of elders. The family council is a more appropriate forum for addressing these issues. Nor should there be extensive discussion in the shareholders' assembly of policy issues or business decisions for which management and the board have primary responsibility. When the entire shareholder group debates these issues, it is a sure sign that the boundaries between the governance structures have not been clearly drawn.

The Shareholders' Agreement

One component is essential for preserving shareholder unity: the shareholders' agreement. The agreement, signed by all family shareholders, is the key to family control of the company. It spells out the rules for transfers of stock, the rules on voting of shares, and the place of trusts in the overall ownership structure. No matter how well members of the extended family get along, it is safe to assume that in later generations at least a few of the sibling or cousin partners will want to sell their stock to obtain cash. The shareholders' agreement is the key to avoiding a dilution of family ownership, which could lead to a loss of family control—especially in companies whose stock is publicly traded and attractive to outsiders. By providing a mechanism for sale of stock within the family, it helps to ensure that the company will remain in family hands and discourages sales of stock to potentially disruptive outsiders. By spelling out in advance the terms of any sale of stock within the family, it also prevents disputes from dividing the family and shaking the foundations of the business.

The agreement may require that the stock be sold back to the company, if a fund has been set up to redeem shares. Or it may include "rights of first refusal" requiring sellers to offer the stock to family members before going outside to look for a buyer. Typically, the agreement includes a formula for establishing the price of the stock when a sale is contemplated, and a method of arbitrating any disagreements that occur over the application of the formula.

The value of stock in such transactions may have a substantial impact on company operations, affecting (among other things) its borrowing capacity if the value is set too low. Many shareholder agreements purposely set a low value on the company's stock to reduce taxes and discourage selling by family shareholders. That strategy often penalizes the family company when it goes to the bank to borrow against its equity, since the amount it can borrow is based on stock value. In such cases the need to pump up the value of the equity for borrowing purposes may run head on into the family's tax strategy.

In later-generation families the shareholders' agreement often lays out rules to prevent sales of stock by cousins from altering the balance of power among family branches. For example, there may be a rule requiring sellers to offer stock to members of their own branch first, before approaching potential buyers in other branches. Or when a cousin in one branch sells to a cousin in another, the rules may require any future transaction to restore the previous ratio of stock held by the two branches. Although agreements of this sort may seem overly legalistic—as if conflicts are inevitable—they actually serve to promote family harmony by anticipating disagreements and putting rules in place to settle them before they flare into major disputes.

Empowering Younger Family Shareholders

The shareholders' assembly provides opportunities for shareholders to question board members and management. Unfortunately, few take advantage of those opportunities. Especially in cultures that emphasize respect for elders and for authority, shareholders at the annual meeting are often reluctant to ask questions or challenge the leadership. This deeply ingrained timidity prevents them from realizing what is at stake for them in the company's performance and from protecting their own economic interests.

In many family companies juniors inherit stock without an understanding of the issues that go with ownership. The seniors may gift stock to their children early for tax reasons, but without turning over any responsibility to them. The seniors may hold on to control of the company through voting stock even though the juniors own most of the shares. If the juniors have never worked in the company, they may look upon it as an inexhaustible gold mine. Even though they are owners, they have the impression that they have little or no active role. They may even believe that because the family business has always been there, providing for their needs, it is invulnerable to downturns. Nothing could be further from the truth in today's rapidly changing markets, in which even huge companies that face stern competitive challenges can quickly disappear.

The shareholders' assembly should have the function of educating shareholders in the responsibilities of ownership. It teaches them that management and the board are accountable to them. It trains them to ask the right types of questions. It also teaches the managers and board members that they are accountable to a higher forum. In well-governed family companies, the board chairperson and the committee heads must be ready to answer questions at the assembly. (To some extent, the board at the annual meeting acts as a buffer for top managers, whose effectiveness might be impaired if they are overly exposed to the questions and criticisms of all shareholders.) Young inheritors are not born with an understanding of where the boundary between business governance and business management lies—this has to be taught to them. In preparing successors, family companies often place a lot of emphasis on management education. They need to give an equal amount of attention to educating young shareholders or future shareholders in the requirements of ownership. Accounting and financial literacy and a basic knowledge of family business governance, in particular of how boards function, are essential for shareholders.

The Board of Directors

Legally, the board of directors exists to protect the interests of the shareholders. In practice, the board in a family company plays a much broader and more positive role in guiding the business and the family. "The objective, confidential and caring counsel of an effective board can help the owners sustain wise and competent leadership," Ward has written.[3] That conclusion is supported by the fact that many sizable family companies that have remained in the hands of their founder's descendants through several generations have such boards.

Just as in a public corporation, the board of a family company is charged with overseeing the operation of the business. It is the directors' responsibility to see that the business is managed as efficiently as possible and earns optimal returns for the shareholders. The board's duties include:

- Reviewing corporate objectives.
- Monitoring the performance of the enterprise.
- Approving major acquisitions and divestitures of businesses.
- Approving the strategic plan and operating budgets.
- Advising the CEO and his or her management team.
- Approving debt/equity ratios.
- Guiding succession planning.

Too often owner managers of family companies are so focused on the policing functions of the board that they tend to overlook the fact that strong boards with experienced independent directors can be an enormous resource for senior executives. The directors can bolster management by bringing an array of skills and expertise to the company. In addition, they play a vital role in keeping managers focused on the big picture, on the long-term goals and strategic direction of the company and the overall performance of the company in meeting those goals.

Beyond its fiduciary duties in overseeing operations, the board in many family companies has another function that is just as important to the owners: It makes sure the management of the enterprise is guided by social and ethical principles that the family deems important.

Some families want their businesses to abide by and foster religious principles. Others feel strongly about the social and environmental impact of the company. Are wastewater streams from its plants polluting local water supplies? Is the company doing enough to recruit members of minority groups as employees? Should executives serving abroad offer bribes to foreign officials in order to do business, if that is customary in the country? Should the company engage in practices that are legal (and practiced by competitors) but run against the values and traditions of the family?

Managers of every type of company come up against decisions involving ethical values and dilemmas almost every day. The board sees to it that management follows the values that are part of the family's legacy and traditions. As we'll see, the articulation and communication of those principles and values to the board is one of the most important functions of the family council.

The Contribution of Independent Directors

Surveys of business owners done in the United States by the Massachusetts Mutual Life Insurance Company and by Arthur Andersen Inc. suggest that most family companies that have lasted for more than one generation have a minimum of two or three independent directors on their board. Another study by Louis Barnes and Marc Schwartz of the Harvard Business School shows that the usefulness of a board, as perceived by owners of the company, increases with each new outsider that is added up to a total of three.[4]

Many business owners are reluctant to have an active board with real responsibilities and qualified outsiders, fearing they will lose control of the company. They worry that their decisions will be challenged and that privacy will be compromised. However, experience suggests that owners who have boards almost always conclude that their initial fears were unfounded and that outside directors have added to the quality of board decisions. S.C. Johnson & Son, worldwide distributors of Johnson's Wax, Raid, and other household products, has a majority of independent directors on its board, even though about 90 percent of the stock is owned by family. Samuel C. Johnson, the current chairman, has written: "My father believed in getting the best outside advice to augment our internal talent, and that is something we continue to do. I'm convinced that one of the reasons for the success of the company was that we were able to attract and hold some of the top outside advisors in the country."[5]

As for the privacy issue, directors are bound by their fiduciary responsibility to protect the confidentiality of information that is shared with them. A careful screening process and explicit confidentiality agreements can help ensure that directors will honor this duty and respect privacy. However, the best insurance against leakage of secrets that might hurt the company or the family is to have nothing unethical or illegal to hide.

Independent directors with broad business experience bring expertise and experience to the company that may be lacking in-house. The CEO can call on them for advice on critical decisions, and family members may turn to them for counsel as well. Some outsiders get to know the family well and even serve as mentors to members of the next generation of leaders.

It should be noted here that all directors serve at the discretion of the majority shareholders. If a director behaves inappropriately—for example, betrays family confidences or becomes a disruptive force on the board—a shareholders' meeting can be called and the individual removed. Family businesses with strong boards, however, are committed to letting the members fulfill their function and freely express their views, whether or not the owners agree with everything they say. They do not drop directors or disband the board summarily when they hear views contrary to their own. For their part, outside directors understand that the shareholders are the ultimate authority, and will usually resign if they no longer have the family's trust. Such incidents rarely occur when the company has an effective screening process.

The Size and Composition of the Board

There is considerable debate in the literature on non-family, public corporations about the ideal size and composition of a board of directors. My own view, supported by research on task-performing groups, is that there is a limit to the number of people who can work together productively in a group. The ideal size of a board is from seven to nine.[6]

Family businesses tend to appoint too many directors, especially in later-generation companies whose leaders often feel obliged to involve as many cousins, uncles, and aunts as possible on the board. Groups with more than nine members become unwieldy, however. Meetings are hard to schedule, work is difficult to coordinate, the sheer number of opinions can be overwhelming, and consensus takes longer to reach.

With limits on the number of board seats, it is important to consider the optimal composition of the board. What is the right mix between inside and outside directors, and between family and non-family directors? When family businesses have a board at all, it often consists almost entirely of family members, some of whom may be less than qualified. This is usually the result of the leaders' well-meaning desire to give everyone in the family who wishes to serve an opportunity to do so. Or it could mean that the leadership does not value the board and is not prepared to give it real responsibilities and independence. In either case, the board with too many unqualified family members frequently ends up being ineffective because its members confuse the family and business agendas. Well-qualified independent directors, moreover, may be reluctant to join such a board.

How many independent directors are needed to ensure that a board stays focused on the key issues? It is becoming more common for large family firms to have a majority of independent directors, like the Johnson's Wax board. Having a minimum of three, however, ensures that there will be a critical mass of support on the board for expression of independent opinions. One or two outsiders may feel isolated and alone; their voices may be muffled.

The process by which independent directors are selected is critical. Business owners often think first of the candidates in their own small circle—their lawyer, their accountant, their banker, and, especially, close friends. Because they may be too close to the owner to provide impartial advice, these are not usually the best choices. Family companies seeking independent directors for the first time can establish a selection committee to define an ideal board member profile and then either develop a list of candidates themselves or hire a search firm specializing in recruitment of directors. Once the board is established, future recruitment and selection may be delegated to a nominating committee of the board that is typically made up of the independent directors and senior representatives of the family.

The best candidates are business owners themselves, people who know what it is to lead a company, manage large numbers of people, make tough decisions, and deal with other stakeholders and the public. One veteran consultant advises family businesses to look not just for their peers but for their "betters," by which he means business leaders whose companies have achieved a higher stage of development than theirs and have successfully gotten over hurdles that they face or are going to face. In general, the following are among the desirable qualities for director candidates:

- Ability to think strategically.
- Experience grappling with issues currently before the company or in its future.
- Capacity to earn the trust of the family and work with both juniors and seniors. (Age is a factor here—directors midway between the younger and older family members in age may communicate better with both.)
- Familiarity with the succession process in other family companies at similar stages of development.
- Desire to make a contribution and not just gain money and prestige.
- Industry and government connections.

Strategic criteria top the list because the future direction of the business determines the types of skills and experience it needs most on the board. The selection committee must consider the skills available on the top management team and what expertise and knowledge that independent directors might bring to the company would be helpful in realizing strategic objectives. Is the company moving into the real estate or credit card business in a big way? Then directors with knowledge of these markets would be extremely useful. Does the company have plans to globalize operations? If so, outsiders with experience in diverse foreign markets would be desirable. Is the company moving into new technologies? If so, a director familiar with those technologies would be an obvious asset.

Some family businesses have reached a stage when knowledge of governments and contacts with investment bankers is critical. One company, for example, foresaw that its business would be profoundly affected by pending legislation in the U.S. Congress; it wisely recruited an outside director with strong Washington connections. Another firm that was adopting a sophisticated new technology brought in a director with a high-tech background. In recruiting directors, companies should cast a wide net and not restrict themselves to candidates in their community or even their country. A company with overseas operations, for example, might consider a foreign national who knows their industry and meets other requirements.

The candidates should exhibit an understanding of and sensitivity to how family companies function. Experience in succession planning or conflict resolution may be among the most useful qualifications. Business owners whose companies have been through a succession from one type of family business form to another can provide valuable advice to a system that is about to go through the same process. On the other hand, CEOs of large public corporations who dismiss family issues as unprofessional or irrelevant are likely to be unhelpful, no matter what their other strengths.

Best friends generally make poor directors. Independent directors should be valued for their impartial views. They are expected to question company policies when necessary. Clearly, good friends, even if otherwise well qualified, may be disinclined to play this role. Nor are service providers such as lawyers and accountants the best candidates. Their services, however valuable, can be paid for directly; they seldom bring significant added value to the board, and the company is better off reserving director seats for people with business experience and talents. Having service providers as directors can also result in conflicts of interest. What if the board takes up a proposal to change the company's accountant or law firm, for example?

Most experienced business leaders agree to serve on a board mainly because they want to help. They are attracted less by money and prestige than by a wish to share their knowledge and by the challenge of helping the company achieve its goals. While outside directors should be amply compensated (I will touch on fees later), chances are that those who are motivated by money and prestige alone are not good choices.

*Insiders versus Outsiders, Family versus
Non-Family*

A proper balance between internal and external directors is vital. A board with too many internal managers may end up functioning like an executive committee; the meetings become too focused on daily business decisions and crisis firefighting and give short shrift to long-term goals, strategy, and the overall performance of management. By contrast, boards with too many independent directors may be out of touch with the everyday realities of the business. When the CEO is the only inside manager on the board, for example, he or she may filter the information going to other directors, thus depriving them of other internal sources that might provide different perspectives. Companies should aim for a point somewhere in the middle: The numbers of insiders and outsiders should be roughly balanced.[7] For example, in a board of seven, having four independent directors or three insiders may be optimal.

Similarly, there should be a balance between family and non-family directors. Like non-family directors, family members should be chosen for the quality of the experience and judgment they can bring to the board. They should fully understand the board's duties and be able to make a strong contribution—to "add value" to the board's work and not just occupy a seat. An "ideal profile" for family directors should also be developed. Among the chief qualifications are familiarity with the business, commitment to its future, and the capacity to interact comfortably with sophisticated independent directors. The candidates should have some knowledge of economics, business strategy, and principles of business management. They should also have an understanding of the basic principles of finance and, at a minimum, be able to read and interpret a balance sheet and income statement. The insistence on director quality, however, is not meant to exclude talented family members who may lack some of the specific qualifications. For those who wish to serve, the family should offer educational opportunities and training programs to help them fill gaps in their knowledge.

Loyalty to the family as a whole is an important requirement of family directors. They must demonstrate by their actions that their reason for serving is not to fulfill a personal or branch agenda but rather to further the welfare of all family members. In larger families, only a few family members at a time can sit on the board, and so a system of representation may have to be worked out. When ownership is divided among several family branches, each branch may have at least one representative on the board who keeps other members of the branch informed of its deliberations. In companies moving from sibling partnerships to cousin companies, the system of representation should be designed to prevent destructive interbranch rivalries and promote unity in the extended family. One way to do that is to have the whole family vote to approve branch representatives on the board. The system can also encourage communication among branches by requiring family directors to report to members of other branches as well as their own. Even under a representational system, of course, family members selected for the board should meet the basic qualifications for directors.

Branch representation on the board, however, can become a double-edged sword. Once established in the transition from siblings to cousins, this principle can get fused into the structure for perpetuity and create dysfunctional dynamics among succeeding generations of cousins. The branches may become irrelevant to future generations. That is why the sooner a system can move to select family directors on the basis of their competence and their commitment to the entire family's interests, the better it is for the purposes of continuity.

Term Limits, Compensation, and Orientation

The terms of both family and outside directors should be limited to between five and seven years. By that time directors have usually shared most of their accumulated knowledge and experience with the board; after more years of service, their contributions may begin to decline. In addition, terms should be staggered so that not too many directors depart at any one time. By rotating a few seats at a time, the board is assured of both continuity and regular infusions of new blood and fresh ideas.

Compensation of directors varies widely and usually reflects the importance that owners give to the board as well as the size of the business.[8] Although pay should not be the primary incentive for qualified independent directors, director fees are a strong indicator of how seriously a family company takes the board's role. One good rule-of-thumb is that the time of a high-level, experienced independent director is as valuable as that of the company's own top officers.[9] To determine the fees of independent directors, a company might tally up the salary, bonus, and stock options earned by its highest paid executive—chairman, president, or CEO—and from that figure derive a per diem rate for the independent directors.

The question of compensation of family directors raises sensitive and difficult issues, which cannot be resolved with any formula. In principle, family directors are entitled to be paid the same fees as independent directors, and usually are in big companies when they are clearly qualified. The trap here is that if family directors are paid, the family may regard board seats as an entitlement rather a critical responsibility. This increases the competition for seats among both qualified and unqualified family members. Appointment to the board may also be seen as a consolation prize for relatives who are denied positions in management, or as a way of distributing income to poor relatives. Some companies reach a compromise by paying family directors a fee that is less than that of independent directors—an arrangement that may make the family directors feel like "second-class citizens." Clearly, the ideal policy would be to pay qualified family members who do the same work as independent directors the same fees. Whether that can work in any given firm will depend upon the company's resources and the family's overall scheme for rewarding participants in governance.

Organizing the Board

Family members and non-family senior executives should have opportunities to meet and get to know board candidates. Independent directors of family businesses usually develop closer ties with shareholders than do their counterparts in large public corporations. In their first meetings with the candidates, members of the selection committee—usually the firm's chief officers and major shareholders—have a chance to assess whether the personal chemistry seems right. When mutual trust and respect exists, outsiders can be a stabilizing influence at board meetings, playing a role that one owner likened to a balance wheel in times of emotional conflict.

Family and non-family appointees should be introduced to key managers and briefed on every phase of business operations and strategy as well as major policy issues on the board's agenda. Most family businesses that have an active board with real responsibilities have a well-planned, formal orientation program which new directors go through before taking their seats.

Most boards meet infrequently.[10] In the large majority of these companies, the board is thus likely to have only a minimal role, if any. Again, balance is key. Boards that hold monthly or even weekly meetings, as some do in Latin American countries, typically become heavily involved in day-to-day operations and tend to micromanage. Quarterly meetings work best because they tend to keep the board's attention focused on big-picture strategy and policy issues rather than details.

This does not mean that the board does not work between meetings. On the contrary, some of the most important work is accomplished in this time. Effective boards are organized into committees that develop expertise in one or more "portfolios." There may be an audit committee, a succession committee, a strategic planning committee, a nominating or corporate governance committee, and so on. The chairperson appoints committee heads who are responsible for coordinating the work of members between sessions, following up on issues discussed in the previous meeting, and preparing reports for the next meeting. The committee heads should be free to hire outside experts and should be given the resources they need to get the job done.

Too often in some companies, directors don't receive an agenda and background material until they walk into the boardroom for the meeting. Using a board effectively requires making certain that important information gets into directors' hands well before meetings so they have time to digest it and formulate opinions. The chairperson and his or her staff gathers information needed by the board for each quarterly meeting and draws up an agenda—a task that involves considerable work in some companies and may thus require a small staff.

This process of collecting information and preparing an agenda for the meetings is an extremely useful, educational exercise for the senior executives who do it. Leaders of family conglomerates often discover the usefulness of a consolidated balance sheet when preparing for holding-company board meetings. Early in their development these companies keep balance sheets for each of their diverse businesses but often lack an overall balance sheet that enables their board to see the whole picture and compare financial results of different business units. One CEO told me that while going through the process of preparing an agenda he discovered serious deficiencies in the way his company collected and used data. Questioning by the board helped him develop more useful yardsticks for assessing business performance. "If you can't measure it, you can't manage it," he said, "and our board has focused attention on the right variables to gauge." By changing the system, he was able to give his managers vital information they needed to do their jobs effectively.

The Family Council

A third category of people associated with a family business have certain rights and responsibilities by virtue of being family members. The broad family group includes not just current family shareholders and managers but other family members whose lives are affected by what happens in the business, such as spouses, parents, and grandparents who own no stock. A whole set of issues having to do with the family's interface with the business must be addressed, but these are rarely discussed in an organized, thoughtful way unless there is a separate governance structure—a family council—to deal with them. Without a separate forum for promoting the welfare of family members and resolving family issues, these matters may intrude upon the work of the board and management—at a significant cost to both family and business functioning.

Many small and mid-sized family companies in the United States have found it useful to organize family councils.[11] A number of sophisticated multinational companies also have such councils, among them Agrolimen and Antonio Puig in Spain, the Bonnier Group in Sweden, the New York Times and Johnson's Wax in the United States, Telemedia in Canada, and Hermes, the French-based manufacturer of leather clothing, men's ties, scarves, and other apparel. Other major companies are also beginning to establish such formal structures as they move into later generations.

The family council plays a vital role in elaborating policies for the family and resolving conflicts over such matters as hiring and firing of relatives, the distribution of business perks, and use of the family vacation home. One of its most important functions is to articulate the family's core values. Although many family businesses have strong values they wish to see advanced through two cultures of the business, they seldom make the effort needed to define these values explicitly.

The council also has other major responsibilities. It educates family members in their rights, responsibilities, and privileges vis-à-vis the business. It provides a forum for discussing issues of continuity and succession. It is responsible for preserving and carrying on the family legacy and instilling a sense of stewardship in the young. In summary, the council's activities may include:

- Articulating family values for the guidance of the board, top management, and the family's philanthropic activities.

- Developing a challenging vision of the future of the family and the company that all members can embrace—a Shared Dream.
- Planning educational programs and events for family members.
- Creating policies regulating relatives' entry into or exit from the business.
- Establishing standards of behavior for family members in the community.
- Developing a family mission statement or credo.
- Furthering the development of young family members, for example, by setting up scholarship and/or venture funds.
- Organizing celebrations of the family legacy.
- Establishing a family office to handle the family's portfolio of investments not related to the family's main business.
- Establishing and overseeing the family's philanthropic initiatives.
- Coordinating measures to protect the personal security of family members.
- Providing fun and leisure activities for the family.
- Establishing policies to regulate conflicts of interests among different business activities of family members.

Changes in Membership and Focus over Time

The council's functions evolve over time as different issues arise and the membership changes. At first, the council may consist of just the parents and their children. The discussions may focus on planning family vacations, on the children's career interests, or on what difficulties they may encounter in school when others discover they are members of a wealthy business family. These meetings may take place only twice a year at first, but may become more frequent.

The early meetings establish a pattern for continued formal discussion of family issues into the future. At the same time, the discussions stimulate the children to think about their own career aspirations, whether or not they have made up their minds about joining the family business. Parents are well advised to use the early meetings to develop a custom of free and open discussions and help their children become the kind of people they want to become.

Through the council discussions, the family lays the foundation for the development of a Shared Dream that the members can embrace. In these early conversations the parents can share their pride and enthusiasm for the family business and the professionalism required to participate in it. When the children are grown, more specific discussions about the requirements of the business and what a career path in the company might be are more appropriate. The family council might then take up what kind of education they should have, whether they should work outside the business for a few years before entering it, and what standards of performance will be expected of them. The council might also organize family events or create publications that emphasize the idea of stewardship.

Councils in large, extended business-owning families are likely to have a system of branch representation and to adopt formal rules for the entry of family members into the business. The council may arrange for mentors to assist the juniors in their careers as well as create other educational opportunities for them. It may also develop retirement policies for seniors that offer them new ways to contribute, such as service in the family foundation. If some family members have developed side businesses, the council may formulate policies to regulate any business dealings between those ventures and the family company.

In addition, some family owners routinely require consultation with the family council before the company makes any major decision to change or broaden the mission of the business, to restructure the company, or take on debt. Some families specify that the council must be consulted on any acquisition requiring an expenditure of $50 million or above, or on contracts with a duration of five years or more.

A typical council agenda may include such issues as:

- What are the central values of our family? How do we express these values?
- How do these values relate to the principles guiding the operation of the business?
- How can these values be preserved and taught to future generations in the business and in the family?
- Who in the family should be allowed or encouraged to participate in the business? What qualifications should be set for family members who wish to enter the business?
- Who has the right to use business facilities and share in company perks?
- How can we improve our communications and conflict management skills as a family?
- Should we develop a code of conduct for family members in the business?

- How is the family perceived by members of the community, customers, and other outsiders? How does the business affect the reputations of the members?
- How can we prepare future generations for the responsibilities of ownership?
- What are the rights, privileges, responsibilities, and roles of inactive family shareholders?
- Should we develop a family history that documents the family's involvement with the business?

Setting Up a Council: Size, Composition, and Organization

The process of organizing a council varies from family to family. Typically, a family meeting is called to establish a committee that will be responsible for organizing the council. As when selecting board members, the committee develops a list of criteria— an ideal profile— for council candidates and nominates the first family members to serve. A strong commitment to the family legacy is obviously important, as is the willingness to spend the necessary time on the council's work. Trustworthiness, the capacity for leadership, and the ability to communicate with and earn the respect of all family branches are essential. Conflict resolution skills can also be very useful.

The same size limitations apply to the council as to the board of directors. Groups with more than nine members begin to get too large to accomplish the work that needs to be done efficiently and in a timely manner. Some families encourage in-laws to serve on the council, which is generally a good idea because it permits them to get information about developments in the business that affect their lives directly rather than hearing it second-hand. A formal structure with procedural rules for meetings is essential. For larger families, I usually recommend that each council member report to a constituency of ten to fifteen family members, including people in other branches as well as in his or her own. As in the case of selection of family directors, the council members should be elected by a vote of the entire family in order to promote unity and loyalty to the whole. The council is likely to work best when a cross-section of the family is represented, however. In constituting the council, the family should think about the voices that need to be heard—including both genders; younger and older generations; family branches, blood relatives, and in-laws; those active and not active in the business; family trustees and beneficiaries; and so forth.

Council members generally have longer terms than members of boards of directors do. Whatever their length, the terms of council members should have a fixed limit. Terms should also be staggered, so that one or two members leave periodically and others get an opportunity to serve. The organization of the council should be roughly parallel to that of the board, with each member responsible for one or more portfolios. Typically, the council is organized into working committees on topics such as hiring and firing policies, the family office, education and family development, trust issues, family history, family recreation, family philanthropy, and the family constitution.

The chairperson is elected to represent the council in dealings with management and the board. In companies that take family governance seriously, the chairperson has a stature roughly equivalent to chairman of the board, with whom the person has frequent contact. Obviously, the council needs to elect someone who is articulate, respected by all branches of the family, experienced at running meetings, and skilled in conflict resolution. Before electing its leader, the council may wish to agree on a profile of characteristics needed in the position with which to evaluate the candidates. In some companies the family is compelled by tradition to give the job to its most senior member. In such cases, if the senior is elderly, a coordinator might be appointed to assist the chairperson in his or her work.

Council members in larger families spend a lot of time and energy on the work, which in many cases takes them away from their jobs and other income-earning opportunities. Thus the question of incentives often arises. Should their work on behalf of the family be considered a labor of love, or should it be paid? Often this becomes a matter of equity, with unpaid council members feeling that family members who sit on the board of directors or work in the company are compensated in other ways, while they receive no pay for their council activities. Some larger companies do, in fact, pay council members a stipend. At the very least, the chairperson, or speaker of the council, ought to be paid and have an office and a budget for staff and travel if the company can afford it.

Paying council members for their time sends a message that the council's work is important. One of the biggest mistakes companies make, however, is to assume that pay is the only reward that produces high motivation. While pay is important, there are other kinds of rewards that can be motivating as well.[12] For example, some families make a continuing effort to celebrate the contributions of people involved in governance activities, at family functions or in the family newsletter. In addition, the participants are often privy to business information that others do not receive. They may get opportunities to meet with outside directors, thereby expanding their own network of contacts. Frequently, they are even allowed to use corporate facilities such as guest houses and the corporate plane to attend meetings.

My own experience has been that the stronger the culture of the family, and the greater the commitment to its legacy, the easier it is to rely on intrinsic rewards rather than pay to spur the work of governance. Quite commonly, however, families organize governance structures without doing a good job of explaining what is expected of the participants and the broader purpose of their work. Preservation of the legacy is a proud duty, like voting in a democracy, and it is up to the leaders to inspire those who are asked to contribute with a broader vision. A committee that is set up to devise rules and requirements for entry into the business, for example, will be more strongly motivated to accomplish this work if they understand its value in sustaining the enterprise over generations. Unless participants have a clear idea of the overall purpose of governance structures, as well as their own specific responsibilities for making the structures work, their enthusiasm and commitment may soon dwindle.

Coaching Council Members on Governance Processes

Some families find it awkward to talk about family matters in regular meetings with bylaws, minutes, committees, and all the other trappings of formal organization. But as an extended family grows larger it will be unable to resolve issues concerning the business in an orderly, constructive manner without formal processes. What happens in many families that lack such a structure is that governance matters are discussed informally—and incompletely—in dinner table conversation or at family social gatherings and celebrations. In these social situations it is difficult to get full and accurate information, resolve family issues in a satisfactory manner, or plan major family events.

The development of a family council is frequently an important event in the life of a family. Many families make the mistake of tackling tough, emotionally loaded issues, such as estate planning, before giving the members time to "warm up" and get used to the process of the meetings. Before taking on serious issues, council members need coaching on process—the scope of their responsibilities, rules and procedures for meetings, preparing an agenda, and so forth. The first sessions might be devoted to learning about the family's history or planning family activities for the year. Some time might be set aside toward the end of meetings to catch up on news of babies, job transitions, or health problems some family members may be having. Ideally, each family member should have a chance to share with the others what is going on in his or her life at that particular time. Such exchanges help to bring the group closer together as a family.

It is important to establish an atmosphere in which family members feel comfortable expressing their views and free to ask any kind of question—even those they are afraid may sound naïve. In a family council, as in most matters concerning family governance, success breeds success. If the early meetings go well and the family finds them useful, there is a better chance that subsequent discussions about the more difficult issues will go well. This should be kept in mind when the council is organized. Some families find it useful to hire a facilitator for the meetings, particularly in the formative stages.

Preserving and Enhancing the Family Legacy

Once the basic mechanisms have been put in place to manage the relationship between family and business, many successful companies look for other ways to enhance the lives and careers of family members and perpetuate the family's legacy. Some of the possible activities that the family council may organize and oversee in larger family companies are shown below (see Figure 12-3):

The structures in the diagram include the following:

- A *family office* with centralized financial planning, which enables the family to invest their wealth as a group, thereby enlarging their buying power and lowering the costs of portfolio management. The family office is a quite separate operation from the business, although a few of the same people may participate in both. Professional managers monitor the investments, oversee tax compliance, group insurance, financial planning, and intra-family transactions such as gifts of stock and estate plans.
- A *family foundation* that channels funds to organizations and causes that are consistent with the family's philanthropic initiative

Figure 12-3   Governance Structure for Family Enterprise

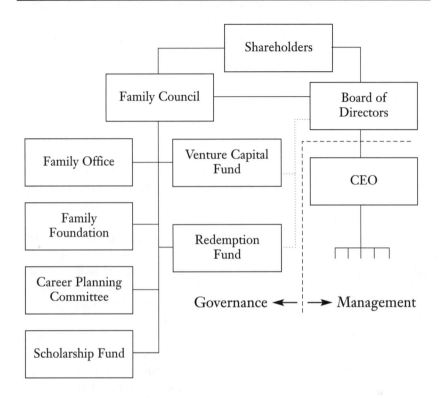

and social values. Along with such well-known institutions as the Ford, Rockefeller, and Carnegie foundations, there are thousands of other private family foundations that support activities in countless communities. These foundations usually confer tax advantages while enhancing the family's reputation and stature through contributions to the community.

- *Scholarship and/or venture funds* that further one of the council's most important functions: supporting the career development and entrepreneurial spirit of the younger generation. Sometimes funded out of company profits, a scholarship program helps qualified young family members to complete university and postgraduate educations. In addition, some larger companies also set up a venture fund for entrepreneurial-minded family members who seek to start businesses of their own.

- A *redemption fund* for shareholders who wish to cash in their stock at a fair price in order to invest it elsewhere, pursue their career interests, or use it for other purposes. Usually the fund is built by contributing a percentage of profits to it each year. A committee of the family council oversees proposed sales and makes sure they conform to the terms of the shareholders' agreement.

These activities broaden the number of possible ways that family members can contribute to the family welfare and legacy. For example, a venture fund provides outlets for members of the younger generation when jobs may be scarce in the family company. The young entrepreneurs get experience in taking risks and managing their own companies that may be useful if they eventually join the family business. Likewise, young family members interested in finance and investing can enhance their knowledge by working in the family office.

The family council is responsible for making certain that these structures work efficiently and achieve their goals. By defining the family's ethical and social values, moreover, the council helps to focus the family's philanthropic priorities. This is particularly important in later generations when diverse pet projects of numerous cousins may threaten to dilute the family foundation's impact.

The resources for the council's budget come out of the pockets of family members—not from the business. Family members sometimes complain about the costs associated with council activities, while ignoring the benefits from its role in promoting family harmony and long-term continuity. In addition, some council activities save money for the family. As a group, the family can enjoy greater negotiating leverage and lower rates for various kinds of services. By pooling resources for investments in a family office, for example, the council can attract top-flight money managers who may be able to earn higher returns for the investors. Similarly, the council can frequently negotiate lower rates on group purchases of insurance. The overall prosperity of the family increases, moreover, when young family members use venture funds provided by the council to build businesses of their own.

Structure, Process, and Coordinating Mechanisms

The relationships among the three family business governance structures we have described are shown in Figure 12-3. Although the name, scope of responsibilities, and composition of the three may vary—their design tends to be tailored in each case to the circumstances of the company and the family—successful multigenerational businesses usually have all three in some form. Obviously, though, putting these structures in place is not enough to accomplish their purposes. Governance structures are useless without an understanding of governance process.

What I refer to as "process" takes time and practice in the beginning to learn, often with the guidance of an experienced facilitator. In fact, a growing group of professionals now specialize in helping families set up and learn to use these governance structures. In addition, some families benefit from talking with other business owners who have established such forums and have had long experience managing them. This educational process is ongoing, since the issues arising in each of the structures may vary over time in substance and intensity.

We will see that some of the toughest dilemmas in a family business do not fall clearly in the domain of one or the other of the three governance structures. Although participants in the business, the family, and shareholder group should be clear on their respective roles—and careful to avoid crossing boundaries into the domains of others—the concerns of the three groups do overlap in places and they need to work in concert. The next chapter will take a closer look at important functions that a board with independent directors can play in a family company, particularly at the time of succession. Chapter 13 will also look in more detail at the pivotal role played by the family council in unifying the family around its core values, in guiding the board in fundamental questions about the future of the company, and in writing a constitution that pulls together the family's vision, mission, values, formal structures, and procedures.

CHAPTER 13

Governance in Action

W HEN family business owners seek advice on how to design a board of directors, too often the only model they have to guide their thinking is the board of IBM, or General Motors, or Citicorp, or some other large, prestigious public corporation. Perhaps seeking to shake off the stereotype of family businesses as inbred and unprofessional, these owners want the most knowledgeable and admired business leaders they can find to serve on their board. Their image of a board fits admirably with what the corporate lawyers or search firms they hire are accustomed to doing—which is designing boards for large public corporations. One consequence, however, is that many boards of family companies, even when well stocked with independent outsiders, tend to focus too narrowly on business issues. Too often independent directors aren't chosen for any particular knowledge or sensitivity to the family side of the business. On the contrary, they are selected for precisely the opposite reason. They come from the larger corporate world and presumably have many lessons to teach the growing family company that wants to become more professional and play in the big leagues.

This approach to selecting directors can be a two-edged sword, however. Independent directors can bring a wealth of business experience and strategic skills to the boardroom table, but without an understanding of the interplay of family and business, the independent

directors may be truly unprepared to help resolve some of the governance dilemmas that arise in family enterprises. When forced to deal
with those issues, they may become disillusioned and quit, or they may
become a detrimental influence, seeking to impose solutions inappropriate to the circumstances of the system they are serving.

Whether they like it or not, independent directors on a family
business board are often thrust into the middle of family issues that will
have a powerful influence on the future of the business. Many take up
the challenge and play a positive role in shaping those forces. The
presence of independent directors is necessary but not sufficient for
getting a board to responsibly address succession and continuity issues,
however. As Mace has observed, it is easy for independent directors on
a family company board to fall under the influence of family owner-
managers and to collude with them in avoiding the planning and management of the succession process.[1]

The board's obligation to look after the best interests of shareholders requires the members to raise questions about how family and
ownership matters may affect not just the economic efficiency of the
business but its long-term viability as a *family* enterprise. For directors
to fulfill this obligation, they must negotiate the kinds of relationships
with key stakeholders that will allow them to enter into discussions
about ownership and family concerns without feeling they are inappropriately meddling in the family's private affairs. The responsible
management of succession and continuity issues requires boards to
adopt a proactive stance toward them. It is impossible for directors to
examine the long-term continuity of the enterprise without taking into
account what the owners have (or have not) done with regards to estate
planning. Likewise, responsible boards of family businesses cannot
ignore the process by which family candidates for leadership are developed, evaluated, and selected.

Helping to Clarify the Dream

The board can play a critical role in helping family members clarify a
vision for the future of the system, without which it is impossible to
plan for succession and continuity. Reconciling the Dreams of family
members and creating a future scenario for the business is never easy.
Directors can sometimes use their personal influence with members of
both generations to help them define what they want for themselves
and for the firm. This process may lead to surprising discoveries that

can totally change the direction of the succession transition. The thoughts of one independent director poignantly illustrate the indispensable role an outsider can play:

When I went on the board [of this company], the president told me that his twin thirty-year-old sons were extremely able, chips off the old block, and dedicated to continuing the heritage and tradition of the family's leadership of an enterprise. . . . During the next few years, I became a good friend of the two sons and an admirer of their imagination and intellect. But as I came to know them better and share their interests and aspirations, it became clearer and clearer that what they wanted to do more than anything else in the world was to get out of the business. One wanted to return to his prep school as a teacher of English and drama. The other wanted to travel, write poetry, and paint. Their father was completely unaware of these carefully disguised and concealed feelings. At a board meeting I asked the sons, "Do you really want to run this company for the next five years and for the rest of your lives?" The sons hesitated and then almost in unison said, "No. I don't really want to devote my life to business." The father was startled, shocked, amazed, incredulous. This was the first disclosure by the sons that the father's dream of continued leadership by family members would not be fulfilled. Over the next several months the chairman became reconciled to his sons' position, and, being the tough-minded old codger that he is, decided that the best solution would be to sell the enterprise to an attractive acquirer. He negotiated the sale of the company, and one son is now a schoolteacher at his prep school and the other is writing poetry in Spain. The father thought he knew his children, but it took over thirty years for him to discover what they were really like. [2]

Boards can play a critical role questioning implicit assumptions about continuity and helping to examine more rigorously the advantages and disadvantages for the business family of a full range of strategic options that can and should include not just the continuity of the company but its potential sale as well. Directors act in the best interests of shareholders when they help the family reach a realistic answer to the fundamental question "Do we want to be together in a family company in the future, and, if so, why?"

While the board should not be expected to work directly with the family on all succession planning tasks—that responsibility falls on senior management—it can be instrumental in getting the family to engage in regular discussions about them. One way the board can influence the system, for example, is to request information from the family about its succession planning just as it asks for regular reports from management on business activities. The board has direct access to the incumbent leaders and can raise fundamental questions with them, such as:

- How do you envision the future of this business?
- How do you plan to divide your shares among your children and why?
- Which of the three family business forms do you envision in the next generation?
- What skills will the leaders of tomorrow need to work effectively in that business form?
- What's being done to help potential successor candidates develop those skills?
- Who among the senior executives do you think might be equipped to lead this company into the future?
- Have you discussed any of these issues with the rest of the family?
- What do they think?

Overseeing Strategic Selection

Boards of directors can also play a critical role helping business owners assess the feasibility of the system they have in mind for the future. By helping family members make explicit the underlying assumptions of their individual Dreams—and of the Shared Dream—directors can be a catalyst for a process of continuous re-examination of these aspirations. One of the virtues of the process of strategic selection of successors is that it allows board members to challenge any assumptions about the candidates that the incumbent leaders have which may be unfounded. In other words, the process serves as a reality check.

Research on corporate governance suggests that the role that boards play in the process of leadership selection has evolved in recent times. Early research by Mace found that the incumbent chief executive rather than the board had primary responsibility for selecting and developing a successor.[3] In fact, boards of large public corporations were reluctant to become involved in the succession process at all. As a recent Conference Board report noted:

Corporate boards have traditionally construed their obligation to select a new CEO as little more than a commitment to fill a vacated post, often with the CEO's handpicked successor. Until recently, few boards and CEOs con-

fronted the host of issues raised by succession. The need to orchestrate a stable transition was not high on most directors' agendas; and the board's role
in persuading a CEO to step down voluntarily in a time of good performance, or yield to the imperative of needed change was seldom discussed.
Directors felt uncomfortable with this duty and even those who were
obliged by circumstances to exercise it rarely shared their experiences in
open forums.[4]

The Conference Board survey of over five hundred large corporations in the United States and Europe revealed that boards of these
companies are becoming increasingly independent and playing a much
more assertive role in the management of the succession process.
"Study participants in all countries report growing involvement of
boards in the development and implementation of orderly succession
plans," the report concluded.

For instance, boards have started to stress the importance of
strategic criteria in the selection and development of potential successors. They have insisted on regular progress reports from the CEO on
what he or she and the human resources department have done to
develop a list of candidates and prepare the successor team. The well-
publicized ousters of CEOs such as Lee Iacocca of Chrysler and James
Robinson of American Express are evidence of the growing involvement of corporate boards with leadership succession. According to the
Conference Board report, this trend is attributable to three basic factors: the increased assertiveness of institutional investors, the media's
enhanced sensitivity to poor corporate performance, and a growing
assertiveness on the part of independent directors.

If boards of public corporations have until recently been uncomfortable about intervening in the succession process, independent
directors of family companies have probably been even more wary
about getting involved in leadership transfers that may arouse strong
family emotions. As in many public companies, successors in family
firms tend to be handpicked by the founder or CEO. The directors
often become part of what I call the succession conspiracy—the tacit
agreement of everyone around the incumbent leader to ignore the
pressing questions surrounding a generational change in leadership.[5]
Practitioners in the field, however, have made family business owners
more aware of the important role that independent outsiders can play
in breaking the conspiracy of silence.

As the time for a generational change looms, boards must become
more active in managing and structuring the process by which the

baton will be passed. They have an obligation to see that the process of selection is conducted in a fair and impartial manner that takes into consideration not just the Dreams and aspirations of the family but the needs of the enterprise as well. The board can enhance the credibility and legitimacy of the process by which future leaders are developed and selected, particularly if directors who are viewed as experienced and impartial participate in the process.

Boards can also play a fundamental role in insisting that reliable performance measures be developed for gauging the capabilities and relative effectiveness of successor candidates. Directors are in a position to insist on receiving information about executive performance on a regular basis. Just as important, they can help to achieve a consensus in the company on the best criteria for measuring the performance of family and non-family executives. Assessment can be a difficult task, and is often riddled with the risk of political conflict between different interest groups. The higher that executives move up the organizational ladder, the more complex their jobs become and the longer the time lag between decisions and results becomes.[6] In multidivisional companies, coming up with meaningful measures for comparing the performance of individual business units can be a complex undertaking. Yet reaching an agreement on performance criteria is critical for assessing the track records of successor candidates.

In one family company I studied, two cousins from different branches of the family were competing with a senior non-family executive for the job of CEO. The board believed the three were roughly equal in leadership and managerial abilities. They had a much harder time coming up with hard data to determine which had the best performance record. A good part of their problem was the lack of agreed-upon criteria for assessing the performances of the three. If profitability was used as the criterion, the non-family executive, who was in charge of a major division, was unquestionably the top performer. When market shares of the businesses run by the three contenders were compared, one of the cousins came out ahead. But when cash flow was used as the yardstick, the other cousin emerged with a slight advantage over the other two. The discussion quickly became politicized as each candidate's supporters on the board endorsed the performance criterion that was most advantageous to their candidate.

The decision became so competitive that, as a last resort, the board decided to delegate the choice of performance criteria (and, by default, of successor) to the three independent directors on the board. In order to determine which of the three performance criteria would be most advantageous for the company in the future, these directors did a thorough industry survey. Their survey revealed that market share would be the key variable for the industry, and thus the cousin who had increased market share the most in his business was chosen as the next CEO.

After this contentious decision was made, the board realized that its ability to handle the succession would have been enhanced had the owners been able to agree, before embarking on the transition, on which performance criteria to use. More important, the board realized that the absence of agreed-upon performance standards had made it much harder to legitimize the final choice of a leader.

Coaching Juniors and Seniors

During the final stages of the transition, both the incoming and out-going leaders are in need of support. Even in the best of situations, the transition can and often does strain the relationship between parting leaders and their successors. Independent directors can play a particu-larly constructive function by serving as an emotional buffer between the generations.

Edwin G. Booz and James Allen, well known founders of the con-sulting firm Booz, Allen and Hamilton, once played just such a role as directors of S.C. Johnson & Son. In *The Essence of a Family Enterprise*, Samuel Johnson, the chairman of Johnson's Wax, recalled how the two directors helped to facilitate the leadership transition from his father, H.C. Johnson, Jr., to himself:

I could tell Jim Allen what was bothering me; I could be straight wrong and use terms that would have gotten me tossed headfirst out of my father's office. Allen would just soak it in, and never get mad. He would say, "Well, Sam, I agree with you on this, but I don't agree with you on that." I never got mad at him for telling me I was wrong about something for there was none of the tension that routinely exists between a father and a son. Moreover, I could trust Jim Allen because he was a consultant with a superb reputation, and I knew how he would deal discreetly with my father. . . . You see, he could lay out my opinion to my father, who might well say, "Sam is way off beam on this. Crazy, in fact, what's that boy thinking?" Should I hear that reaction, our working relationship would sink faster than the Titanic.[7]

Johnson's comments suggest that independent directors can coach aspiring successors to pick their battles and focus on the truly important issues. Seniors in family businesses tend to be attached, for symbolic and personal reasons, to the functions and activities that they have been most responsible for, and the juniors—partly out of their own insecurities about recognition—often focus their attention on acquiring those roles early in the transition rather than on consolidating their control over the actual management of the business. Directors can offer next-generation leaders valuable advice on what to insist on at the beginning of the taking-charge process and what can be left for the end. For instance, the transfer of those roles that have a great deal of public recognition but do not directly pertain to the day-to-day affairs of the company may often be left until the end of the succession process.

In view of the resistances to succession planning by many senior leaders, the boards of family companies can play a major role in monitoring the transition process and keeping it on track. We have seen how some incumbent leaders attempt to delay the progress of the succession plan and redefine its terms, in part perhaps because of their ambivalence about letting go, but also because they are never quite sure that the juniors are up to the task of taking charge. Sometimes they delay the process even after the would-be successors have demonstrated outstanding success. The board can help establish milestones that define progress on the transition journey.

In one family company, for example, the business owner constantly renegotiated how much time his daughter needed before she could take over particular organizational functions under his direct command. With the approval of the board, both the father and daughter had agreed to a two-year schedule under which new responsibilities would be transferred to daughter in each quarter, provided she had demonstrated her ability to carry out the most recent set of new tasks. The most important and difficult functions were to be passed down toward the end of the process. But whenever the father had even the slightest doubts about the daughter's performance on any of her assigned functions, he would immediately and arbitrarily postpone the transfer of any additional responsibilities. This happened even when it was abundantly clear that external financial factors, and not the daughter's managerial decisions, were responsible for the problems. To the disappointment of the daughter and her managerial team, the transition that was to take two years was stretched out to four years. When the directors finally caught on to the fact that the process was being unduly lengthened, they confronted the father and insisted that there be no further departures from the timetable.

As I described in Chapter 11, the departing leaders must address many complex psychological and organizational issues associated with their withdrawal from management and ownership responsibilities. Much of their resistance to planning for succession stems from the fact that they feel very alone with these issues. One of the most important contributions that board members can make is to coach key family and non-family executives as they contemplate the implications that succession has for them as individuals. This role is particularly critical with regard to helping incumbent leaders to understand and manage their retirement.

Departing leaders need someone they respect to act as a sounding board and help them articulate their own perspective on the succession. Even more important, they need help in answering questions they face about their personal future, such as: What will my work life be like once I retire from active involvement from the family business? How will my retirement affect my relationships with people I've been close to almost all my life, such as clients, suppliers, senior executives, the community at large and, indeed, the board itself? How will this transition affect my role in the family? It is often advisable for family companies approaching the succession transition to have at least one independent director who is about the same age as the incumbent leader and who has successfully managed his or her own transition to retirement. Such a person can serve as a role model on retirement issues for the senior leader and help to focus his or her attention on the positive elements of retirement. The director thus provides the encouragement that can motivate the leader to carry out the timely implementation of succession.

The Pivotal Role of the Family Council

At the time of succession, the family council can be a rock of stability that makes a substantial contribution to shaping the future of the system. We have seen that as a leadership transfer approaches, competitive pressures often challenge previously held assumptions and call for a strategic repositioning of the business. Market realities frequently rub up against family values and traditions and may spark generational clashes that, depending on how they are handled, can either facilitate or hinder the system's ability to adjust to the demands of the transition. It is the fundamental responsibility of the family council to create conditions that will allow the system to sort through these complex decisions. The council is responsible for defining the family's involvement with the business and preparing family members to operate within the governance system in a constructive manner.

First and foremost, the council must send clear signals to the board about the mix of family and non-family leadership structure it wishes to see in the next generation. If the council decides it wants management to remain in family hands, it must direct the board to develop a pool of younger family members who are qualified for the top positions. If there are no outstanding family candidates for the CEO's job, or if the family wishes to avoid a potentially destructive competition for the job, the council may ask the board to develop a list of non-family professional managers who might run the company in the next generation. Or the family may wish to have the board develop a team of family and non-family leaders to manage the company.

Apart from the succession process, the council plays an ongoing role in guiding the board and management on the principles and values they are expected to uphold in their policies. First, the family has to give general guidance to management and the board on what the priorities in the business are to be. When the values of the business and the values of the family are in conflict, which comes first? Second, the family should be clear about any social, religious, and political values that they feel strongly about and want to see promoted by the business, or, at the very least, not violated in its dealings.

Coordinating the Work of Board and Council

In many companies that do not have a family council, the board is left in the dark about the family's preferences on issues involving conflicting values. Consider the case of a U.S. insurance company, owned by a Jewish family, that had an opportunity for a lucrative deal to insure a shipment of arms to the Palestine Liberation Organization (PLO). The non-family CEO had negotiated the million-dollar deal, which was perfectly legal and would have boosted company revenues. Unsure whether the family owners would approve, however, the CEO asked for guidance from the board. The board chairman, who also sits on the family council, then raised the issue at a council meeting. After discussing the matter, the family decided that as Jews, they could not help a group that was at that time dedicated to the destruction of Israel. The family's opposition to the PLO was more important to them than the profits they would have earned. The deal was scrapped.

Decisions that require value judgments come up in business more often than families commonly suppose. Take the case of a company whose managers wanted to move its main plant to the South in order to gain a competitive advantage on wages. The newly appointed successor determined that the move was necessary in order to restore healthy profit margins and capture lost market share. But the family was very attached to the local community where it has lived for four generations and is the principal employer. Although they understood the economic advantages of the move, many family members opposed it. It was up to the family council to weigh the options carefully and convey their preferences to the board, which ultimately must decide the issue.

In other situations, family input may be inappropriate and even disruptive. One example is provided by the company mentioned in Chapter 10 that sought measurable ways to compare the track records of three successor candidates. This company also wanted to develop a bonus system for rewarding exemplary performance. In the past, the company had used net profits as the variable for gauging performance. Some directors, however, felt that growth in market share should be adopted as the critical variable determining bonuses. The industry, in contrast, was moving toward cash flow as the preferred performance variable for bonuses. Whether the board continued to use net profits or adopted market share or cash flow as the measure would make a big difference in the size of the bonuses of senior managers, some of whom were family members. A strong case was made, however, that compensation systems should be "family neutral," and that this was strictly a business decision that should be left to the board. The board ultimately adopted a weighted bonus system that rewarded all three measures, although it assigned a heavier weight to market share than to profitability and cash flow.

Governance mechanisms are absolutely essential for resolving shareholder disagreements. Without such mechanisms, these disputes often lead to costly litigation and even sale of the company.

Up to now we have emphasized the importance of keeping discussion of different issues in the right forums. The paradox here is that the components in the family business must first be effectively differentiated before they can be effectively integrated. The owners have to fully understand the essential differences between the functions, and learn to respect boundaries, before they can work constructively and without confusion. In the final analysis, many issues will require concerted action by all three forums. The three constituencies must come together around a vision of the future and sense of stewardship that unify and inspire all.

Some difficult issues do not fall exclusively within the purview of either the board or the council but require a dialogue between the two. The ultimate decision on dividend policy, for example, is the responsibility of the board. But the board cannot set the policy arbitrarily; it has to take into account the liquidity needs of the shareholders, conveyed to the board members through the family council. The family may be willing to forgo dividends in a year when its other investments, unrelated to the business, have appreciated in value; the council may inform the board in that year that profits could be plowed back into the business. At other times the family may need cash in order to fund an important philanthropic initiative and may ask the board to increase the dividends.

The membership of the two bodies should overlap to some degree. At the very least, the chairman of the board should sit on the family council, and the chairman of the family council ought to have a board seat. This is important for ensuring good communication between the two bodies. Unless the most powerful leaders in the business are active on the family council, moreover, other family members may feel that the council's work is not taken seriously and that their policies and wishes will carry no weight with the board. In some family companies, the board and the council meet at least once a year for an open-ended discussion of mutual concerns.

A statement of family values, approved by the council, can help the board reach policy decisions in many cases. If board members have doubts about the application of those values in the context of any specific decision, they are obliged to go to the family council for guidance—as they did in the insurance company case. Finally, a family constitution can lay out guidelines for coordinating the work and policies of the three structures and clarify any gray areas in jurisdiction and responsibilities.

Writing It All Down:
A Family Constitution

Although few families have until recently seen the need for a comprehensive family protocol or constitution, those who have put such a document together have found that it is well worth the time and effort. The creation of a family constitution can be important from a substantive as well as a process perspective. In terms of substance, the development of a family constitution offers the family an opportunity to make explicit the values, principles, and policies that will guide family governance and thus help regulate the family's relationship to the company. In terms of process, the writing of the constitution ideally enlists the participation of the entire family and reinforces a sense of ownership in the final document, which can increase the odds that it will be respected and followed.

The constitution defines the family's vision of the future and its core values and beliefs. It spells out the purpose and responsibilities of the family council, the board of directors, the trustees, and the shareholders' assembly, the criteria for membership in each of these groups, and the checks and balances that regulate the relationships among them. With regard to succession, the document may spell out the process by which the leaders in the family and in the business will be chosen. Further, the document may spell out how family members who serve on the board of directors are to be selected. In addition, the constitution may specify that the family council is responsible for developing family members interested in serving on the board and ensuring they have the necessary training and qualifications.

Other possible components of a family constitution include:

- *A mission statement that defines the family's fundamental desire to be in business together.* A typical statement might read: "We the descendants of Mary and George Dow vow to preserve and enhance the legacy of the founders for the sake of our children, our employees and their families, and our community at large. We will do so in a way that promotes harmony in our family and opportunities for each individual to realize his or her potential to the fullest."
- *A statement of the family's fundamental values and beliefs.* The statement may embrace wise sayings and quotations that express the family's shared experiences as well as its ethnic and religious roots. For example: "It's better to have a good name than to be well known." "Give someone a fish and you'll feed them for a day; teach someone how to fish and you'll feed them for a lifetime." "Our family name is our most important asset." "Austerity and a low profile are essential for success."
- *A family code of behavior that specifies the family's norms and expectations with regard to how the members treat one another and conduct themselves.* A typical code makes explicit such norms as: "Family members are expected to protect the privacy of the family at all times and never to do anything that may put family members at

risk." "Family members should not argue in public." "Family members will try to resolve their difficulties directly with one another, rather than unduly involving innocent third parties."

- *Policies for regulating the relationship between the family and the business.* For example, a clause on employment of family members may specify: "Any member of the family who hopes to work for the company must have completed a college education in a subject relevant to the business, earned a graduate degree in business or have had comparable work experience, and must have worked outside the family company for at least five years." Another rule might be: "During the first five years after entry, family members will be assigned only to line positions in which their performance can be reliably measured."

- *Performance policy.* The constitution may state, for example: "We expect those family members who come to work at the company to excel in their performance. If after the first two years they are not performing at a level comparable to that of the top 25 percent of our executives, they will be asked to leave." Another rule might be: "In order to facilitate performance reviews, family members working at the company should not report to another family member, if at all possible."

- *A retirement policy.* For example: "No family member should continue serving in an executive position in our business past the age of seventy. No family member should continue serving on the board of directors past the age of seventy-five."

- *A dismissal policy.* For example: "The authority to fire a family employee rests squarely with his or her direct supervisor. Prior to dismissing a family employee, the superior should inform the family council so that the family ramifications of the dismissal can be anticipated and constructively managed."

- *Stock redemption policies.* The document may outline goals for a liquidity policy under which shareholders interested in selling their stock can be bought out with a minimum of family disruption. It may, for example, establish a goal in all such transactions of maintaining the balance of power among family branches.

- *A non-competition agreement that all family shareholders are willing to abide by.* Such an agreement may, for example, spell out restrictions on the commercial uses of the family name.

- *Job descriptions for the key positions in the governance structure.* This section spells out the duties, terms, responsibilities, and privileges of the chairman of the family council, the chairman of the board, and the chairman of the family foundation's board. Some family constitutions also establish the process by which each of these positions will be filled.

- *Funding mechanisms for governance.* Board activities are paid for by the business. But some regular source of funds may be required for the activities of the family council and shareholder group. The constitution may, for example, set up an annual levy on family members that is based on a budget.

The Constitution-Writing Process

It is the responsibility of the family council to design a process through which family members come together to learn about family governance and make decisions that are consistent with the family's values and traditions. The writing of a constitution is itself a powerful way to motivate family members to work together to make sure the board focuses on the difficult issues associated with succession and continuity. Because the authority of the family constitution depends entirely on the willingness of the family members to abide by its mandates, the process of writing it is as important as its contents. Unless the entire family has a sense of ownership in the process, the document may be filed away and forgotten.

Once the constitution has been drafted, then it is important for the family council to gather the entire family and explain the document and its implications in detail. The constitution should be formally voted on by all family members in order to foster the sense of shared ownership necessary to make the document work in practice.

One view of constitutions sees them as envisioning governance structures as Platonic ideals that never change and can only be approached through constant effort. My view is that there are no perfect ideals and that structures must be constantly re-examined and readjusted to take into account changing realities. Not all the details of a constitution can be worked out ahead of time. Indeed, constitutions are often written in very general terms—much like the U.S. Constitution—to allow room for reinterpretation in each succeeding era. Periodically, new policies will have to be added on issues that were not foreseen when the constitution was drafted. For a constitution to work, it must become a living document.

Questions about Governance Structures

Families that dedicate themselves to preserving their cohesion and unity understand that they are acting not just for the good for the family—it is also good for the business. A united shareholder group is a tremendous asset for a family company. It is one of the singular competitive advantages that well-run family enterprises have vis-à-vis nonfamily counterparts. Successful family companies know that it is substantially more expensive to raise financial resources in the open capital markets than it is to invest time and energy in keeping the family shareholders involved and committed to preserving the family's business legacy.

Nevertheless, some families are uneasy when cautioned about all the possible issues that may arise in the future and the planning that they must do in order to maintain control of the business and harmony in the family. They frequently ask why they have to deal with these decisions now, when the issues are far off into the future—when, in fact, they may never occur? Why has life gotten so complex when everything seemed so simple in the past?

The answer, of course, is that both the family and the company *have* become more complex. Governance structures and policies are fundamentally preventive. Time and time again, experience has taught me that unless formal mechanisms are in place to resolve certain issues that inevitably arise in business families, they seldom get dealt with constructively.

Nan-B de Gaspé Beaubien, the Canadian woman whose family has devoted considerable effort to developing such structures, put it this way: "It is important . . . to put the rules in place before they are needed." Phillipe and Nan-B de Gaspé Beaubien of Telemedia, Inc., are convinced that complex structures are essential for dealing with the issues that they and their four children will face in the future. They make it a habit to talk with the leaders of similar family enterprises around the world to get ideas for governance of their company.

Governance structures are essential for ensuring that the complex issues that arise in many family businesses will be dealt with in an open, orderly manner. When governance structures are well managed, they are active, vibrant forums that promote ongoing discussion in the family and make the participants feel they have been heard and fairly treated. Structures, policies, and procedures are not a panacea, of course. They solve some problems, but not others. Ward cautions that too much emphasis on the role of governance structures for resolving and preventing conflict may lead families to dwell on the negative, disheartening aspects of owning and managing a business. In establishing governance structures, therefore, leaders should stress their positive value in planning an exciting, fulfilling future for the family and in preserving and passing on the business.

Participants in a family business are most satisfied with their lives together, in my experience, when they approach the challenge with a deep commitment to preserving and continuing a legacy. Those that manage to remain in business through generations typically see themselves as responsible for preserving, enhancing, and then handing on the business to their descendants in better condition than they received it. This concept of stewardship views a business enterprise as a human system on which many people depend for a livelihood, including employees and their families as well as other stakeholders. Very successful and long-lasting family companies make an effort to instill this sense of social responsibility and enlightened ownership in each generation.

Embodied in the notion of stewardship is the expectation that the current family leaders will do everything possible to keep the family "ship" in good shape during their tenure and then turn over the helm of an even bigger and more magnificent ship to the stakeholders and, especially, to their children and grandchildren.

CHAPTER 14

Conclusion:
Improving the Odds of Success

THIS book has examined the challenges that business families face as they approach a generational transition. Two assumptions underlie the ideas presented. First, that succession and continuity can indeed be planned for, and, second, that planning does in fact improve the odds of continuity. At the very beginning, we noted the opinion of experts on the high mortality rate of family businesses in the second and third generations.[1] There are undoubtedly many reasons why countless companies are sold or close their doors after only one generation of family ownership. Many simply lack a qualified successor who wants to continue the business. Others are in rapidly consolidating industries and lose out to larger competitors. Although it is difficult to prove, large numbers undoubtedly fail because they do not engage in succession planning at all or don't do so until very late in the game.[2]

I have emphasized that the odds of transferring a business to the next generation are greatly improved when the process begins early and families get into the habit of talking together about their Dreams. To a great extent, success depends upon how well the family, the shareholders, and the senior executives are educated and prepared to face up to the challenges of the transition plan, upon the structures that are put in place to ensure that key stakeholders communicate with one another and problem-solve together effectively, and upon adhering to the timetable for implementing the changes spelled out in the plan. Above all, the process must be *managed* every step of the way, painstakingly and thoroughly.

Even with the best preparation and planning, however, there are no guarantees of success. With all the planning in the world, a successful company can sometimes go downhill quickly because of critical mistakes or drastic changes in the economic environment. As I mentioned at the outset of the book, this lesson was brought home to me most painfully by the failure of the substantial insurance brokerage business that my father built in Venezuela.

Adversity is a great teacher, and the demise of so many family-owned businesses has taught me much about how successions should, and should not, be handled. One of the biggest lessons was that succession plans must be continuously monitored to ensure that corrective action is taken when evidence begins to mount that they are failing. Drastic and embarrassing though such action may be, leaders must be vigilant and ready to change course when circumstances warrant.

Some successions fail because the family anoints new leaders without having demonstrable evidence of their competence. Others end in disaster because the family goes ahead with its plan despite ample and trustworthy data about the lack of fit between the successors and the needs of the business. As we noted in Chapter 10, dynastic Dreams can blind the most enlightened families to information that contradicts their assumptions about the successor candidates. Proceeding with a succession plan when there are doubts about the leadership capacities of the chosen successors puts the whole enterprise—and the family's wealth—at risk. If families are to succeed at succession, they must make courageous choices based on hard evidence.

Given the grim statistics on the continuity of family companies, how can I justify the optimistic perspective on planning in this book? How can I explain my confidence that many families can do better, that they can improve the odds of continuity?

Undeniably, for many families the transfer of a business from one generation to the next represents an unachievable goal. If we imagine the universe of companies wishing to preserve family control as being distributed along a bell-shaped distribution curve, probably as many as one-fourth of business families at one end would be, for one reason or another, incapable of making the transition. Maybe the Dreams of the younger and older generations cannot be reconciled, or the resources of the company are inadequate to provide for both the needs of the retiring owners and continuity in the business, or perhaps the demands for liquidity of increased numbers of passive shareholders have imposed impossible pressures on the leadership. Whatever the reason, the wisest course for these families may be to acknowledge that they are not able to sustain the business. Their task is then to sell the family business under the best possible terms, in a way that creates the least amount of family conflict. The ideas in this book may thus heighten the awareness of families in the lower quartile that they may be better off ridding themselves of the burdens and responsibilities of being a business family. It is also possible that in exploring the alternatives, another solution will present itself—such as a buyout of one group of shareholders by another or a clean division of the company into two or more smaller businesses.

I would expect to find at the other end of our imaginary curve another quartile of firms that naturally possess the blend of skills and capabilities needed to negotiate the leadership transition. For these firms and recommendations in this book may provide helpful supportive material for a process they probably would have been able to figure out intuitively for themselves.

The vast number in the middle of our bell-shaped curve—the other 50 percent of families—stand to benefit most from the growing body of experience and knowledge of what effective succession planning requires. It is these families that can get the most help from professionals in sorting out whether or not they can manage the transition, and what they can do to improve the odds.

I harbor no fantasies that the ideas and perspectives in this book can be easily applied to the complex realities of any given family enterprise. Nevertheless, I have observed many approaches that have plainly worked and produced impressive results. The most successful business families, in my experience, pay an extraordinary amount of attention to scanning the environment in search of good ideas. In that spirit, let me summarize ten key lessons that I hope readers will take away from this book.

> *Lesson 1: An active, deliberate investigation of the*
> *full range of options, and the implications of each,*
> *is vital to successful planning.*

Many families make fundamental choices about the future by default. One of the most important messages in this book is that the avoidance of choice is what ultimately gets family businesses into trouble. Facing up to choices is critical not just because it helps the family formulate a plan for the transition, but because it strengthens the commitment of those who will be responsible for sustaining the enterprise. There can be no real commitment without choice. Like an arranged marriage, a family's ties to a business will be weak and perhaps unsustainable if the members feel that continuity has been forced on them rather than chosen by free will.

Choices are easier to avoid when the universe of possibilities is vague and when there is little valid information about the advantages and risks of the various options confronting the system at a given juncture in time. Unfortunately, business owners are frequently not clear about what they want for themselves, for their families, and for their businesses. Even when they are clear on their Dream, they often lack a detailed understanding of specific steps they will have to take to realize it.

We have also seen that procrastination results when the fundamental choices are entangled in complex family dynamics. If there are emotional conflicts in the family, the leaders often ignore the long-term issues involved in planning, and bury themselves instead in the day-to-day decisions over which they feel they have more control. The issues that are critical thereby get postponed, perhaps indefinitely.

The first and most fundamental choice is deciding whether or not to continue the business at all. For many families the very idea that they have such a choice comes as a revelation. The family enterprise is such an integral part of their identity that to question it seems inappropriate and even heretical. But no matter how long the company has been in business, it should not be passed on unless the members make a deliberate decision to do so—and commit themselves to doing the work required.

A generational transition also confronts many individuals in the family with a basic choice about whether or not they want to retain any involvement in management or ownership. Here again it is often assumed that family members will want management or ownership roles. Many drift into the business because they don't know anything better and think they might fail in the outside world. Later on, they feel trapped in roles they never wholeheartedly chose and may not be cut out for. In numerous companies, family members inherit shares or receive them as a gift. While such gifts come from caring and generous relatives, they do not come with any education in the responsibilities of ownership.

Obviously, succession and continuity planning are not just a matter of choosing among alternative leadership structures and selecting new leaders. After choices have been made, the hard work of thinking them through and implementing them begins. The process requires that families give careful attention to such questions as What is the right time to make the key decisions? What needs to happen so that the decisions made are successfully implemented? Who should be involved in the planning? How will the change process be monitored? Who will take responsibility to see the process through?

> *Lesson 2: Create an atmosphere in which family*
> *members feel comfortable discussing their Dreams*
> *and their common future.*

I have maintained that traditional approaches to succession planning do not give sufficient attention to the aspirations of members of a family and how they combine to form a vision of the future. It is true that Dreams are intangible and even at times amorphous; to many practical business people, the very concept may sound like New Age fantasy. But Dreams have a real existence and cannot be ignored. Professionals who treat succession and continuity planning as if it were a purely rational/cognitive activity run a twofold risk: First, they stand to develop elaborate plans that the family cannot realize because they do not address the deeper emotional and developmental needs of individuals in the system. Second, they fail to harness the enormous motivational power of the Shared Dream.

The Shared Dream is the emotional reservoir from which business families gather the strength to accomplish great deeds. The Dream provides the inspiration, the higher purpose and sense of direction necessary to cope with adversity. Above all, it helps business families answer the question, "*Why* is what we're doing worth doing?"

Families can nurture the development of a Shared Dream in a number of ways. First, they can create an environment that helps their members articulate their aspirations in mutually respectful and supportive ways—an environment in which children from an early age can nourish their own "imagined possibilities." Families are at their best when the members help one another to realize their Dreams. By sharing their enthusiasm for their work and stories about their experiences, the seniors help their children appreciate the satisfactions of a career in the family business.

Ideally, work on the articulation of a Shared Dream *precedes* more formal steps in the continuity planning process, such as the development of strategic and succession plans. There are some families for whom launching right into discussions of Dreams may be too threatening, however. For those families it may be wiser to the first start a formal process of deciding practical strategic and succession issues, in the hopes that such conversations will help them to address more emotionally loaded issues associated with Dreams later on. We have seen, though, that such plans may turn into a futile exercise without agreement on the yearnings and ambitions of family members.

Giving Dreams the importance they deserve also helps the family get through the drudgery and frequent discouragement that are endemic to the planning process. After all, much of that work requires paying careful attention to what can go wrong, so that appropriate preventative measures can be designed. It is easy, consequently, to lose sight of the real opportunities for growth and development that the family business offers. Focusing on the Dream can help families engage in active problem solving with the purpose of actually realizing their deepest aspirations.

Lesson 3: Continuously reassess the feasibility of the Shared Dream.

A business and a family are like Heraclitus's moving stream: The participants never set foot in the same stream twice. When conditions change, as new information is sorted and assimilated, people's Dreams change. The Shared Dream must be revised accordingly. If at some point in a sibling partnership the work relationships between the partners become seriously frayed, it may be best to sever them completely and work to develop a new Dream. A family with several branches may be very committed to a cousin consortium, but if the business is not big enough to sustain a large group of shareholders, they may have to adjust their expectations. Sometimes a business is simply no longer producing the returns that were anticipated when the original Shared Dream was articulated. Likewise, a family that has been in the same business for several generations will have to modify its Dream if it becomes clear that the business is no longer competitive and is destined to be driven from its markets by stronger competitors or technological developments. In such cases, the family should consider selling the business and investing in another around which to rebuild their Dream.

It is also common for to families face new *opportunities* that they need to factor into their Shared Dream. A family enterprise that strongly identifies itself with the heritage, symbols, and aspirations of its home country, for example, may need to learn how to recognize the potential profit in expanding across borders to neighboring markets.

Not to take these constraints and opportunities into account is the engineering equivalent of building a house without first exploring the bedrock and soil on which the foundation will be laid. This exploration of family Dreams and business conditions must be a continual process, since opportunities and constraints may not be evident at the time a strategy or project is initiated and the planning process is launched.

Paying attention to the needs of the business means instilling in family members a deep appreciation and respect for the professionalism required to run a successful enterprise. Even large companies can be buffeted by market forces, and there is a danger that families accustomed to success can become so overconfident that they develop a sense of invulnerability. Often in such cases they ignore the need for even the most elementary continuity planning until it is too late.

> *Lesson 4: What is best for the business in the short run may not be good for the business in the long run if the family's needs are ignored.*

This seeming paradox may be explained is a simple observation: Those who assume that the family must make every sacrifice for the sake of success in business are likely to discover that a broken, dysfunctional family is the greatest threat to continuity.

Members of business families are often asked to subordinate their individual Dreams to the needs of their business. The assumption here is that if all goes well for the business, the family will take care of itself and be all right. Nothing could be further from the truth. Family business must be thought of as a hyphenated term, in which family and business are mutually supportive and the health of one depends upon the health of the other.

Researchers and consultants often divide family firms into those that usually put the business first when faced with difficult decisions and those that give priority to the family. To my mind, this business-first versus family-first dichotomy is misleading. Continuity planning must seek solutions that work for *both* the family and the business.

One could easily argue that from a business standpoint having a single leader is a more efficient leadership structure than a leadership team, but imposing a single leader and a rigid hierarchy on a group of siblings who want to work together may destroy their capacity to collaborate and may create problems in the family. In terms of the family's quality of life, shouldn't the risks of such a plan be taken seriously? If a solution is not the best for the business but is *good enough* and, in the bargain, secures twenty years of peace and family harmony, isn't it worth adopting?

The best solutions to succession and continuity problems are those that bring into alignment the needs of the family and the needs of the business. Mapping out that territory is precisely the job of professionals interested in helping family businesses. Any solution that does not cover the entire territory is, by definition, *not* a solution.

> *Lesson 5: Continuity and succession planning*
> *require the development of effective governance*
> *structures and processes.*

Business owners make a serious mistake when they move their companies in the direction of more complexity without putting in place the structures and policies necessary to manage the realities of the new circumstances. Every stage in the evolution of a business raises particular issues and dilemmas that call for flexible solutions. The governance structures that I have described—the family council, the board of directors, and the shareholders' assembly—monitor the system to ensure that it is adequately attending to the myriad issues associated with leadership and ownership changes.

Governance structures institutionalize the social contract among critical stakeholders, define the power relationships among them, and develop fair procedures and rules of conduct. Governance bodies should serve to continually educate the members of each constituency about their rights, responsibilities, and privileges. They deliberate on such issues as Who will have responsibility for making the critical decisions regarding succession and continuity? Who will define what the various leadership roles will be, and how will the people best equipped to serve in those roles be selected? Where in the system will the family's deepest values be articulated and preserved? Who will monitor the system to make sure that its decisions adhere to those values? These are all fundamental governance issues that must be resolved if the enterprise is to move from one generation to another.

Lesson 6: Continuity planning requires anticipating future challenges and developing policies to address them before *they happen.*

By its very nature, planning is about the future and maintaining a long-term perspective on the needs of both the business and the family. While some families do a good job of thinking through the strategic and financial challenges that the business will face, they are often less attentive to the psychological development of their members and what that portends for succession planning. Adult development theory, as I've shown, can be a powerful tool for helping families anticipate the kinds of issues and concerns they are likely to face at different stages of their lives. Families can learn much about the road ahead through the simple exercise of listing the ages of their members and systematically projecting those ages forward year by year for, say, fifteen years.

They can also learn by visits to other family enterprises that have successfully managed a recent generational transition. Cross-family learning is becoming increasingly common and can benefit both the visiting and host families. Before such learning can take place, of course, the two families have to get to know and trust one another in order to ensure that the exchanges will be candid and that confidentiality and privacy will be respected. If they do, the visiting family usually finds this form of benchmarking is one of the best ways to learn what the succession journey will be like, the obstacles that will be encountered, and the techniques that can be used to get over the bumps in the road.

Lesson 7: The successful implementation of succession and continuity plans requires a consultative style of leadership.

Strong leadership is required of those who have the power to make change happen, but not just any kind of leadership will do for succession planning. The effective management of generational transitions calls for strong *consultative* leaders. They are leaders who are not afraid to seek the opinions of others in order to make decisions that are better informed and more likely to be accepted by those who have to live with the consequences. They are leaders who understand what is required and are willing to devote the time necessary to develop members of the next generation and help forge commitment and consensus among them. They are people who can look at the performance histories of members of the younger generation and not flinch at taking corrective action when necessary to bring the process back on track. In short, the process calls for *servant* leaders,[3] who can subordinate their personal needs and egos in order to maximize the odds of a successful transfer of the business.

Likewise, successors must show not only that they can provide strong leadership for the business, but that they have a commitment to the long-term benefit of the whole family. Successors, too, need to have a rare blend of assertiveness and empathy. They have to be sensitive listeners, willing to engage in dialogues with family members and respond to their needs and concerns. To establish their authority, they have to be proactive in seeking and developing the most talented family members for management roles. They must be able to discipline family employees whose performance is sub par or whose behavior is an embarrassment, but they should do it in a tactful, caring way.

Weak, insecure leaders surround themselves with yes men and shy away from appointing capable board members who might question their decisions and policies. Strong successors are protectors of the system's competence. One of the best tests of the security of new leaders, indeed, is whether or not they appoint people to their team whose talents and experience exceed their own.

*Lesson 8: Good leadership in implementing a succession
plan depends upon responsible followership.*

Leaders cannot implement a succession plan without the cooperation and support of many others who are in a position to influence the outcome or even derail the process. Among those who have this power are family shareholders who don't work in the business, spouses who may lack a formal role in the business yet command considerable influence in the family, and minority shareholders who are not in the family. A successful transfer of leadership will depend on the extent to which these individuals are responsible followers.

Responsible followers understand the need to empower leaders to spearhead the process of change; they participate in the process and contribute anything they can to support members of the two generations and facilitate the leadership transfer. For example, they invest the time necessary to understand the complex issues and dilemmas posed by the transition. They also work within the governance structures and serve on committees to provide ideas and help generate support for the plan among employees and outsiders.

Often in generational transitions people criticize the process but contribute little to solving the problems. They are like the masses of people in a democracy who complain endlessly about their leaders but then fail to vote in elections. In any governance system, both leaders and followers must be held accountable. Good citizenship in family companies requires acceptance of responsibility and sustained participation. The stakes in succession are too high for the stakeholders to be indifferent to the important process that is unfolding. President Kennedy's admonition might be paraphrased in this context: "Ask not what your family can do for you, ask what you can do for your family."

> *Lesson 9: Family business continuity requires*
> *developing a spirit of inquiry and a commitment*
> *to lifelong learning and exploration.*

The most successful business owners, in my experience, know they do not have all the answers and are always seeking new information. Families such as the Lombardis constantly encourage their members to seek the best education and training available, and they invest the time and resources necessary to develop the family as a problem-solving system.[4] These families embrace a spirit of inquiry, constantly reflecting on how they do things and whether they can improve by adopting more innovative approaches. They arrange regular educational programs for their families and senior executives. They become avid readers of family business books and articles, and frequently join support networks that put them in touch with other business owners.

An estimated 42 percent of family businesses will change hands within the next five years.[5] Our growing experience with and knowledge of what is required to make the leap successfully gives cause for optimism. Business owners now have many more opportunities to educate themselves about the issues they face, and they have become much more open to discussing these issues within their families and with other business families. Today, for example, in the United States there are more than 150 university-based family business forums where they can do so. The quality of advice and support they are receiving has also improved as professionals from diverse disciplines—law, psychology, accounting, family therapy, banking and insurance, to name a few—

learn to work in concert and define best practices in the field. Indeed, recent surveys suggest that increasing numbers of family business owners are engaging in succession planning.[6]

> *Lesson 10: The whole process stands or falls on the family's capacity to build trust and foster collaboration.*

A central theme of this book is that silence and secretiveness are enemies of succession and continuity planning. Only through open communication and debate can the sensitive issues that inevitably come up be addressed and resolved. Almost every solution to the problems requires the family to be able to discuss issues together and collaborate across generational lines and, in more complex systems, across family branches.

Collaboration, in turn, depends on maintaining and strengthening the bonds of trust in the family. Trust is a complex phenomenon which has five major components—what I call the "five Cs." First, trust grows in families when the members have confidence in one another's *competence*—that is, when each can depend upon the others' experience, skill, and reliability in completing assigned tasks. Second, trust is enhanced when a family member's behavior is *congruent*—in other words, when others can rely on the person to do what he or she says.[7] Trust also depends on *consistent* behavior that is predictable and not erratic. In family businesses, the people who are most trustworthy consistently demonstrate that they will put the interest of the family as a whole above their own self-interest. Ultimately, families cannot raise the level of trust just by talking about it. Developing trust requires trustworthy behavior. By the same token, it requires consistently showing trust by giving family members who make mistakes the benefit of the doubt until a pattern of untrustworthy behavior is unmistakable.

Another requirement of trust—the "fourth C"—is *compassion*. When leaders must make tough decisions for the good of the enterprise that disappoint other people or threaten their financial status, they should do so in a way that shows the various stakeholders that the decisions have been made fairly with the interests of all in mind and with a true understanding of—and empathy for—the impact on those affected.

The "fifth C"—*communication*—is the foundation on which trust is built. Families that are committed to continuity understand that it is critical for their members to learn how to communicate their feelings and ideas in ways that are clear, consistent, and timely. They place a great deal of emphasis on developing better ways of talking and listening to one another, and they continually practice and celebrate these acquired skills.

Families don't usually think of themselves as systems that require regular maintenance. The successful family businesses I have observed, however, invest considerable time and effort in promoting collaboration and preserving harmony among their members. Each of the members makes a strong personal commitment to doing his or her part to uphold standards and maintain the level of trust in the group.

A book on succession and continuity planning should not end without noting the tremendous satisfactions of operating a family enterprise and seeing it passed on through the generations. Although I have emphasized the risks in planning and the enormous amount of work that goes into it, I hope that I have also shown the great rewards reaped by those who do it effectively. Few experiences can match the challenges of steering a major enterprise that touches the lives of so many people in its employ and in the communities where they are located. When these enterprises are managed with competence, grace, and humanity, their owners experience profound spiritual rewards as well as economic ones. Participants in a family business constantly wrestle with life's great questions: "What do we stand for?" "What good do we serve in the world?" "How will we be remembered?" For children, being part of such a legacy creates not just burdens but opportunities, not just wealth but a sense of belonging and pride. A business that has lasted for generations and is widely admired pushes people to excel, to learn to collaborate with others, and to transcend narrow self-interest. In short, for those who are successful at it, the family enterprise offers a way around the alienation of modern life and the dissolution of families. The journey is well worth the effort.

Notes

Introduction

1. There have been many studies on the frequency and causes of entrepreneurial failure. In one well-known study Altman found that in 1970 more than 279 million-dollar firms went broke. He reports that one-third of bankrupt businesses were less than three years old, 53 percent were younger than five, and 23 percent were over ten. Altman et al. 1971. See also Kimberly 1980.
2. See Ward 1987.

Chapter 1   Designing New Road Maps for the Journey

1. Christensen C.R. 1953.
2. Levinson 1971.
3. Becker and Tillman 1978, 278.
4. Benson et al. 1990, 169.
5. Ibid., 36.
6. Ibid., 228.
7. Danco 1992.
8. Danco 1975.
9. Interestingly, 42.3 percent of the respondents said that one of the two co-CEO's might be a woman, suggesting that mixed gender leadership teams will be more prevalent in years to come. This finding also reinforces the notion that many companies are seriously considering leadership teams because primogeniture is difficult to justify as a selection criteria. Arthur Andersen/MassMutual American Family Business Survey 1997.
10. Selz 1994.
11. *Forbes* (Oct. 16, 1995), 56–64.
12. Spector and McCarthy 1995.

13. Hollander 1990.
14. Toffler 1990, 180–182, 187–189.
15. Simon 1996.
16. Vancil 1987. For a more detailed treatment of the behavioral dynamics of "teamwork at the top" in non-family companies, see also Nadler, Gerstein, and Shaw 1992, 209–232; Katzenbach 1998; Hambrick 1995 and 1997.

Chapter 2   A Typology of Successions

1. Berle and Means 1932; Galbraith, 1967, 2; Mason 1958, 1.
2. Zeitlin 1976.
3. Ward 1991. See also Herschon 1975. For a similar typology of family business in a Chinese context, see Wong 1993.
4. Colby 1984.
5. Muson 1993.
6. Danco 1975, 37
7. Schein 1985, 209–222.
8. Gersick et al. (1997) have proposed an additional type of sibling partnership, the "quasi-parental" form, in which one of the siblings acquires so much influence over the others as to behave in a parental way toward them. In the quasi-parental form, there is typically a very close, longstanding special relationship between the parents (or at least the surviving parent) and the lead sibling. Sometimes the dominant sibling adopts some of the symbols of the parental role, such as living in the parental home and hosting all family functions. The lead sibling in quasi-parental partnerships is often quite autocratic and derives a certain pride in making the other siblings dependent. Sam Steinberg, the second-generation leader who built Steinberg, Inc., the Canadian supermarket giant, is a typical quasi-parental leader of a group of siblings. The partnership rapidly fell apart after Sam's death because of the resentments that his siblings had harbored for years over his pervasive influence.
9 Marcs 1991.
10. Johnson 1988. In recent years three highly regarded successors have been working in senior management at S.C. Johnson & Son, suggesting that for the first time in its history, the company may evolve into a sibling partnership.
11. Given the high incidence of blended families—in which as a result of a divorce and remarriage a business owner may have a second family with young children relatively late in life—recycled sibling partnerships from older to younger (half) siblings may become more common in the coming years.
12. When only one sibling in a partnership is active in management, the ground rules may be easier to define. But even in these relatively rare cases the sib-

ling in management still has to find ways of collaborating with the other siblings in shareholder roles on matters of corporate governance such as succession and continuity.

13. Friedman 1964.

14. In a number of cases I studied that clearly showed this type of succession, the infusion of fresh capital came from sources such as a windfall from the sale of a very successful venture that was owned by one of the cousins, the sudden inheritance of wealth from another side of the family, or wealth acquired by marriage that allowed the individual to buy the stock.

15. I am indebted to John Ward for suggesting the metaphor of the soccer club for a cousin consortium.

16. By "structural conflict" I mean conflict that is induced by the circumstances that people find themselves in. Even though these conflicts often seem to result from a clash of personalities or styles, they are in fact a by-product of the changes in the "deep structure" of the system.

Chapter 3   The Lombardi
Family Business

1. While the issues in this case are true to life, the names and places have been changed as requested by the family in order to protect their anonymity.

Chapter 4   Family Dreams

1. For a more detailed treatment of this approach see Nanus 1992.

2. I capitalize the first letter of Dream to emphasize the specific use of the word in this context.

3. Levinson 1978, 91.

4. See Winnicott 1971.

5. Schein 1985. The precise process by which the individual Dream of a leader is infused into the culture of a family company is similar to what Schein has described. The organizational culture is shaped by (1) what the leader focuses on; (2) the leader's reactions to critical incidents and organizational crises; (3) deliberate role-modeling, teaching, and coaching provided by the leader; (4) the criteria the leader uses to allocate rewards and status; and (5) the criteria the leader uses to recruit, select, promote, retire, and "excommunicate" people.

6. Shapiro and Sokol 1982.

7. Reiss 1981.

8. In the family business literature only Ward has paid much attention to the issue of how business families develop a vision of the future. His typology for different types of visions that families can develop is based primarily on constructs from political science. Hence he distinguishes among family visions that are associated with different political ideologies, such as: laissez-faire, royalty, socialism, social democracy, democratic capitalism, representative democracy, pure capitalism, and utopia. There are two fundamental differences between Ward's approach and my own. First, I base my examination of vision on constructs that are fundamentally psychological rather than political. My interest is in how the fundamental continuity choices derive from and shape the personal experiences of family members. Second, I argue that the Shared Dream must grow out of the personal Dreams of individuals if it is to harness the motivational force necessary for implementation. Although I believe that there are certain archetypal forms of visions that recur among business families, the substance of the individual Dreams provides the raw material from which a Shared Dream must be constructed, in that sense, families are not free to choose any vision they want at any point in time. While Ward acknowledges that there needs to be a fit between the vision, the values, and the distinct ideology of a family, his underlying assumption seems to be that a family can instrumentally select from the full range of visions available to them at any given juncture.

9. Lansberg 1992. This point suggests a number of interesting questions: Is the passage of major developmental milestones slower for participants in family businesses? Do they, for example, face the usual mid-life upheaval later than usual? Contrary to Minuchin's perspective, Levinson's adult development theory would suggest that the transition points are not context specific but result from relatively fixed temporal punctuations. Hence the fact that the mid-life transition occurs in the early forties is not coincidental —it happens then because that is the "half time" period of our lives in which a fundamental reassessment is critical. See Gersick (1988) for a theoretical discussion of the impact of time of human behavior.

10. See Correll (1989) for a personal account of what happens when a successor's Dreams are subordinated to the interests of the family business.

11. Gilligan 1982. See also Brown and Gilligan 1992.

12. For a detailed (and discouraging) discussion of this issue see Levinson 1996.

13. "Dover Beach" by Matthew Arnold.

14. The motivational force of the Dream may well be intricately connected to the fact that it is forged during the early adulthood transition and hence captures the excitement and vitality associated with that era. We may hypothesize that if the circumstances in a young person's life are such that they are unable to develop a Dream at this stage, it may be extraordinarily difficult to recapture the passion associated with a Dream later on in life.

15. Selz 1994.

16. Watson and Petre 1990.

17. For a detailed analysis of the unconscious relationship between fraternal collaboration and the French Revolution see Hunt 1992.

18. Marcus 1991. See also Marcus and Hall 1992.

19. This example is based on my interviews with the woman known as Greta in a case published in 1988 by the Harvard Business School. The Precista Tools AG case concerns a Swiss company founded after World War II by the Huebels (the names are fictional). It was written by Prof. Louis B. Barnes and a former participant in the business school's Owner President Management Program.

Chapter 5   Working with Dreams

1. Benson 1990; Dyer 1989; Poza 1990.

2. Beckhard 1977, 25. This idea was originally developed by David Gleicher in his formula: $C = (ABD) > X$ where C = change, A = level of dissatisfaction with the status quo, B = clear desired state, D = practical first steps toward the desired state, and X = cost of change.

Chapter 6   Assessing the Feasibility of the Dream

1. The term "enmeshed" comes from family systems theory. Enmeshed families are characterized by the tight psychological interlocking—or fusing— of its members. In these families the quality of connectedness is such that attempts by one member to change will elicit immediate resistance from the others. In contrast, families with a disengaged style have little, if any, interconnectedness. In an enmeshed family the intensity of relationships is such that a relatively small problem confronting a member rapidly escalates into a major issue that preoccupies the whole family. In a disengaged family, a member experiencing serious difficulties may well go unnoticed by the rest of the family. Extreme forms of enmeshment or disengagement are typically associated with serious family dysfunction. For a more detailed treatment of these concepts see Hoffman 1981; Minuchin 1974.

2. Lansberg 1985. See also Lansberg and Astrachan 1994.

3. For an interesting illustration of a father-son team who play competitive tennis as a vehicle for cementing their relationship outside work, see Drozdow 1989.

4. Selz 1994.

5. Murdock and Murdock 1991.

6. For more details on how the financial structure may be implemented see de Visscher 1995.

7. Bowen 1978.

8. Bank and Kahn 1982, 197.

9. Deutsch 1975.

10. For a more detailed review of the research on group composition and performance see Jackson 1992. There is still debate as to the degree of heterogeneity that is most conducive to high performance. Hackman and Oldham (1980) caution against too much heterogeneity in work groups because "insufficient 'common ground' among members makes communication difficult and provides for less-than-needed interchangeability among members." Their research suggests that balance between homogeneity and heterogeneity is most conducive to group performance.

11. The Sherman brothers, creators of the some of the best-loved songs in Disney movies (including *Mary Poppins*), provide an interesting example of sibling synergy. In a radio interview, one brother described how a lifetime of mutual experiences had supplied the two of them with an abundance of material to draw upon for their songs. The trips to the park with their father as children, their adolescent struggles, their careers in the music industry— all were grist for the Sherman brothers' remarkably successful collaboration.

12. Sulloway (1997) argues that birth order tends to produce this effect among siblings. Each child develops skills and a personality in order to establish a unique identity and voice within the family. The pressures for differentiation may push a pair of siblings to adopt personalities that are mirror images of each other. The first-born sibling may be outgoing and gregarious, for example, and the second-born more reserved and introspective. The same pressures may produce complementary skills: A brother who is gregarious may develop a talent for sales, while a sister who is good with numbers becomes a strong CFO. Sulloway's theory also has implications for choosing a leader to fit the strategic needs of a company at a particular time in its history. First-borns, in his view, tend to be highly responsible and conservative—a good choice as leaders for companies striving to maintain the status quo. Later-borns, who tend to be more rebellious and innovative, may be a better choice as leaders in times of radical change.

13. The concept of triangulation, which comes from family systems theory, suggests that a two-person emotional system under stress has a tendency to form a three-person system. For instance, if tension arises between the two, and the one who was more uncomfortable would relieve tension by "triangling in" a third person, perhaps by telling a story about that person. Then the tension would shift to the new twosome, relieving the tension between the original pair. But the outsider, once he or she becomes drawn in, may respond to the tension by accepting an alliance with one of the others, so that the outsider of one moment becomes the insider of the next. For a detailed treatment of triangulation see Hoffman 1981. Also see Bowen 1978. For a similar construct in the social psychological literature see Cartwright and Harary 1956.

14. Friedman 1991.

15. Gibbon and Hadekel 1990.

16. This theme is found in a Greek myth about a revolt on Mt. Olympus. In the story, Zeus leads a group of his siblings in overthrowing their father, Cronos, as chief of the gods. As a result of the rebellion, Zeus becomes the leader of the gods. But he is really a first-among-equals, and when he starts bossing his siblings around—demanding that they address him as "Father Zeus"—they tie him up in one hundred knots in order to teach him a lesson in humility. Zeus wasn't even the oldest of his generation (Poseidon was), which made his bossiness more unpalatable to his siblings. For a fuller description of this myth see Graves 1955, 53–55.

17. Marcus 1991.

Chapter 7   Developing Successors

1. Those challenges and issues have been described in detail in Gersick et al. 1997.

2. Erik H. Erikson's ideas on developmental stages are described in a number of his books. The most detailed is Erikson 1963.

3. Daniel J. Levinson's model of adult development is described in detail in Levinson 1978. Also see his posthumously published book on the adult development of women, Levinson 1996.

4. Levinson's perspective has much in common with the theory of "punctuated equilibria" in biological sciences. In evolutionary theory, this view postulates that species develop not continuously but by jumps, whenever environmental conditions change dramatically or a new, mutant life form makes a superior adaptation to conditions. For a detailed treatment of punctuated equilibrium and its implications for adult development and group behavior see Gersick 1991.

5. Davis and Tagiuri 1989.

6. Lansberg 1991.

7. Gilligan 1982.

8. Lansberg 1991.

9. Bettelheim 1988.

10. Bibb 1993.

11. Ibid.

12. Bandura 1986.

13. Bateson 1972; Watzlawick, Jackson, and Beavin 1967.

14. Levinson 1978, 255.

15. Rogal 1989.

16. Some family business owners have made informal arrangements with the leaders of other family firms in the same industry sector to hire each other's

children for beginning positions. Such exchanges obviously carry some risks if the companies are competitors—especially in industries where proprietary information yields a competitive advantage. Many companies, moreover, may not want to invest time and resources in training young executives who will not remain with them very long and will ultimately join their own family firms.

17. Detailed information on family business compensation practices is hard to come by, but a 1994 survey by Coopers & Lybrand suggests that while the average compensation for top executives was comparable between family and non-family companies, middle executives (second to fifth place) received 17 percent less compensation in family companies than in their counterparts. Presumably, middle-tier jobs are more likely held by junior family members and by non-family employees. Sincdelar 1994.

18. Kotter 1979.

19. Rogal 1989.

Chapter 8   Mentoring

1. Davis and Taiguri 1989.

2. The mentoring of the young by more experienced seniors is deeply ingrained in the traditions of virtually every culture. In Homer's *Odyssey*, Mentor was the friend whom Odysseus chose to look after his son, Telemachus, while he was away on his ten-year adventure. That Mentor was not a blood relation to Odysseus is particularly significant for mentoring in family businesses. Another significant aspect of this story is that Mentor was really Athena, the Greek goddess who assumed a variety of disguises and had fostered the development of Odysseus as a hero. The myth thus suggests that true mentoring incorporates both masculine and feminine components, both being essential to the developing "hero."

3. For a more detailed description of the guild system in the Middle Ages see Mitterauer and Sieder 1977, and Gies and Geis 1987. For standards in the medical profession, consult the Code of Medical Ethics: Current Opinions with Annotations. American Medical Association (1994), #8.19, p. 124.

4. Watson and Petre 1990.

5. Hackman and Oldham 1980.

6. Simurda 1995.

7. Hollander 1983.

8. Levinson 1978, 253.

9. Ibid, 101.

10. Kramm 1988.

Chapter 9   Anointment and
Taking Charge

1. Kenney 1992.
2. Levinson 1978, 144.
3. Machiavelli 1981.
4. The names are disguised to protect the anonymity of the actual persons.
5. J. W. Ward, personal communication.
6. Brown 1997.
7. Menninger 1995.

Chapter 10   A More Systematic
Selection Process

1. Simon 1996. In contrast, the average tenure of CEOs in public corporations is only about four to five years. Empirical studies suggest that when public companies or sports teams do not perform up to expectations, the removal of the leader or coach is seen as the first remedy. The untimely removal of a leader of a family company is a lot tougher for both the business and the family. For a detailed discussion of the effects of organizational performance and leadership succession, see Allen Panian, and Lotz 1979; Gamson and Scotch 1964; Gursky 1963; Gursky 1964; and Brown 1982.
2. Hall 1989; Gilmore 1988.
3. For a more complete treatment of the concept of strategic selection see Gerstein and Reisman 1983.
4. Rifkin and Harrar 1992, 197.
5. Adapted from Gilmore 1988, 134.
6. For a detailed discussion of the three circle model of family business see Gersick et al. 1997.
7. J. W. Ward, personal communication 1997.
8. See Vancil 1987. In 1996, Corning once again turned to non-family leadership. Roger Ackerman was named the first non-family CEO of the company after James Houghton retired. Houghton had a son and nephew working their way up the corporate ladder, but they were regarded as too young to be included in the top management team.
9. Fombrum, Tichy, and Devanna 1984.
10. Mintzberg 1994.
11. Ward 1987, 162.
12. Gilmore 1988.

Chapter 11   Letting Go

1. Rosenblatt, de Mik, Anderson, and Johnson 1985.

2. For a more complete treatment of the multiple forces that conspire against succession planning in family businesses see, Lansberg 1988.

3. Ward 1987, 22–23. The problem is so pervasive that at least two states, New York and Illinois, concerned with the loss of jobs when family companies close their doors, have set up agencies to help aging owners plan for continuity when they have no family successors.

4. Herbert de Vries, of the Andrus Gerontology Center at the University of Southern California, suggests that a seventy-year-old man in a moderate physical conditioning program can enjoy a 30 percent increase in work capacity. See de Vries 1986.

5. Merck Manual of Diagnosis and Therapy 1992, 1542.

6. Seabrook 1995.

7. Erikson 1968, 140.

8. Erikson 1963, 268.

9. Erikson 1968, 140.

10. Sonnenfeld 1988.

11. Narcissism has been defined by the psychiatric profession as a distinct personality disorder. The *Merck Manual* (16th Edition, p. 1546) describes the syndrome as follows: "Narcissistic personalities have an exaggerated sense of self-importance and are absorbed by fantasies of unlimited success. Paradoxically, such persons are also often preoccupied with envy. They exhibitionistically seek constant attention. Extreme swings between over-idealization and devaluation characterize the relationships of these persons, who also display marked entitlement, interpersonal exploitiveness, and oversensitivity to failure or to criticism." See also Williams 1994. 168–189. For a discussion of this personality type in business organizations, see Kets de Vries 1984.

12. Sonnenfeld, 1988.

13. Quoted in Sonnenfeld, 1988, 199.

14. Sigelman and Shaffer, 1995. See also Posner 1995.

15. Fry 1992; Seleen 1982.

16. Atchley 1976.

17. Ibid.

Chapter 12   Governance Structures and Processes for Continuity

1. "In Boards We Trust" 1996.

2. Giving this much influence to family shareholders who are in management, however, can create a conflict of interest that manifests itself in governance

decisions (such as decisions about dividends or the sale of the business) in which the interests of owners and those of management might not be in alignment.

3. Ward 1991.

4. Schwartz and Barnes 1991.

5. Johnson 1988.

6. Hackman and Oldham 1980. Opinions on the optimal size of a work group varies. After reviewing the extensive research in this area Johnson and Johnson conclude that "Taken in its entirety, the evidence concerning group size indicates that the optimal size of learning groups might be four to six members. Such a group is large enough to ensure diversity and a variety of resources and small enough that everyone's resources will be utilized and everyone will participate and receive rewards for his or her contributions." Johnson and Johnson 1997.

7. Attitudes regarding best governance practices in public companies are fast moving in the direction of having fewer insiders on corporate boards. The latest survey of corporate governance by *BusinessWeek* stipulates that having more than *two* insiders (presumably the Chairman and the CEO) begins to compromise a board's independent judgment. See *BusinessWeek*, December 8, 1997. See also Corporate boards and corporate governance 1993.

8. An Arthur Andersen survey of 3800 family businesses in 1995 found that nearly two-thirds of them (65.5 percent) offered their directors no compensation at all. Nearly 10 percent paid their directors $4,000 to $25,000 annually, and less than 5 percent paid more than $25,000. The Andersen survey, however, included relatively modest-sized businesses with median sales of $9.5 million and an average of 50 employees.

9. Ward 1991.

10. The Arthur Andersen survey found that 53 percent of family businesses in the United States have only one or two board meetings a year, and 17.3 percent hold none at all. Only 18.1 percent call three or four a year, while 11.6 percent have five or more.

11. The idea of a formal organization for accomplishing the goals of the family has a number of precedents. Family councils organized in the French Revolution provided a voice for family members long disenfranchised by the dominant patriarchal authority. See Hunt 1992. The Mormons have a long tradition of regular family meetings. Mormon "home evenings" serve a similar function to family councils in such Mormon families such as the Huntsmans of the Huntsman Chemical Co. (mentioned in Chapter 2). The meetings foster communication in the family, support the members in their religious observances, relationships, and careers, provide moral guidance to the young, and plan family activities.

12. Psychologists have identified two broad categories of rewards—intrinsic and extrinsic—that motivate people to do any kind of work. Intrinsic motivation refers to psychic satisfactions, for example, the playfulness and sheer joy that comes from accomplishing a given task, or the deep satisfaction of exercis-

ing one's skills and talents and seeing the fruits of one's labor. Extrinsic rewards, in contrast, come from the outside. We get a bonus, a promotion, an award or a public pat on the back for a job well done. It is essential to address questions of motivation up front, when governance structures are created in family companies. The leaders need to find the right mix of the two types of incentives to motivate those who will be asked to devote substantial amounts of time to these activities. For a more detailed analysis of intrinsic and extrinsic rewards see Deci 1975, also Staw 1976.

Chapter 13   Governance in Action

1. Mace 1986.
2. Ibid. 186.
3. Ibid. 65.
4. Berenbeim 1995, 40.
5. Lansberg 1988.
6. This basic idea was originally developed by Elliot Jaques (1976). Jaques referred to the phenomenon as "time span of discretion."
7. Johnson 1988.

Chapter 14   Conclusion

1. The most prominent study of survival rates was done by John Ward of Loyola University, Chicago, who followed the course of two hundred manufacturers listed in the *Illinois Manufacturers Guide*. The annual lists included dates when the companies were founded as well as names of officers and directors—a reliable guide to whether or not they were owned by families. By studying sixty years of listings, Ward was able to conclude that less than two-thirds survived the second generation and only 13 percent lasted through the third. See Appendix G in Ward 1987.
2. The Arthur Andersen/MassMutual Family Business Survey 1997 of over 3,000 firms showed that 23 percent of senior-generation stockholders had not completed any estate planning other than writing a will. Only 31 percent had written strategic plans. A 1995 survey of 4,000 firms by Arthur Andersen showed that only about a third—32 percent—even hold family meetings.
3. The concept of servant leader comes from: Greenleaf 1983.
4. For a fuller treatment of the idea of lifelong learning and the enhancement of the family's human and intellectual capital see Hughes 1997.
5. Arthur Andersen/MassMutual Family Business Survey 1997.
6. Ibid.
7. In Argyris's terms, this is when the "theory-in-use" is consistent with the espoused theory. Argyris 1966.

References

Allen, M., S. Panian, and R. Lotz 1979. Managerial succession and organizational performance: A recalcitrant problem revisited. *Administrative Science Quarterly* 24: 167–180.

Altman, E. I., 1971. *Corporate bankruptcy in America.* Lexington, Mass.: Heath.

Argyris, C. 1966. Interpersonal barriers to decision making. *Harvard Business Review* (March–April).

Arnold, M. Dover beach. 1960. In *The pocket book of modern verse*, revised edition, edited by O. Williams. New York: Washington Square Press.

Arthur Andersen/MassMutual Family Business Survey 1997.

Atchley, R. C. 1976. *The sociology of retirement.* Cambridge, Mass.: Schenkman.

Bandura, A. 1986. *The social foundations of thought and action.* Englewood Cliffs, N. J.: Prentice Hall.

Bank, S. P,. and M. D. Kahn. 1982. *The sibling bond.* New York: Basic Books.

Bateson, G. 1972. *Steps to an ecology of the mind.* New York: Ballantine Books.

Becker, B., and F. Tillman, 1978. *The family-owned business.* Chicago: Commerce Clearing House.

Beckhard, R. 1977. *Organizational transitions: Managing complex change.* Reading, Mass.: Addison-Wesley.

Benson, B., E. T. Crego, and R. H. Drucker. 1990. *Your family business: A success guide for growth and survival.* Homewood, Ill.: Dow Jones-Irwin.

Berenbeim, R. E. 1995. Corporate boards: CEO selection, evaluation and succession. Report #1103-95-RR. New York: The Conference Board.

Berle, A. A., and G. C. Means. 1932. *The modern corporation and private property.* New York: Macmillan.

Bettelheim, B. 1988. *The good enough parent.* New York: Vintage Books.

Bibb, P. 1993. *It ain't as easy as it looks.* New York: Crown Publishers.

Bowen, M. 1978. *Family therapy in clinical practice.* New York: Jason Aronson.

Brown, B. 1997. Arming your firm against crises. *Family Business* 8 (4): 34–42.

Brown, L. M., and C. Gilligan. 1992. *Meeting at the crossroads.* Cambridge: Harvard University Press.

Brown, M. 1982. Administrative succession and organizational performance: The succession effect. *Administrative Science Quarterly* 27: 1–16.

Cartwright, C., and F. Harary. 1956. Structural balance: A generalization of Heider's theory. *Psychological Review* 63: 277–293.

Christensen C. R. 1953. Management succession in small and growing enterprises. Boston: Graduate School of Business Administration, Harvard University.

Code of Medical Ethics: Current Opinions with Annotations. American Medical Association. 1994. #8.19.

Colby, G. 1984. *DuPont dynasty: Behind the nylon curtain.* Secaucus, N.J.: Lyle Stuart, Inc.

Corporate boards and corporate governance, Report # 1036. 1993. New York : The Conference Board.

Correll, R. W. 1989. Facing up to moving forward: A third generation successor's reflections. *Family Business Review* II (1): 17–30.

Danco, L. 1975. *Beyond survival: A business owner's guide for success.* Cleveland, Ohio: University Press.

———. 1992. Greed and animosity in the second generation. *Family Business* 3 (3): 11–12.

Davis, J. A. and R. Taiguri. 1989. The influence of life stage on father-son work relationships in family companies. *Family Business Review* II (1): 47–77.

de Visscher, F. 1995. Financing transitions: Managing capital and liquidity in the family business. *Family Business Leadership Series.* No 7.

de Vries, H. 1986. *Fitness after 50.* New York: Scribner's.

Deci, E. L. 1975. *Intrinsic motivation.* New York: Plenum Press.

Deutsch, M. 1975. *The resolution of conflict.* New Haven, Conn.: Yale University Press.

Drozdow, N. 1989. A conversation with Tory and Victor Kiam. *Family Business Review* II (5): 277–292.

Dyer, W. G. 1989. *Cultural change in family firms.* San Francisco: Jossey-Bass.

Erikson, E. 1963. *Childhood and society.* 2nd Edition. New York: W.W. Norton.

———. 1968. *Identity: Youth and Crisis.* New York: W.W. Norton.

Fombrum, C. J., N.M. Tichy, and M. A. Devanna. 1984. *Strategic human resource management.* New York: John Wiley & Sons.

Friedman, L. M. 1964. The dynastic trust. *Yale Law Journal* 73: 547–592.

Friedman, S. D. 1991. Sibling relationships and intergenerational succession in family firms. *Family Business Review* IV (3): 3–21.

Fry, P. S. 1992. Major social theories of aging and their implications for counseling concepts and practice: A critical review. *Counseling Psychologist* 20: 246–329.

Galbraith, J. K. 1967. *The new industrial state*. Boston: Houghton Miffin.

Gamson, W., and N Scotch. 1964. Scapegoating in baseball. *American Journal of Sociology* 70: 69–72.

Gersick, C. 1988. Time and transition in work teams. *Academy of Management Journal* 31(1): 9–41.

———. 1991. Revolutionary change theories: A multi-level exploration of the punctuated equilibrium paradigm. *Academy of Management Review* 16:10–36.

Gersick, K. E., J. A. Davis, M. M. Hampton, and I. Lansberg. 1997 *Generation to generation: Life cycles of the family business*. Boston: Harvard Business School Press.

Gerstein, M. S., and H. Reisman. 1983. Strategic selection: Matching executives to business conditions. *Sloan Management Review* (Winter): 33–49.

Gibbon, A., and P. Hadekel. 1990. *Steinberg's: The breakup of a family empire*. Toronto: Macmillan of Canada.

Gies, F., and J. Geis. 1987. *Marriage and family in the middle ages*. New York: Harper & Row Publishers.

Gilligan, C. 1982. *In a different voice*. Cambridge, Mass.: Harvard University Press.

Gilmore, T. N. 1988. *Making a leadership change*. San Francisco: Jossey-Bass.

Graves, R. 1955. *The Greek myths*. London: Penguin Books.

Greenleaf, R. K. 1983. *Servant leadership: A journey into the nature of legitimate power and greatness*. New York: Paulist Press.

Gursky, O. 1963. Managerial succession and organizational effectiveness. *American Journal of Sociology* 69: 21–31.

———. 1964. Reply to scapegoating in baseball. *American Journal of Sociology* 70: 72–77.

Hackman, J. R., and G. R. Oldham. 1980. *Work redesign*. Reading, Mass.: Addison-Wesley Publishing Co.

Hall, D. T. 1989. Dilemmas in linking succession planning to individual executive learning. *Human Resource Management* 25 (2): 235–265.

Hambrick, D. C. 1995. Fragmentation and other problems CEOs have with their top teams. *California Management Review* (Spring): 30–39.

———. 1997. Conflict and strategic choice: How top management teams disagree. *California Management Review* 39 (2): 43.

Herschon, S. A. 1975. The problem of management succession in family businesses. Unpublished doctoral dissertation. Graduate School of Business Administration, Harvard University.

Hoffman, L. 1981. *Foundations of family therapy*. New York: Basic Books.

Hollander, B. 1983. Family owned businesses as a system: A case study of the interaction of family task and marketplace components. Ph.D. dissertation. University of Pittsburgh.

———. 1990. Hail to the chiefs. *Family Business* 1 (3): 40–43.

Hughes, J. E. 1997. *Family wealth: Keeping it in the family*. Princeton Junction, N.J.: NetWrx, Inc.

Hunt, L. 1992. *The family romance of the French Revolution*. Los Angeles: University of California Press.

"In Boards We Trust," quoted in *Across the Board*. 60–61. 1996. New York: The Conference Board.

Jackson, S. 1992. Team composition in organizational settings: Issues in managing an increasingly diverse work force. In *Group process and productivity*, edited by S. Worchel, W. Wood, and J. Simpson. Newbury Park, Cal.: Sage.

Jaques, E. 1976. *A general theory of bureaucracy*. New York: Halsted Press.

Johnson, D. W., and F. P. Johnson. 1997. *Joining together: Group theory and group skills*. Needham Heights, Mass.: Allyn and Bacon Publishers.

Johnson, S. C. 1988. *The essence of a family enterprise*. New York: Curtiss Publishing Co.

Katzenbach, J. R. 1998. *Teams at the top*. Boston: Harvard Business School Press.

Kenney, C. C. 1992. *Riding the runaway horse: The rise and decline of Wang laboratories*. Boston: Little, Brown & Co.

Kets de Vries, M. 1984. Narcissism and leadership: An object relations perspective. *Human Relations* 38 (6): 583–601.

Kimberly, J. R. 1980. *The organizational life cycle*. San Francisco: Jossey-Bass.

Kotter, J. 1979. The psychological contract: Managing the joining-up process. In *Career management for the individual and the organization*, edited by M. Jelinek. Chicago: St. Clair Press.

Kramm, K. E. 1988. *Mentoring at work: Developmental relationships in organizational life*. Lanham Md.: University Press of America.

Lansberg, I. 1985. Family firms that survived their founders. Paper presented at the annual meeting of the Academy of Management, San Diego.

———. 1988. The succession conspiracy. *Family Business Review* I (2): 119–143.

———. 1991. On retirement: A conversation with Daniel Levinson. *Family Business Review* IV (I): 59–73.

————. 1992.The family side of the family business: A conversation with Salvador Minuchin. *Family Business Review* V (3): 59–73.

Lansberg, I., and J. H. Astrachan. 1994. The influence of family relationships on succession planning and training: The importance of mediating factors. *Family Business Review* VII (1): 39–60.

Levinson, D. J. 1978. *Seasons of a man's life*. New York: Knopf.

————. 1996. *Seasons of a woman's life*. New York: Knopf.

Levinson, H. 1971. Conflicts that plague family businesses. *Harvard Business Review* (March-April): 134–135.

Mace, L. M. 1986. *Directors: Myth and reality*. Boston: Harvard Business School Press.

Machiavelli, N. 1981. *The prince*, translated by G. Bull. New York: Penguin Classics.

Marcus, G. E. 1991. Law and the development of dynastic families among American business elites: The domestication of capital and the capitalization of the family. *Family Business Review* IV (1): 75–113.

Marcus, G. E., and P. D. Hall. 1992. *Lives in trust*. Boulder Col: Westview Press.

Mason, E. S. 1958. The apologetics of managerialism. *Journal of Business* (January): 1.

Menninger, R. W. 1995. In the shadow of giants. *Family Business* 6 (1): 40–47.

The Merck Manual of Diagnosis and Therapy. 1992. 7th edition. Rahway, N.J.: Merck & Co.

Mintzberg, H. 1994. *The rise and fall of strategic planning*. New York: The Free Press.

Minuchin, S. 1974. *Families and family therapy*. Cambridge, Mass.: Harvard University Press.

Mitterauer, M., and R. Sieder. 1977. *The European family*. The University of Chicago Press.

Murdock, M., and C. W. Murdock. 1991. A legal perspective on shareholder relationships in family businesses: The scope of fiduciary duties. *Family Business Review* IV (3): 287–301.

Muson, H. 1993. How to build a dynasty. *Family Business* 4 (3): 25–30.

Nadler, A. D., M. S. Gerstein, and R. B. Shaw. 1992. *Organizational architecture*. San Francisco: Jossey-Bass.

Nanus, B. 1992. *Visionary leadership*. San Francisco: Jossey-Bass.

Posner, R. A. 1995. *Aging and old age*. The University of Chicago Press.

Poza, E. J. 1990. *Smart growth*. San Francisco: Jossey-Bass.

Reiss, D. 1981. *The family's construction of reality*. Cambridge, Mass.: Harvard University Press.

Rifkin, G., and G. Harrar. The ultimate entrepreneur. Quoted in Kenney, C. C. 1992. *Riding the runaway horse*, Boston: Little, Brown & Co. 197.

Rogal, K. H. 1989. Obligation or opportunity: How can could-be heirs assess their position? *Family Business Review* II (3): 237–256.

Rosenblatt, P. C., L. de Mik, R. M. Anderson, and P. A. Johnson. 1985. *The family in business*. San Francisco: Jossey-Bass.

Schein, E. H. 1985. *Organizational culture and leadership*. San Francisco: Jossey-Bass.

Schwartz, M., and L. Barnes. 1991. Outside boards and family businesses: Another look. *Family Business Review* IV (3): 269-286.

Seabrook, J. 1995. Spinach kings. *The New Yorker*, February 27.

Seleen, D. R. 1982. The convergence between actual and desired use of time by older adults: A predictor of life satisfaction. *Gerontologist* 22: 95–99.

Selz, M. 1994. Family portraits: Scions rue the sale of parents' firms. *Wall Street Journal*, March 24.

Shapero, A., and L. Sokol. 1982. The social dimensions of entrepreneurship. In *Encyclopedia of entrepreneurship*, edited by C. A. Kent, D. L. Sexton, and K. H. Vesper. Englewood Cliffs, N.J.: Prentice Hall.

Sigelman, C., and D. Shaffer. 1995. *Life-span human development*. 2nd edition. New York: Brooks/Cole.

Simon, H. 1996. *Hidden champions*. Boston: Harvard Business School Press.

Simurda, S. J. 1995. Eric Monsen's mentoring team. *Family Business* 6 (1): 24–30.

Sincdelar, K. 1994. Unequal pay at the top. *Family Business* 5 (1): 25–29.

Sonnenfeld, J. A. 1988. *The hero's farewell: What happens when CEO's retire*. New York: Oxford University Press.

Spector, R., and P. D. McCarthy. 1995. *The Nordstrom way*. New York: John Wiley & Sons.

Staw, B. M. 1976. *Intrinsic and extrinsic motivation*. Morristown, N.J.: General Learning Press.

Sulloway, F. 1997. *Born to rebel: Birth order, family dynamics and creative lives*. New York: Pantheon Books.

Toffler, A. 1990. *Power shift*. New York: Bantam Books.

Vancil, R. 1987. *Passing the baton: Managing the process of CEO succession*. Boston: Harvard Business School Press.

Ward, J. L. 1987. *Keeping the family business healthy*. San Francisco: Jossey-Bass.

———. 1991. *Creating effective boards for private enterprises: Meeting the challenges of continuity and competition*. San Francisco: Jossey-Bass.

Watson, T. J., Jr., and P. Petre. 1990. *Father, son & co.: My life at IBM and beyond.* New York: Bantam Books.

Watzlawick, P., D. Jackson, and J. Beavin. 1967. *Pragmatics of human communication.* New York: W.W. Norton.

Williams, N. 1994. *Psychoanalysis diagnosis.* New York: Guilford Press.

Winnicott, D. W. 1971. *Playing and reality.* New York: Basic Books.

Wong, Siu-lun. 1993. The Chinese family firm: A model. *Family Business Review* IV (3): 327-340.

Zeitlin, M. 1976. Corporate ownership and control: The large corporation and the capitalist class. *American Journal of Sociology* 79 (5): 1073–1119.

Index

About the Author

IVAN LANSBERG, who grew up in a business family, is an organizational psychologist in New Haven, Connecticut, with broad consulting experience to complex family businesses in the United States, Canada, Europe, and Latin America. He is also a co-founder and a senior partner of Lansberg•Gersick, a research and consulting firm specializing in family enterprise and family philanthropy. He has taught at the Columbia University Graduate School of Business, was on the faculty of the Yale School of Management, and served as a research fellow at Yale's Institute for Social and Policy Studies.

Dr. Lansberg is a frequent speaker to university and industry groups and a regular teacher at leading family business centers throughout the world, including El Instituto de la Empresa Familiar (Barcelona), the Escuela Adolfo Ibanes (Santiago), the International Institute for Management Development (Lausanne), and the Montreal Institute for Family Enterprise. He has helped establish research and executive programs on family business in many colleges and universities. In addition, he participates on the boards of directors of a number of family companies.

Dr. Lansberg is a founder of the Family Firm Institute and the founding editor of the *Family Business Review*. He is also a columnist for *Family Business* magazine. His writings on family business issues have also appeared in such publications as *Fortune, Newsweek,* the *New York Times,* and the *Wall Street Journal.* With Kelin E. Gersick, John A. Davis, and Marion McCollom Hampton, he is a co-author of *Generation to Generation: Life Cycles of the Family Business.*

Dr. Lansberg holds Ph.D., MA, and BA degrees from Columbia University. He lives in Guilford, Connecticut, with his wife, Margarita, and his two sons, Daniel and Simon Emilio.